Second World War
Europe

Courtesy of: A History of War At Sea, Helmut Pemsel, Naval Institute Press, Annapolis, MD: 1979
Resized and enhanced by David Hazelden.

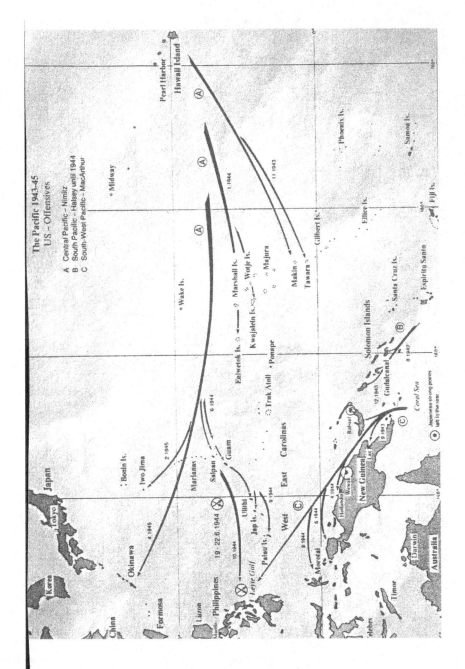

Courtesy of: <u>A History of War At Sea</u>, Helmut Pemsel, Naval Institute Press, Annapolis, MD:1979. Resized and enhanced by David Hazelden.

The Star in the Window

Select Stories of World War II Veterans

LOUIS C. LANGONE

iUniverse, Inc.
Bloomington

iUniverse books may be ordered through booksellers or by contacting:

iUniverse
1663 Liberty Drive
Bloomington, IN 47403
www.iuniverse.com
1-800-Authors (1-800-288-4677)

ISBN: 978-1-4620-1425-5 (sc)
ISBN: 978-1-4620-1426-2 (hc)
ISBN: 978-1-4620-1427-9 (ebook)

Library of Congress Control Number: 2011908792

Printed in the United States of America

iUniverse rev. date: 5/18/2011

Front cover by R. James Mahoney, DDS. Patterned after the Blue Star Banner–
Original design by Captain Robert Queissmer – 5th Ohio Infantry, 1917.

To my wife Shirlee, who has been so tolerant.

To my mother and father, Louis and Catherine Langone, whose three "stars" returned home safely.

To all the mothers and fathers of those who served – especially to those who displayed the gold stars – for those sons and daughters who made the supreme sacrifice.

Acknowledgements

Numerous people have contributed in various ways toward making this book a reality and it is impossible to list all of those who did help in one way or another.

First and foremost, I am grateful to all the World War II veterans who were so cooperative and patient with me regarding the numerous interviews, phone calls, and responses to my questionnaires.

I am very appreciative of my friend and high school classmate, Dr. R. James Mahoney of Lakeland, Florida, dentist and artist, who did the artwork for the cover.

Thanks to Richard Searles, friend and retired English teacher from Mount Markham Central School, West Winfield, New York, and to Kim Todd of Annapolis, Maryland, who assisted me in copy editing and contributing constructive recommendations.

I am grateful to the Colgate University Library and the Mid-York Library, especially the following member libraries and their staffs: — Waterville, Utica, Rome Jervis, and New Hartford Libraries.

Thanks also to the following people I contacted on the Internet who have compiled information for the Dictionary of American Naval Fighting Ships website: Yves Hubert, Patrick Clancy, Michael Hanson and their project manager, Andrew Toppan. The website led me to the actual nine volume *Dictionary of American Naval Fighting Ships* published by the Navy Historical Center, Department of the Navy. To CDR George King, Pensacola, Florida for the verses in the prologue and epilogue.

Appreciation is extended to the _Waterville Times_ for the use of the 1945 Waterville Honor Roll. Thanks also to Dorothy McConnell of the Town of Marshall Historical Society; Millie Miner, Gaylene Fairchild, Stella and Leo Cieslak of the Town of Augusta Historical Society, Town Clerk, Carol Fanning of the Town of Bridgewater for obtaining the Honor Rolls of their communities. Thanks to Harold Maine for the use of *A Book of Remembrances* that contained Honor Rolls for Brookfield, Leonardsville, and

North Brookfield. To Stephen Evans, a former student, of West Winfield, who assisted me with the Town of Winfield Honor Roll of veterans. To members of the Will family and Edward Gates of West Winfield for their help in providing information on Walter Will.

To Althea Zweifel Browne of Waterville and Nancy Sango of Clinton, New York for information regarding their deceased husbands. To Bertha Moyer of Westmoreland, New York who provided me with a copy of her husband's (Francis Moyer's) diary. Thanks to Phyllis McNamara of Oriskany Falls, New York for information regarding her late brother, Charles Rigaud, and I am also grateful to Elizabeth Cowen Kane and the Cowen family who gave me permission to use Richard's personal military memoirs and letters. To Helen Adsit, John Behrens, and Betty Lanigan, Mohawk Valley Institute for Learning in Retirement facilitators at SUNY Institute of Technology, for their helpful information.

Thanks to the authors and publishers of various references that contained facts that helped supplement the personal memoirs of the veterans. Also, to the _Waterville Times_ and _Utica Observer-Dispatch_ for information from their newspaper articles. To Allen Brooks, Deborah Bauder, John Cleary, Kelly Falk,(for assistance in copy editing), Ronald Foppes, David Hazelden., John Peterson, and my daughter-in-law, Jennifer Enos Langone for her help in editing the additional eleven chapters.

And, special thanks to my son, Christopher, who combined files, organized tables, and solved so many layout and computer problems. And to my granddaughter, Trisha Cowen, who alphabetized and entered information in the preparation of the Waterville area list of veterans. To all of my family and friends for their support and encouragement —my sincere appreciation.

Preface

In the past few years, there has been a renewed interest in the wars of the twentieth century and in the military experiences of millions of men and women who have served in our armed forces. This re-kindled interest is especially true with World War II.

While recording the stories in this book, I often thought of the anxiety felt by family members of those who went off to war. Mothers and fathers, faced with the possibility of losing a loved one, suffered the most wartime anxiety. Three of my brothers served in different parts of the world during the war and I remember my father telling the local railroad ticket agent, who also handled western union telegrams, to deliver any War Department telegrams to him only and not to my mother. Fortunately, our family received no telegrams with the following opening words: "I deeply regret to inform you..."

I recall the homes, including my own, that displayed the service banner with stars representing the family members serving in the armed forces. There were so many young boys and men who enlisted or were drafted –leaving school even before they graduated, to confront a world much different from civilian life, and sometimes a world that was not always friendly. To be away from home and family was the first obstacle one faced, and adjustment to the new life without the comfort and protection of family had to be made. The transition to adulthood was swift.

I was too young to realize how much a serviceman missed home and family and little did I know that within a few short years, I would be in the Navy also trying to adjust to my first extended stay away from home.

The homesickness and feelings of loneliness one faces during peacetime cannot be compared of the young soldier, sailor or marine, as he stands in his landing craft that is propelling toward the beach. What were his thoughts of home and family as the ramp of the boat descended and he rushed ashore to meet the enemy—or the thoughts of the airman as he faced aerial "dogfights" and flak from the anti-aircraft guns—or of the sailor on board his ship under attack from bombers or sailing through rough seas and typhoons—or of the submariner under hundreds of feet of water as his boat is being assaulted by depth charges?

For many years I have had an interest in recording some memories of World War II veterans, and in 1998 I decided to send out questionnaires and interview veterans of the immediate Waterville, New York area. After reviewing the questionnaires, I interviewed the veterans and then wrote some narratives with the object of creating a book.

An article in the Utica Observer-Dispatch by "Bill" Farrell led to numerous phone calls and letters from veterans or their family members. Many were from outside the Waterville area. Their interesting stories influenced me to expand my book and I had no idea that it would develop into a project of this proportion. I regret that I have not been able to include more narratives in the book.

So much time has elapsed since World War II that a problem was memory on the part of the veterans. To ensure as much accuracy as possible, I conducted extensive research to supplement and verify the accuracy of as many of the recollections as possible. Twenty years of active and reserve duty in the Navy, and 30 years of teaching history helped to augment the memoirs of the veterans. Nevertheless, errors do occur and I have recorded, with few exceptions, the facts as the veterans recalled them to the best of their ability.

A newer method of footnoting (parenthetical citations – using the author's last name or first significant word in the source cited) has been used and the alphabetical bibliography will connect the source used with the footnoting.

Several community Honor Rolls compiled during World War II of veterans who served from December 7, 1941 to September 2, 1945 are listed at the end of the book. In cases where questionnaires were returned, I was able to update the ranks/rates and add additional data. Included in the Waterville list are names of some veterans who moved to Waterville after 1945 and completed my questionnaire. Using information supplied by veterans, family members, news clippings, and miscellaneous lists of veterans, some modifications were made by adding significant facts to the lists.

Originally published in 2002 (second printing-2003), this book has been a challenging, exciting and satisfying experience. During the past few years I have interviewed eleven more veterans and have added these accounts to the original publication.. Several more photographs have also been added. Since 2002 over a third of the veterans featured in this book have died. Over 850 World War II veterans pass away each day. More than once while conducting over a 100 plus interviews including these eleven additions, the veterans had difficulty holding back their tears. It has also been an emotional experience for this author. I often think of those young 17, 18, 19, 20, and 21 year olds who did not make it home to become employed - to marry – to raise a family.

It is my desire that this book will be part of a lasting record of the military experiences of each of those individuals whom I have chosen to call –*The Star in theWindow.*

Louis C. Langone- 2011

Table of Contents

PART 1   ARMY

PART II   THE ARMY AIR FORCES

ADDITIONAL PHOTOS

PART III   THE NAVY AND COAST GUARD

PART IV   PRISONERS OF WAR

PART V   AMPHIBIOUS WARFARE

PART VI   PEARL HARBOR/HICKAM FIELD

PART VII   MARINE CORPS

EPILOGUE

APPENDIX

INDEX

Prologue

"When we were young we fought the wars, and then,
  A little older, fought the wars again.
  We rode machines all barebacked in the sun,
  Repelled invaders, put them on the run!

  (Commander George King, (QTD. in Prados 8)

ARMY TROOPS LANDING AT OMAHA BEACH-JUNE 6, 1944
(Courtesy of National Archives)

Part I
The Army

SGT CARLTON ALSHEIMER

1

Carlton Alsheimer

BANDSMAN

Few things are more inspiring to the military man than hearing the sounds of John Philip Sousa parade music. Every branch of service, division, or capital ship has a band and throughout history the soldier, sailor, and airman have appreciated the entertainment and morale boosting that the band provides.

From the Revolutionary War fife and drum music to the modern huge military bands serving around the world, these music men and women have served their country well. Today, the Army, Air force, Navy, and Marine Corps bands also perform for the civilian community including assembly programs at secondary schools and colleges.

During World War II there were 500 bands serving the Army and were divided into three categories- Special – Separate and Organizational. Examples of the Special Band were the U.S. Band (Pershing Band), the U.S. Military Academy Band, and the U.S. Air Corps Band. Separate Bands were bands attached to training units. Organizational bands were infantry division bands assigned to a combat command. The Army also had dance bands, which helped boost morale of the troops. The drafting of men into the service helped to bring excellent musicians into the Army and Army Air Corps/Air Forces (Army 1).

* * * *

Carlton Alsheimer of Waterville was one of these outstanding musicians to serve in an Army Organizational Band – the 69th Infantry Division band.

Carlton "Carl" Alsheimer graduated from Waterville Central School in 1937 and then attended the Capital Engineering Institute at Washington, D.C. where he studied electronics and engineering. He had also performed with local bands at hotels and nightclubs.

At the age of 23, and months before Pearl Harbor, he enlisted into the army. His basic training, which he referred to as "rigorous and complete," took place at Fort Benning, Georgia.

After basic training, Alsheimer was assigned to the 78th Division, 101st Tank Destroyer Battalion. Between 1941 and when he became part of the 69th Division band, Alsheimer was a member of Headquarters Company at

Camp Shelby, Mississippi. He was assigned to Publications and his duties involved distributing army regulations. He also ran the movie theater and played in small group bands at service clubs during off-duty hours. Promoted to sergeant by 1943, he was transferred to the 69th Division in June of 1944 and to the Division band in August of 1944. While stationed in the United States, the 58-member Division band was required to entertain at concerts, parades, service clubs, and enlisted men's clubs. The band also performed for arriving and departing dignitaries, and embarking and disembarking troops. They also performed for the USO and with celebrities such as Bob Hope, the Marx Brothers, and Peggy Lee when they visited to entertain troops. (Alsheimer's wife, Anne, also sang with the USO in the States.)

According to J. A. de Mond's book, <u>What the Hell</u>! - the 69th Division left Camp Shelby November 2, 1944, destination unknown. "Our instruments and equipment were loaded onto freight cars. For three to four years the band had played for departing troops. Now it was the 65th division playing for us as we left"(2). Thanksgiving Day was spent aboard the troop train and in the early hours of November 23, the 69th arrived at Camp Kilmer, New Jersey.

de Mond's book goes on to relate that at Camp Kilmer there was training in security, censorship regulations, lifeboat drills, abandon ship drills, and films on escape methods if captured by the enemy (2-3).

The time came to board ship so they packed up and took a train to Staten Island for the ferry ride to Pier 10 in New York City. The Band was playing for the troops at Pier 10 and the Red Cross was there with coffee and doughnuts. They boarded the USS LEJEUNE and the sleeping quarters, named One Peter Baker, were not very favorable. They were located in the most forward part of the ship. It was very crowded and the lighting was very bad. The LeJEUNE left New York on December 1, and joined into a convoy following a zigzag course to avoid submarines. The ship headed toward the Bahamas and then swung northward and joined another convoy and continued the voyage across the Atlantic.

"While crossing the Atlantic," Alsheimer related, "the Chaplain gave us some instruments and our band performed on decks for various shows. One day aboard ship we heard these loud noises. Our destroyers had sighted some submarines and dropped depth charges destroying one sub."

On December 12th the troops arrived at Southampton, England. Their quarters were about two hours from Southampton at a Boy's School called West Downs.

On January 23, 1945, the 69th left England for the continent. They got aboard a British ship and went to the port of LeHavre. On January 24th, the troops landed on French soil. LCT landing boats transported them from the ship to the shore.

By the spring of 1945 the 69th division was in Germany and by late April had met up with the Russians but the band instruments were 300 miles behind. On April 23 several men took off by bus, truck and a quartermaster truck to bring back the instruments. They returned on the 28th(deMond 31-2).

On May 1st, the band performed for General Reinhardt and two other high-ranking officers. "The 1812 Overture," "The Red Cavalry March", and a Glen Miller version of the "Song of the Volga Boatman." were played. The band's arrangement of "Der Fuhrer's Face" was also included in the performance The Russian officers were very pleased and they said good music could promote good relations between nations. (deMond 36). On May 3rd the band went to the allied prisoner of war camp and played for the prisoners who were mainly French.

In addition to England and France, Alsheimer served in Holland and Germany. Most of the time overseas was spent in Germany. The 69th suffered no casualties but lost one man through sickness.

While overseas, the 69th Division band performed many times. "We played for dignitaries, kings and queens. At the same time we entertained our own troops with concerts, dance music, and parades - similar to what was required of us in the States," Alsheimer explained.

The author asked Alsheimer if he could recall some of his most memorable experiences. He said he had performed for generals as they deplaned at various air bases. One time he was in a marching band, which performed at a Duke University football game. He also mentioned that the band had performed at shows for servicemen.

A talented musician, Alsheimer had written musical arrangements for the band and played in concert and marching bands. They marched in a lot of cities and he played in dance bands before he was shipped overseas. A versatile musician, Alsheimer has played guitar in dance band, the tuba in marching band, and the trombone in concert band. Also, he remembers that because of his talent in electricity he was nicknamed "Sparks".

In addition to his music assignment he stood guard duty with Headquarters Company, guarding post perimeters, warehouses, and supply trains. "At times, Alsheimer said, "the Germans were very close."

DeMond recorded in his short history of the 69th Division Band that at Kassel, Germany:

...Eight of our men were sent to a captured Nazi warehouse, which was filled with rations, liquor, and thousands of cases of sardines. Their duty was to guard the warehouse and of course its contents. Several cases of sardines and a number of cases of

Schnapps were requisitioned for our own use, which resulted in many stomachaches and even more disastrous consequences. (25).

In concluding his history of the 69th Division Band, de Mond further writes that "We didn't win the war by playing in the band or by standing guard duty -but we like to think that we were an intricate part of the machine. We did not spend the entire war without hearing a malicious shot fired. And, we have one battle star to our credit at least"(37).

By May 12, 1945, after the Germans had surrendered, the 69th Infantry Division was located at Naunhof, Germany. Alsheimer said that he remained in Germany until it was time to return to the United States.

Sergeant Carlton Alsheimer was discharged from the Army on October 18 and worked in heavy military equipment engineering at General Electric for four years. Following that he was proprietor of Modern Electric, a former Waterville, New York TV appliance and repair business. His talent in electronics was evident by his development of TV test equipment for a prominent television manufacturer.

He died November 30, 2003.

2

Lester Barnes

ARMY FARRIER/CLERK

The soldier on horseback has been a part of warfare for over 2500 years and these cavalrymen charged into battle ahead of the infantry. Glorified in countless novels and movies, they have left an indelible mark on history as part of our romantic and adventurous past.

The horse cavalry was not used much in World War I and between the two world wars. The cavalry was changed into armored cavalry units and in the Viet Nam War; air cavalry used helicopters for rapid transport of men and materiel. (Cavalry -Encarta).

When World War II began there were about fifteen horse cavalry regiments maintained by the army. "In 1941, the cavalry arm was an elite element of the Army's front line troops"(U.S. 1).

Lester Barnes of North Brookfield was assigned for a while with one of the last of the horse cavalry regiments of World War II and also served as a personnel clerk.

* * * *

After graduation from Waterville Central School in 1939, Lester Barnes worked as a farmer and at the Savage Arms defense plant in Utica, New York. On October 20, 1944 he enlisted into the Army and was inducted at Fort Dix, New Jersey.

Following induction, Barnes was transferred to Fort Riley, Kansas for several weeks of basic training. At Fort Riley, in addition to the regular basics of military life, Barnes worked in the horse stables, took long rides on horses, and performed KP (kitchen police) duty.

During basic training he rode horses almost every day. "A lot of rides and quite a bit of time in bivouac," he said. The author asked Barnes as to why he was assigned to a horse cavalry unit. "We were asked if anyone could ride a horse. I told them that I had ridden horses on the farm so I was assigned to the unit and had to take care of two horses," he said.

Following basic training Barnes was selected to attend cavalry horse shoeing school at Fort Riley to learn all about horse shoeing. He said that he had had no previous experience with horse shoeing and that he attended the school for twelve weeks. At the school the students learned how to make a horseshoe from a bar of iron and he would put small shoes on little donkeys. "They were corkers to shoe," he laughed. I'd pick up a front foot and the donkey would stand on its hind feet. I would have to pick up the other front foot – couldn't do a damn thing. They'd kick like a son-of-a-gun. The horse manure was stacked and it looked like big hills. There must have been a thousand horses in ten or eleven barns at Fort Riley," he explained.

From Fort Riley, Barnes rode to Monterey, California aboard a passenger train (not a troop train). There were no available seats, he remembered, so he had to ride between the coaches (area where coaches are connected). The area was covered with soot and there was a lot of smoke from the engine. "I had to sit on my barracks bag and the trip took two days and nights," he stated.

From Southern California Barnes boarded a navy ship bound for Japan. Sailing across the Pacific the ship went by Pearl Harbor, Wake Island and Corregidor. "We had good 'eats' on the ship and I was lucky since I didn't get seasick. We stopped at the Philippine Islands, probably Manila, for two overnights," he recalled. There, it was the first time that Barnes, the upstate New York farmer from North Brookfield, swam in the ocean. Barnes described his attempt to crack open a coconut.

...I cut my thumb trying to open a cocoanut with a knife. Boy, they are tough. There was a guy there with a bulldozer and I put the cocoanut behind the bulldozer and had him back up to crack it open. I lost all the milk that I was after and it was hot and dry that day in the Philippines.

From the Philippines the ship headed in the direction of Japan. Barnes said he remembered when the first atomic bomb was dropped on August 5, 1945 and pointed out that he was near Japan when the war ended on August 14. He could not remember any Japanese submarines in the area and things were very quiet.

After the Japanese surrendered the ship docked at Yokohama and the troops spent a few days there. He then took the train to Nagoya, which he said was an ordinary train that was full of people.

Searching his memory about his arrival in Japan, he thought that the trip on the train to Nagoya took place just before Christmas of 1945. Barnes said that it was real nice in Nagoya where he stayed while in Japan. His main duty was working as a personnel clerk in the office of his company, and he made sure that the men received their required inoculations and he did general office work.

When it was time to leave Japan he took an all day train ride from Nagoya. Along the way there was a spectacular view of beautiful Mount Fujiyama. While riding the train, he said, he noticed again how crowded the train was from Nagoya to Yokohama "It was really packed with people."

Leaving Japan by ship, he crossed the Pacific again and returned to the west coast of the United States. There he boarded a train for the cross-country trip to the east.

He was discharged at Fort Dix March 26, 1946, where he had been originally inducted into the Army seventeen months earlier. Upon his return to civilian life, he again engaged in farming in North Brookfield, and married Betty Ford in September of 1946.

Lester Barnes passed away January 9, 2001 at the age of 78.

3

Ebenezer Belfield

QUARTERMASTER TRUCK COMPANY

The oldest logistic branch of the Army, the Quartermaster Corps, provided supplies and transportation. During World War II the quartermaster truck regiments, though not front line combatants, drove their trucks to the front lines, often living in and out of foxholes.

****

Ebenezer, "Ebb," Belfield, originally from Bridgewater, and later in Sangerfield, New York, enlisted in the Army on November 12, 1942. He was then twenty years old. Before entering the military at the age of 20, Ebb Belfield worked on the assembly line at a General Motors plant in Buffalo, NY At the time Belfield was there, the plant manufactured Pratt and Whitney aircraft engines.

Ebb Belfield's first orders sent him to Fort Dix, New Jersey and then to Fort Custer, Michigan for ten weeks of basic training. Of his time in boot camp, in the winter, in Michigan, he recalled that while crossing the Kalamazoo River a few men fell through the ice and needed an ambulance to take them to the hospital. After basic training, Belfield was transferred to Camp Phillips in Salina, Kansas. His longest lasting memory of his time there was of the 35-mile strenuous marches in full gear and pack. Belfield laughed when recalling the officers on the training marches. In particular, Belfield remembered one lieutenant filled his pack with paper to lighten his load. After Camp Phillips, Ebb Belfield traveled to Camp Shanks, New York before boarding the Queen Mary ocean liner on September 1943 for Europe. Belfield described his rough crossing of the Atlantic as follows:

...On the third day out, the ocean really got rough. The waves seemed as high as mountains. I heard that three men who were afraid of going into battle, committed suicide by jumping off the bridge of the ship into the water. On the third deck of the big ocean liner, a few of these men were slammed into the inboard windows of the former passenger ship. It took us four and [a] half days to cross the ocean and get to Scotland. We then got on a train

for Liverpool, England and stayed at the Seaforth Barracks. We spent nine months at Liverpool and put 48 trucks and three jeeps together to haul cargo off the docks. During those nine months we loaded trucks and went to farmlands in Scotland and Wales where troops were located. We put the supplies and some eight-man tents there and we also went to airfields in England and hauled bombs for the bombers. We saw quite a bit of England and Wales.

In preparation for the Normandy invasion, we went from Seaforth Barracks and gathered at Gladstone Docks in the heart of Liverpool... We then boarded a Liberty ship and the trucks were placed in the holds of the ship and waterproofed in preparation for crossing the Channel. We crossed the Channel June 6, 1944. "There were so many ships – hundreds of them in the channel. [The] Army guys had to man the guns of the Liberty ship. [And], the sailors ran the ship. We were on that ship for eight days and sometimes, at night, the Germans were dropping bombs. I saw the third ship over from us, another liberty ship, get hit. It sank and there were no survivors.

Finally, on June 14th, after more than a week onboard, Belfield went ashore at Utah Beach. At the time, he was assigned to the 3881st Quartermaster Truck Company as a truck driver of a 2 ½ ton truck. "We were soon ordered to the front lines. I was a sergeant at the time and I took eight men back and forth to and from the waterfront transporting supplies. Omaha Beach was to the left of us [and] on Utah Beach."

In the days that followed the Normandy invasion, Belfield was the first of the 3881st truck company in Cherbourg, with his eight men, to find billets for the motor pool. He reached the front lines by July 14th, a month after landing. Belfield was in Europe from the time he landed on Utah Beach June 14th, 1944 until the war ended. From the Cherbourg area, Ebb Belfield then went to Rouen, France to prepare to go to the Pacific. (From Belfield's handwritten note in the margins of a page in the book titled: Remember Normandy by Rene Garrec. Belfield's noted ended with these words: "God bless Harry Truman for dropping the bomb. He saved our necks."

After experiencing V-E Day, on May 8, 1945, in Cherbourg, Belfield and his Company relocated to Rouen in order to haul equipment and supplies from the beaches (Utah, Omaha, etc.) to other parts of France and to Belgium. Tanks and some equipment were trucked to airports in Belgium and Berlin. Some of the equipment was declared "not in operable condition" and dumped into the ocean as junk.

Belfield remembered observing German prisoners in the months after the official end to the war. He recalled that "the younger were friendly, but the older ones were diehard Nazis and had to be guarded closely." Before the 3881st left Europe, they went to concentration camps and hauled Polish prisoners out of them. He said that he had seen the extermination ovens used and the skeletons of those killed.

At Rouen, Belfield was assigned to the 3595th Quartermaster Truck Company. That unit had been hauling tanks for General Patton. While with the 3595th, Belfield's most memorable experience was driving General Eisenhower in a jeep to the front lines. According to Belfield, a photographer following in another jeep took a picture. Belfield pointed out the photograph in a book entitled I Remember Normandy by Garrec.(page 60). The photograph showed Eisenhower and part of the jeep. While driving Eisenhower, Belfield mentioned to the General that he saw his birthplace when he was stationed in Kansas. While at the front lines, a mortar shell hit one of the buildings shown in the photograph. Just after it made contact, Belfield remembered Eisenhower remarking, "Let's go!."

While in Paris on a three-day pass (leave), Belfield ran into American men trading goods on the black market. "I saw these guys and they said they were Americans. One was an American deserter from World War I and living in Paris. I saw many others working on the docks in Brussels and Antwerp. They said they didn't dare to go back," Belfield explained.

As part of the 3595th Company, Belfield served with Patton's Third Army. Before the German counter-attack at the Battle of the Bulge (in the Ardennes), he saw a group of soldiers pass by saluting him and other enlisted men. This surprised Belfield since they should have known better than to salute other enlisted men. Belfield suspected they were Germans dressed as Americans. As it turned out, this was an actual known tactic of the Germans during the Battle of the Bulge.

During his time with the 3595th Company, Belfield saw General Patton a number of times. Once he saw him when Patton's trailer got stuck. Belfield also remembered seeing pontoon bridges being constructed and later crossing the Rhine River on one of them.

Belfield left Europe from LeHavre, France on a Liberty ship that took two full weeks to cross the ocean before arriving in Newport News, Virginia. By the time he departed, he had covered much of France, Belgium, and Germany. Sgt. Ebenezer Belfield was honorably discharged from the army at Fort Dix, NJ and returned home to upstate New York.

Belfield married Theresa, an English woman whom he had met in Liverpool, England. Following his return, Belfield became self-employed and presently lives in Sangerfield, NY.

4

Joseph Billings

THE FIRST INFANTRY

S/SGT JOSEPH BILLINGS

The First Infantry Division is known as "The Red One" or "Big Red One" because its insignia is a red "number one" centered on a shield. Also called the "Fighting First," it saw action in North Africa, Sicily, Normandy, northern France, the Ardennes, the Rhineland, ending at the Elbe River in Germany, where American forces were ordered by Eisenhower to wait for the Russians (Baldwin Introduction).

The division arrived in Scotland in the summer of 1942. By November, it was engaged in the "Second Front" in North Africa, landing at Oran, and advancing across Algeria joining the British forces in Tunisia.

During the African campaign Ernie Pyle, the famous war correspondent and author, wrote the following:

.... A salute to the infantry - the Goddamned infantry, as they like to call themselves. I loved the infantry because they were the underdogs. They were the mud-rainforest-and wind boys. .... In the end they were the guys without whom the Battle of Africa could not have been won (Pyle 247).

From Africa the First Division invaded Sicily and returned to England to prepare for the June 6, 1944 invasion of Normandy.

Of the 50,000 men in the First Infantry Division, 4,325 died in battle (Baldwin Introduction). Over the years, 250,000 to a half million have served in the "Fighting First." War correspondent Don Whitehead wrote that General Eisenhower with General Bradley visited the First Division Command Post in Normandy in early July 1944 to present 22 Distinguished Service Crosses and two Legion of Merit awards. Following the ceremony, he addressed the group informally: "You are one of the finest regiments in the Army. I shall always consider the16th my Praetorian Guard. I would not have started the invasion without you...(QTD. in Whitehead 219).

Joseph Billings of Oriskany Falls, New York was a member of "The Red One" and the 16th Regiment. He was engaged in all of the above campaigns and was shot in one leg in North Africa, and shrapnel hit his other leg as he stormed Omaha Beach as part of the first wave on D-Day. For his battle wounds, Billings received the Purple Heart with one bronze Oak Leaf Cluster, and the Bronze Star for meritorious service, and five Battle Stars.

* * * *

Joseph Billings attended Oriskany Falls Central High School and was working in farming and drove a truck before enlisting in the Army at the age of 18 in 1939. He would earn $21 a month and net $18. His first duty station was in New York City at Fort Jay, which was located in New York harbor. While in the New York area, he participated in parades at the 1939 World's Fair and would go to Pine Camp, New York, which is now Fort Drum, for training in cannons. The troops trained with dummy guns with telephone pole attachments for barrels because cannons were scarce. Pre -war America was not ready for war and cannons were scarce.

Billings said that one of the best jobs he had was that while in New York City, prior to Pearl Harbor, he had to act as a guard on trains transporting gold bullion to Fort Knox, Kentucky. The United States was holding gold for foreign countries and a million dollars per trainload was shipped to Fort

Knox. Billings showed the author a copy of the orders for the sentries traveling the train. They were as follows:

> *…1. I will remain on my post and alert at all times until properly relieved.*
>
> *2. When the train is moving slower than 20 miles per hour, I will remain at my Post in observation.*
>
> *3. I will allow no unauthorized person to approach the train at any time.*
>
> *If necessary to fire in protection of the train I will shoot to kill.*

He said that every week they made a trip to Fort Knox and on the last trip, a few in their group had an opportunity to go through the vault and they saw gold bars being weighed. Billings said that 80% of the world's gold was stored there.

Billings was transferred to Fort Benning, Georgia. There were no buildings there, so in addition to their training, the men helped in construction of the installation. At Fort Benning he engaged in maneuvers with the northern boys against the southern boys. "The north usually won," he grinned. The Air Corps dropped flour bombs and those hit by flour were dropped out. While on maneuvers he had to walk from Georgia to Louisiana, which was almost to the Texas border. Horses were still used and he said the trip proved a man could out walk a horse. The horses had problems with hooves since they had to walk on concrete so much.

At Arsenal, Maryland, he learned about chemical warfare and Army amphibious training. Landings on the beach were practiced and he worked on diesel engines because he had attended diesel school. He learned how to operate the Higgins boat (LCVP), which was used extensively in the amphibious invasions during the war.

Billings explained how the Army Amphibious Force was the first to land on Normandy in June 1944. He said the Army, which did many of the amphibious landings, should not have been involved with boats, and that the Navy should have taken us in to the beach.

The departure date for the overseas voyage had arrived:

> *…The First Sergeant yelled, 'Pack up!' 'You're shipping out!' On August 1, we boarded the Queen Mary in New York City and were packed in like rats. We only had two meals a day. I didn't know it at the time, but Ray "Budge" Kennard of Deansboro was on the same ship.*

The Queen Mary docked in Scotland on August 8 and the troops went by train to southern England to Tidworth Barracks where the British West Point is located. Billings was attached to the 16th Infantry Regiment.

After a time in England, Billings boarded a British freighter and didn't see land for thirty days.

> *...We were on that ship so long we got soft. We were in a convoy and traveled almost to New York and then headed back toward England. Many more ships joined our convoy. Sometimes our ship was on the outside where there is less protection and sometimes we were on the inside. The formation in the convoy would change every other day at about three o'clock when one of the ships would fire a gun as a signal to change formation. We sometimes were positioned on the outside but there was more protection on the inside."* The destination was North Africa.

The invasion of North Africa, "Operation Torch," was called the Second Front. At 6:00 A.M., on November 8, the landing was made at Oran in Algeria. It was the first landing for the First Division and the first amphibious landing (Knickerbocker 34,35). The landing was made without opposition and the Vichy French troops at Oran surrendered. As the African campaign progressed into Tunisia, Billings was wounded by a sniper in the lower leg at the Battle of El Guettar and was taken to a field hospital in Oran. El Guettar "was one of the most savage engagements in which American infantrymen ever took part, and one of the first of many actions in which "The Red One" division has achieved high honors." (War Department Interview 1).

> *...For a while things looked black for me. I couldn't walk. Our position was threatened and I began to resign myself to being taken prisoner or perhaps being shot. A company aid man, one of the bravest men I ever saw crawled out to me, shielded me with his body while he bandaged my wounds and then managed to get me back, under heavy enemy fire to the battalion aid station. I don't know how he did it, for I passed out just as we started. But I do know that I'll always be grateful to that medic. (War Department Interview 1-2).*

Billings told how he worked for two or three weeks with the Foreign Legion, teaching them how to use U.S. guns and equipment. "Boy they were strict," he related. He said he had met an American who was in the Legion and found out that they are in the Legion for life. They were stationed way out in the desert. Billings asked him why he was there and he told Billings not to ask too many questions. If they lived through the war they were free. While working with the Legion, Billings lost his mess kit. "I threw it in their dishwasher and I never saw it again."

"One day while working with the Legion, I was riding back in the truck and I had this awful headache. I had never felt such pain." Billings said that he had to go into the hospital a second time because he had contacted meningitis. The doctor told him he almost died and that another soldier had not been as lucky.

Billings described the Goums, a ferocious group of native North African irregular troops in Morocco and Algeria. He explained that these tribesmen really frightened the Germans and that our military paid them to kill Germans. The Goums would start a large fire at night that would expose the German artillery positions. "They would go after the Germans and cut off their heads. Some brought back ears or a head to collect payment. I said to my buddy, 'Let's get away from here.' "They were crazy," Billings said.

In another remembrance, Billings recalled the following:

...Once, while walking up the Kasserine Pass, which was a very narrow road just large enough for a jeep, we spotted two Germans at the top of a very high hill. It was scary and we got on a jeep and the driver went so fast that it was a wonder we stayed on the road. We did get them. Our early tanks were light and thin-skinned antiques and the Germans beat our tanks awful. Later we got new tanks. From the hill and at a distance of about thirty feet, I saw a tank battle involving one of our new tanks. Our tank shot three shots that got three enemy tanks. The tank could keep the barrel straight and shoot on the go.

Billings explained that in the early stages of the North African campaign, the Germans had captured some American tanks that got stuck in a swamp and "we later ended up fighting against our own tanks."

Eventually, the American forces joined with the British at Tunis. "The British said, 'How did you Yanks get here before us?' The Germans were glad to see us. They didn't want to fight anymore," Billings said.

The invasion of Sicily followed North Africa and Tunisia. Billings described General Mark Clark and General Theodore Roosevelt in Sicily.

...We got lined up and Clark shook our hands. Boy, he was tall. Clarks' troops went up the coast of Sicily and the First Division

went through the center. Patton was a phony. Always showing off with his pistols and all. I liked General Teddy Roosevelt (Son of President Theodore Roosevelt). He was with us throughout Africa and Sicily. He was a little short guy. In a jeep he would have to stand so you could see him. At Tidworth Barracks in England, Roosevelt told us, 'this is not a picnic. Some of you will be killed. Some of you will lose an arm or a leg.' He would throw cigarettes out to us and tell the Sergeant to give us a break (Roosevelt died of a heart attack at Normandy July 24, 1944).

In Sicily, Billings went thirty-three days without changing his shoes or clothes, and acquired many sores on his body. Near Palermo, Sicily, the troops took off all of their clothes and walked in up to their necks in the salt water of the Mediterranean. "We were covered with salt when we got out and the salt sure stung, but it was supposed to help the healing of the sores," he stated.

Also, in Sicily one of the war's worst blunders occurred.

…We had been told that about twenty planes with paratroopers were being flown in for support and to hold our fire. They were due at about at 0100. During the day a German plane was in the area and bombing the ships which were unloading tanks and trucks. I was telling everybody to hold their fire because American planes would be coming in. That night someone on one of the ships probably still thinking of the daytime raids, must have started the firing and when the American planes approached, many of the Navy guns fired and as a result they shot down all twenty-one of our planes. I was working with the Army Amphibs, what a mess! Two of the falling paratroopers almost landed on me. The people back home were never told about this.

After the Sicilian campaign, the First Division went back to Scotland and England to train for D-Day. A few weeks later the division would participate in the biggest invasion of the war.

It was June 6, 1944 and the largest armada of ships ever assembled was in the English Channel and set for the invasion of Normandy. Billings describes the landing:

…I was in the first wave that went in at Omaha Beach and it was the worst mixed up landing. The tide came in and many drowned and many more came close to drowning. You should have seen the boats. There were obstacles made of steel rails set in concrete and

the landing boats would come in and hit the obstacles and sink. Going in to the beach I heard a photographer yell 'Help! Help'! He got hit in the hand and he was carrying these large reels. He wanted help in loading his camera. I loaded the camera with this big reel for him. We were standing on the beach and I said, 'Let's get out of here.' We lost every officer in my company K that day. Boy, they were good officers.

Before Normandy, an officer had given his wife's address to Billings and asked him to write her if he were to die. The officer was killed in action but Billings said because of being wounded he had lost the address and wasn't able to write her. Of the 2,000 men that went in on the first wave, 107 survived, he recalled. At Normandy, Billings received his second wound going ashore. This time it was his other leg and it was shrapnel that hit him. Some of the shrapnel is still in his leg. "You can't imagine that beach - all that concrete and the boats running in to it. The Germans were firing from the top of the cliff." Billings described the pipeline, which was laid out from the boats. Gasoline for the trucks and tanks would be pumped from the boats and followed the pipeline to the areas where the trucks and tanks were. "We had to guard the pipeline because the Germans would sometimes disconnect it and gasoline poured out all over."

The hedgerows were a problem. "They were sons-of-guns," he said. In a war department interview in 1945, Staff Sergeant Billings said he didn't mind the hedgerows of Normandy. "You see, I had a chance to do a lot of sharp shooting in Normandy," he exclaimed. His regular job was that of a machine gun section sergeant in a weapons platoon of a rifle company. In North Africa and Sicily, he saw plenty of action but he didn't get an opportunity to fire a rifle. However, Normandy with hedgerows full of Germans gave him the opportunity to use a rifle. "We often sprayed the hedgerows with machine gun fire but what I liked best was spotting German snipers and picking them off with an M1. That may sound bloodthirsty but I had buddies killed by snipers and every time I knocked one off I had a feeling that I was paying the enemy back for what he had done to us." (War Department Interview 1-2).

Billings also saw action in the Ardennes, which is also referred to as the Battle of the Bulge, where Hitler ordered a counter-offensive in a desperate attempt to stop the allies. The First Division had been scheduled for a rest and almost pulled out but the German counteroffensive postponed this. At the Northern flank of the "Bulge," the division took the full force of the attack on December 17.

Billings was allowed to come home in January of 1945, but he had to go back to his unit in Europe in April of 1945. The First sergeant said, 'What in hell are you doing back here?' 'Why didn't you go over the hill?'

In Germany on V-E Day, May 8, 1945, the First Division received orders to cease firing at 8:15 A.M. On June 23, Billings was ordered back to the United States for discharge and he had a choice of flying or taking a ship. Many of the planes were being flown back to the States. He chose the ship since he thought he would let some of the others fly since he had already been home in January. It turned out to be a stroke of luck for him, because the plane he had decided not to take home, went down in the Atlantic and 18-20 died in the crash.

He boarded a merchant ship on June 23. He offered to help in the kitchen doing KP and as they got closer to New York Harbor, the merchantmen brought out sides of beef and dumped them into the harbor. He was surprised to see this meat being wasted and he asked why they were doing this. They could give it to the poor. He was told that the seamen might be out for six or seven months on their next trip and they wanted to make sure they stored all fresh meat. The ship docked on July 2, 1945.

While viewing a display of his various medals, the kind and aging veteran said with a grin, "This is the one I like the best. He pointed to the honorable discharge lapel pin, which veterans for years have referred to as "The Ruptured Duck."

Staff Sergeant Billings was discharged from Fort Dix on July 7. This time, he was home to stay. Billings went to work for Eastern Rock, which is now (Hanson Corporation) in Oriskany Falls. He also worked in maintenance at SUNY Morrisville, retiring in 1978.

He passed away March 18, 2002.

5

Ralph Butrym

MONTECASSINO, ANZIO, FRANCE

In 1944, the allied forces fighting in Southern Italy were made up of Americans, British, French, French Goums (Moroccans), New Zealanders, Poles, Italians and Gurkha troops of India fighting with the British.

After the invasion of Sicily and the invasion of the Italian mainland in 1943, Italy was the first of the axis powers to capitulate. However, Nazi troops still occupied the peninsula and continued to fight fiercely. Hitler ordered his troops to fight to the death. Consequently, the combat was extremely bloody and ferocious and the conquest of southern Italy took longer than expected.

The American 5th Army was under the leadership of Mark Clark and General Alexander commanded the British Eighth Army. General Clark insisted that the 5th Army would enter Rome first.

Fierce fighting took place at the town of Cassino and the area of Montecassino Monastery or Abbey where the Germans had set up the Gustav Line and the Allies found it almost impossible to take Cassino. The monastery was located on a hill overlooking the town of Cassino. It was believed at the time by the allied high command that the Germans were occupying the Montecassino Abbey and were using this high point as an observation point for directing their artillery down the hill at the allies. The monastery, one of the oldest of the medieval Benedictine abbeys, was built in 529 A.D. over an ancient Roman fortification. Destroyed three times prior to 1944, it was decided that "military necessity" required that the Abbey be bombed. On the morning of February 15, 1944, a great many bombers attacked and destroyed the Abbey killing over three hundred civilians who were either inside or scrambling down the hill in an effort to escape the bombing. "It was the end of fourteen hundred years of tradition, devotion, art and learning"(Trevelyan 124). It was later learned that the Germans had not occupied the Abbey and it has been argued as to whether the bombing was justified and who was really to blame for declaring this very tragic event of World War II a "military necessity" (124-125).

With aspirations of going around the Gustav Line in the Cassino area and to complete the offensive march northward to Rome, a beachhead was established at Anzio on January 22, 1944. Anzio became one of the bloodiest battle areas of

World War II. It took months to make the beachhead effective against the enemy (Pictorial 247).

Eventually, the allies broke through the German lines and advanced toward Rome, which was declared an "open city" by both the Germans and the allies, to preserve the ancient ruins and the art treasures of Vatican City. American troops entered Rome victoriously on June 4, 1944.

The following two narratives are about two infantrymen - Ralph Butrym and Rocco Zito. Originally from Utica, New York, they served in different infantry divisions at Cassino in southern Italy and in southern France.

Butrym was assigned to the 36th Infantry Division and served in the combat areas of Montecassino, the Anzio invasion, and the invasion of southern France while assigned to an Intelligence and Reconnaissance unit.

* * * *

Ralph Butrym was born in Utica, where he attended Utica schools and was employed at the Savage Arms Corporation before entering the military.

On February 20, 1943, he was drafted into the Army and was ordered to report to Fort Dix. He did his basic training at Camp Croft, South Carolina and said it was not too difficult for him, since at age 14 or 15, he was in a voluntary Civilian Military Training Camp for two summers. He felt that this had given him some experience in the rigors of military life.

From Camp Croft, Butrym reported to Fort Benning, Georgia where he attended the Automotive Truck Mechanics School. Upon completion of this school, Butrym was transferred to Fort Dix again for embarkation overseas. In late 1943, he boarded the "Empress of Scotland," a converted British passenger liner. The destination was North Africa. "I was very sick going over," Butrym recalled. After seven days he landed at Casablanca, French Morocco.

The second front in North Africa had already taken place (1942) and the allies had already invaded Sicily and the Italian mainland. Butrym spent about ten days in Casablanca and then left for Naples, Italy, about two weeks after the September 9, 1943 invasion of Salerno, Italy. Salerno became the staging ground for the upcoming Anzio invasion.

Butrym was assigned to Headquarters Battalion of the 141st Regiment of the 36th Infantry Division. He was engaged in combat in the vicinity of the Rapido River near the Montecassino Abbey. The strong German defense line was called the Gustav Line. "Night after night we tried to cross the area. The road was flat and the Germans would watch it and pinpoint the road and then drop artillery," he said. It was thought that the Germans were using the Montecassino Abbey as an observation point. Traveling along the road driving a jeep on reconnaissance patrol, Butrym said that he did not really know what speed to go by the intersection. "I got up in that area, supposedly doing reconnaissance work, but we were actually directing artillery into the high point where the Germans were. The Germans would fire artillery shells firing at us at night without seeing their targets. But they knew where we were. In the Cassino area I was not engaged in infantry combat but assigned to INR - Intelligence and Reconnaissance, which was attached to Headquarters Company," he explained.

Butrym emphasized the fact that the work was more difficult for him because the other men in the unit had received Ranger training.

He spent about five to six months in the Montecassino area and then ordered to the vicinity of Naples, which was a staging area for the Anzio invasion.

Butrym participated in the January 21, 1944 invasion of Anzio (Operation Shingle). He was on board an LST (Landing Ship Tanks) and went on to the beach on a landing craft. Trucks were being unloaded from the LST and Butrym explained how the going was very rough on the first day. After getting off the landing craft he drove a jeep on recon patrol.

"The Germans used big guns," Butrym recalled. "I think they were mounted on railway cars and they could be heard in the distance winding up. Those guns were big and to listen to the winding sound was terrible," Butrym related. The Encyclopedia of the Second World War notes that, 'Anzio Annie' was one of two 280mm monster guns mounted on a railway car and were 135' long and weighed 215 tons. (Wheal, Pope, and Taylor 22).

Butrym spent about two months in the Anzio area and after the break in the German lines he went on to Rome. The 5th Army occupied Rome on June 5, 1944. In Rome he saw civilians fighting with one another. The Partisans were fighting the Nazi collaborators. Italy had surrendered in July of 1943. After a stay in Rome, Butrym returned to Naples in preparation for the invasion of southern France.

On August 15, 1944, Butrym took part in "Operation Anvil," which was the invasion of southern France, known as the "underbelly" of France. He boarded an LST in Naples and after heavy naval and aerial bombardment of the beach, he went aboard a small craft launched from the LST, and went ashore at Green Beach in Marseilles, France.

...The landing was not bad until we got up a ways. The vehicles (my jeep included) were waterproof and they can go into five feet of water but I didn't have to drive my jeep through that depth. There was a large ship right where I landed. The ship had a lot of vehicles, which did get everything unloaded. It was the first time

I saw a ship get hit and it was something like a guided missile or bomb, which came off a plane. It glided perfectly into the ship.

After landing at Marseilles, he was still with reconnaissance and his job was to locate the enemy and then pull back as soon as he spotted the retreating troops. "The Germans were moving back very fast and the roads were all mined and we had to be very careful. At night, which is kind of scary, I did reconnaissance and we used no lights. One time we did a good hundred miles and never found the enemy," he recalled.

On one patrol he did remember having close contact with the Germans. His jeep had a 50-caliber gun operated by a buddy. "I forgot to turn the jeep around but the guy had to keep firing. There were three of us on the jeep and one or two would man the 50 caliber gun," he remembered.

"One time we were caught on the ground with just our raincoats. It's no fun crawling around on the ground in a raincoat. I had lost the jeep after it got hit but we did not confront any of the enemies and we managed to crawl away," he related.

The Division moved rapidly through Lyons, France to the Alsace-Lorraine region. Butrym was close to the allied troops from the north. and the 7th Army made contact with Patton's Third Army at Autun, France.

From the northern Alsace area the 36th Division moved through Bavaria in southern Germany and crossed the Danube into Austria. Butrym said that while doing reconnaissance patrol he did not have head to head confrontation with the enemy.

Butrym was in Somers, Austria not far from the Italy-Austria border on V-E and V-J Day. He had been awarded the Bronze Star, five battle stars, and was entitled to wear the Combat Infantry Badge. He said that an officer in his Headquarters Battalion, Lieutenant Burke, and a ten-man patrol had captured Field Marshal Gerd vonRunstedt. This field marshal had masterminded the Ardennes campaign (Battle of the Bulge) and was one of Hitler's outstanding generals. Also, Field Marshal Hermann Goering, leader of the Luftwaffe, surrendered to Butrym's Assistant Division Commander, General Robert I. Stack on V-E Day (Huff 192).

Sgt. Butrym left Europe in December of 1945 and was discharged at Camp Kilmer, New Jersey, January 1, 1946. He returned home to Utica where he started his own business and later moved to Waterville.

He passed away September 30, 2004.

5 (Cont'd)

Rocco Zito

MONTECASSINO, CASSINO, ANZIO, SOUTHERN FRANCE

Rocco Zito attended Proctor High School in Utica and had worked at the Hatheway Bakery before entering the Army on April 5, 1943. He attended basic training at Camp Blanding, Florida. and after further infantry training; Zito left Newport News, Virginia aboard an old British ship. Several days later he reached Casablanca in French Morocco in September of 1943. From Casablanca he was moved to Oran, Algeria and boarded a ship for Naples, Italy. Zito said that the Salerno invasion had already taken place, and the front line was a little above Naples. He soon joined Company A, 7th Infantry Regiment of the 3rd Division as a replacement at the Volturno River. The location was south of Rome near the town of Casino.

The 3rd Infantry Division, which had gained fame in World War I, was commanded by General Sharpe and during World War II was engaged in many battles from North Africa to Sicily, Italy, and southern France and most of the major battles of Western Europe. Their members won 37 Medals of Honor and its most famous member was the late Hollywood actor and Medal of Honor winner, Audie Murphy, the most decorated soldier of world war II, and the author of *To Hell and Back*.

Zito said that he was a rifleman and the fighting in the Casino area was tough and the troops were bombarded heavily by German artillery. The battle was prior to the invasion at Anzio and that he was at the Cassino area from September to early January. He was relieved there and brought to Naples, a staging area, to practice with Higgins boats for the Anzio invasion.

From the staging area in Naples they boarded an attack transport and headed for Anzio. The invasion began January 22, 1944 at 0200 and Zito said he boarded a Higgins boat, the landing craft what would transport him to the beach. The author asked him about his thoughts as he headed toward the beach.

...What was I thinking when the boat headed toward land? I worried that we would hit a sandbar or something and as we left the boat the water would become deep. I am not a good swimmer.

When we got on land, there wasn't much resistance since we had caught them by surprise. They didn't expect us to come in there.

The Anzio invasion took place with aspirations that the Germans would leave the Cassino area and head north to Rome to fight other American troops there. However, the Germans did not leave the Cassino area. Instead of leaving, the enemy brought in troops from southern France to reinforce the Anzio line. Anzio became a tougher battle than had been anticipated and it took five months to reach Rome. "I say it was a long battle – the forgotten battle. The U.S. should have brought in more support. One time at Anzio we made a move to Cisterna, which we had taken, but after taking it, we were pushed back, Zito recalled.

Kenneth Sliter of Lowville, New York, who was a Navy signalman attached to the First Beach Battalion at Anzio, said that of all the five campaigns in which he had participated in World War II, Anzio was the toughest. He pointed out that if it weren't for the Navy's heavy shelling of the Germans, the beachhead at Anzio would have been lost. When he left the beachhead, the assault troops had advanced only fifteen miles. Sliter further explained that the Germans had brought in two divisions from northern Italy. "Our troops were held up and just dug in."

Zito told of how some Americans were killed in January and that their bodies were not found until the first week in June. The bodies were between the lines and could not be reached and by the time they were found they were badly decomposed since they had been left there for so long. "The morale at Anzio was very bad. We felt that we were the only ones doing any fighting and everyone was talking about the big upcoming invasion (Normandy). After a while we thought it was a big joke – and they were never going to pull the big invasion off," he explained.

Zito was critical of our American planners and leaders and said that our American troops could have gone to Rome the very first day had General Clark, the general of the Fifth Army, done things differently.

...If two or three divisions had been available to follow us in, we would have been able to advance north to Rome the first day. General Clark had hesitated on going in since it was felt that it was easy for the Germans to surround us. They did surround us until we took Rome on June 5, 1944. "*What happened, he said, was that the Germans pulled troops off the Casino line and it was very easy to surround us. The Germans used a lot of 88mm guns and they were devastating. They were used as direct artillery, but were primarily used as anti-aircraft guns. It went on day and*

night and after a while we were able to tell by the sound of the shelling whether it was German or American.

Zito showed the author an illuminated newspaper clipping which he said was in the *Utica Daily Press* in January of 1944. The newspaper interviewed his mother shortly after the Anzio invasion and the article mentioned an associated press dispatch written by World War II war correspondent Don Whitehead. According to the AP dispatch ("On the Fifth Army's Beachhead South of Rome"), Rocco Zito had participated in the landing at Anzio in January 1944 and quoted Zito as saying that an old woman standing by the roadside was very happy to see American troops, and was waving and kissing the hands of all the troops that came along. The article stated that there must have been 200 troops going through the area (*Utica Daily Press*, January 1944).

Zito explained that Anzio should be called the forgotten battle. He feels that there hasn't been as much publicity about it as there has been of other battles. It seems that much more has been publicized about the bombing of the Montecassino Abbey and the battle of Cassino.

After Rome was taken, the 3rd Division was relieved and was sent back to the Naples staging area to practice dry runs in preparation for the invasion of southern France. At Naples, Zito boarded an LST and departed to an area between Marseilles and Toulon on August 15, 1944 to invade the "underbelly" of France. He describes the division's northward advance in France as follows:

…There wasn't much resistance, but after advancing, the Germans engaged us in combat as we were trying to meet our troops in the north. Along the way we would take a town and there was no resistance and at the next town, there was hardly any resistance. At the third town, the artillery was coming in like crazy. They had us pinned down in an open field, and the only thing we could do was to get up and run toward the Germans to try and stop the artillery. However, when we got close to the Germans the machine guns would open up and would spray the whole area. I got shot in the stomach with a machine gun bullet. The troops moved on and I got up, bleeding badly, and supported myself by lying against this tree. I almost bled to death. I saw this boy who was about 10 years old coming down the road. I waved to him and he came up to me and his eyes got as big as half-dollars. I talked to him in English and a little Italian so we could communicate. All of a sudden he takes off up the hill from the direction from which

he came. I don't know how long it was but in a few minutes our American ambulance is speeding down the road. It came right to me, picked me up and I then passed out. When I came to, I was in a field hospital. That little boy was my hero. He saved my life. This took place in the area of Valence, France on September 14, 1944, the day I became 20 years old. I have never gone back to France but I would like to find that boy. He's probably in his late forties.

Thinking of what the boy did for him, Zito said that if he ever finds the boy, he has a speech prepared and he wants to mention how nice it is to meet him, and remind him of how frightened that he, the young boy, had looked, and let him know how grateful he is, and that it was he, and not Zito, who was the hero on that day so many years ago.

Rocco Zito earned the Combat Infantry Badge and was awarded the Purple Heart and three battle stars. He returned to the United States and was discharged in April 1945 from the Army from Rhodes Hospital that was located in what is now the Business Park in New Hartford, New York. Rocco Zito passed away December 28, 2010.

6

Elmer Ford

QUARTERMASTER/TRANSPORTATION

L-R – "WILLIE", CPL ELMER FORD ,AND "BASTOGNE"

The U.S. Army Quartermaster Corps is the Army's oldest logistic branch and during World War II provided supplies and transportation. During World War II, the Quartermaster Truck regiments, though not front line combatants, drove their trucks to the front lines, often living in and out of foxholes. Driving by day or by night, the trucks rolled on and at night drove with limited lights since the headlight covers were designed to hinder detection by the enemy.

* * * *

Elmer Ford of Waterville and Clinton, New York, was a truck driver in a quartermaster corps regiment and participated in most of the major battles of Western Europe during World War II. His duties involved transporting ammunition, fuel, and other essential supplies to and from the front lines from June 1944 to May 1945.

Before entering the Army, Ford lived on Crow Hill Road in Clinton and worked for Savage Arms in Utica. "I had been getting all of these deferments and all my friends had been drafted or enlisted so I went to the draft board and enlisted on February 24, 1943," Ford said.

From the induction center at Camp Upton, New York, Ford was ordered to Fort Custer at Kalamazoo, Michigan for basic training. "First thing in the morning we would go outside in our winter overcoats for calisthenics. It was awful cold. We would take off our coats and fold them up beside us and then do our exercises," Ford related. My battalion stayed for two months at Fort Custer before convoying to Camp McCoy, Wisconsin to finish our basic training.

Following basic training Ford traveled to Camp Tyson, Tennessee where he participated in maneuvers. He was assigned to the 3806 Quartermaster Truck Regiment as a truck driver. He remembered that at Tyson in October through December of 1944 they lived in pup tents while on maneuvers and there was a great amount of snow. While stationed at Camp Tyson, Ford married Hazel, his fiancée from Sauquoit, New York. They were married on October 14 in the chapel and a corporal was the bridesmaid, and a sergeant was the best man.

Ford referred to Camp Tyson as the barrage balloon "capital of the world," at that time. Barrage balloons were all over the place and special troops took care of them. They were usually tethered about 200' above ships to discourage planes from strafing ships. Planes would get tangled in the barrage balloons if they came too close. Ford explained that when his ship went across the English Channel these barrage balloons were tethered about 200' above the ships as a defense against planes.

In late February of 1944, Ford went by train to New York City. "We went right through Utica in the middle of the night. So close to home," he laughed. In New York harbor the troops went aboard the "Queen Mary" and after five days at sea reached Glasgow, Scotland. The troops went by train from Glasgow to Rugely, which is located in central England about twenty-five miles north of Birmingham. They were put on maneuvers and Ford, now a corporal, said they had to learn how to drive on the left side of the road.

While in England, Ford said that he had observed German V-1 Missiles that had been launched against English cities. "You could hear them going over and when you could no longer hear them and their motors were shut down you would know then that they were coming down. The Germans had them timed as to when they would go off."

...On D-day plus six, June 12, 1944, we crossed the Channel on an LST (Landing Ship, Tank) and headed for Omaha Beach. Before landing we had to prepare the trucks for passing through deep water as we went ashore. The LST would go in so far and

we had to disembark in about two to three feet of water. The ship had to return to England for another load and would not wait for the tide to recede. Since the truck's engine would be under water going toward the beach, it was necessary to apply a dark green stuff like putty called Duc Seal all over the engine. We had to do it twice. The first time was practice and we would put it all over the engine, the spark plugs and wires. There was a ventilator and exhaust coming out of the carburetor and out the top of the truck. Everything on the engine was sealed so that when we got in the water the wires would not short out and water would not get into the carburetor. All of that preparation took a lot of time and then after it was inspected, we were told to clean it up and get the Duc Seal off. This was a couple of days before the landing and then after the practice dry run, we did it again. We wanted to do a good job because we didn't want to get stranded in the water. We didn't even bother to test it after the practice.

"As we landed at Omaha Beach and after driving through about two to three feet of water, we drove on the road to St. Mer d'Eglise. Our trucks had to haul troops, ammunition, and supplies to the front, and we had to travel by night with partially covered parking lights, called Cats'-Eyes. We would follow the tail lights of the trucks ahead of us, which would help us to keep up. Every place we stopped we had to dig a foxhole for the night. Once in a while shells would pass over us. They were from German 88mm guns. We had to camouflage our trucks from the planes even though the Germans did not have much air power at the time. There were many hedgerows and the tanks had trouble getting through at first, but our guys finally wised up and put big blades in front of the tanks and they acted as bulldozers," Ford explained

Ford's daily routine was trucking supplies and ammunition to the front. His major campaigns included Normandy, Northern France, the Ardennes, Central Europe and the Rhineland. He said that he was bivouacked near Bastogne and that was their operating area. It was their home base where they had gasoline and ammunition dumps for supplying the troops (Before the Battle of the Bulge). After the break through which created the bulge in the allied lines, we had to retreat.

He remembered that he visited Paris and attended the Follies on May 3. It was his first three-day pass since he had left the States.

Ford said that just before the Germans surrendered on May 7, 1945, he was on the way back to bivouac areas such as Weimar and Nuremberg, where he would stay about two or three days in one place and then move on to another place.

Recalling other memorable experiences, Ford showed the author some pictures of Nuremberg where Hitler had made many speeches during the height of Nazi rule, and of Cologne, which had been demolished by allied bombing. He said that it was the first time he saw the German autobahns, the super highways. The Germans would park planes alongside the autobahn and use the roads as runways. He also displayed a picture of a friend, Willie, and of himself holding a dog named "Bastogne," since that is where the scared and hungry pet was found when the Germans were driven back.

On V-J Day, August 14, 1945, Ford was in Germany and the trucks were used to move some of the displaced people back and German prisoners were also being transported since they were allowed to go home. One time, at a concentration camp, they were directed to go into the village and bring some of the local people to observe these concentration camps. Many of them said that if they had known about these camps, they wouldn't have happened. "I remember at one camp that had been liberated, I saw bodies stacked and lined up for burial. Only the hands were sticking out. Just a terrible sight," Ford described.

In November, Ford traveled to Marseilles in southern France and waited for two weeks to board the S.S. CHAPEL HILL, a victory ship to take him back to the United States. He said it was a rush to get them there, "the old hurry up and wait game," and after arriving they stayed in eight man tents - four sided pyramidal tents - and waited for the ship to arrive. Ford said he remembered hearing the song, "Going To Take A Sentimental Journey," being played over the P.A. system. I bet I heard that song a hundred times a day," Ford said with a loud boisterous laugh. The only thing we had to look forward to was that they had ice cream available. Once a day in the early afternoon we'd take our mess cups to go and get our ice cream. They'd charge a nominal fee, which was not very much. Boy that tasted good," he said. "Quite a line-up there! It was the only thing to look forward to. No one in my outfit came home on the ship with me." They probably came at the same time but in another group," he said.

Corporal Elmer Ford arrived in New York City and was discharged on December 8, 1945. He worked at various jobs including thirty-four years employment with General Electric repairing electrical equipment. He retired in 1987 and in his spare time he built three homes.

7

Robert Garrett

MAIL GUARD

The 103rd Infantry Division, which was formed between the two world wars, was known as the "Cactus" Division and during World War II was involved in three campaigns including the Battle of the Bulge. The division was disbanded in September 1945.

The 42nd Infantry or Rainbow Division was formed during World War I and General Douglas MacArthur, a colonel in World War I, stated at the time "The 42nd Division stretches like a rainbow from one end of America to the other"(QTD in Rainbowvets 1).

During World War II, as part of the 7th Army, the 42nd Division attacked German defensive positions and liberated the Dachau concentration camp on April 29, 1945. The division also swept through Munich on April 30 and after the war ended served as occupation forces in Austria (Grunts 1).

In the last few months of World War II, Robert Garrett, formerly of Clinton and Utica, served in the 103rd Division and the 42nd Infantry Division in Germany and Austria where his duties involved guarding German prisoners of war and acting as a mail guard.

Shortly after the war ended, he and his family moved to Waterville.

* * * *

After graduation from high school in Utica, Garrett enlisted into the Army at the age of 18 in November of 1944. "I wanted to enlist so badly that I would have been disappointed if I had been rejected," Garrett remarked. His basic training was at Camp Croft, Spartanburg, South Carolina, and he recalled how damp and cold it was during his training. He said that since it was the latter part of World War II, the Army was only interested in infantry replacements. "I always remembered a guy saying to us, 'Well, you will be taking an aptitude test tomorrow, but I want to tell you one thing, all the good jobs are gone, boys. All we need are replacements,' Garrett explained with a laugh. The training which included M-1 rifle, bazookas and machine guns, was tough and Garrett recalled saying to himself at the time - 'If others could get through it, so could I.' Many recruits had difficulty with the 20-mile march or with the obstacle course, but since he endured them, Garrett said that it gave him a good feeling of accomplishment.

Following basic training, they left for Camp Myles Standish in Boston, Massachusetts. In March of 1945, he boarded a troop transport, the MARIPOSA that was bound for France. The MARIPOSA sailed with no convoy escort and Garrett recalled the zigzagging maneuvers of the ship with the purpose of avoiding possible torpedo attacks by enemy submarines.

After seven or eight days the ship docked at Marseilles, France and the troops were placed in "Tent City" where they were quartered inside tents. "You would think the Mediterranean would be warm but we slept in cots and it was cold. Someone said to place a blanket over the cot so that it would drape to the floor to keep out the cold air," Garrett described.

The troops boarded French railroad boxcars and were transported north to a redeployment center at Worms, Germany. He said that he was not ordered into combat since the war in Europe would end within two months of when he had arrived.

Garrett was assigned to the 103rd Infantry division as a replacement and he saw American troops (that they were replacing) withdrawing from the area. They had been in combat at the Ardennes (Battle of the Bulge) and other battles, carrying all sorts of German souvenirs, helmets, sabers, etc. they had collected. Only 18 years old at the time, Garrett remarked how this was quite a sight and it seemed to stick in his memory. "When we arrived, there were so many replacement troops – hundreds of us. They didn't know what to do with all of us." The Germans were in retreat and his unit's main duty was rounding up prisoners and moving them to stockade compounds.

> *...In May of 1945 we were at a small town of a couple of hundred, called Westenderf, in the Austrian Alps. There, we were berthed in chalets and assigned to "I" company. We were there for a few weeks and we guarded German prisoners of war. Since there was a need for firewood, the prisoners were trucked each day to the woods with two guards and we would watch them as they cut wood and stacked it. At the end of the day they would be trucked back to the compound. The prisoners were content and made no attempts to cause trouble or escape...*

In September of 1945, the 103rd Infantry Division was disbanded and went back to the states. Garrett was then assigned to the famous "Rainbow Division," the 42nd Infantry, as part of the occupation forces.

Garrett was in Vienna, Austria, and at first was guarding the railroad yards. Later he was assigned the duties of a mail guard. While in Europe, he spent most of his time in Austria at Vienna, Innsbruck, and Salzburg.

He said his most memorable experience was serving as a mail guard.

> *...I was made a mail guard and I traveled from Salzburg to Vienna twice a week on a train called the "Mozart" which ran from Paris to Istanbul. The train would stop at Salzburg and Vienna. Mail was placed into the mail car and sealed. I was only a Private but as mail guard, I received special treatment riding the train, which had private sleeping compartments. We traveled with officers and often shared compartments with captains and colonels. I carried a 45 pistol and the trip was slow, since all of the bridges had been destroyed and pontoon bridges were used in place of the regular bridges. We had three days off between trips. When we weren't riding the train we stayed at a small hotel in Vienna and ate at a restaurant taken over by the Army. We would walk to the restaurant and once, while walking, I saw General Mark Clark walking with a group of officers and we were surprised and startled to see him.*

Garrett added that all of his time in the Army was a memorable experience. He said that one time in the Alps, he was at an old German youth camp and for some unknown reason there was not enough food. To compensate for this, the troops had to hunt for wild game such as deer.

Garrett said that on V-J Day he was on occupation duty in Vienna, Austria. He left Europe and returned to the United States and was discharged on August 16, 1945.

After returning home, his family moved to Waterville where he helped his father who owned and operated Garrett's Grill. The business was located at the west end of the village on the corner adjacent to the Stewart's parking area.

In 1950, he purchased Steve Congelo's small grocery store where the Waterville Times is located and he also built a new store in 1966, which he operated until 1989.

He presently lives in Waterville and spends his winters in Florida.

8

Frederick Hilsinger

28ᵀᴴ INFANTRY

Organized in 1879, the 28ᵗʰ Infantry Division, a Pennsylvania National Guard Division, is the oldest Division in the Army and elements of the Division can be traced as far back as 1747(Twenty-Eighth 1).

The Division arrived in England October 8, 1943 and after several months of training in England and Wales, landed on Utah beach in July of 1944.

The Division, which was in five major campaigns —Normandy, Northern France, Ardennes-Alsace, Rhineland, and Central Europe, saw action at the Seigfreid Line, crossed the Rhine River April 1945, and was part of the occupation forces north of Aachen, Germany. The fierce fighting of the 28ᵗʰ Division led the Germans to label it as the "Bloody Bucket" Division (Twenty-Eighth 1-2).

Frederick Hilsinger of Waterville, New York was attached to Company G of the 110ᵗʰ Infantry regiment of the 28ᵗʰ Infantry Division.

* * * *

Frederick "Fred" Hilsinger was born in Waterville and prior to entering the Army in February 1942, worked in Dorney Park in Allentown, Pennsylvania. He was drafted at the same time as Hank Blair and Lincoln Stafford who were also from Waterville.

After basic at Fort McClellan, Alabama, Hilsinger went to Pass Christian, Mississippi and was berthed at an abandoned hotel. He was assigned to an Aviation Construction unit and about two months later; equipment was loaded on to a railroad flat car and shipped to New Jersey. The troops followed.

On July 1, 1942 Hilsinger boarded the S.S. ARGENTINA for a twelve-day trip across the Atlantic. The ship was packed with troops and most of the troops slept every night on the main deck or in a passageway.

…We arrived at Glasgow, Scotland and then went to Great Dunmore and stayed there about two months building runways. We ate English rations, which included tea, porridge, and mutton stew. English equipment was used since the equipment we had sent over had not been received. We used about six small cement

mixers with a bucket. The cement came in at night in bags and we had to unload them by hand and put them in a tent. The big cement mixers came in the week that I left.

After six months at Great Dunmore, Hilsinger was transferred to Watford, England and helped form the EBS-SOS Headquarters unit.

…I was a courier and carried secret documents to all of the outfits including my old outfit. It was a long run. Though I did not see them, the documents were their orders for the day. I used a jeep and traveled alone with an M1 rifle and a Thompson sub-machine gun. I had to memorize the route because I couldn't carry any maps with me and I couldn't stop to ask any questions. Driving on the left side of the road wasn't bad except for the roundabout. One night I went around one three times and a "Bobby" had to help me find the right road off the roundabout.

After acting as a courier for two years he was eventually transferred to Company G of the 110th Infantry of the 28th Division. He said he had signed up for this in Pennsylvania when he volunteered for the draft. The 28th Division, known as "The Bucket of Blood," was from Pennsylvania.

While in England Hilsinger's brother, Richard, who was stationed at Ipswich in a B-17 squadron, visited Fred.

…He heard I was there at Watford and he said - 'Why don't you come back with me and we'll get a B-17 and see if we can go flying. We went and got a crew together and we took off. There were two Texans – pilot and co-pilot and they did everything. They tried the loop, and tried to barrel roll it over. One time we dropped 5,000 feet and that put everybody right up to the ceiling. Richard was going to have the crew fly me back to Watford but an announcement over the loud speaker said that all planes were grounded so I had to take a train to Watford. I got the MP's to give me a ride back to the train station and I had to climb over a fence to get to the station and a guy on the platform directed me to the right train. After changing trains twice, I was able to go directly to Watford and didn't even have to buy a ticket.

Richard came down again and he thought it would be a good idea to look up another brother, Paul, who was stationed at Southampton. Paul was in an artillery unit. There were four Hilsinger boys and all were serving overseas.

The oldest, Harry, was an air- crewmember flying the "hump" from India to China. Unfortunately, they were unable to locate Paul. No one there could help them. It was a staging area and the troops were getting ready to cross the channel. It was just before D-Day.

Fred Hilsinger crossed the channel during the summer of 1944 on a Liberty ship. "We couldn't get to the beach since the tide was out so the equipment and troops were loaded on barges. We were on a barge all night and landed on Utah beach early next morning," Hilsinger related.

Staff Sergeant Fred Hilsinger earned two battle stars and the combat infantryman's badge while serving with the 28th Division, a part of General Patton's Third Army. He said that one time he walked 63 miles without stopping, and actually fell asleep while walking and fell in a ditch. "Falling down woke me up," Hilsinger added.

During the winter of '44-45, at one of the battles, (not sure which one), Hilsinger slept in a foxhole and in the morning he said that he would find himself covered with snow. "I usually stayed awake at night. It was no fun spending a winter in a foxhole and I never did get winter shoes."

Hilsinger remembered that one time some of them were pulled off the front line to guard displaced persons. They were placed on a hill which had a stonewall around it. There was a road going to it and the bombs hit the roadway. There was a big sewer pipe that got broken and every hole along the roadway was full of sewage. He described his ordeal with the sewage as follows:

> *...It was night and we couldn't see a thing. Two guys went in headfirst. I slid in right up to my neck. When we got back to where we were staying, we went to Supply to get new uniforms and they wouldn't give them to us. We were staying in an architect's house, which had a cellar with an air raid shelter. There was a big stove with a bucket on it. We filled it with water and GI soap and we threw everything in there and boiled the clothes, rifles, leggings, and cartridge belts. The leggings and cartridge belts were bleached white. That soap was strong and it even took the varnish right off the rifles.*

Hilsinger said he turned down an opportunity to become a warrant officer since he would have had to sign up for another year overseas. "I already had three years overseas. At that time you could get out on the point system, I had more than enough to get out but they wouldn't release me. In fact, the guys in my outfit couldn't believe that I had so many."

Hilsinger returned to the States and was given a thirty-day leave. He then had to report to Fort Oglethorpe, Georgia to train on chemical mortars. "We said we were afraid of them and wouldn't train. They were going to send us back overseas and they wouldn't let us out until some of us wrote a letter to our congressman. I could have been a first sergeant but I turned that down, too. I said. 'Why should I take it?' I'm eligible to get out.' -"

He was discharged on October 2 1945, after three years and eight months in the Army and he returned home to Waterville and worked 27 years as an automobile mechanic, and service and parts manager for Chevrolet dealers.

He passed away March 12, 2003.

9

Leeman Huff

26ᵀᴴ INFANTRY

The 26ᵗʰ Infantry Division was formed from the New England National Guard shortly after World War I had started. It was named the "Yankee Division" and its insignia is a dark blue "YD" monogrammed on an olive background. Arriving in the European Theater of Operations September 7, 1944 and on the European continent September 19, the troops entered combat for the first time in October. The Division had an outstanding record by V-E Day and had suffered almost 10,000 casualties. In October the division was in Normandy and was ordered to the Third Army front in Lorraine, France. At Lorraine the YD relieved the 4ᵗʰ Armored Division and it was in the hills of Lorraine where they went into combat. By December of 1944, the YD would also be involved in the Battle of the "Bulge" and other major battles. One regiment of the 26ᵗʰ Infantry Division was the 104ᵗʰ, which had a long and noteworthy history. "The 104ᵗʰ dates back to 1639, fought in seven wars and 26 major campaigns. From Lorraine to Czechoslovakia, the 104ᵗʰ received more decorations than any other regiment or unit of the "Yankee division" (Reis 1-2).

Leeman Huff, an infantryman with the 26ᵗʰ Infantry Division, 104ᵗʰ Infantry Regiment, was attached to the Third Army and was a part of the bitter combat at the Battle of the "Bulge," and the Rhineland (Alsace-Lorraine). He was subsequently awarded the Bronze Star for meritorious service. Three weeks later at another battle, he sustained shrapnel wound in the back and was awarded the Purple Heart.

* * * *

Before World War II, Leeman Huff had worked for Savage Arms in Utica. He was twenty when he was drafted in August of 1942. "I really didn't have to go," he laughed. "Since I was working on a sub-machine gun at Savage Arms, I could have been deferred." Huff turned down the deferment opportunity and reported to Camp Upton, New York and Fort Dix, New Jersey.

Huff did his basic training and some infantry training at Fort Jackson, South Carolina where he endured a twenty-mile hike when he almost starved. "They served us liver! I didn't like liver but I got used to liking it," he said.

At Fort Jackson, Huff also participated in maneuvers where he received more infantry training.

Following that training, he went in a cadre (in a group) to Augusta, Georgia for military police school for six months and was transferred to Fort McPherson in Atlanta, Georgia where he was assigned to town duty there. The MP's were assigned to patrol duty in the city of Atlanta and Huff was the squad leader.

Huff was also assigned MP duty on trains from Atlanta to North Carolina and Atlanta to Macon and for a time acted as an MP desk sergeant at the Atlanta police station.

Desiring a change in duty, Huff decided to volunteer for the infantry and was transferred to Greenville, Pennsylvania, where he was placed in the 26th Infantry Division.

Sgt. Huff boarded the troopship George Washington, a converted ocean liner, at Hoboken, New Jersey and left on June 16, 1943 for England. He was placed in charge of all of the military police on board.

The troop ship docked at Liverpool, England after a fourteen-day trip across the Atlantic. Huff said that he was stationed in England for quite a long time and explained that he was in Chester, England on June 6, 1944 when the Normandy invasion took place. "In England I did quite a lot of weapon and general infantry training. I was very active and was stationed near Chester, England all this time," Huff stated.

In September of 1944, 105 days after the invasion of Normandy, Huff boarded a troopship in England and set out across the channel. Off the coast of France, the troops were ordered over the side of the ship and they climbed down the net to board the landing craft that transported them to Omaha Beach.

The 26th Infantry Division moved from Normandy across France to Lorraine to the Third Army front to relieve the 4th Armored Division. Huff's regiment, the 104th Infantry, went through Lorraine taking several towns near Nancy, France. The Third Army was spread along a 75-mile front and the 26th Infantry Division had to face the tough German 11th Panzer Division (Twenty-Sixth 2).

The History of the 26th Infantry Division noted that the 104th Infantry Regiment took Benestroff on November 10, Montcliclier on November 21, and Albestroff on November 24. On December 1, Huff's Company C moved against Saar Union. By noon of that day Company C was met by heavy fire in the woods and was delayed until 1630 and.. then moved forward again. By the end of December 3rd, after 62 hours of fierce fighting, the town was taken (Twenty-Sixth 5, 7, 8).

Metz was captured and it was there that the 104th heard about the

German counter-offensive at the Ardennes. In December of 1944, Huff's division, a part of Patton's Third Army was ordered to go to the Ardennes, which became known as the Battle of the "Bulge" area near Luxembourg.

"Heading north, the 104th hit into the flank of the "Bulge" on the right flank of the 4th Armored Division and went on to relieve Bastogne. The Germans were determined to stop the 104th and bitter fighting ensued. The 104th took Arsdorf on Christmas Day and moved on and took the town of Wiltz" (Reis 2).

Huff did not want to say very much about his combat infantry experience at the "Bulge" or of his other major battle at Lorraine. "I can't say much. Guys were being blown to hell. I don't talk about it much. There were a lot of heads flying off. They were throwing everything at us," he explained.

Huff won the Bronze Star for action at the Bulge involving enemy snipers and described the incident as follows: "We had a sniper nest with quite a few snipers and my squad went out to get rid of them. Three good soldiers got killed on this expedition," he related sadly.

Three weeks later at Bettborn, Luxembourg he was struck in the back with shrapnel and he was moved to a hospital in Comercy, France for about six weeks.

After he was released from the hospital, he was put on limited service and then transferred from the infantry to the Army Air Force and Air Force personnel were being placed in the infantry.

Sgt. Huff was assigned to the 9th Air Force at Louvain, Belgium, which is located near Brussels. Looking at pictures, Huff thought that this occurred during the spring of 1945 when he was at Louvain. In the Air Force, he had an interest in working as an auto mechanic. For a couple of days he said he had enough of this and did not continue in this capacity. Huff said he was treated well in the Air Force and that the food was better than that of the infantry. "All we had was K-rations in the infantry," he added.

Huff showed the author his array of medals and campaign ribbons that included the Bronze Star, the Purple Heart, New York State Conspicuous Service Medal, and Combat Infantryman Badge. He also received two battle stars.

Huff commented on his feelings about the War with the following words:

.... Oh, I'm sure everyone felt the war. When you are over there in it, you don't think there's anything else in life. You can't believe that somewhere people are sleeping in comfortable beds or sitting in a restaurant eating. In Europe, everywhere you walked, you would see a bombed out building and you live with the constant

reminder of it. But when I came back here, all the death and bloodshed seemed so remote. It seemed that it couldn't have actually happened - that it was some hellish nightmare. And you realize that time is the most precious thing. Because time is life!

Sgt. Huff came back to the United States on a Liberty ship. "What a God Damned ship that was!" Huff shouted with a loud laugh. It was evident that Huff did not enjoy his ride home on a Liberty ship.

He was discharged at Fort Dix on November 9, 1945 after thirty-nine months in the Army and Army Air Forces. After the war, Huff was employed at Drop Forge (now Homogeneous Metals) in Clayville, New York and as Traffic Manager for the RCA Service Company. He also operated the "Huff Brau" tavern in Earlville until 1982. He lives in Hamilton, New York.

He passed away November 10, 2007.

10

Raymond Kennard

INFANTRYMAN

The Infantry, the largest of all branches of the army, is as old as history and in earlier times followed the horsemen or cavalry into battle. With the advent of mechanized warfare, the infantry often followed the tank and is sometimes moved about in battle riding on armored vehicles, trucks, planes, and helicopters. The infantry has also included special units of paratroopers. Fighting in all kinds of weather, they have sloshed and slashed their way through swamp and jungle and have agonized in blazing desert heat and snow- covered sub-zero battlefields. The "foot soldier" frequently endured ridicule for being a part of the military, which, in the eyes of many, lacks the glamour of other fighting forces. Nevertheless, history has shown that wars have not been won without the efforts of the infantry.

Raymond "Budge" Kennard of Deansboro and Waterville, was one of these "foot soldiers." He was in combat for over 300 days in North Africa, Sicily, Normandy, and the Battle of the Bulge in Belgium, France and Germany. When the war in Europe ended May 8, 1945, he was in Franzenbad, located on the Austria-Czechoslovakia border.

* * * *

Kennard left his job on Claude Hinman's farm in Deansboro and enlisted in December 1940 into the army. The United States had not yet entered World War II. With $.25 deducted from his pay of $21.00 a month for the Old Soldier's Home, he would net $20.75. By the end of the war with a rank of sergeant and his years of service, his monthly income would grow to $110.00.

Kennard did his basic training at Fort Hamilton in Brooklyn and did further training at Fort Devens, Massachusetts and maneuvers in North Carolina and other parts of the U.S. The training included familiarization in firing 30 mm machine guns and 60 mm mortar firing. Since the country was spending less on the military, readiness for war was lacking. The troops trained with antiquated and makeshift artillery. "We were not really prepared," Kennard pointed out.

On August 2, 1942 he boarded the luxury liner Queen Mary that would transport 20,000 American troops across the Atlantic to England. Kennard described his trip:

> *…The Queen Mary was big and fast and traveled without escort. Even with the weight of the troops, it was too fast for submarines. We had two meals a day because there were so many people on board and we alternated between living and sleeping 24 hours on the deck and living in the staterooms for 24 hours. I didn't get seasick going over but did get sick on the British ship going from England to the North Africa invasion. They fed us mutton stew and tomato sauce. My God! If that wasn't enough to turn your stomachs, the waves would…*

Landing at Roseneath Bay, Scotland, Kennard was transported by train on August 7, 1942 to where he engaged in night training with a compass to get used to operating in the dark. They would mark out certain spots. As a member of the First Infantry Division, 18th Infantry Regiment, Company I, Kennard's training was with 30 caliber machine guns and 16 mm mortars. "The Germans had superior equipment, and they even had better shovels for digging. We had 16 inches of steel on the front of our tanks, but their 88mm guns would penetrate ours. Our tank men had to shoot the tracks off of the German tanks or we could not stop them. Machine gun fire and mortars were the primary fire and the object was to keep the enemy down so the soldiers carrying rifles could move," Kennard explained

On November 8, 1942, the second front started with the invasion of North Africa. Kennard describes his first invasion as follows:

> *…The opening battle was at St. Cloud in Algeria and the resistance was not heavy, but it was enough for our first time. I used to get so sick of getting up in the morning – breakfast, more training, the bayonet course, —had to do that thing so many times – so many times. The training was great. When you get to the point when you are scared and knees start buckling, the training tells you what to do and you just keep going.*

After Algeria the regiment moved into neighboring Tunisia on December 7 to fight alongside French and British troops. The Regiment remained in combat for 48 days.

After the Tunisian campaign, the Regiment sailed for Sicily and landed at Gela on the night of July 10. The campaign in Sicily took 39 days and the Regiment was in combat 33 days. The regiment, not needed in the invasion of the "boot," was ordered back to England in the summer of 1943. In England the regiment was split up and Kennard tells of enjoying some time off and then engaging in amphibious training in preparation for the invasion of Western Europe.

The long awaited time for the attack on Hitler's "Fortress Europa" had arrived. It was D-Day- June 6, 1944 and the point of invasion would be Normandy, France - the approximate location of where American troops disembarked in World War I.

The loaded landing craft (LCVP'S, LCM's and others) rocked and bobbed in the choppy waters of the English Channel as they headed in towards the beachheads. On that gloomy gray morning, the 16th Infantry was part of the first wave that stormed Omaha beach. Kennard's 18th Infantry Regiment would strike Omaha Beach as part of the second wave. "Lots of people drowned in the first wave as they left the landing craft. Kennard maintains that as many drowned as were shot. The Nazis had laid out many barriers including barbed wire and the navy coxswains manning the helm of the three boats dropped their ramps too soon. They didn't want the screws of their boats to get tangled in barbed wire. They had to get back so they could transport more troops to Omaha Beach. As a result of this many drowned in the deep water. Some of the troops had landed in deep water holes caused by artillery shells and the water would be up to their heads. "If you couldn't swim, you were in trouble. Some would grab a rifle butt from a buddy and be helped to shallow water. As part of the second wave to assault Omaha Beach, we were lucky that some of the coxswains knew just where to drop the ramps and avoid the deeper areas," Kennard recalled.

By evening of the first day troops had moved only three miles inland. Kennard said that of all the campaigns he was in, Normandy seemed the toughest for the allies. In place of fence wire, farmers used hedgerows to keep the cows enclosed. These sectioned off the land with openings to allow passage for cows (Houston 37). Germans would conceal themselves in the hedgerows and also place their machine guns in the openings thereby controlling the whole field. "I would anticipate where these openings were and lob in mortars in that direction. We had to use tanks to get over the hedgerows and the advance was slow. The Germans used MG 34 machineguns and could fire 1150 rounds a minute compared to our 30 calibers which fired only 850 rounds a minute," Kennard explained.

When asked how close he was to the enemy, he replied, "At times I was so close I could see their eyes. They were just as scared as we were." Commenting on fatigue and the winter of 1944-45, Kennard remarked that he dug the deepest and best hole of all – down two to three feet. At that depth the temperature was about 52-54 degrees. Then he would make a seat at the side of the hole. "Man! That dirt was warm. Didn't dare to take our shoes off because then we couldn't get them back on," Kennard explained.

The history of the 18th Infantry Regiment indicated that beginning July 14, 1944, after 39 days of continuous combat, the men enjoyed four days of rest a little west of St. Lo, France. On July 25, the 18th Infantry with the help of the 3rd Armored Division, brought about what some have called the greatest achievement of the war – the breakthrough at St. Lo. By August 17 the enemy front had disintegrated and another rest followed. "In the short span of 60 days, the 18th regiment had been assigned to two of the most difficult and momentous missions in its history. The first was that on the night of June 6, the Normandy beachhead was expanded...The second was the breakthrough at St. Lo. Both missions were fulfilled at a high cost of lives and suffering (Commanding Officer, "History of the 18th Infantry Regiment" Nov.8 '42 to Nov. 8, '44 – Algeria to Aachen, Germany). Following this engagement, Kennard said that the troops rode a lot. The history of the regiment further indicated that the troops rode 120 miles into enemy territory. By September, they passed through Belgium and moved on to Aachen, Germany.

In December, the Germans initiated their last counteroffensive with the objective of gaining Antwerp in an attempt to capture fuel. The breakthrough created a bulge in the allied lines, which led to the naming of this campaign as the Battle of the Bulge. SS Colonel General Dietrich was in charge of the German Panzer Army. His policy was – "take no prisoners."

The Battle of the Bulge took place around Christmas 1944 and lasted until February of 1945. "The terrain was covered with snow and you couldn't see if there was a creek in the area. You would take a step and then fall in. Most of the casualties were the result of artillery fire." The 18th Infantry crossed the Rhine River on Bailey Bridges(rapidly constructed metal bridges) and Kennard added that after Aachen, Germany, the division advanced rapidly across Germany and into Austria.

He was wounded once in Germany in January 1945. A self-propelled gun on a tank hit a roof and a piece of the roof fell and hit him under the right shoulder blade. After receiving some sulfa and morphine for the wound, he kept going. In February he refused a chance to go home. "I decided to stay until it was over, and then I wanted to be the first to leave," Kennard remarked.

On V-E Day, May 8, 1945, he was at Franzenbad on the Austrian border. The regiment was sent to Bamberg, Germany, where they were given new clothes and began to eat better. Later they left for LeHavre and came home on Liberty ships. He landed at Boston and was discharged at Fort Dix, New Jersey. He was dissatisfied with the way the war ended because he thought American troops should have been allowed to take Berlin. General

Eisenhower, Commander of the Allied Expeditionary Forces, stopped the American advance at the Elbe River in Germany, permitting the Russians to conquer Berlin. American and Russian forces eventually met at the Elbe.

On V-J day, August 14, 1945, Kennard was in front of Altieri's Restaurant (still in business) in Clinton. "The country owes you a lot, "Budge," the author declared. Kennard replied," I was proud to serve in World War II and the country doesn't owe me a thing."

Raymond Kennard passed away October 3, 2000.

11

Michael Kucirka

9TH ARMORED

The 9th Armored Division commanded by Major General John W. Leonard had a proud and glorious record during World War II. Arriving in England in August of 1944, the division, a part of the First Army, crossed the Channel and moved swiftly across France, Belgium, Luxembourg and the Rhineland into Germany and finally into Czechoslovakia. The division participated in one of the most bitter and bloody battles in history - the Ardennes Forest Campaign - better known as the "Battle of the Bulge". At the "Bulge" the 9th Armored and 101st Airborne Divisions were encircled by the enemy and ordered to hold at all costs.

Another major engagement was the capture of the Ludendorff Bridge at Remagen in March of 1945. The 9th Armored Division tanks crossed over the Rhine River before the Germans could blow it up. "It was the first time in 140 years-since the great days of Napoleon-that a hostile invader had crossed the German River"(Miller 798).

Michael Kucirka of West Winfield, New York, was attached to Company C of the 9th Armored Engineer Battalion and participated in the Battle of the Bulge and the seizing of the bridge at Remagen as the allies moved through Europe. Though wounded at the Battle of the Bulge, he never received a Purple Heart medal.

* * * *

Kucirka, who was born in Conemaugh, Pennsylvania, was a farmer and construction worker before being drafted into the Army on November 10, 1942. He was 26 years old.

After induction at Camp Upton, New York he went to Camp Polk, Louisiana for basic training, and then to Fort Riley, Kansas in July of 1942 where he was assigned to Company C, 9th Armored Division, Engineering Battalion. At Fort Riley he suffered an injury while supervising the building of a pontoon bridge with his men. The crane's swinging arm struck him on the side of his head and broke his helmet and injured his right eye requiring stitches over the eye.

Kucirka's next duty station was in California for desert training and maneuvers. He was injured again one night in 1943 while removing caps from a land mine. The mine explosion resulted in his losing sight in his left eye.

After six months he was released from the hospital and returned to his company and then was shipped overseas. He arrived in England in August 1944 and while there, a few of them built two communications trailers for the officers for combat use.

After drawing equipment the division crossed the channel to France and his first combat experience was in Belgium and Luxemburg in October. The location was a section of the front at St. Vith and "it was bad," Kucirka recalled. The fighting lasted until November and the forces then advanced to Echternach and it was there that Kucirka's said that he froze his feet. "I was in a foxhole and they got me out and lit a cigarette and held it close to my foot." He had no feelings in his feet and was placed in a jeep and taken to a building, which resembled a hop house in America. He lay on his back with his feet in the air and after recovering, his friend Allen Wilhite took him back to his division.

After some time elapsed and as they were crossing some fields, he said, the Germans were continuing their artillery attacks and he remembers that he managed to get into a gorge. Some vehicles were destroyed but some did escape the shelling. Later, at night, when he was alone and the German artillery was causing many casualties, he was running and was picked up by the company's half-track and was glad to be back with his buddies.

Kucirka said that one time while he and his buddies came to a road where more of his company vehicles were located, they advanced to a small hill and exchanged shots with a German machine gun, which was firing at them. "We shot back and destroyed the machine gun nest. Some white flags appeared and some of my buddies went there to get prisoners but as we went along a little ways the enemy shelling started again and we shelled them back hard and we killed them," Kucirka explained.

Kucirka said they then moved toward another town and the enemy was firing at us. An officer and some men went into the town and it was decided before they went that if they did not return after a set time, the town would be hit hard.

...We waited and they didn't show up and we couldn't see them. We hit the town and I mean hard." The town was on fire from the heavy shelling. The white flags went up again. The smoke was bad and as we went through the town we didn't see any of our buddies or the officer that had gone into the town...

Kucirka explained that at Bastogne they were told to dig in and hold.

Bastogne, which is located in Belgium, is the most well known battle site of the Ardennes Campaign (Battle of the Bulge), the largest land battle by U.S. armed forces in World War II (Wheal, Pope, Taylor 75,76). Elements of the Third Army rushed from the Alsace-Lorraine area to the Bastogne area.

At Bastogne, Kucirka said, "There was no place to stay and it was cold. The men dug holes in the ground and filled them with leaves to stay warm. It was December 1944 and it was snowing at times." He said that during the day fires were started to keep warm and at night they would put the fires out so the enemy did not spot them. They were told that help was on the way and planes came after the weather was cleared and dropped supplies.

...In a day or two the 101ˢᵗ Airborne Division came down and General MacAuliffe was their commander. After a few days we were told to hold our fire since a German officer was coming up the road where we were. The German officer came and returned on the same road.

Kucirka said they had found out later that General MacAuliffe was asked to surrender and that his answer was "Nuts."

We were on the line and had no place to go. That night the German artillery was like hell. I lay on the ground and a plane came over that was shot up and on fire and it came right down at me. The great God was with me. The plane turned off to the right and then I heard the trees being crushed and the plane crash and explode. It was cold and I cried aloud at times. I went to sleep and when morning came we were told to go to a field with other buddies...

He said that as they moved along some of his buddies were killed. "I got back to my foxhole and stayed a few days and nights and received new socks," he recalled. It was night and he stayed there with no place to go and the food, which was in cans, was cold. At times he had canned heat for heating the food and for keeping warm. "Sometimes, we placed sleeping bags over the foxhole."

Kucirka described German tank fire at an American machine gun position in the Bastogne area.

...A line had been set up and since it was almost evening, we had set up a line there. There was a machine gun nest ahead and the Germans directed tank fire at it. One shell from the tank hit the

machine gun nest. One of the men must have had his hand on the machine gun trigger and the gun was turning toward me. I hugged the ground until I heard the machine gun stop turning. I raised my head up and looked over there and called my buddy's name. I did not see or hear anyone. I was there by myself. I cried and did not know what to do so I stayed there all night. After a time the shelling stopped...

Next morning Kucirka heard a tank and he looked up and saw an enemy tank coming toward him. The tank stopped and someone in the tank opened the hatch. He stood up and "I took my weapon and shot him in the head. He went down fast. I was mad for what they did to my buddies," Kucirka shouted with determination in his voice. The German tank rolled back down the hill. He struggled back to his foxhole where he had been previously.

Kucirka continued his recollection of the battle as follows:

...It was as if I had a dream. I couldn't run or walk very fast. It was hard going back. After getting back into my foxhole, I saw a person climb a tree and he was looking at me with field glasses. I took my weapon and shot him. He dropped down and he didn't move. I stayed in my foxhole. I could see the Germans to my left in the hedge. Soon I heard one of our tanks heading for my foxhole. I took my helmet and weapon and put it up. I don't think he saw it because he came close to my hole and stopped. I got out of my foxhole and he opened the tank hatch door. I told him to hurry and also told him where the enemy was located. So the tank fired a few shots with the 50 calibers to help give a position for the big gun of the tank. The 50-caliber gun hit the exact spot I had pointed out to him. The tank then fired the big gun and you could see the bodies fly in the air. I then told him that I had better be going and let him take over....

As he was walking along he met an officer and some others in his company and he was asked where he was going. "I told him and he said help was on the way." I, and my buddies, went back to our foxholes and stayed there all night. It was cold and the moon was shining. "We got word to go back to the town and so we left," Kucirka stated. Along the way a German plane fired at Kucirka and his group. "The bullets landed right in front of me. I could see the dust fly in front of me. I stopped and froze and I could hear bullets hit the wall of a building to my left and a piece of the wall hit me in the face," he recalled. As they went along further they came to a building and were told to go inside. They were told that General Patton was coming in the evening. Inside the building they lie on the floor and could hear a plane go over and then come back. It dropped a bomb on the building he was in knocking him unconscious. Kucirka didn't know how long he had lain there. "I was out and when I came to I looked up at the ceiling. And it's hard to explain this, but looking up, I could see the sky and stars," he stated. He removed the debris from his body and he was in his sleeping bag, which was carried in his duffel bag. Someone helped him get out of the building and it was dark and he could neither see nor hear his buddies. Blood was on his hands and his ears were ringing. He said that his head was roaring and that he had lost part of his hearing. As he left the building some men also helped him on to a truck. It was morning and they were standing on the road. Kucirka said that in a short time General Patton drove by and as he went by in his vehicle he looked at Kucirka and stuck his stick out and said, "Get that God damned vehicle off the road!" After about a half- hour, Kucirka said that he and his group moved on.

The Battle of the Bulge was over in January. "This futile attempt cost the Germans 20 divisions, 100,000 casualties and 1,000 airplanes. At the end of January, Hitler had ordered a retreat"(Wheal 76).

Kucirka remarked that after the "Bulge" he thinks the division moved to Metz, Germany. There was a lull in the fighting. "It was good to not be fighting and it sure was great to take a shower, shave, eat good food and sleep inside," he remarked joyfully. They were issued new clothes and after a few weeks the division was re-equipped.

Continuing with his recollections, Kucirka said that at one place an officer told him to go through a building and check it out. He said that when he went inside he heard a shot behind him and that it didn't sound like a German weapon. It was dark and soon a nurse tapped him on the shoulder. Speaking English, she told Kucirka that an American officer had been shot and she needed his help. She said that she was a German nurse.

> *...After we got to the officer who had been shot, she said to take his watch off so she could take his pulse. I said to her, 'you take it off! She said she couldn't since she was a German nurse. So I took the watch off the officer and at the time I didn't know if he was an officer or not. She then took his pulse and she said he was dead and I put the watch in my pocket and asked if that was all she wanted of me. She said 'Yes'. I went on and checked out the building. Later, we were all called out and told to stand in line. My battalion commander said that an American officer had been shot and he had a watch. 'Does anyone here have the watch?' I*

stepped out and showed him the watch and two men came toward me, but my battalion commander said-'Let him go. We need that man.'

A day or two later Kucirka was called in and told that the nurse had verified what he had said about the watch and the dead officer. "I was free," Kucirka explained, but he never found out why the German nurse was in that building, and under what circumstances the officer was shot.

The 9th Armored Division was on the move passing through Aachen through German territory and heading toward the Rhine River. On the way to Remagen he said there were smoke pots on the road and powerful lights. They were being shelled but they were able to knock out the lights and they saw trenches twelve feet deep and four to six feet wide with dead bodies in them. As they went by they smelled gas and someone said it was a gas chamber. "I had to put my hand over my mouth and nose because the smell was so bad," he described. "I said 'What the hell was that?' The gas-like smell was so bad I had to put my gas mask on and I could see a person with his hands on the bars of a window." Kucirka said that he could not remember the name of the town and never learned the reason for the gas smell.

Kucirka described the capture of the bridge at Remagen.

...It was spring. March 7, 1945, and we reached a bridge (Ludendorff Bridge) at Remagen. Companies B and C worked together and we were the first ones there and we captured the bridge. B Company went on the bridge and cut all the wire connections to prevent the Germans from blowing up the bridge. We stayed there two days and nights...

The following quotation taken from a military booklet entitled <u>The Bridge</u>, commemorates the seizure of the "Bridge:"

...The Ninth Armored Division under Major General John Leonard joined the "immortals" of military history, March 7, 1945, by its spectacular capture of the Ludendorff Bridge at Remagen, and its subsequent swift establishment of the first Allied foothold east of the Rhine. This brilliant military coup electrified the entire world, and hastened the end of the European War (Gasque 1).

As the weather improved in the spring, the division advanced to Limburg and Warburg, Germany where prisoners of war were liberated at both places. "It was still March and the war was going our way," Kucirka related.

Kucirka told how they were moving along from morning to night and German prisoners were going by all day long in the opposite direction. "We were told just before sunset to come back and follow the Germans. We followed with a half-track vehicle to a big field and all the Germans were ordered into a circle and a fence was put up around them. At Erfurt we saw another 12,000 German prisoners and they were also encircled."

It was the middle of April and the Ninth Armored Division had reached Leipzig. There the division encircled the city but there was no combat. The 2nd and 69th Infantry Divisions relieved them. They then proceeded to the Mulde River and were told to stay there and wait for the Russians to arrive. In early May they were at Hof - a place that had railroad lines and many railroad cars including tank cars that they were supposed to destroy if they contained war supplies. One tank car had been damaged by gunfire and liquid was pouring from it. Kucirka said that he saw guys going back and forth to the tank car filling their water cans and putting them on trucks. "I said, 'What the hell are they doing? They must be carrying water and putting it on trucks.' Next day an officer poured some liquid from the can into his cup. He tasted it and spit it out. He thought it was water but it was 'booze'. The officer said 'What's going on?' The men told him that the tank car had alcohol in it. They were then ordered to dump it and replace all the water cans with water," Kucirka seriously disclosed with much emphasis and excitement in his voice.

From Hof, the division went into Czechoslovakia to a place called Karlsbad where some German troops surrendered on May 7. The war in Europe was over.

In relating some other experiences, Kucirka described how he had slept outdoors at Bastogne for two weeks dug into a foxhole and sleeping inside a sleeping bag at night. One time something was inside his sleeping bag and bit him. Jumping up he shook his bag thinking it was a snake. A field mouse jumped out. He often wore two pairs of socks inside oversized shoes to keep his feet warm.

Kucirka related again how his feet were badly frozen at Echternach, and feels that he is entitled to at least one Purple Heart medal because of the frostbite and for his head wound at Bastogne. He has not been able to prove that he was wounded at Bastogne when the injury occurred, was unable to obtain immediate medical attention at that time, and he had never mentioned the incident while he was in Europe. However, he was granted disability for the head injury incurred at Fort Riley, Kansas and for the frostbite injury.

T-4 Kucirka returned to the United States and before being discharged, he did mention to the Army the injury he had received at Bastogne.

His records were destroyed in a fire at the Military Personnel Center in St. Louis and there is no known record of the injury he had received at Bastogne.

He was discharged on November 20, 1945, at Fort Dix. After leaving the service, he worked in construction and cabinet making until retirement.

Michael Kucirka passed away January 2, 2002.

12

Rocco Langone

SERVICE COMPANY

PFC ROCCO LANGONE
(Courtesy of Linda Nichols)

Service companies in the Army provided support transporting supplies, equipment, and personnel to the front lines. Two and one-half ton trucks carried the fuel to keep the tanks rolling.

The following is about the author's brother who was a member of a Service Company attached to the 748th Tank Battalion. In August of 1944, he and several friends from Waterville who were in the same tank battalion, landed at Omaha

Beach in France. Their unit advanced through France and Germany and into Austria where the war ended in early May of 1945.

Since they are all now deceased, much of the following is taken from conversations years earlier with the author's late brother, and a pamphlet entitled "Saga of the Rhinos - Or A Brief history of the 748th Tank Battalion from 1942 to 1945." Information was also obtained from a farewell address entitled "So-Long Tankers," delivered by the Commanding Officer, Lieutenant Colonel, Robert R. Glass near Linz, in June of 1945.

The author's eldest brother, Rocco Langone, and two of his friends from Waterville were truck drivers in the 748th Tank Battalion. His next-door neighbor in Waterville, Harold Youngs, was a tank driver and during Christmas 1944 they were at the south flank of the Battle of the Ardennes (Battle of the Bulge). Before the war ended, Langone, Harold "Chesty" Youngs, Robert "Mose" Ruane and his brother Leo "Honk," earned four battle stars for their part in the campaigns of northern France, Ardennes, Rhineland, and Central Europe. William Howe, from Waterville, and "Bud" Kirley from Oriskany Falls also participated in these campaigns. They were all attached to the same tank battalion of General George Patton's Third Army. Harold "Chesty" Youngs, who loved racing his father's old Model T Ford around town, was selected to become a tank driver. Youngs was wounded a few weeks before the war ended.

* * * *

Always a hard worker, with a desire to help support his family, and not always in love with his studies, Rocco Langone dropped out of school. He went to work at the old Conkling-Rogers box factory in Earlville, a short walk from home, which was located at the end of Preston Street. After employment at the box factory, he worked for his section foreman father on the DL&W Railroad as a track worker.

At age 20, he was drafted into the Army on December 1, 1942 and the first blue star on the World War II service banner appeared in the front window of the house on East Bacon Street.

"Rocky" Langone and the boys from Waterville went to Camp Rucker, Alabama for basic training. According to the pamphlet "Saga of the Rhinos – A Brief History of the 748th Tank Battalion, on December 5, 1942, five hundred and six recruits reported from Camp Upton, Long Island. The men were placed into companies and the training began with M4 tanks. (Saga 2).

Langone and the Ruanes were attached to Service Company, 748th Tank Battalion and they drove 2 ½ ton light trucks transporting personnel, fuel, and other equipment.

On the 15th of April, the 748th left by train for Fort Knox, Kentucky. The training consisted of close order drill, scouting and patrolling, and gunnery and tanking.

On July 15, 1943, the battalion boarded a train once again for the Desert Training Center located near Needles, California. "Saga of the Rhinos" relates how the Santa Fe Railroad dumped them in the middle of the California desert with 72 M4 tanks…"one of the cooler days was 120° in the shade" (4).

In September the new location for desert training was Camp Bouse in Arizona located 85 miles from Phoenix, Arizona where weekend passes were sometimes enjoyed. Some beautiful ladies from Hollywood called the "Desert Battalion" came to sing and dance for the troops. The book "The Desert Battalion," written by Mrs. Edward G. Robinson includes "a great deal" about the 748th Tank Battalion (Saga 5).

Orders to leave for overseas arrived on March 21, 1944 and the battalion left Camp Bouse for New York. After a brief stay at Camp Shanks they boarded the Queen Elizabeth for the trip overseas. Langone, Youngs and the Ruanes boarded the huge luxury liner and left New York Harbor and after the fast trip across the Atlantic, the ship docked at Glasgow, Scotland April 6, 1944. The battalion went to South Wales to Crymnychin Pembroke County where the troops lived in tents.

More training followed and. on D-Day, June 6, 1944; the 748th was at a British training camp. Receiving orders to cross the Channel to France, the troops boarded the Liberty ship, SS Daniel Heister and six LST's. There were some submarine alerts before they landed on Omaha Beach.

After a while the battalion went to a new training area near Genets, France, near Mont St. Michel. There they lived in foxholes. After a few weeks the battalion moved to Joullouville, a resort town, and the whole battalion lived in a schoolhouse. Mines left by the Germans along the coast had to be avoided and they had the job of protecting the coast from German invasion or raids located on some islands (Saga 11-12).

In November the battalion moved thirty miles southwest of Rennes in Brittany and lived in barracks. There the troops were placed on reserve in case of an enemy breakthrough and more training took place before they were ordered to move up to the front lines.

The German counter-offensive in the Ardennes Forest began December 17. The "Saga of the Rhinos" stated that by mid-December 1944 the battalion "had the opportunity of becoming eligible for the famous Forty and Eight – the famous Quarante Hommes Huit Chevaux." "Forty & Eight" refers to French railroad boxcars used during World War I and II to transport troops to the front. Stenciled on the outside was the capacity of the little boxcars—Forty men or eight horses. "Quarante hommes at huit chevaux." This was the origin of the veterans organization known as the "FORTY& EIGHT") (Forty 1).

The tanks, trucks, and jeeps were put on flat cars and the troops were jammed into boxcars and set out for Hagondange near Metz, Germany. "When we arrived before, during, and after Christmas Day we knew we had arrived in the combat zone" (13). The author remembers his brother describing the heavy shelling on Christmas Eve.

There were two occasions when things got exciting. Some paratroopers came into the area and weapons were fired at them. It turned out to be a crew from a B-17 that had bailed out. Also, "a patrol was sent out to investigate a 'mysterious' vehicle and captured our own garbage truck."(Saga14) In a conversation with the boys from Waterville who were there, the author learned that it was Langone on a garbage detail, and he had strayed behind enemy lines.

Around the middle of January 1945, the battalion moved toward the Siegfried Line between the Saar and Moselle Rivers. On the 19th of February, an all out attack on the Siegfried positions was launched and the Line was broken. The battalion moved forward through the area toward the Rhine River, which was crossed at St. Goar on the 26th of March. The author remembers reading one of Rocky's letters stating that he crossed the Rhine at St. Goar, which is located below Coblenz, Germany.

Shortly before the war in Europe ended, the author recalls a telegram received by Harold Youngs' parents informing them that their son had been wounded. A shell struck Youngs' tank and one crewmember of his tank was killed. William, "Pete," Howe, also a tank driver in the 748th Unit, was two tanks behind Youngs' when the shell attack occurred. According to Donald Howe, a nephew, "Uncle Pete" told him the American tanks were travelling single file down a road in Germany close to the Austrian border in late April 1945. Pete Howe said the top turret of his tank was open and he observed a sniper in a church tower launch a bazooka at Youngs' tank. Donald Howe also recalled Youngs telling him after the war that he still occasionally felt pain from shrapnel that was never removed from his back.

On the 4th of May, the division went into Austria reaching Linz on May 6 and the war in Europe ended May 8. The author recalls reading letters from his brother that were written in Linz, Austria.

On June 22, 1945, near Linz, Austria LTCOL Robert Glass, the Commanding Officer of the 748th Tank Battalion said goodbye to the Battalion as he was being transferred to XX Corps. Some quotes from his farewell address summarize quite well the highlights of the 748th and the experiences of the boys from Waterville and Oriskany Falls that served in the Battalion.

> *Do you remember Alabama – the driving rain, mud*
> *and biting cold?*
> *Do you remember the desert? - - The scorching*
> *heat and the scorpions and the rattlesnakes?"*
> *Do you remember the Queen Elizabeth — the*
> *first thrilling sight of land?"*
> *Do you remember the ride across France in the*
> *forty and eights?"*
> *Do you remember the day the first of our*
> *companies came back from its baptism of fire?"*
> *Do you remember the thirty-six hour drive from*
> *Hagondange right up to the Formidable Rhine River without*
> *even a break?"*
> *Do you remember the first tank in the Third Army*
> *ever to cross the Rhine?*
> *Do you remember the uncompromising pursuit through Germany*
> *and over the borders of Austria?" (Glass 2-3).*

Private First class Rocco Langone and the Ruane brothers sailed home on a fast cruiser in November. They reported to Fort Dix and were honorably discharged December 4, 1945. Youngs had returned home earlier.

Langone worked as a Section Foreman on the DL&WRR (later the Lackawanna-Erie RR, and Conrail) until his retirement.

He passed away in 1982 at age 60.

13

Daniel Mahoney

MP/ESCORT GUARD

During World War II there were 425,000 enemy prisoners captured by the American forces and placed in 511 camps throughout the United States (German 1). Once taken into custody, they were escorted by units that transported them under guard to different parts of the United States to be used as part of the labor force. The state of Texas had 78,000 German prisoners of war- more than any other state.

* * * *

Daniel Mahoney of Utica, NY, who lived in Waterville for several years after World War II, was a member of the Military Police Escort Guard whose primary duty was guarding and transporting prisoners of war from Europe back to various parts of the United States.

The draft was signed into law by President Franklin D. Roosevelt in 1940 and months before the attack on Pearl Harbor, 25 year-old Daniel Mahoney was drafted into the Army in March of 1941.

His first duty station was Governor's Island, New York. "I had the best time of my life there," Mahoney said with a big smile. They treated us so well in New York City – especially after December 7, 1941." While at Governor's Island, Mahoney said he did administrative work but had no basic training.

The attack on Pearl Harbor occurred during Mahoney's ninth month in the Army. At the time of the attack, I was lying in my bunk and after hearing the announcement, I jumped up so fast that I hit my head on the bunk above me." Mahoney recalled. "All I could think of was that I had nine months to go before I could get out since I had only been drafted for a year." However, Pearl Harbor automatically extended Mahoney's Army time to last the duration of the war.

Around October 1942, Mahoney was transferred to Fort Custer, Michigan for basic training. During basic his company was being made up and he was assigned to the 475th Military Police Escort Guard (MPEG).

For a while the unit had guard duty assignments at a prisoner of war camp in Illinois. During the time he was stationed at Fort Custer, several trips were made to New York City for German prisoners of war who were transported back to Michigan to work as agricultural field workers. He also escorted prisoners to Texas. Mahoney explained that the prisoners were happy to be in the United States, and the guards even got to know some of them. He recalled one German saying, "I knew we were defeated when I saw how good things were in the United States."

Mahoney said that his first trip overseas was in July 1944, about a month after D-Day at Normandy. From England he crossed the channel and landed at Omaha Beach. His unit was at St Lo. France when the Germans finally gave up the area and the big breakthrough occurred, putting the Germans in retreat. Many of the enemy were captured and among them were members of the German staff including a general.

> *...You would think the German staff was going on a vacation. The general and the others had their gear with them including fishing poles. A general even had his own dog –an Irish setter dog. The Company commander said to grab four guys and take them to England. We gathered them together and put them on a plane for England. I had never flown before. The five of us plus the company commander escorted the prisoners.*

Mahoney made five trips back and forth escorting POW's and he recalled what he believed was the worst situation he observed while in the Army. He was on a hospital ship traveling back to Germany and it was about September of 1945. I was in Cherbourg one day when some of our boys were brought in and put on the hospital ship to return to the United States. They were in real bad shape with severe mental problems. "They were really shot," he said, and they had to sleep in cramped quarters below deck."

"One-half of our unit boarded a ship for the trip back to the States, but the ship developed a problem and we had to pull into St. Johns, Newfoundland for repairs. At St. Johns, the GI's on board were not allowed off the ship, but the escort guard was given permission to leave the ship and visit St. Johns.

"The ship was repaired and we arrived in New York City. After a night and a day we boarded a train for Georgia. One-half of the 475th unit had arrived in New York earlier by way of another ship but they had already left for Georgia," Mahoney said.

Corporal Daniel Mahoney was discharged in October of 1945. He worked for Langdon and Hughes as an electrical General Electric distributor. After General Electric absorbed Langdon and Hughes, he worked for that firm until he retired in 1982.

He passed away April 30, 2010 at the age of 94.

14

Charles Miner

30ᵀᴴ INFANTRY

The Thirtieth Infantry Division traces its origins to World War I and was made up of National Guard troops of North and South Carolina and Tennessee. The division built a proud reputation participating in various battles in France and Belgium and especially for penetrating the famous German Hindenburg Line in September of 1918, which helped bring the war to an end. The division bears the nickname "Old Hickory" in honor of Andrew Jackson (Old Hickory 1-2)

In 1940, the division was federalized at Fort Jackson, South Carolina and fought in all of the major campaigns on the western front. Army Historian S.L.A. Marshall called the thirtieth the "Finest Infantry Division in the European Theater of Operations"(Old Hickory 1).

* * * *

Charles B. Miner of Oriskany Falls joined the 119th Infantry Regiment of the 30th Infantry Division a few months after D-Day in September of 1944. The regiment would take part in the cracking of the Seigfreid Line as the 30th Division broke the Hindenburg Line in World War I in 1918. Miner fought in several campaigns and ultimately won a battlefield commission.

After graduation from high school in 1939, Miner worked in his uncle's garage. On May 29, 1942 he enlisted into the Army at the age of 22 and did his basic and tactical training at Fort Meade, Maryland.

In 1942, the war was well underway and the Army needed officers so Minor was selected to attend Officer Candidate's School at Fort Benning, Georgia. He and several others were surprised when three days before the end of the course they were not allowed to graduate. They were told that they lacked leadership ability and that men would not follow them into battle. "The irony was that they also "bounced" a first sergeant that had seen combat in the Pacific. Figure that one out – if you can," Miner asked with some bitterness in his voice. "I didn't always agree with them because I didn't follow their school solutions as to how to conduct a battle. Strangely, I was then put into a regiment that did demonstrations for the OCS personnel."

After a period of one year of this duty, Miner heard that the Army needed pilots, navigators, and bombardiers so he applied for this and was transferred to Miami and entered the Army Air Forces.

In Miami, in 1944, he received Air Force training, which included qualifying tests. Before starting Air force training, the Army decided to transfer him to Fort Jackson, -a replacement depot. He was there about two months and during that time the invasion of Normandy took place.

In the latter part of September 1944, he left New York on the "Idle de France," a French luxury liner operated by the British. After a seven-day trip he arrived in England.

In October, he was assigned to the 119th Infantry Regiment of the 30thDivision and joined them as a replacement at Bardenburg. Miner said that the division was at the Seigfried Line, which extended for miles along the border of Germany.

Miner said that on the second day after arriving there, he viewed a grisly sight- a dead American officer draped over a barbed wire fence. He was sent on patrol and made contact with the First Division, and he said that a battle occurred at the town of Wurselen and he displayed an article that his former company commander, Colonel Edward Arn (a Lieutenant at that time), had sent to the <u>Waterville Times</u> a few years ago. Arn praised Miner, who had been in combat less than a week, for his true leadership. The article is an account of Miner saving some lives at Wurselen and is quoted, in part, as follows:

...On October 11, 1944, Co. F, 119th Regiment of the 30th Infantry Division was attacking south in the Seigfried Line toward Aachen, Germany and reached Wurselen, a suburb of Aachen. Sgt. Charles B. Miner who commanded one of F Company's rifle squads, was ordered to place his squad in a defensive position in a bombed out café in Wurselen. The enemy was very close and firing mortars and machine guns. Entering the café, Miner searched for booby traps and during the search found several buckets of sand. After he was sure there were no booby traps, he ordered his squad into the café. F Company was to remain in a holding position for several days. Enemy fire continued to strike the café. As Miner and his men were waiting for orders to move out, men from a relieving unit brought a portable gasoline cook stove and set it up in a narrow passageway leading from the cellar to the first floor. Fuel spilled out and a fire occurred trapping the men in the cellar. Without regard for his own life, Miner raced up the stairs to the second floor as enemy shells were striking the building. He seized two buckets of sand and at great risk put out the blaze thus saving the lives of at least a dozen men. Lieutenant

Arn praised Miner, who had been in combat less than a week, for his true leadership…(Arn).

Since they had been advancing so fast, supplies were not able to keep up. Miner explained that they were placed in a holding position at Wurselen for a couple of weeks.

In the latter part of October, the regiment was ordered back for R&R – rest and recreation at Kolsheid. Following the R&R, Miner described the taking of the town of Merzenhausen as follows:

…After Kolsheid we went through several towns and reached Merzenhausen in November. There had been a seesaw battle there and we were very tired of that. On the 26th E and F companies, after enduring much German machine gun fire, mortar fire, and bazooka fire, took the town. We took about 80 prisoners one afternoon and that was my first house-to-house combat. We used grenades and we kept the enemy inside until they surrendered. Most of them were in the cellar. We also captured a German battalion commander…

That night, about mid-night, Miner recalled, the Germans made a counter-attack but they were stopped at a bridge.

…We called for artillery to stop the attack even though it was coming right in on top of us. A German tanker with a .50 caliber swung his turret around so I ducked and hit the ground. As I did I inadvertently shoved my M1 rifle into a sugar beet pile. I said to myself, 'What do you do next'? I couldn't shoot the thing but I was able to get someplace so I would not get hit and I then dismantled the rifle in the dark. I took it apart, cleaned it, and put it back together again. I was well trained since I had to do it many times in training and I had shot it a lot.

"After we took Merzenhausen, we were pulled out of combat. It was Thanksgiving and we were treated to an excellent Thanksgiving dinner. Most of the time we had only K-rations" Miner explained. After Thanksgiving the troops were ordered back again and were then put on line with the British for a few days.

There was some snow on the ground and it was the middle of December. The Battle of the Bulge took place causing a huge dent in the American lines. Miner was transferred from Merzenhausen to a rear area and assigned to central communications. He was put in charge of all of the radiomen, map-readers, and telephone men. He was made a communication sergeant and remained in that status to the end of the war. Miner said that there was a lot more to it than just communications.

> *...I felt it was my job to go up to the front lines if there was a problem. I would make recommendations as to what to do about it, and sometimes I would get into a few skirmishes. I would move around quite a bit and there was one skirmish in particular near Malmedy. At Malmedy, I remember that it was the first time we got bombed by our own Air Force. We would look up and say, 'which way should I run? – Or should we just stand there. We were in the northern part of the "Bulge" with the 9th Army. The date was December 17 – when the German counter offensive began.*

Miner also said that the Americans did stop the Germans and their Field Marshal Piper. He described how the German advanced units came up on these troop carriers. It was dark and they were coming up on one side and American tank destroyers were going down the other side. Suddenly, their column stopped and they turned their headlights on and the tank destroyers fired the 90mm guns and got the Germans. One of Miner's men shot a bazooka three times and knocked out three troop carriers. They turned around and headed down the road toward Liege. The 119th was involved in skirmishes at Malmedy and other areas of the "Bulge."

Miner said that Stoumont was a very hot spot, as he described the bitter battle that was fought there.

> *...Our troops were hit with more 'friendly fire.' Part of the unit was in a brick building. We could tell by the sound that they were American planes and we saw their smoke shell that mark targets, come down so we headed for the cellar in a hurry. This was at Bellevue and they laid a pattern of bombs that hit just across the street and we were in a building close to the street. We did have a few close calls.*

Another time, after the "Bulge" battle, Miner recalled, the squad was held out by German artillery fire and I went to check on them. "I was walking by a former member of my squad and I was about 20 feet from him and all of a sudden he wasn't there. He had been hit by artillery fire. He was gone just like that. That was a close call for me and I was pinned down in a snow bank,"

Miner said with emotion. He continued to describe the battle that went on into February as follows:

> *...We then were set up in a chateau at the end of the woods. Another guy and I thought we'd check the woods without getting hit. Anyways, there were a whole row of trees across the road and in the branches the Germans had planted mines. We checked these over and called the engineers in to clear them out. In the meantime we captured a young kid who was supposed to be guarding the trees. He had fallen asleep. We then left the area...*

Miner said that his Assistant Squad Leader took off in the middle of the night. "He just dropped everything and left. He came back after a week but he was never the same. He was wounded at a later engagement but he was a good man and could speak German. 'Shell shock', I guess," Miner concluded.

"There was this one guy at the "Bulge" who was always firing his bazooka and going out looking for booby traps to set off. He just wanted to do something. He was a good southern boy and eventually earned the Distinguished Service Cross," Miner recalled.

Minor continued with another memory. "After we went through a few more towns and lost a few more men, we ended up near the small town of St.Vith. This was a crossroads that the Germans were determined to hold. They did not hold it very long. The 7th Armored Division did a job on the Germans there. After that we were pulled back to the rest area at Kohlsheid. This was a coal-mining town and coalmines were in operation. We enjoyed hot showers there and showered right along with the coal miners," Miner explained.

"Another time while we were in a rear area the quartermasters or engineers had set up a portable shower assembly with a canvas around it. It was the first of February and we took the hot showers outdoors," Miner laughed. The troops received a re-issue of winter clothing and then boarded the trucks and returned to Kohlsheid. He said that they rode in the back of the trucks and that it was very cold.

Training for the Roer River crossing in February was underway and the Germans had flooded the river. "We crossed the Roer River by walking across a wooden foot bridge which went under water from the weight of the men crossing the river. The crossing was interesting because it was kind of a show," Miner explained. The British had the habit of using big search- lights and they would set them up on a hill back of the river and about midnight they would put the lights on at a low angle creating artificial moonlight, which would illuminate the area. (Artificial Moonlight was a British idea used during night attacks. The British used several large powerful searchlights set up behind the line of attack. They reflected the lights off the clouds and down the faces of the enemy, which gave the attackers the advantage.) All the artillery, machine guns and everything else would cause what was called a "creeping barrage" providing protection for the British and American troops as they were crossing the river. The Germans were looking into the light, which was going overhead of the troops crossing. "It was quite an operation, Miner explained. A typical military maneuver and it worked. After crossing, we then took a couple of towns and regrouped. From there we went on to Koenigshoven."

Miner showed the author a 1940 German field map (reproduced in 1944) pointing out Koenigshoven and the Roer River. He traced his route of travel from October 1944 to May 1945. He pointed out the German Superhighway the autobahn with its clover leafs that bypassed all of the towns. He said the allies took advantage of these highways to move tanks and trucks rapidly despite the fact that the Germans had blown up bridges along the autobahn.*

From Koenigshoven, Miner was pulled out of the front line, and with four others from his unit sent to the rear to train replacements. This was March 1945 and he had been in combat for four months and this was the end of direct combat for Miner. He was ordered to Hasselt in The Netherlands for about two weeks to train troops in weapons and general combat training in preparation for the Rhine River crossing. "I was not at the Rhine crossing, Miner clarified. I started with the troops but was pulled back to go to Hasselt."

Miner joined the 30th Division at the Elbe River where Eisenhower ordered the advance to halt. Miner said that he did not cross the Elbe but some of the outfit did cross and was called back. "I was at Magdeburg until the formal surrender on May 8, 1945. The Russians came over across the Elbe and I saw some of them. One of our boys could speak Russian."

After the Germans surrendered on May 8, Miner's unit pulled back to Ocherleicher and remained there for occupation duties. At Ocherleicher the company commander informed him that the regimental commander wanted to see him at regimental headquarters. Miner reported there and the colonel said, "Well, come in Lieutenant. Needless to say, Miner was surprised. The battlefield commission he just received was the result of all of his past meritorious experiences. The new second lieutenant reflected on his days at OCS where he was not allowed to graduate for "lacking leadership ability." Miner was also awarded the Bronze Star for "meritorious service while serving in ground combat against an armed enemy."

---

* The autobahns impressed General Eisenhower and after he was elected president, he promoted the building of interstate highways in the 1950's.

Miner was transferred from his occupation duty to Hirschberg, Germany, "a nice little town in the Alps." It is a small town on a river, which provided waterpower. The town had the largest leather factory in Europe. "They made leather things for us and I hated to leave there," Miner explained.

After a stay at Camp Lucky Strike at LeHavre, France, the whole regiment boarded a Liberty ship, the GENERAL BLACK and they were bound for the USA. About halfway across the Atlantic, the word came over the loud speaker that an atomic bomb had been dropped on Hiroshima.

"We were supposed to go to Japan but we landed in Boston and then took a train to Fort Jackson. At Fort Jackson our unit was broken up and I went to Indiantown Gap, Pennsylvania and was discharged in 1946. At Fort Jackson, I had a choice of being advanced to first lieutenant or be discharged. Thinking back I guess I should have stayed in the Army," Miner said with a grin.

Miner said that in combat he did get tense but we knew we had to be there. The war was my first time away from home. And when I got home - I was no longer a boy."

Miner came home to Oriskany Falls and joined the Army and later Air Force Reserves. He worked at various jobs and then constructed a nine-hole golf course (Barker Brook Golf Course) and subsequently sold it after work on the back nine had commenced.

Charles Miner passed away December 14, 2010.

15

Sewell Morgan

INFANTRYMAN

The Ninth Infantry Division has had a long and glorious history dating back to World War I. The division participated in battles in France, Belgium, and Germany. On March 7, 1945, the group crossed the Rhine River at Remagen. Private First Class Sewell Morgan joined the division in late December 1944 after he arrived in France. The division ended up at the Mulde River near Dessau. (Wikipedia). Below is an account of Morgan's experience with the Ninth Infantry Division, 47ᵗʰ Infantry Regiment.

* * * *

Before entering the military, Sewell Morgan of Unadilla Forks, New York was employed by the Grange League Federation, the forerunner of Agway. He worked in Ithaca, Bainbridge, and Greene, NY. Morgan was married before the war to Ada Dillman. She was a grade school teacher who taught at Waterville Central School.

Morgan entered the Army in October of 1944, at the age of 24. He was first ordered to Camp Wheeler, Georgia for 17 weeks of basic training. Asked what he recalled about basic, Morgan's most amusing memory basic training is his memory of a First Sergeant saying "there was nothing frozen in Georgia only a poor soldier's back side."

Morgan also remembered that during boot camp, he received training firing the 50 caliber machine gun. One time when it malfunctioned, Morgan disassembled and fixed it. While reassembling the gun, he heard someone say "Nice job!" Morgan looked and saw that it was General George Marshall, the Army Chief of Staff. Another positive basic training memory for Morgan was the visit there (Camp Wheeler) by his wife, Ada, and especially, when she helped him out while he was on KP (Kitchen Police) duty

After basic training, Morgan left Camp Wheeler, traveled to New York City in order to board the Queen Elizabeth ocean liner en route to his first duty station overseas. During his sail across the Atlantic, Morgan discovered just how rough that ocean can be. Throughout the six days it took to get across the ocean, he suffered repeatedly from seasickness. The zigzag course the ship took to evade possible presence of submarines aggravated his condition. "The ship even dropped depth charges at times." Morgan wryly recalled that "the mess hall was really a mess room [because of] the rough seas and the hallways stunk from the vomit."

After six days, the Queen Elizabeth arrived in Glasgow, Scotland. As a security measure for the port, the submarine nets were opened to let them through and closed immediately after the ship passed. After disembarking he boarded a train for Southampton, England. Morgan said that while at Southampton, he contacted pneumonia and spent some time in the hospital. Because of his illness he was unable to continue with the 65th division. In about a week he was assigned to the 9th Infantry Division.

In December of 1944 Morgan's unit crossed the Channel and landed at LeHavre, France. At that time he was assigned to the 65th Replacement Division and later assigned to the 9th Infantry Division, 47th Regiment -a part of General Patton's Third Army. Morgan recalled that U.S. troops were held up at the Siegfried line bordering Germany. He was assigned as an automatic rifleman carrying a BAR (Browning Automatic Rifle). Asked about his crossing of the Rhine River into Germany he remembered crossing on a pontoon bridge which was quite common in the Rhine crossing by American troops in the last year of the war. Morgan remembered later that a shell had exploded near him and the next morning when waking up in a field hospital, he couldn't hear out of his left ear.

Morgan grimly remembered that he was at one of the concentration camps where European Jews and others were imprisoned. "Probably the worst smell I have ever smelled was when we liberated the prisoners about April of 1945.

We met up with the Russians a few days before the war ended. I was on guard duty one day at a bridge on the Danube. The Russians were on one side and our troops were on the other side. A woman was attempting to cross and an American guard yelled at her to stop. She kept going and the American shot at her. She lost part of her ear. The lady was riding a bicycle and didn't stop for three large signs. One in English, one in German, and another in French. We heard later that she was deaf."

When the war against Germany ended, for V-E Day, Morgan was somewhere on the Danube in Austria. "I remember a day after the war ended I was in a little town in Austria. I saw some water coming down a hill and I put my shirt in the water. The shirt was pretty hard since I hadn't changed it in quite a while and then ended up at Linz, Austria." Morgan was still in Austria when the Japanese surrendered. "I guarded SS troops that were in the stockade and also was assigned as the colonel's driver."

...One time while driving for the colonel, the SS Germans in a stockade had tried to break out and the colonel had me bring him back in a hurry to the stockade. Another time I drove the colonel to Hitler's hideout—at Berchtesgaden. And saw the famous Crow's Nest I visited where Hitler lived and took a picture of it. I saw this big parking lot and there was an elevator to the Crow's Nest – a part of his house.

Morgan said that he also was assigned as honor guard for Patton's funeral in December of 1945.

Private First Class Sewell Morgan received the bronze star for meritorious service. He was discharged in April of 1946 as a Private First Class. Morgan returned to his home and job. Morgan also spent several years mentoring young boys as a Boy Scout Scoutmaster. He and his wife Ada currently live in the West Winfield area.

16

James Nelson

SERGEANT-MAJOR

Army divisions are made up of regiments, battalions, and companies and each have their own Headquarters Company. The headquarters company, made up of the officer staff and senior enlisted, is the nerve center and the senior enlisted man is the sergeant major. The main duty of that individual is to keep on top of everything that occurs in the unit. Written orders are cleared through the sergeant major and entered in a daily journal by the clerk, and the sergeant major on a daily basis is frequently involved in conversations with the officers in the headquarters. The sergeant major also wrote citations. James J. Nelson of Utica, New York was a battalion headquarters sergeant major attached to the 76th Infantry Division.

* * * *

An Army recruiter told James Nelson that if he enlisted rather than wait to be drafted he would be able to choose his branch of the Army. Nelson enlisted in June of 1942. However, he soon discovered that the Army does not always fulfill its promises. After signing up, he was informed that the quotas had been filled and he would be sent to Fort Dix and assigned to an infantry regiment. As expected, Nelson was not too pleased to hear this but later considered himself lucky because his infantry division would stay in the States until the fall of 1944.

He was transferred to Fort Meade, Maryland for three months of basic training and it was at Fort Meade the 76th Infantry Division was being formed. He volunteered to be a clerk-typist and was assigned to Headquarters Company. Nelson explained how he was able to become sergeant major so quickly. In his office, Nelson was seated next to an old sergeant major that had served in World War I. Since he was too old to go overseas, they replaced him with a younger man. Shortly thereafter, Nelson replaced that person and became sergeant major of the battalion. This was comparable to the rank of Technical Sergeant and he was in charge of all of battalion communications and was responsible only to the officers.

Nelson remained at Fort Meade for about one and one-half years and the division was then transferred to Camp A.P. Hill, Virginia, a maneuvering area. From Camp A.P. Hill, the division went to Camp McCoy, Wisconsin. Nelson said that for about a year the troops had more infantry training and winter maneuvers at Watersmeet, Michigan on Lake Superior.

Following this training, the 76th Infantry Division received orders to go to Boston harbor to board the SS BRAZIL, a converted ocean liner. The BRAZIL and other troop ships joined a huge convoy off Cape Cod, which included destroyers, destroyer escorts, and even an aircraft carrier. They sailed over the rough waters of the Atlantic for England.

After a few days at sea the troops reached England. "Bouremouth, England in December was a climatic oddity," Nelson said, describing the lack of snow and green foliage.

In January of 1945, the division crossed the channel. In France, Nelson recalled that outside of LeHavre the troops had to stand in a large field in a foot of snow. After a few hours they were put into 40-8 French boxcars and shipped out. At Rheims they became part of the 3rd Army under General George Patton. From there they were transferred to the Ardennes area (The Battle of the Bulge). "We went into Bastogne where the carnage of the battle just fought was a shocker, Nelson further described in his memoirs. After seeing the terrible sights at Bastogne, some men took some extreme measures to avoid combat. Some men in a truck took off their shoes in the freezing weather to induce frostbites. Nelson said that some others in the truck convoy thought that frostbite wouldn't be sufficient to get out of combat so they shot off a few toes.

The 76th Division was replacement for another infantry division and while traveling through the Ardennes Forest he compared the scenery to the Adirondacks in the winter. His thoughts would drift home to earlier times of driving through the mountains of northern New York State.

After a thaw, he saw bodies in the snow and they were Germans who had died during the Battle of the Bulge. "We stacked them up like cord wood," Nelson had written in his memoirs. Nelson explained that going through and observing the post-battle area was to help prepare us for upcoming combat.

General Patton was headquartered at Luxembourg City after Bastogne and Nelson mentioned that Patton wanted the glory of being the first to cross the Rhine River. His plan was to head into the Moselle Valley to the Rhine and to accomplish this, the 76th Division was to be the spearhead.

Nelson was attached to Headquarters Company, 3rd Battalion, and 410th Infantry Regiment of the 76th Infantry Division. The Third Battalion would lead the attack and this was made at Echternach on the Sauer River. Nelson said that the West Wall was all along the border of Germany (Siegfried Line) and the Wall at Echternach was heavily fortified with bunkers and pillboxes, five trenches and artillery positions. They were protected with barbed wire, anti-tank obstacles and mine fields. The bunkers were very large and dug into the ground about thirty feet. "The Sauer's current was ten to twelve miles an hour and it was a raging torrent," exclaimed Nelson, as he described the precarious situation. He said the pillboxes and barbed wire started at the river's edge. Rubber assault boats with green troops were used to cross the raging river. Some boats were swept downstream.

Nelson said that the sergeant major ran the Command Post, which is actually a safe location during combat. The first CP was located on the side of the road going toward Echternach. Enemy artillery was very heavy.

In his memoirs, Nelson described the shelling and seeing General Patton.

> *...A shelling is a frightening experience. As I went for shelter, there he was, the big ham himself, standing on his jeep all bright and shiny as if in a parade. It was 'Old blood and Guts' in all his theatrical glory. He paid no attention to all of the shelling... the battalion officers got their pep talk and he (Patton) was on his way.*

The memoirs further describe the scene as the troops move into Echternach.

> *...The thunder of guns, flashes of gunpowder, tracers from automatic weapons, and star shells bursting made it look like a scene out of Hollywood. Some of it was too close for comfort and the cellar of a building became the battalion headquarters (6).*

Nelson was awarded the Bronze Star for "meritorious service in connection with military operations against an enemy of the United States from 12 February to 10 April 1945 in Germany"(Excerpt from the citation). Nelson said that the Captain was supposed to write up the citation but found out that Nelson could write better so he said to Nelson, 'this is your job.' Nelson said that he interviewed them and wrote up the citations. "Lot's of us got the Bronze star," he said.

Nelson described how the operation of breaking through the Siegfried Line was terrible, and the 417th was the first to break into the line. Patton was in the Luxembourg operation. The town was all shot up when they went in, he said, and they stayed in the cellars, since only the cellars of the buildings were left.

"We left the bunker the next morning and crossed the river. There was death and destruction on all sides. We reached our advance command post. The attack lasted several more days and finally we were relieved," he recalled.

Sergeant Major Nelson related some heroic stories of some men in his battalion.

First, he told how a lieutenant and his rifle platoon had been attacking pillboxes for about a week. Since all of his men were dead or wounded, the lieutenant attacked and destroyed the last pillbox by himself by placing dynamite against the wall. He was awarded the Distinguished Service Cross but had suffered a nervous breakdown. The doctor said that the man was out of his mind for two weeks.

Nelson's memoirs also mention a Company Supply Sergeant who got lost and then captured by the enemy. After a few hours in a bunker with the Germans, the Sergeant, 'a street wise Brooklyn Jewish boy' talked to his captors in German and was able to persuade them to quit the war.

Another buddy, a rifleman private, bragged that he was going to knock out a Tiger tank. Nelson said that the opportunity did come one day while the private was in the woods. A Tiger tank came out in front of him and he decided to run but as he was running he suddenly stopped. He remembered that he had bragged about getting a tank. He hid behind a tree and after putting a rifle grenade in his M1; he aimed at the tank and squeezed the trigger. The tank was fighting infantrymen and the top was open. The grenade "looped through the air like a shot put, found the opening in the tank setting off the ammunition inside. "The tank was knocked out and I have never been able to figure the odds on this happening," Nelson said.

Nelson said that on the road to Trier near Bitburg, he killed his only "German" – a big German rooster. As it was strutting around, Nelson shot its head off. He said the troops started eating off the land and raided farmhouse cellars. One evening they cooked potatoes, vegetables, steak, and pies and even enjoyed some wine. The table was set but the whistle blew and they had to leave before they enjoyed the meal.

Nelson explained that by the time the unit reached Trier, they had been in combat about a month. He said that one duty was to report casualties. For thirty days the battalion had mustered about 1,000 men and 50% were listed as casualties (killed, wounded, missing or sick). Replacements, arriving at night most of the time, were assigned to units and sometimes didn't last through the night, Nelson had written in his notes.

After Trier, conditions began to lighten and Patton no longer needed the division so his armored positions took over and "Patton rode to glory," Nelson said.

The division was in the Moselle Valley and fine wines were plentiful.

"There were bottled goods for breakfast, lunch, and dinner", Nelson recalled. The battalion reached the Rhine at Boppard and he visited an old castle at St. Goar. They crossed the Rhine in Army "Ducks." He said that the Germans had disappeared and they just mopped up small pockets of resistance. The first mopping up took place at Schmitten. There an armored column was ambushed by some SS troops and the battalion was assigned to clean them out of the area.

Nelson praised his battalion commander – a major, but was quite critical of his regimental commander – a colonel who countermanded the major's order to direct artillery on the town of Schmitten prior to sending the First platoon into the town. Nelson said this blunder cost the loss of thirty men and it was the colonel's fault. Over the next two days we lost one hundred men and ten tanks in house to house fighting. No artillery was used. Later, the Colonel placed the blame on the major saying that the major had made a bad decision. The generals agreed with the colonel at the hearing, Nelson explained.

At Weimar, Nelson visited the Buchenwald concentration camp. "It was horrible. Nelson noted that the German civilians said that they knew nothing of Buchenwald.

Traveling along a road in April of 1945, Nelson said he saw planes flying by that were different; their approach could not be heard and as they flew by, and smoke came from their tails. They were German jets.

Technical Sergeant Nelson told of looters in his outfit. Several men engaged in looting such items as stamp collections, saddlery, jewelry, and cameras. He said his only souvenir was a pair of wooden shoes worth about ten cents.

At Greitz, the Americans waited for the Russians, Nelson noted. "We waited over two weeks." It was May 7 and the war in Europe ended.

He was injured in a baseball game and he went through five hospitals before he was shipped home. He boarded an Italian hospital ship and arrived in New York on VJ Day, August 14, 1945. After three months more in a hospital he was discharged and he returned home.

Nelson ended his memoirs with the following words:" I have never put on a uniform or marched in a parade since then. I have had enough of them." After the war, he worked as an agent for the Metropolitan Insurance Company until his retirement.

17

Louis Randazzo

INSTRUCTOR-CHINESE ARMY

During World War II Americans were often assigned to help train troops of other countries in marching, military tactics and in the use of various weapons. Cultural differences and different methods of warfare often contributed to disagreement and conflict, which made it difficult to achieve the desired ends. Since his main concern was defeating the Chinese Communists after the war ended, the Chinese Nationalist leader, Generalissimo Chiang Kai-shek, uncooperative and stubborn at times, was more than willing to leave the defeat of Japan to the United Nations forces.

Activated in November of 1944, the Chinese Training and Combat Command provided American training to Chinese divisions. It was located in Yunnan Province in southwestern China (Records 1).

As a member of the Headquarters Company, Chinese Combat Command (Provisional), Louis Randazzo of Utica, New York was assigned to a remote part of China for about two years training Chinese troops in military methods.

* * * *

Louis Randazzo enlisted into the Army in 1938 and first reported to Fort Ontario in Oswego, New York. Eventually he was assigned as a Drill Instructor and a Sergeant in the 32nd infantry Training Battalion at Camp Croft, South Carolina.

He was discharged on June 12,1941 and subsequently drafted into the Army on March 4, 1942 and was attached to various infantry battalions at Camp Croft, and Fort Jackson, South Carolina.

From Fort Jackson, he was transferred to Camp Blanding, Florida in 1943. After sending his wife to New York City, he was ordered overseas and he boarded a luxury liner in San Francisco for overseas duty – destination unknown. For the next 36 days his ship carried him westward across the Pacific. After crossing the Equator, he sailed on to New Caledonia, Australia, and Bombay, India.

Arriving in the summer of 1943 during the monsoon season, he crossed India by rail and arrived in Calcutta. After a few weeks, he traveled to Assam in northeastern India and by plane crossed the "Hump"(the Himalayan Mountains to Kunming, China. Flying the "Hump" referred to a 500-mile trip from Ledo in India to Kunming in Yunnan Province in southwestern China).

At Kunming, S/Sgt. Randazzo was attached to Headquarters Company, Chinese Combat Command (Provisional). He said that when he first arrived in Kunming in 1943 there were only about 100 American soldiers that were assigned there.

"While I was there," Randazzo explained, "They assigned me to a Chinese regiment. I instructed Chinese soldiers in American military methods and technique and supervised their training. The training, he said, consisted of instruction in marching, weapons, mortar and bayonet practice and Americans were assigned to various areas to train Chinese. In actual combat between Chinese and Japanese, Randazzo stayed in the rear and made suggestions and also ordered ammunition. He said that he tried not to interfere in the operations of the Chinese, since he was there at the courtesy of the Chinese government.

> *...I went out to the Regiment by myself - the only American with them, but I had a Chinese soldier as an aide and an interpreter. When I left Headquarters I became a muleskinner. With the help of some 'Coolies', I packed up the mules and the packs for the three to five men with food and supplies. We would then go out into the field and train all of the time we were there. Since the government could not feed me, I. would get $3.00 a day. I ate a lot of rice that was prepared in every possible way. At times, I would go back to HQ where there were more Americans stationed to get more supplies. I would walk and ride a mule on the old Burma Road and then return to the Chinese Regiment in the field. This would take five to seven days. The supplies consisted of mountain rations and C-rations, which was mixed with rice, and it was not too bad. Once in a while the aide would go out and bring back a chicken or something. I also had to requisition ammunition to bring back.*

Randazzo said that the Chinese Regiment was about 100 miles from Headquarters. "I would travel from sunrise to sunset and along the way I sometimes slept in temples, which were of every size and shape and they were clean. My aide would find the temples, which were the only clean places in the towns. I was always leery of the Japanese since they were out to get the American who was instructing the Chinese.

Randazzo related some of his most memorable experiences while working with the Chinese. He said that during one incident when the Chinese were in combat against the Japanese, there was one town that must have had a neutral status. The Chinese troops would enter the town - have a good time at night, and then return to the field. After the Chinese left, the next day the Japanese would come in and have a good time. There was an agreement between the Chinese and Japanese to leave that town alone. I couldn't understand that and wondered, 'Are we fighting the Japanese or aren't we?'

Randazzo said that he did contact malaria and had to take Atabrine and quinine. He said that one time on his way back to Headquarters, he had stopped to see a lieutenant who was doing the same kind of work as he was doing in training the Chinese. The lieutenant had contacted dysentery so bad that he went to get stretcher-bearers and then helped transport him all the way back to Kunming. There was a hospital and doctor there who took care of the officer. The doctor said that he would have died if he had not been brought back.

Randazzo describes the Chinese and their fighting methods as follows:

...To the Chinese- life was cheap. I would take them out on a forced march and if a soldier fell down, they would take his shoes kick him off to the side of the road and let him die there. Of course, it was better not to fall down because if they just lay there, the next guy would take his shoes and even strip him of his clothes. Also, the Chinese would go into a town and take all the young men out to fight with the Army. You could always tell when you were entering a town because of the smell. The Chinese used human waste on the soil. It made good fertilizer.

In the cemeteries there would be a stone to mark the dead but they did not name the daughters. Women meant nothing in China. One time in combat, the Japanese were dug into a hill in tunnels and the Chinese had to capture that hill. I was just an observer in the rear but could see the combat. I didn't even carry a rifle. I would order ammunition and also advise the generals on directing artillery fire, the 105's at the hill, barrages of 30 seconds apart. Then a lapse of three minutes then fire for another 30 seconds. But life being cheap- the Chinese leaders would order their men against the Japanese with machine guns and the Chinese would be mowed down. I would make suggestions and they would say, 'You, I hear, you are a guest of China.' I would order ammunition and the Chinese would not always use it. They would hoard it for future use against the Chinese Communists after the war ended.

Staff Sergeant Randazzo spoke of dining with Chinese generals and would drink a rice whisky comparable to the strength of corn whisky ("white lightening").... He said that when dining and drinking with the generals, they would give him all kinds of salutes and try to get him drunk.

Randazzo recalled going fishing with the generals. "You know how they fished? Not with a hook, but with a pelican," he exclaimed excitedly with laughter. "They would send a pelican out and the pelican got a fish in its pouch and after the pelican returned to the boat they would hold the pelican by the neck. They would then take the fish out of its mouth. What a way to do things!" Randazzo concluded.

He recalled that one time he had a big argument with the interpreter. He had come to town where the Regiment was supposed to be but he found that it was nowhere to be seen. The interpreter saw some of the local people and started to run off to talk to some of the local people in an effort to find out where the troops were. The Regiment had moved.

> *...I told the interpreter to wait and not leave me alone with the mules scattered all over. I had to run out after the mules by myself. The argument led to the interpreter calling me a son-of-a-bitch. I grabbed him and I felt like killing him. We found the Regiment but he had reported me, and the Chinese commander ordered me back to Headquarters. However, the lieutenant that I had helped previously had patched things up for me and I was sent right back.*

Randazzo trained the Chinese for about two years. He was still in the field training the Chinese when Japan surrendered on V-J Day. Included amongst his medals is a Bronze Star that he received for meritorious service. The Chinese awarded Randazzo a medal but he had put it in his duffle and the medal was lost.

Randazzo left Kunming and traveled to Calcutta and boarded a plane for Karachi in the western part of the subcontinent. He said he flew over the Taj Mahal in Agra, India on the way to Karachi. From there he boarded a ship and went up the Red Sea through the Suez Canal through the Mediterranean and crossed the Atlantic to New York City. He had completed a trip around the world.

In October of 1945, Staff Sergeant Louis Randazzo was discharged from Fort Dix and returned home. He worked at various jobs and then moved to Utica and was employed at Griffis Air Force Base for 25 years with special police attached to the 416th Police Security Squadron. He retired in 1980.

18

Douglas C. Rogers

CHEMICAL DEPOT COMPANY

SGT. DOUGLAS ROGERS
(Courtesy of Royce Rogers)

During World War II the Chemical Warfare Service prepared gas weapons and non-chemical weapons. Poison gas was not used in combat. Though American governmental leaders were opposed to the use of poison gas, some military leaders favored it. The battle of Tarawa in the Gilbert Islands in the Pacific occurred in November of 1942. In three days of fighting, the U.S. suffered 3400 casualties. Major General William Porter endeavored to get approval for use of poison gas against Japan. Some newspaper editorials even endorsed the idea. However, public support for use of poison gas as a weapon never rose above 40%.

*   Douglas C. Rogers served in the 194th Chemical Depot Company. His unit worked with loading, unloading, and transport of gas bombs, non-chemical flame*

throwers, flame tanks, as well as chemical mortars. These munitions were used to support armor and infantry units. The following account of his military experience is taken primarily from letters he sent to his brother, Gerald, during the war years. Information has also been acquired from one letter to his son, Royce, in 1978, which is a brief overview of his father's experience.

* * * *

Douglas Rogers was born in Brookfield, New York on July 24, 1924. Before entering the military he worked on the family and other area farms. Reminiscing about farm life, Rogers wrote: "Growing up on a farm was something that every child should have a chance to do. During the thirties I am sure the farm had it all over city life. We didn't have the frills but I can't remember ever being hungry or cold." After graduating from high school, Rogers was drafted into the Army on July 5, 1943. He left home, boarded a train for a military camp on Long Island where he received his uniform. From there, he went to Camp Sibert in Alabama for one month of basic training. Like many others, he was assigned some time with kitchen police - "KP." In one letter to his brother, Rogers wrote

> *...I was on KP yesterday and I think it was the hardest day I ever put in. We had to report at 5:00 a.m. in the morning and did not get through until 8:00 last night. You ask me how I like Army life. The sergeants here are pretty good. There are five of them and they were at Pearl Harbor and have seen quite a bit of service. For the work part, as long as you keep going and trying- everything goes all right. There are plenty of things that I am learning that will come in handy all through my life. This training will make a man of me, if anything will. We have plenty to eat and a good place to sleep. If it wasn't so hot I wouldn't mind the long hours out in the sun. The only thing that I don't like to any great extent is that I won't get home. You never miss the old home town and surroundings until you go away and don't know when I get home again.*

In the same letter to his brother, Rogers also mentioned really wanting to join the Army Air Forces.

After basic training, Rogers was assigned to the 194th Chemical Depot Company. Of that time, he wrote "[w]e will start having more about chemicals and less about Army drill. That's all right by us. I had trouble with the heat but I could drive a truck real well." Rogers then added that he had spent several days in the hospital for an infected hand. Rogers subsequently went to a military driver's school to learn how to operate eight and ten wheel trucks. Three months later, having finished the program, he was assigned to the motor pool.

As was common with all servicemen, thoughts of home and family emerged in several of Rogers' letters. Missing Christmas was perhaps the most difficult for many of them. "My outfit is going on maneuver and I should get a furlough for Christmas. I asked for mine (furlough) for Christmas. If they don't give it to me they will probably be reporting me "over the hill". It will be my luck that we will be moving just about that time." Rogers' prediction was accurate and luck was not with him at that time.

On Thanksgiving Day of that year Rogers was transferred to California and Arizona for desert training. "It was a land of dust and dirt." Rogers also wrote he hoped he wouldn't lose his new Eversharp pen in the sand. During his time out west, he did manage to see Hollywood and the coast of California. "We were glad to head back to Massachusetts at Easter time of 1944."

From Massachusetts, but before going overseas, Rogers was transferred to Camp Upton, New Jersey for special training. At the harbor in Boston, Rogers and his fellow troops boarded what he referred to in a letter to his brother as "the USS United States," arriving five days later in Liverpool, England. Author's Note: There was no troopship named the 'USS United States' during World War II. Rogers likely meant to write SS United States Victory; a victory ship-hull number 4 that did carry troops.

...We didn't go in a convoy because we had a fast ship that could out run the German submarines. We did zigzag all the time. We were packed in pretty good and got fed twice a day if your tummy could take it. Oh well, what else could you do when you are getting all that money anyway - $30 a month. As soon as we got off the ship we loaded on a train for Southampton which is on the English Channel. I remember a "Bobby" leading us through the fog in the dead of night to board the train. At Southampton we loaded onto the worst looking ship I ever saw. It wasn't very big and was bought for a one way trip by the allies. We thought it was held up by the barrage balloon that was tied to the center mast. Headed into a small cabin, twenty of us were to spend one of the longest nights of my life. We had seen what the bombs had done in England the day before [and] here we were headed for another land of uncertainty. Didn't know so many fellows had a jacket bible and you could read so well in the dim lite [sic]. With the help of the LST we landed the next day in France wet, tired, and

bewildered. We made our way through rubble and landmines and in a few hours we had our trucks and were moving gas bombs and shells off the beach on to high ground and hiding them in the hedgerows that surround all the fields there. This country kid has already made a reputation as a truck driver and crane operator but seems like they always had to get a farm kid to get a truck out that was stuck in a sea of mud that now covered the land along the channel. Our big ten wheel cranes all had winches but it was hard to find something to hook to that would hold. We worked from evening to first lite [sic] of dawn so the enemy could not see us. Could not use lite [sic], mud to your knees, and handling shells full of poison gas and fifty gallon drums full of flame thrower fluid that leaked, and being watched all the time by German prisoners that were hoping for you to turn your back or make a slip, can make you a bit edgy. Nobody knew what day it was and didn't care. It got cold that winter and snowed a little and we stole boots to keep our feet warmer in the ever lasting mud. I also trucked water and captured Germans to the lock up. We slept from about 11 AM to 4 PM then got something to eat. Worked all night. - day after day.

In a letter written during September of 1944, Rogers indicates he was somewhere in France reports that it "didn't look much different in France than back home in Brookfield." He described the farming country writing that it "was not too level, with small fields with red and white cows that grazed between the shell holes and bomb craters,… the hedgerows have a lot of blackberries, [and that] the berries looked bigger than those back home… not long[,] but very sweet and the apple trees were heavy with fruit." As part of the same letter, Rogers also writes "The Battle of the Bulge came and went."

After the company moved closer to the German border, Rogers and two of his men were dispatched with a truck to the south of France for a month-long "transport mission." By the time they returned, they had already been put on the missing list. A sergeant, and commanding officer of the trio, also went on the mission. The sergeant was a Greyhound (bus) driver before being drafted into the Army. Rogers thought that he would have help with the driving, but his experience was only with hard paved roads, not "the country lanes they call roads," as he put it, in France.

…We got lost and crossed the border into Spain and back. Got stuck in the snow in the French Alps and finally had to have a new motor put in the truck in Lyons, France." Our stay in Charleville,

France will never be forgotten cause it was there I saw a whole train blown up that we were unloading shells and flame thrower fluids [from]....Some leakers in a steel floored box car of flame thrower fluid were ignited by the hobbled nailed shoes that the Germans prisoners wore that were helping to unload. I just missed it, because I had loaded and went into the woods three or four miles away to unload. Where the train depot had been was just a big hole in the ground and there was nothing left but twisted steel where the box cars and track had been. Live, unspent mortar shells were laying everywhere on the ground.

Our next move was into the country of Luxemburg between France and Germany. Here we started to set up another gas depot closer to Germany. German airpower was at a nothing and we could work days in the light......I was here also [when]... in the good old mixed up U.S. mail I learned that my brother Royce had been killed March 15, 1945 near there [while] in Germany crossing the Rhone River. The last that I knew, he was sailing for the South Pacific, but at the last minute he got appendicitis and was transferred to a different unit. I checked a cemetery in Luxemburg nearby and found he was buried there." After the war ended, Royce Rogers' remains were brought home to Brookfield, N.Y.

Douglas Rogers was in Luxembourg on V-E day and wrote that he expected pictures of the Victory Day parade to be saved for him. "I drove through Paris a while ago. It is real big and is quite exciting." Soon after, peace was declared in Europe and Rogers' 194th Chemical Warfare Company was sent to the South Pacific by way of the Panama Canal.

In September 1945, Rogers wrote of his trip across the Pacific after leaving Panama. "Here we are still in this darned ship. I think it is about 45 days now. It's crowded as all get out and hotter than the devil." He said that censorship of letters and blackouts have been lifted when they had left New Guinea. "We are laying off some island I don't know the name of, taking aboard mail to take to Manila where we will be getting off." He wrote that many of the men are heading back to the States and expected that the company would be disassembled. "Who knows- I may land in Japan yet. Might as well see the world, I guess -longing to get home-though."

Rogers arrived in the Philippines later the same month. He left there a short time later, in February of 1946, embarking on another long trip over the Pacific. This time, though, he would be returning to the "eternal hills" of

Brookfield, New York Douglas Rogers was discharged from the military as a Sergeant at Fort Dix, NJ on March 25, 1946.

After returning to Brookfield, he engaged again in farming. To pay for its operating expenses, Rogers worked at Mohawk Containers. However, after finally selling the farm in 1968, Rogers worked at Wicks Lumber Company for the next eight years. In 1976, he decided to relocate to Tucson, Arizona In Arizona he operated a washer and dryer rental business until retirement. He also became an active church member there and in later years enjoyed volunteering at the Veteran's Hospital.

Doug passed away June 14, 2008 at the Tucson, Arizona Veteran's Hospital after a long battle with cancer. His wishes were to be buried near his brother and that is where he now lays in rest.

19

Lincoln Stafford

FIELD ARTILLERY

T-4 LINCOLN STAFFORD

Though the artillery can be traced to the early Romans and other people of the ancient world, it was not until the 1800's that the artillery became a moveable-supporting unit in warfare. The Field Artillery is one of many branches of the Army and supports our "doughboys" or infantrymen. It is comprised of mortars, cannons such as 105-mm and 155 mm howitzers as well as rocket launchers. Since World War II, they can also be equipped with atomic shells and have proved to be the most destructive weapons on the battlefield (Cass 1).

T-4 Lincoln Stafford who was originally from Waterville, served in the Eighth Infantry Division, assigned to the 56th Artillery Regiment, Battery C.

His duties included carrying ammunition, serving as a cook and doing carpentry work for his unit.

* * * *

Stafford had attended grade schools in the Town of Paris and Waterville High School. He had worked as a machinist and also for Lincoln Davics, before being drafted at the age of twenty-three. He was among the first five men of Waterville to be drafted.

Following his basic training at Fort Bragg, he was transferred to Fort Jackson, South Carolina, where his unit, the 56th Field Artillery Battalion, Battery C, was organized. At Fort Jackson, he received training in 105mm howitzers, 50 caliber machine guns, and small arms. The unit later did more training in 105mm howitzers at Fort Sill, Oklahoma.

In March of 1943, he participated in desert training at Camp Laguna, Arizona. In November, the Unit participated in maneuvers near Manchester, Tennessee where the troops slept in tents in cold and rainy weather. After a short stay, the Unit was then transferred to Fort Leonard Wood in Missouri. From Fort Leonard Wood, the division traveled to Camp Kilmer, NY for departure overseas.

On December 5, 1943, the Eighth division boarded ships for the voyage across the North Atlantic. "I went across on a small "tub," Stafford pointed out. The trip on a rough sea took ten days and submarine scares required zigzag maneuvers. A rudder problem caused steering difficulties that headed the ship toward the battleship, USS NEVADA. Fortunately, the ships didn't collide "We had trouble keeping up so a destroyer was left to look around for us," Stafford said.

The troops arrived in Belfast, Ireland, on December 15 and settled at Camp Blessingborne at Fivemiletown during their six-month stay in Ireland. Stafford mentioned that they did not do much in the way of maneuvers while they were in Ireland. He recalled that General George Patton paid a visit and a demonstration was put on for his benefit. During the demonstration, one of the men was injured, because he had placed his hand in the breach of a 105mm howitzer and it drew some blood. (Once they got to France, Patton had kept them on the front for 11 months, Stafford added.) Stafford also recalled that, as a cook's helper in Ireland, the mother of Field Marshall Bernard Montgomery was served in the Officer's Club.

It was July 1944 and the time came for the Eighth Infantry Division to make their landing on the continent. Stafford boarded a ship in Ireland and he explained that they were on the water for a very long time considering the short distance from Ireland to France. After the convoy was finally organized they headed toward the Normandy peninsula.

On the evening of July 3, the troops went over the side into landing craft and went into Omaha Beach. "We got one gun in but the winch broke on the ship and we spent most of the day unloading the rest of the howitzers," Stafford explained. He said his unit moved into position behind the 121st Infantry Regiment to provide them with artillery support. Their baptism to combat was at La Haye du Puits where there were German 88's and larger guns firing at the 121st Infantry and the 56th Artillery. Following that they were clearing up some hot spots on the Cherbourg peninsula. "This was hedgerow country and the fighting was vicious," he reflected.

Stafford's Company C had fired the Eighth Division's first artillery round in France. And another company also claimed this honor. (Later, Company C also claimed to have fired the 100,000th round).

At Dinard the Germans were firing what Stafford thought was an 88 on a flat car on a railroad track. He said that the Germans would shoot it and then they would wheel it back out of sight and nobody would be able to see it. It was able to do considerable damage and one Monday morning, "C Battery with 100 men, moved up to support the infantrymen who were alongside the road. "The infantry wondered where we were going. We told them we were going to support them. The colonel believed in close support of the infantry so our Unit, C Battery, kept close to the infantry," Stafford related.

At Dinard the 56th did quite a bit of firing and everyone wondered why the German 88 couldn't be sighted. As the troops advanced many Germans were taken prisoner. The unit finally succeeded in tracing the 88 and "then we fired," Stafford said with emphasis. "The gun was located on this island and was way back in. The Germans were good at hiding things," Stafford added.

The 56th Artillery Regiment continued cleaning up a lot of hot spots and by September the troops were moving across northern France through Belgium and Luxembourg, entering Germany in early October of 1944.

By mid-November the unit moved into the Hurtgen Forest where the winter of 1944-45 was spent near the village of Hurtgen. The forest is located outside the village and it was in the Hurtgen Forest that the 56th spent some of the bitterest days of the war. Hurtgen fell at the end of November. It was wet and cold there but Stafford described the woods as "just perfect." He showed pictures of the area with the snow covered coniferous trees. "We built our own shelter," he said. One picture showed the rustic structure where he spent the winter and he pointed out the cookhouse, a small shack like building where Stafford helped with the cooking. His main duties were cooking, some carpentry work, and carrying ammunition for the 105 howitzers. Stafford described his cooking duties and meal preparation on the front lines. He said that his artillery unit did have meals at the front. The unit carried two stoves and large two by two pans and a serving line would be set up. "I enjoyed my cooking duties, he said. At Eppeldorf, "We were being shelled by enemy artillery so we left our stoves on the truck. We took them off after the shelling ended," he added.

In the area of Duren, Stafford recalled, the Germans used V-2 rockets. "They sounded like an old Ford when the V-2's flew over us. If you heard one - it was over you. Then you knew it wasn't going to hit you. When the V-1's came they were quiet. These rockets were used by the Germans against our troops," he said. Stafford mentioned that he had heard that the German rocket scientist, Werner von Braun who was the head of our space program, was kept hidden by the Americans toward the end of the war and that Eppeldorf was Von Braun's last stop before going to the United States. Eppeldorf is a small place, which was captured by Stafford's unit in October of 1944 where the unit suffered many casualties amounting to 10%. "Normally, an artillery unit would have only 3% casualties. Our Colonel believed in close support," Stafford explained.

The 56th advanced toward the Roer River crossing it in February, and then moved on to Cologne and it was near Cologne where the unit crossed the Rhine on March 30' 1945 (Griesbach 36).

The 56th moved further into Germany and the history of the Eighth Infantry Division recorded that some elements of the division crossed the Elbe River even though the U.S. was ordered by General Eisenhower to stop at the Elbe River and wait for the Russians. However, Stafford said that the 56th did not cross the Elbe River and that he remembered advancing as far as Schwerin, which is near the Baltic Sea. Schwerin was one of the cities in Germany that had not been bombed. "It was a nice city with a railroad depot," he added.

T-4 Stafford was in Schwerin when the Germans surrendered on May 7, 1945. From there, the division went by truck to France to Camp Old Gold. Along the way, they had stopped at the Maginot Line, which was built in World War I to prevent the Germans from invading France. He said it was something to see and he had noticed that the gun stations there had been dismantled.

At Camp Old Gold, the battalion boarded the GENERAL SQUIER at LeHavre and left on June 30. It was a bigger ship and they had a smoother ride than the ship that had taken them to Europe. It took five days and the Regiment arrived in New York in July. They went by train to Fort Leonard Wood and after a one-month furlough; "We were packing up to go to the Pacific since we were considered to be a crack outfit. Then we found out that the war was over," he exclaimed.

Stafford pointed out that the four guns of the 56th Regiment had fired over 100,000 rounds while in combat. Stafford explained that he had about 100 men in his regiment and they had four batteries, which included a service battery. There were about 20 men assigned to a gun.

T-4 Stafford received four battle stars for Normandy, Northern France, the Rhineland, and Central Europe. When asked what he thought about his time in service he replied, "I just took the war day by day."

Stafford was discharged on September 22, 1945 from Fort Leonard Wood, Missouri, and returned home. He became involved in construction work and was clerk of the works on several projects.

20

Charles Thompson

CONSTRUCTION OF THE LEDO ROAD

S/SGT CHARLES THOMPSON

During World War II the Japanese had conquered much of eastern China, and shipping supplies to China had became a major problem. To assist China in her efforts to hold back the Japanese, it was decided to build a new road to connect to the damaged Burma Road that had been started in 1920 and completed just before World War II.

Since the Japanese had blocked and severely damaged portions of the Burma Road, the Ledo Road was to bypass a segment of the road and construction by U.S. engineers began in 1942. Since the Burma Road had been heavily damaged, it was decided to repair 600 miles of road from Mung Yu in northern Burma to Kunming, China. Following that a new road would be constructed for 600 miles from Ledo in Assam, India to Kunming.. This would be called the Ledo or "Stilwell Road," since the project was planned by General "Vinegar Joe" Stilwell.

For more than two years, over 17,000 engineers and thousands of natives worked to complete the Ledo Road, which cost about 150 million dollars (Anders 235). Completed eight months before the war ended, it was a subject of controversy as to how much, if anything, it contributed toward winning the war in Asia.

During the war, American troops were sent to the far-flung corners of the world – some glamorous, some not so glamorous. Many Americans served in the China-Burma-India Theater of operations – the CBI-, as this area became known. The jungle, extreme heat, torrential rains, and malaria of Burma and India, were often as much an enemy to our troops as were the Japanese.

The following two chapters relate the war experiences of Charles Thompson of Deansboro, New York and John Langone of Waterville and Utica, New York. Both Thompson and Langone served in two separate units, but had never met. Thompson served in the Army Air Forces with an Engineer Aviation Battalion that helped build the Ledo Road. Langone served in the Army as a member of a Quartermaster Group and was a truck driver on the first truck convoy that carried supplies to China.

* * * *

Among the Americans who served in this distant part of the globe was Charles "Chuck" Thompson. The son of a day laborer, Thompson was drafted into the Army Air Forces in 1943 at the age of 23. This former truck driver and farmer was one of the few black individuals to be living and working in the rural Waterville-Deansboro area of the early 1940's.

After basic training at Camp Upton he was assigned to an Engineer Aviation Battalion engaged in construction. More training followed at Jefferson Barracks, Missouri, and McDill Field in Tampa, Florida.

Following his training, he received orders to travel to Patrick Henry, Virginia, the 23rd of May 1944 to board a ship bound for India. After a 47-day trip half way around the world, he arrived in Bombay on the western coast of India. Boarding a train, he traveled to northeastern India where the mode of transportation shifted to a side-wheeler riverboat on the swift Brahmaputra River carrying him to Ledo, India. From Ledo he then traveled by truck further into the Assam province into the Naga Hills where the once fierce headhunters of the Naga tribe dwelled. Having been converted to Christianity by Baptist Missionaries years earlier, the Naga tribesmen were to become good friends of the Americans.

Thompson rose to the rank of Staff Sergeant in the 823rd Engineers Aviation Battalion (Headquarters and Service Company) and had many memorable experiences while stationed in the CBI. He said that when he was in the hospital undergoing treatment for a back injury, he had the opportunity to meet the famous Burma surgeon, Dr. Gordon Seagrave. Dr. Seagrave was a medical missionary who spent many years before World War II serving the Burmese people. During those years Seagrave built a hospital and also administered nurse training to Burmese women.

When Thompson arrived in Assam, India in 1944, the Ledo Road had already been under construction since 1942. The road was to extend from Ledo in India to Lashio, connect with the Burma Road, and continue on to Kunming, China.

Thompson's unit was engaged in construction all of the way from Ledo to Kunming, China. The Burma Road would have to be repaired and 500 miles of new road would have to be carved out of the jungle from Ledo to Mong Yu. Thompson said that the engineers were made up mostly of black Americans who used light D-7 bulldozers. Big earth moving machinery was scarce. Much of the area was in enemy hands and bulldozers often carried a man with a rifle giving the bulldozer operators protection from the Japanese snipers who had killed 130 engineers. Working close to the front lines, Thompson explained, the lead bulldozers were armor plated and the survey parties carried heavy arms. Many bridges needed to be built and bulldozers pulled flatbed trailers down the road while cleaning and picking up debris along the way. A military highway, the Stillwell or Ledo Road, was an idea of General Joseph ("Vinegar Joe") Stilwell and had to be constructed through jungles, mountains, and across swift rivers. Since the Japanese occupied much of the area, the American troops (Merrill's Marauders) and Chinese infantrymen battled the Japanese in bloody combat. The Irrawaddy River near Myitkyina, Burma was crossed with the largest floating bridge in the world. Supplies for the road had to come in by ship from the U.S. to Calcutta and then transported by train over two different rail gauges. Work often had to be interrupted so that the Japanese could be driven back (Buchanan and McDowell 65).

Completing a mile a day, the Road passed through 102 miles of mountains. General Lewis Pick took over the road in October of 1943 and when told that the Ledo Road could not be built because of the obstacles, he said, "It is going to be built - mud, rain and malaria be damned" (QTD. in Fischer 31). The road was completed in 1945 and General Pick led the first truck convoy into Kunming, China, delivering much needed supplies to Chiang Kai-shek's troops.

During World War II, black servicemen such as Thompson, were segregated and served in all black units commanded by white officers. Total segregation was the order of the day and blacks were not treated as equals. Many of the black units, including the Tuskegee Airmen, excelled in combatant and non-combatant roles. Their achievements were often not appreciated and decorations were few and/or not awarded until years later. Some Congressional Medals of Honor have only recently been awarded.

Assigned to an all black unit, Charles Thompson relates how in Tampa at Fort McDill black soldiers were required to sit in the back of the bus. If the busses were filled, blacks were told to get off the bus so the white soldiers could get back to the Fort or camp on time and not be AWOL. One night, Thompson remembers a white Colonel, sympathetic to the blacks, took over the bus and made the whites give the blacks preference. At times, Thompson recalled, the food served the black soldiers was not good. Objecting to the food, they rebelled by not obeying an officer's order to "fall out" for formation. A higher ranked officer was informed of the situation and went to the mess hall and after tasting the food, threw it out. Returning to the barracks, he then ordered the troops to "fall out."

"In the rush to get out, we broke the door down – (not in a malicious manner), and the food did improve after that," Thompson added.

Thompson described an incident where he was called on the carpet for refusing to salute a white officer. He admitted that he didn't do this intentionally. In Missouri at the Jefferson Barracks, he met an officer who refused to return his salute. A superior officer who had witnessed this called the junior officer aside and chewed him out. The senior officer took off his own hat and placed it on a pole and said to the Lieutenant, 'Now- salute the uniform.' Thompson did not like being addressed as "boy" and often confronted officers on this.

One of his most memorable experiences was a visit by movie stars Pat O'Brien and Jinx Falkenburg who entertained the troops. The officers had planned on dining with the stars, but Pat O'Brien chose to eat with the troops rather than sitting with only the officers.

Thompson recalled that the time spent in the CBI Theater of operations was not too comfortable. The heat was often unbearable, and the monsoons and mosquitoes made life miserable. "I spent some time in the hospital since I had contacted malaria and dysentery. I receive $11 month disability for having contacted dysentery. The army said it would recur, but it has not." In spite of this, Thompson said that he was happy to have done this duty.

On March 26, 1946, Thompson was discharged from the Army Air Forces. He was awarded two battle stars for the Central Burma and India-Burma campaign and his unit won the Presidential Unit Citation.

Returning to the Waterville area, Charles Thompson resumed his work as a truck driver and joined the Army Reserve. He was recalled to duty in 1950 when the Korean War began and served as a heavy equipment instructor and was promoted to Sergeant First Class.

A civilian once again in 1953, he returned to his job as a truck driver. He passed away August 27, 2005.

21
John W. Langone
FIRST CONVOY OVER LEDO ROAD

Left (Identity Unknown) (Bottom Right)
T-5 JOHN LANGONE

With construction completed by the engineering units, the trucks were loaded with supplies for the Chinese and were ready to roll by January 1945. John Langone, as a member of the 472nd Quartermaster Group, was one of the truck drivers selected for the first convoy to travel over the road from Ledo, India to Kunming, China. "The reopening of the Burma Road did not have much effect on the outcome of the war. ...As a story of human endurance under some of the worst conditions to face soldiers in wartime, it holds a special place in the annals of World War II and American military history"(Halbert and Watson 26)

Corporal Attilio Cucci of Utica served with Langone from the date of induction-March 3, 1943 to the date of discharge in December 1945, and has added considerable information about Langone's experiences. They were members of the same unit and both were selected for the first convoy.

★ ★ ★ ★

It was quite common during World War II for young high school boys to drop out of school before graduating. The author's brother, John, an excellent soccer goalie, discouraged with some aspect of school, or frustrated by a subject he disliked, dropped out during his senior year. Unfortunately, so few returned to high school after the war to resume their studies for a high school diploma.

He was eighteen when he was drafted in 1943. Since brother Rocco had already been drafted into the army, a banner with two stars was placed in the living room window (The third star would be added about eighteen months later for brother Anthony who enlisted in the Navy).

From Camp Upton in New Jersey, the new recruits boarded a troop train, which would take them to Monroe, North Carolina, the location of Camp Sutton. It was there that the Third Battalion and the 472nd Quartermaster Truck Company was formed.

According to a brief history of the 472nd Quartermaster Truck Company, Colonel Kenneth Hapworth wrote that at Camp Sutton the men were directly assigned to the regiment without military training. The regiment would "provide all training, basic and advanced, and also training in vehicle maintenance and convoy operations." The history also noted -"only the best of the officers and enlisted personnel were selected for the final organization which would include the group that would make up the first truck convoy to China over the Ledo-Burma Road" (Hapworth 1).

John's friend, Attilio 'Til Cucci, described the training they received from March -July 1943, which emphasized rifle indoctrination and truck driving. They would later drive two and one-half ton trucks. Langone was a T-4 Corporal. Cucci was a Corporal with duties as a Company Clerk and truck driving.

From Camp Sutton in July of 1943, the troops boarded four troop trains and traveled across the country to Camp Stoneman in Pittsburgh, California. "This began a journey that was to take the Regiment completely around the world by train and ship taking two and one-half years before arriving back for discharge in New Jersey in December of 1945. It was to cross India twice by troop train."(Hapworth 2).

After physical examinations they went to San Francisco, got on a ferryboat in the Sacramento River and traveled up the river where men and equipment were loaded. On July 31, 1943, after 5,000 men and equipment were loaded onto the SS BRAZIL, a luxury liner owned by the McCormick Lines, the long sea voyage began. The destination was the subcontinent of India. On August 20, 1943, the ship docked at Tasmania, Australia. Two days shore leave was granted here and the town was cleaned out of baked goods and candy.

The SS BRAZIL sailed on to Perth on the west coast of Australia and waited for a convoy escort - two destroyers. The troops arrived in Bombay, India September 11 and they had to stay aboard for a couple of days. There were no orders for the group but there was shore leave and the sights of Bombay were enjoyed. There were many cows roaming the streets, which was a common sight in many cities of India. The author's interview with "Til" Cucci revealed that the troops then went to a British rest camp near Bombay called Deolali. "We had tea and hard biscuits when we arrived", he recalled.

Boarding a troop train they then traveled over the narrow gauge railroad across India and boarded a riverboat to Chabua, Assam in northeastern India where there was an American Air Force base located. Following this, the Regiment split up and some went to the Army Air Forces.

The 3rd Battalion was assigned the mission of getting the truck convoys ready.

The author recalls that his brother, John, told stories of living and sleeping in tents in the steaming hot jungles and rainforest inhabited by snakes, blood sucking leeches and mosquitoes. The deadly Cobra and Kwait and Pythons are also located in India and Burma. Snakes were seldom seen, but the mosquitoes, leeches, and mites were the worst enemies. (Buchanan and McDougall 9). The summer monsoons brought tremendous amounts of rain to the sub-continent. Both Langone and Cucci had visited Darjeeling in Assam, which is not too far from Cherrapunji, a place noted for holding the world's record for the greatest amount of rainfall in a twelve-month period.

Cucci said that hammocks were sometimes strung between vehicles and if they didn't stay at a place very long, the natives would build straw shacks called Bashas. He said that sometimes when lying down on a cot inside the Basha, you would look up and see a snake dangling from the trees and upon getting up in the morning you would have to tip your boots over and check them.

The truck drivers in Company K (120 men) were rotated and they would make overnight stops along the Ledo road when moving vehicles from Pandu to Ledo. These vehicles would later be used on the Burma Road portion when it was repaired and cleared of Japanese.

It was January 12, 1945 and the first convoy was about to commence. Thirty-five men were selected from Company K, which was later named the 3730th Truck Company, to drive on the first convoy over the Ledo Road to

China. The CBI Roundup magazine's May 1982 issue wrote that each truck had a shamrock painted on the bumper as an insignia since Colonel Ralph F. Ireland was the Commanding Officer of the 472nd Quartermaster Group. "Watch the Shamrocks go by," was a phrase often used by the onlookers in the Assam Valley (6).

Cucci said that he and John were close enough to the front to receive two bronze meritorious battle stars for their Asiatic-Pacific Ribbon. They were for the Central Burma Campaign and the India-Burma Campaign. The truck drivers, armed with rifles, often saw blood soaked areas where recent combat had taken place to rid the area of the enemy.

The Salween Gorge was a very treacherous part of the journey. The Japanese had bombed the bridge over the Salween several times and the engineers rebuilt it each time and the trucks had to cross one at a time. "It is a huge gorge. Talk about being scared," Cucci shouted with emphasis.

The Ledo Road was built through valleys and gorges and over swift rivers with pontoon bridges constructed by engineers. "It was 1079 miles of the roughest driving you'll ever experience" (Buchanan and McDougall 9).

Before the war ended, both John and "Chuck" Thompson of Deansboro were to contact malaria. Langone brought home pictures of the Burma Surgeon, Dr. Gordon Seagrave. Seagrave, who had retreated from Nankham, Burma in 1942, returned to Nankham after Burma was recaptured from the enemy (Buchanan and McDowell 16,17).

Two days out of Kunming, the convoy reached the highest point on the Burma Road, 9,200 feet, and arrived at its destination on February 4, 1945. The second convoy did not take as long and was considered more enjoyable. Cucci said that the trucks pulled 105 howitzers but would often disconnect them since they could not make the curves during inclement weather. Every sixth truck had a machine gun mounted on the top and each driver carried a carbine rifle.

Before entering the city, General Lewis Pick called the drivers together and said: "I am proud of you men. You have brought every one of the 113 vehicles through safely. I'm going to see that each of you drivers get a letter of commendation" (Cook, 6).

In a *Waterville Times* article dated April 1945, an army press release reported that Langone was selected to drive in the first convoy because of the outstanding work he and his Quartermaster Trucking Company had been doing on "the American built road during the 20 months he had been overseas."

The army press release also indicated that the first convoy over the new road left Ledo in Assam, India, and before long "was climbing the hundreds of curves on the treacherous Patkai Hills, crossed the Hukawng and Mogaung

Valleys, through the Burmese cities of Myitkyina and Bhamo and on to Mongyu where the Burma and Stilwell Roads merged." On January 28, the convoy arrived in Wanting, China. After celebrating in Wanting, the trucks then traveled through the "Salween Gorge and on to Paoshan where the Chinese greeted General Pick and his men with fireworks, streamers and merrymaking." On February 4, 1945, the first convoy rolled into Kunming, China where ceremonies were held attended by dignitaries of the United Nations. Pick delivered the goods to the government of China. The trucks were turned over to the Chinese and Langone and the other drivers boarded a C-46 and were flown back over the Himalayas ("the Hump") to India to prepare for another truck convoy to China. (1)

Attilio Cucci concluded his comments by describing the celebration after the trucks had reached their destination. "We got to Kunming and there was a big dinner put on by Chinese officials. We had Chinese and American flags mounted on the vehicles, which I still have." Cucci showed a picture of the Chinese governor's invitation indicating that Lily Pons and Andre Kostelanetz as well as Chinese folk and war songs made up the entertainment. "I made three more trips and the second was more enjoyable. John made more trips than I did. We were in China when the first atom bomb was dropped and I remember saying, 'Oh boy, we are going home.'"

The 472nd QM Group received several decorations including a Presidential Citation and an award from the leader of China, Generalissimo Chiang Kai-shek.

The U.S. Office of Public Relations pamphlet, which was published immediately after World War II, explained that the CBI Theater of Operations was a forgotten theater of war during World War II, and was often on the short end for supplies. "The brave and determined troops who served there were farther from home than any soldiers in the war. - Living in jungles and rainforest areas – much of which had been slightly penetrated by civilized people" (Buchanan and McDonald 3).

The war ended August 14, 1945 and later in the year, Langone and Cucci crossed India again to Karachi (in present day Pakistan) to board the USAT TORRENS. On November 24, the ship left port and steamed down the Arabian Sea, up the Red Sea through the Suez Canal to the Mediterranean Sea, and across the Atlantic Ocean to New York City. Fond memories of home and family made the long journey home more enjoyable and less stressful than the trip two and one-half years earlier.

The TORRENS arrived in New York harbor on December 7, 1945 and Corporal Langone's trip around the world was now complete. He was discharged from the Army on December 11 at Fort Dix, New Jersey.

As is true of so many veterans of the "Big One," John Langone, "Til"

Cucci, his wartime buddy, and Chuck Thompson, the construction engineer on the Ledo Road, didn't think the world owed them anything. They served in the most distant theater of operations of the War, performed their duty honorably, and returned home to happy and proud families.

John Langone worked at various jobs including the DL&WRR as a telegrapher and ticket agent and mechanic and later worked as a mechanic for the New York State Department of Transportation.

He passed away at the age of 58 in 1983.

22

Colonel Oscar Tonetti

WEST POINT

Located on a plateau high above the Hudson River on 16,000 acres, the U.S. Military Academy at West Point, N.Y. has trained some of America's finest men and women since 1802 to become professional army officers. About 56,000 cadets have graduated from West Point since it was started and the Corps of Cadets each year is about 4,000. More than 900 graduate each year and many have become famous generals, engineers, statesmen, and diplomats (Walker 625).

Upon graduation they are commissioned as second lieutenants and granted a Bachelor of Science degree. They are then given an opportunity to choose the branch of the army and duty station where they wish to serve, and class standing will contribute greatly as to what extent their requests are granted.

The following is about one member of "the long gray line" who served thirty years in the army and retired with the rank of colonel in 1967.

* * * *

Oscar Tonetti, the son of an immigrant coal miner, was born in the coal mining town of Universal (Bunsen), Indiana that is located seventeen miles from Terre Haute. When he was about twelve years old, he and his brother would pick up the winter's coal off the mining site to heat their home. It was bituminous or soft coal that was used as fuel in the miners' homes. The harder, cleaner burning anthracite coal, more suited for heating homes, was not available. His father was a Punching Machine Operator, which undercut the coal and drilled holes for the necessary explosives to break up the coal. The Shot Firer would set off the explosives and the next day the miners would come in to shovel and load the coal into the little rail carts on tracks.

After high school, he worked for two years in a lacquer plant in Terre Haute and attended Rose Polytechnic Institute - an engineering school. He learned about the military academies in civics classes in high school and applied to all of the academies including the merchant marine academy hoping to obtain an appointment. After a period of two years, he received a congressional appointment from a congresswoman. She called him and said that he had an appointment if he could pass the physical. It was 1937 and at the age of 21 had just made the age limit by six months.

Riding a train for the first time in his life, Tonetti traveled to West Point, New York. Upon his arrival he went to the administrative building and told the secretary that he was reporting in and he was told to take a seat. With a hearty laugh he remembers that a colonel came out of an office and introduced himself. Totally unfamiliar to the military life, Tonetti remained seated. With a very stern voice, the colonel told him to stand up. "I came out of that chair like a shot," Tonetti said. After that it was all regimentation. A delegation of cadets arrived and took him to the central area located right on the Plain - the quadrangle. The barracks is on one side and the mess hall is on the other side of the Plain. When you are in that area it is all "double time." A cadet is assigned to you who takes you with the squad. He is what we called a 'yearling.' since he had finished his first year. This 'yearling' wanted to treat us like he had been treated. He would rake us over the coals, make you stand up straight with shoulders back. "Here," Tonetti recalled with a grin, "was raw meat."

Discussing assignments after graduation and class standing, the author mentioned that General Custer had graduated last in his class. Tonetti pointed out that no one forgets who ranks last and he told of a friend of his who ranked last in the class and was struggling with mathematics. Tonetti helped him go from basic mathematics to advanced math in seven weeks. After 10 o'clock at night, lights were out and there was to be no radio playing. Sometimes studying was done under a blanket under a desk to prevent being caught studying after ten o'clock.

"At that time we all took the same courses. It is different now since it is possible to specialize", he stated. Just before graduation, a class meeting is held and the cadets would select the branch of the army of their choice and the duty station where they wish to serve. The assignments are handed out according to class rank. "I selected the first armored division at Fort Knox, Kentucky." Tonetti graduated with a Bachelor of Science degree in June of 1941 and was commissioned a second lieutenant. Usually the graduates would get a three-month leave but it was cut to one month because of the approaching war.

Arriving at Fort Knox, Lieutenant Tonetti was assigned to the 27th Armored Field Artillery in the First Armored Division. He had just enough time after arriving to get his field equipment and go on maneuvers at Fort Bragg, North Carolina. Following the maneuvers, he went home for the weekend to Terre Haute, Indiana where the family was living.

...I was getting ready to return to Fort Knox and I was just pulling out of the yard when my brother came running out and

said that he had heard on the radio that Pearl Harbor had just been bombed. I said, 'I guess I better be getting back.' I said to myself, 'that's it! There's the next thing.' I was driving a 1941 Ford business coupe - the cheapest car you could get. It cost $600. Fort Knox was 150 miles away and as I was driving along that night when a state cop stopped me for speeding and asked if I was going back for the emergency. I said, 'No. Just going back - reporting in for duty.' The cop didn't give me a ticket but said, 'well, just take it a little bit easier.' I got away from him and I went the same speed as before. When I got to Fort Knox I had to get rid of the car so I gave it to my brother - my next older brother.

At Fort Knox, Tonetti was assigned to the 5th Armored, pending the activation of the 7th Armored, pending the activation of the 10th Armored Division (all based at Camp Polk, Louisiana).

The author asked Colonel Tonetti to explain the difference between the armored field artillery and the regular artillery.

...We had six armored artillery carriages - a 105mm howitzer mounted on an open medium tank chassis -an M-7 full-track. The tank chassis did not have armor and no turret. Regular tanks have a 75-mm with a crew inside. It was more advantageous to have a 105 howitzer. It was larger mm and fired semi-fixed shells. Semi-fixed means that powder bags were used to fire a 50-lb. projectile in a brass case - seven bags to a case. If the range were up to 5,000 yards we would use two powder bags. Seven powder bags could go up to 12,000 yards. We usually went into position so we would have a range of 5,000 yards. The powder bags were quite small compared to those used for 16" guns on a battleship. Our battalion had a headquarters company, three gun batteries and a service battery. There were six howitzers to a battery.

He was transferred to Camp Polk, LA in 1942 and engaged in more maneuvers and as representative of the battalion division artillery, assigned recruits that reported to Camp Polk.

After a stay at Camp Polk, Tonetti engaged in six months of desert training at Camp Coxcomb, California and further training at Fort Benning, Georgia. The time was approaching for shipment overseas so the next stop was Camp Shanks, New York for pre-embarkation.

On June 6, 1944, the whole division, 17,000 troops and some ancillary personnel boarded the ocean liner Queen Mary in New York Harbor for the trip across the Atlantic. There was no escort or convoy and it took five days at full speed to get to Firth of Clyde, England. "After we were out one day we were surprised to hear loud gunfire. The ship trembled and I thought, 'Oh God, we have been torpedoed'. Without any warning, the 6" deck gun had just been test-fired by the crew," Tonetti said with a laugh.

Tonetti said that his rank was major when he was shipped overseas and he was the training and fire-direction officer for the battalion. He was in charge of the fire direction center. There were two majors and a colonel in the battalion and the captain commanded the firing batteries. There was also a service company and headquarters company in the battalion. Tonetti did the training for the whole battalion and ran the fire direction center. In the firing battery there were three forward observers, and if they had been assigned to a tank battalion, would ride in the M-4 tanks. If the forward observers had been assigned to the infantry, they would ride in the half-tracks. A half-track was a lightly armored vehicle with a half-track instead of rear wheels. In an armored division there were three tank battalions and three infantry battalions. All of the infantry battalions were mounted on half-tracks.

After landing in England, the troops boarded a train and went to Tidworth barracks - an armored center area near Winchester. At Tidworth all of our equipment was drawn, and we removed the cosmolene preservative off the weapons and vehicles and radios were put into the vehicles. We also engaged in one training session on the artillery firing range on the Salisbury plains to further prepare us for the weeks ahead. About two months after the Normandy invasion, near the middle of August 1944, Tonetti said that they boarded LCT"'s (Landing Craft, Tank) which were loaded with M-4 tanks, and they landed across the Channel at Utah beach. The rest of the division was made up of half-tracks and trucks. All ammunition was supplied in trucks towing armored trailers.

The front line at that time was near St Lo. The mission was to close the Falaise gap and to get there in time for the breakthrough at St. Lo. However, the breakthrough had already occurred. The next objective was the Falaise Gap. That was the division's first combat order and the first combat was at Falaise.

...The town we first had to liberate was Chartres where the famous Gothic cathedral is located. We went through right at the base of the cathedral at dusk and the division we reported to, which was the 19th or 20th corps, was part of General Patton's Third Army. We thought we were going to liberate Paris but we crossed the Seine River at Melun twenty miles south of Paris. The Seine

River was quite an obstacle but there was no problem in crossing. We headed across northern France through all the famous World War I trench warfare areas. We engaged in skirmishes at Verdun and were close to Toule. Tonetti pointed out that Toule was the place where the famous WWI Lafayette Escadrille airplane squadron was based. We would go into position and succeeded in liberating various towns. The division was separated into three combat commands. Combat Command B was the lead command - commanded by a Brigadier General. The assistant division commander was General Walton Walker. Also, there was Combat Command A and then the reserve combat command.

He remembered how they ran out of gas at Metz on the Moselle River.

...We were supplied with gasoline and ammunition and it took three days to re-supply the division. From there we crossed the Moselle south of Metz. The Germans had been reinforcing this area for three days and we crossed after they reinforced. The Germans were using officer candidates to reinforce the river and they gave our division quite a tussle. The officer candidate school was located nearby. We crossed the Moselle on a pontoon bridge and right across the Moselle was a line of hills that looked similar to the hills around Sangerfield and Waterville. We attacked and went through along the river line and secured the heights across the river. We thought if we stayed there we would be out of range and we had to displace on the forward slope of the hill to further the attack. We got counter battered there.

Tonetti was then assigned to the British Second Army near Maastricht, Holland. The big plan was being argued by the high command as to how, and whether or not, to attack Berlin by going across the mouth of the Rhine and Maas rivers. That plan was never completed.

His unit was then ordered to go down to St. Vith - the focal point of the northern shoulder of the "Bulge" (Battle of Bulge). The Germans had to go through St. Vith. and my unit, the 434th field artillery which was part of the 7th Armored Division, had to defend St. Vith," he explained. Tonetti was told to go down and pick assembly areas for the battalion. Given a map, which portrayed the route to St. Vith, he left to go there at about 5:30 in the morning. Arriving about mid-afternoon on the 16th of December, he waited for the battalion to come down. He and his jeep driver just sat there along side of the road near Malmedy. It was at Malmedy that the Germans massacred about 81 American prisoners from an artillery battalion.[*]

Tonetti said that after a while the division commander, assistant commander, artillery commander, and a few staff officers came by and were headed for division headquarters of the 106th Infantry Division (the division that took the brunt of the first and second German panzer group that was at Bastogne on the southern flank). The Germans had to come through both the northern and southern areas of the Bulge. The 106th division headquarters was in a school or hospital. The division artillery commander waved and said to get on the tail end of the group. At division headquarters, two generals walked in - General Jones was commander of the 106th. The group I had just joined was told to reinforce the 106th. General Jones recommended that the division would form a hedge defense (actually a horseshoe on high ground) to the west of St. Vith.

From 106th division headquarters, Tonetti returned to the Malmedy massacre area to meet his battalion. He noticed that colored tracer shells (German) were being fired across the assembly area. He remembered saying at that time that this was stupid so he had better pick firing positions. He picked three positions and waited for the battalion to come down. "Well, they never came down. I decided to go up the route that they were taking down and had gone about three miles up the road when a lieutenant from our signal company came down the road and stopped me. He asked, 'What is your battalion?' I told him the 434th armored field artillery and he also asked, "Who is your battalion commander?" I told him and then got to wonder and said 'And just who the hell are you'? The lieutenant told me and I knew his battalion commander," Tonetti said. Tonetti also pointed out that it was about this time that a German general had outfitted a German organization with American uniforms and had weapons, obtained passwords, and had infiltrated American lines. Their job was to create havoc and they accomplished that pretty well. This explained the questioning by the lieutenant who Tonetti had just met. The lieutenant went on to say that a Colonel Matthews, the division chief of staff, ran into an ambush a short piece up the road and was killed. (Tonetti had him as an English instructor at the academy.) The lieutenant said 'You can go ahead - but it is up to you'.

...I thought this over. All I had on me was a 45 pistol and not a good shot at that, a radio, and my jeep driver had a carbine. I

---

[*]   Raymond Vitucci, (nicknamed V-2 by his Army buddies), lives in Utica and was an artilleryman in the 75th Division. He wrote in his War Memoirs that he learned of the Malmedy massacre while he was at Septurn, Belgium and commented: "This massacre so infuriated soldiers that we then became demons in battle (7).

said to myself, 'here, by God, is my battalion up ahead with all this firepower - 18 self-propelled howitzers, and 50 caliber guns in every half-track and tank that we had.' I said to the lieutenant that I would just wait for the battalion. I then went across the road to a barn and went to sleep. In the morning I heard tracked vehicles moving. I came down to the road and who the hell was there but the Lieutenant Colonel, the battalion commander. I said, 'Boy am I glad to see you. You don't know how glad I am to see you.' He said, 'Oscar, It's good to see you.'

Tonetti said that at one point there had been an operations plan to sacrifice the 7th armored division at the Bulge in order to delay the German panzer group for 24 hours. However, General Ridgeway of the 82nd Airborne was persuaded into changing the plan.

...We defended St. Vith for five days. This was the Battle of the Bulge on the northern flank. On Christmas Eve, the Battery A Executive Officer called for a fire mission. We were out of ammunition. I told him he could have three rounds per gun. He said, 'Number one has fired. Merry Christmas.' I said, 'Bart, Merry Christmas to you.' We had fired all the high explosives and we had put in all the white phosphorous we had. White phosphorus shells were casualty-producing shells that would burn you if pieces landed on you. The last firing mission I had was from Lieutenant Chapin with the 23rd Infantry. I told him we hadn't seen our ammunition officer in quite a long time and that we only had smoke ejection propaganda shells. Chapin said, 'Let's fire them.' so I loaded 4" shells with surrender leaflets and shot them out and they would raise about 200 yards in the air.

At reunions held after the war, Tonetti and Chapin would enjoy talking about this. Chapin recalled how the Germans would get out of their foxholes and stuff the leaflets in their pockets. Chapin said, 'You know, you were the only battalion that ever fired propaganda leaflets.'

Following this, Tonetti said, "We were relieved by the 82nd airborne and we pulled back to the town of Viesalm and were re-equipped and supplied with ammunition. The next objective was to liberate St.Vith and we went through and captured it. Following the Battle of the Bulge, we then went towards the Roer River where there was a group of dams."

At the Roer River, a dam was captured and the troops proceeded across the Ruhr River into the industrial area. "We engaged in skirmishes fired on the town while tanks located on the outskirts were also firing shells. We crossed the Rhine River at Remagen," Tonetti explained.

Tonetti was awarded the Bronze Star, a decoration that was established in 1944, and is awarded for heroic or meritorious achievement during military operations.

On V-E Day, "we were at the base of the Denmark peninsula on the Baltic Sea. The purpose was to cut off five German divisions in Denmark. We went from Denmark to Frankfort, Germany and I became part of the 188th field artillery. We were to retrain for shipment to Japan and we were still in Denmark when the Japanese surrendered on August 14, 1945.

After the war Tonetti did tours of duty in Paris and Berlin before returning to the United States in 1947. He had extended his stay in Berlin with the understanding that he could attend the University of Michigan to obtain a degree in mechanical engineering.

In 1949, he received his degree in mechanical engineering and did a tour of duty at West Point teaching mathematics and automotive engineering to Plebes.

Tonetti served 18 months in Korea during the Korean War and was assigned to ordnance and supply.

Before retiring he did duty at Fort Ord, California and the Pentagon (Office of the Chief of Ordnance). He was then assigned to the arsenal at Watertown, Massachusetts where various explosives and Nike missiles were manufactured. After two years, he received orders to close down the base.

Oscar Tonetti retired in 1967 after 30 years service in the regular army and moved to Sangerfield, New York and taught twelve years at the Morrisville Agricultural and Technical College.

He passed away August 7, 2007

23

Robert W. Treen

ANTI-AIRCRAFT BATTALION

Anti-aircraft warfare tactics defend against aerial attack by employing a variety of ground-based guns and cannons to combat the enemy. These techniques have been used to counteract   military aircraft since the latter were first introduced during World War I. Though infantry guns were used to shoot down enemy planes, they had limited capacity and were unable to prevent aircraft from droppig bombs.

During World War II different guns, cannons, and even rocket powered missiles, were used as anti-aircraft weaponry. Among these were the 20mm, 40mm, and .50 caliber cannons 8mm rifles were also utilized on the smaller mounts. The U.S. Army anti-aircraft systems were highly rated. An example of their artillery was- "Four M2 .50 caliber machine guns were linked together and mounted on the back of a half-track."(Wikipedia Website). However, the allied forces in turn greatly feared the 88mm gun developed by the Krupp company in Germany. It became "one of the best and most famous artillery pieces in the world. (Id). Anti-aircraft battalions also served as a defense against ground attacks. The 90 mm gun, as was true for the 88mm, was also an anti-tank gun. Barrage balloons were another element of anti-aircraft warfare. Anchored to the ground, these blimp-like balloons impeded low- flying aircraft, forcing them to higher altitude. After the war, various studies revealed that, despite the AA guns, 90% of the bombers reached their targets. Ultimately, in the decades following the second World War, Surface-to-Air Missiles (SAM's) superseded anti-aircraft artillery.

The following account relates the experiences of the late Robert Treen who was attached to an AAA Gun Battalion and served in the European African Middle Eastern Theater of Operations during World War II. Information for this chapter has been compiled from a newspaper article (probably the Waterville Times) and from his son, Robert Treen, Jr.. Unfortunately, very little information regarding Treen's AA battalion is included therein.

* * * *

Prior to joining the military, Robert W. Treen worked as a mechanic with his father in the gas station on Main Street in Waterville, New York. He decided to enlist into the Army in late February of 1941, several months before the bombing of Pearl Harbor. In March of that year, he was assigned to the 62nd AA Battalion at Fort Totten, Long Island, NY. After Pearl Harbor, he was transferred to Prospect Park, Brooklyn, NY. From there, the English ocean-liner, the Queen Elizabeth I, transported Treen and his battalion overseas for European deployment.

For many years before the war, Treen would spend part of his summer vacations at his aunt's campground in Sherburne, NY. Beginning when he was six, he found a new summer friend there, Elsie. English by birth, Elsie also visited the campground annually. They visited every summer thereafter in July until the war broke out. Elsie and Treen made plans to marry, but had to sideline their engagement when Elsie, who was still a British subject, told Treen that she was returning to England to fight for her country.

Robert Treen related to this author the following story about what turned out to be very coincidental experiences of his father and mother:

> *...My father's ship idled at sea about two days out while they waited for the rest of the convoy to form for the voyage to England. Among the ships joining this convoy was the HMS CITY OF HONG KONG. [M]y mother, Elsie, was a passenger on that ship... this was a fact unknown to either my mother or father until after the war. My mother joined the Royal Air Force and [remained] in Britain until after the war.*

After the usual rough ride over the Atlantic, Treen's ship first docked on the Clyde River in Scotland before continuing south into England where Treen and the other soldiers had further training. Later that year, Treen left England as part of the 'Second Front' of invasion forces heading for North Africa. This troop offensive, named "Operation Torch," started on the morning of November 8, 1942, would be a godsend for the British armies fighting the Axis powers in North Africa. Troops landed at three task force areas known as Western, Center, and Eastern.

Treen was in the Center task force landing at Oran, Algeria. He saw action at Chateaudun, Algeria and in the Constantine vicinity. In that area, where General Doolittle oversaw the North African Air Force and his unit, the 62nd AAA Battalion, Treen's group provided AA protection In short order, Treen's portion of the offensive soon moved on to cross through Algeria, Tunisia and Libya. In the last of these countries, particularly in Bizerte, Libya, combat was especially intense.

Following action in North Africa, Treen's unit invaded Sicily and southern

Italy. In August of 1944, two months after the allies landed at Normandy, Treen's unit invaded the "underbelly" of France. His mission was to join allied forces in the north and surround the German armies. By then, the allies there had advanced west of Cherbourg and the 62nd, Treen's unit, moved up through the Vosges mountain area, and on into eastern France, Alsace Lorraine, and then into Germany.

In Strasburg, Germany, Treen's unit was the forerunner of the allied forces moving into that city. Even before the infantry or military police, Treen and his fellow soldiers were the first of American troops to enter the area. His unit also struck at locations in Germany, such as Hagenau, Colmar, Forbach, Bitsch, Saarbrucken, Worms, and Mannheim. The 62nd crossed the Rhine, ending up on the Danube River in Bavaria. In one place he viewed incredible inhumane sights of dead prisoners in a concentration camp. By the end of the war, the 62nd was both an anti-aircraft and field artillery unit. Treen then became part of the 108th Anti-Aircraft Battalion, receiving an assignment to police and guard duty.

Corporal Treen received six battle stars, each commemorating one of the six major battle areas where he served. His son, Robert, recalled an incident his father had told him when he was near a tributary of the Rhine that Germans had pinned down twenty-two Americans and a rescue of them was attempted. After three failed attempts, Cpl. Treen and one other volunteer took a half-track vehicle and a gunner in another endeavor to rescue the men. On the way back from the rescue mission, the Germans succeeded in getting two of them. Treen thought later that he had failed in thinking that the mission had not been a success. When questions were asked about who had volunteered, he did not step forward, thinking the mission was a failure. He found out later that they could have been nominated for the Congressional Medal of Honor for what they did accomplish that day.

Treen's son, Robert, Jr., also explained that the AA guns were 90mm and the recoil sometimes bruised their hands. At his discharge he learned that some in his unit received Purple Hearts for this. The appropriateness of this is questionable since Purple Hearts were not normally issued for injuries of that type.

Treen boarded the Queen Mary in the fall of 1945 to return home. Enlisting as he had, before the attack on Pearl Harbor, Treen spent 33 of his 54 months of active duty in the Army stationed overseas. He never received a furlough. Cpl. Treen was discharged 18 September 1945.

Returning home he was employed by the GLF (Grange League Federation,). Treen and Elsie were reunited and married shortly thereafter on December 22, 1945 at the campground in Sherburne, N.Y. where they first met. After GLF, Treen joined the police force and eventually reached the rank of Chief of Police in Waterville. Later, he also served as a Deputy Sheriff in Oneida County before finally retiring in 1981 because of complications from heart disease.

Robert W. Treen passed away in 1982.

24

Walter J. Will

MEDAL OF HONOR

The Medal of Honor is our nation's highest and most prestigious military decoration. It is granted to those who have displayed conspicuous bravery above and beyond the call of duty. Since its origin in 1861, over 3,400 Medals of Honor have been awarded and the medal has often been referred to as the Congressional Medal of Honor since Congress signed the bill authorizing the medal. Four hundred and sixty-three Medals of Honor were awarded in World War II and the medal has been awarded to one woman.

Walter J. Will of West Winfield, New York, won the medal during World War II in Germany. His incredible acts of bravery and devotion to duty would lead to his being posthumously awarded our nation's highest award, the Medal of Honor. In addition to the Medal of Honor he was also the recipient of the Silver Star, the Bronze Star with an Oak Leaf Cluster, the Purple Heart with Cluster, and other medals.

What drives a person to risk his life in battle above and beyond the call of duty? What compels him to face a deadly machinegun nest to rescue wounded members of his unit? A niece, Marjorie Palmer, describes Walter Will as having been slow to anger, quiet, and a caring person. He enjoyed cars but never hunted. One time when he was home on furlough, he took time to read stories to his young niece. Palmer added that she had learned from a local man who attended a reunion of the First Infantry Division that men who fought with Walter had a tremendous respect for him and his leadership before and after he was commissioned. She was also told that someone at that reunion had described Will as a quiet, intensely determined, competitive person, and 'One hell of a fighter.'

Much of the following information was compiled from official Army citations and a War Department Public Relations Press Release provided by his family of West Winfield.

Born in Pittsburgh, Pennsylvania, his mother and father, John and Theresa, were born in Germany, but Will's German ancestry did not deter him from eliminating many soldiers of Hitler's Nazi regime.

* * * *

Walter J. Will attended the old West Winfield Central School (now known as Mount Markham Central School), and enlisted in the Army at age 17 on December 14, 1940. After basic training and further training at Fort Benning, Georgia, he was assigned to the 1st Division, the "Big Red One" (see chapter on Joseph Billings), and 18th Infantry Regiment.

Will arrived overseas on August 2, 1942 and as part of the 1st Division, participated in three major invasions, Africa, Sicily, and Omaha Beach in Normandy, France. For gallantry in action, he was awarded several decorations.

In Tunisia in North Africa, Corporal Will received the Silver Star. The citation stated that in the face of German artillery fire Corporal Will made 15 round trips on Christmas Eve and Christmas night, transporting food and ammunition to men who had been pinned down by enemy fire, and then he removed the wounded from the area.

On January 1, 1944, as a Staff Sergeant Will received the Bronze Star for meritorious achievement in ground operations against the enemy in Sicily.

He received an Oak Leaf Cluster for a second Bronze Star for "heroic achievement" near Normandy, France, on June 13, 1944. The citation included the following words: "When his patrol leader was mortally wounded, Sergeant Will unhesitatingly assumed command, and disregarding heavy fire, directed a successful assault upon enemy positions..."

In London, a few months prior to the invasion of Normandy, S/Sgt Will met a friend, Leo Zweifel, originally from Bridgewater, New York. They had tried to locate each other in Africa and Sicily. Will had gone to Zweifel's outfit when they were in Sicily, but Zweifel had been sent back to a base hospital in North Africa with malaria and two cracked ribs.

In November of 1944, Will accepted a battlefield commission as second lieutenant to Company K, 18th Infantry Regiment of the 1st Infantry Division. In addition to the Normandy invasion, he saw action throughout northern France and at the Ardennes (the Bulge), the Rhineland, and Central Europe. On November 25, 1944 he was slightly wounded for which he received the Purple Heart.

Shortly after being promoted to first Lieutenant on March 26,1945, he was engaged in combat once again. His incredible acts of bravery and devotion to duty would lead to his being posthumously awarded our nation's highest award- the Medal of Honor.

The citation reads as follows:

...Lieutenant Will, displayed conspicuous gallantry during an attack on powerful enemy positions near Eisern, Germany, on March 30, 1945. He courageously exposed himself to withering hostile fire to rescue two wounded men and then, although

painfully wounded himself, made a third trip to carry another soldier to safety from an open area. Ignoring the profuse bleeding of his wound, he gallantly led men of his platoon forward until they were pined down by murderous, flanking fire from two enemy machine guns. He fearlessly crawled alone to within thirty feet of the first enemy position, killed the crew of four and silenced the gun with accurate grenade fire. He continued to crawl through intense fire to within twenty feet of the second position where he leaped to his feet, made a lone, ferocious charge and captured the gun and its nine-man crew. Observing another platoon pinned down by two more German machine guns, he led a squad on a flanking approach and, rising to his knees in the face of direct fire, coolly and deliberately lobbed three grenades at the Germans, silencing one gun and killing its crew. With tenacious aggressiveness he ran toward the other gun and knocked it out with grenade fire. He then returned to his platoon and led it in a fierce, inspired charge, forcing the enemy to fall back in confusion. Lieutenant Will was mortally wounded in this last action, but his heroic leadership, indomitable courage and unflinching devotion to duty live on as a perpetual inspiration to all those who witnessed his deeds.

President Harry S.Truman signed the citation.

A War Department press release dated October 14, 1945 includes accounts by two witnesses. S/Sgt George H. Johnston of Peru, Indiana observed the following:

...I watched him crawl through that fire to the first man and somehow come alive to our lines. With the dirt kicking up all around he went after the other. About halfway he was hit. But he pulled himself together and went ahead. He got to the other man and came back with him." Going after one machine gun, Will got within 20 feet and charged like a madman. The rifleman and the machine gunners, nine of them, threw up their hands and surrendered (1).

The second witness, Private First Class Leland E. Lloyd of Detroit, Michigan, in a squad behind Will, described Will rushing the third and fourth machine gun nests. "Bleeding badly he got to his feet and fired a rifle grenade that knocked out the nest that killed the crew. The enemy riflemen fell back with scattered firing and it was one of those shots that got him. He (Will) fell as we were driving the enemy before us," Lloyd concluded. (1-2).

Walter J. Will was killed in action on March 30, 1945, a few days after his 23rd birthday and about 38 days before V-E Day when Germany surrendered. On April 8, 1945 in a letter to Will's mother, Theresa, Lieutenant Colonel John Williamson, Commanding Officer of the 18th Infantry Regiment, wrote the following words of praise and gratitude.

> *...During the time that your son served with the 18th Infantry, he distinguished himself by his cheerfulness and courage in all missions assigned to him and under the most rigorous conditions of combat, he rendered invaluable service to his Regiment, his Division and his Country. Your son was promoted to the grade of 2nd Lieutenant and subsequently to 1st Lieutenant on the field of battle, a feat most difficult to attain. The awards of the Silver Star and the Bronze Star Medals which were made to him, reflect in only a small way the splendid record he achieved.*

First Lieutenant Walter J. Will is buried in a cemetery in Margraten, the Netherlands. A simple cross that bears his name, rank, and service number, home state, unit affiliation, and the words," Medal of Honor," mark his gravesite.

In 1997, Walter J. Will was inducted into the Mount Markham Central School Hall of Fame.

FIRST LIEUT WALTER WILL
(Courtesy of Walter J. Will)

25

John Williams

ANTI - AIRCRAFT BATTERY

Anti-aircraft weapons were used to provide protection for cities, military bases, ships at sea and ashore, and our troops on the battlefield by destroying approaching enemy aircraft. The shells would burst in the air releasing numerous pieces referred to as flak. During World War II, special 20 mm, 37mm, 40mm, 3 inch, and 5-inch anti-aircraft guns were used against highflying aircraft.

Jack Williams, who lived for many years in Waterville, served as an officer attached to the 460th Antiaircraft Unit, D Battery in the European Theater of Operations during World War II.

* * * *

Prior to Pearl Harbor, Williams was a student at Hamilton College and in June of 1942, at the age of 21, was drafted into the army. He summarized the following about his early Army experience:

> *...The only guy in Waterville to go in with me to the army was Roy Clark. He and I were first assigned to Fort Niagara and we ran into an old girl friend who was dating the Sergeant in charge of making assignments. She said she could probably help us get the assignment of our choice. The sergeant looked us up and I told him I had an interest in the engineers but there wasn't a need for engineers, so we ended up being assigned to the cavalry. Transferred to Fort Riley, Kansas for basic training. Clark was assigned to horses and I to motorcycles. I was scared to death of motorcycles. I had seen a man killed with one. However, I got licensed and got through basic training. After basic a Lieutenant Colonel who was with the Illinois National Guard picked three or four of us and we were sent to Camp Livingstone, Louisiana as part of the 106th Cavalry of the Illinois National Guard.*

At Camp Livingstone Williams was asked if he wanted Officer Candidate School.

> *...I didn't want to go since I didn't want the responsibility. They were assigning us jobs and said we were going to schools. The lists were put on the board and they needed three W's and a Z to go to KP school. I said 'bull.' That sounded more like work not school. I got mad since I was not allowed to participate in anything. They wouldn't even let me play on the baseball team. So I decided to go to Officer Candidate School to become an officer and was assigned to anti-aircraft.*

Williams attended OCS at Camp Davis, North Carolina and while there, he saw Kenny Rankins, a high school friend from Waterville. After being commissioned a second lieutenant he was sent to Camp Hulen, Texas. and assigned to the 460th antiaircraft unit, D Battery. There we trained on several types of antiaircraft guns finalizing on the 40mm gun.

In February of 1944, Williams boarded the British ship HMS AQUITANIA docked at New York City and set out across the Atlantic for Europe. Aboard ship he was assigned as Recreation Officer of the ship and was told to have a play presented to the troops every night. It would be presented in A and B Mess, and the officer's lounge.

> *...Where was I going to get the men for this? I went around the ship and found this guy who had done burlesque but the colonel got me aside and said no off color stuff. The officer's lounge would have nurses and WAC's. I told the burlesque man what the colonel said and instructed him to keep it clean. Of course he ignored the order and his first comment in the opening introduction was off color. However, the performance went over well and everyone enjoyed it, including the female audience.*

After a few days on the high seas, Williams landed in Yeovil, England, in Somerset County near Nottingham. He spent about four months undergoing further training and preparing the guns with cosmolene and getting them ready to go. "No one knew the exact date for D-Day," Williams recalled. Just prior to D-Day, Williams said that the colonel got five of the officers in the battalion together and asked for volunteers. He said a unit was being made up of American convicts. They would be in the first landing craft to hit the beach on D-Day. An officer was needed to lead them. A guy from Texas was finally picked. When they did finally hit the beach on D-Day, 75% of them were killed. The officer survived by digging a foxhole and staying there about two days. He won the Silver Star.

Williams remembered the following about D-Day:

> *…I remember hearing Hitler saying on the radio that the allies would be driven back into the sea. 'I said, 'Good', they are gone and I'm still here but that very afternoon I was on the ship. On D+ 2 we were off Omaha Beach. The USS TEXAS was alongside shelling the beach. I watched, as the battleship would actually slide back and forth in the water each time the guns were fired. We had to stay on the landing craft for two days before we went ashore on D+4. We finally got ashore and the beach had not yet been secured. It is hard to believe that the Rangers had scaled the high cliff on Omaha Beach successfully. After the cliff scaling the troops were able to advance forward. Without that achievement, the beachhead would have been lost. Williams related how he was in the big bunker on the right as you go up the hill at the beach.*

Williams said that his unit was in on the liberation of Paris and was at the bridge at Remagen. He said it was there at the Rhine where five buddies from the first platoon were killed:

> *…As we crossed the bridge across the Rhine we were trying to locate gun positions. My platoon had already made a reconnaissance and came back across the bridge. One officer, four corporals, and a driver were on a reconnaissance mission to set up antiaircraft guns beyond the bridge. They ran over a land mine and six were killed. One had his dog tag blown off and he couldn't be buried until he was identified. The Captain wanted me to do it. He was almost crying and couldn't do it himself. "I went back and identified the body and signed the paper. God, I remember they were cooking chili where the body was.*

As a member of the First Army, Williams was involved in most of the campaigns including the Battle of the Bulge.

> *…In the area of the "Bulge" we knocked down fifteen planes in three days. Our boys did a hell of a job. Prior to the major German offensive at the Bulge we were stationed on the road to Bastogne. I was at the command post and had perfect ground position for our guns. One day a guy came down the road with orders to take my gun position. (I later found out that if I had*

stayed at that point I would be dead.) An officer named Wade had a 360mm and was going to shell Aachen. The 360mm was made up of two gun parts, and so large that it had to be put together with cranes, and the barrels so big that a man was able to climb down inside them to clean them. They were much larger than the German 88mm guns. Wade was in the wrong position and couldn't read a map. When the Germans did launch the Bulge offensive, they came right over the top (our former position on the Bastogne road). However, I was no longer there. In relation to Aachen we were on the other side of the Rhine and north of the big action. We were closer to Aachen than to Bastogne.

The author asked Williams about his most memorable experience and he said that it occurred after the war.

…We thought we were going to Japan but a directive came out wanting to know who could speak German. I took it in college and could speak very little. I was transferred to military government, which was a mistake because everyone else in my outfit went home. This extended my stay. Our job in military government was to handle displaced persons throughout Germany. We handled 5,000 Germans, Poles, Estonians, Latvians, and other nationalities. We had to see that they received food and clothing. Where were we going to get all this food and clothing? We went to the burgomaster, the mayor, and he said he couldn't help us. We said, OK, we would let all of these Russians out. It wasn't long before the wagons showed up with the food and clothes. One time we were invited to a wedding banquet involving the displaced persons. They married 25 couples at one time. We handled these displaced persons all over Germany but didn't get to Berlin. The best experience I had was in Czechoslovakia. It was when the Germans were coming back the other way and we were assigned to the Reichsbank in Frankfort.

Williams said that his job was to do an inventory of all the stuff the SS had stolen and he saw things he couldn't believe.

…In Austria I held a Crown in my hand, which was loaded with jewels. I am not sure of the origins - perhaps the Emperor Constantine. A sergeant tossed it to me and it knocked me down and the crown fell on the floor. I was shocked when I picked it

back up. The cross was bent but I found out that the crown had been made that way. After the war on a trip to Europe I listened to a tour guide talking about this crown. I said I had held it in my hand. He thought I was a hero by helping to save it. If I had been a crook I could have obtained a lot of things that were worth a lot of money. The SS had stolen ingots of gold, silver and platinum and even fillings from the teeth of those in the concentration camp at Buchenwald.

After his duty with military government he was sent back to the US and was discharged from the army as a Captain in January of 1946.

He returned to Waterville and later became a physical education teacher and coached wrestling at Watertown High School in Watertown and North Syracuse, New York. Williams was elected to the New York State Wrestling Hall of Fame, on his retirement in 1983, after 29 years of teaching and coaching.

26

Richard Woodman

JUDGE ADVOCATE

In the armed forces, the Judge Advocate General is the officer-in-charge of legal affairs and is either a major general in the Army or rear admiral in the Navy and is in charge of all legal affairs. Judge advocates are lawyers of officer rank who work for the "JAG," and they prosecute, defend, and/or review records of courts-martial. They also serve as legal advisors to their superiors and to members of the military (Lough 147).

* * * *

On July 23, 1943, Richard S. Woodman, a law partner with the late Harold Fuess, received his "greetings" from the president drafting him into the Army. "My wife was in the hospital at the time since our first child had just been born on that day," Woodman related. He reported for duty on August 23, 1943. "At the time", Woodman commented, "The Army wasn't quite sure what to do with the attorneys that were drafted. I was sent to Fort Custer at Battle Creek, Michigan for basic training for military police." The thirty-year-old Woodman trained with recruits who were younger and it was difficult to keep up with them. "It was tough — but good," he indicated. The training included infantry tactics, military government and military police training. Following that, at the same camp, he attended and graduated from the Civil Affairs branch of the Army. From Fort Custer, Woodman went to an embarkation camp located in Pennsylvania and the barracks there were tarpaper shacks. It was a frightening experience since some of the barracks burned down because of coal stoves that burned soft coal and got out of control. The stoves had to burn off the gas and it was difficult to do this and still control the heat. One morning he awoke with his face all red and he had inhaled a considerable amount of coal dust and the stoves he was attending were all glowing red and ready to explode.

While awaiting orders to be shipped overseas, someone in the Supply room told Woodman - "I can't tell you where you are going, but you better bring sandals and an umbrella." From Pennsylvania he traveled for five days by troop train to Camp Beal, California. He described a lengthy illness he endured before going overseas.

> *...I had a terrible cough and cold all the way. At Camp Beale I was given an x-ray and went on a 25-mile hike. I had contacted pneumonia and after going on the hike was taken to the hospital by ambulance." The doctor thought I had a lung condition similar to that of some soldiers who had contracted a bad lung condition from maneuvers in the desert and some had been actually discharged because of the serious condition. Consequently I was kept in the hospital for forty days. It was the coal dust I breathed and it made me sick with a bad cold that developed into pneumonia. They offered to let me come home on furlough but I refused, for once you have said your good-byes it is hard to go through it again. You know how it is. It can be very traumatic.*

In 1944, Woodman left the United States for the South Pacific. From the West Coast, it took 21 days to arrive at his base on the island of New Guinea. He was a passenger on a Dutch freighter that had been taken over by the British and manned by the American Navy.

When the freighter arrived in New Guinea, he went ashore on board an amphibious vessel called a "duck." After landing, he saw a sign that read "the 38th Division. Woodman's brother was in the 38th Division and must have landed just before him, and he said he wanted to see his brother. Alone, he found a shortcut though the jungle and saw a couple of herds of wild boars. He got there and they thought he was his brother, but Woodman was unable to locate his brother. The division had left him behind at Schofield Barracks in Hawaii recovering from an injured knee received on maneuvers. The Mess Sergeant saw Woodman and thought he was underweight since he weighed only a 140 pounds – so the mess sergeant gave him five pounds of powdered milk to fatten him up.

Woodman explained that since he had had infantry training at Fort Custer, he thought he would transfer as a rifleman. He had also been trained as a military police officer and had received training in military government, and was carrying an application for Officer Candidate School, which had become quite dog-eared. The Army wouldn't accept the application earlier since he was on overseas shipment.

However, in New Guinea, before he could make an application to transfer to the 38th Division, he was interviewed to be an investigator for the Counter Intelligence Corps. They asked him a lot of questions and he was also asked if he wanted to volunteer for a dangerous mission. Woodman answered, "I'm starving here – and nothing could be more dangerous. They told me that some morning we will wake you up and you will be on your way."

When that morning arrived, Woodman was transported to the middle of the island of New Guinea to a large airport and from there flown to Port Moresby. He then traveled to the top of Australia where he was "bumped" off the airplane to make room for someone else. After a couple of days there he was flown to Brisbane, Australia by C-47. He remembers the long take off on the overloaded C-47. Since the tail section was weighted down, they were told to get out of that section and move in front so the plane could get off the ground. The plane finally was able to take off.

When he arrived, he made a telephone call to meet someone downtown. When he arrived he then submitted his application for Officer Candidate School. Later, he took the Counter Intelligence Course and was told that if captured he would be executed without a trial. During this course, which he said was a "snap", he learned some Tagalog, which is the main language of the Philippines. He was attached to Headquarters unit, which was in the governor's mansion. However, he lived in a tent – six to a tent.

After graduating from the Counter Intelligence Corps School, he left Brisbane, traveling by a PBY aircraft, going to New Caledonia, a French island located in the Loyalty Islands of the South Pacific. He landed at Noumea – the capital. Noumea was "the prettiest French town. I'd love to go back." He was based in the mountains and attached to the 25th Infantry Division. No fighting was going on there. Woodman related how he lectured troops on how to act. The outfit there had been through Guadalcanal and New Georgia and was listed to go home on furlough. They were bored with lectures on how to act. However, MacArthur wanted top troops for the upcoming invasions and they were disgruntled about this. This outfit had a high mortality rate because their attitude was – "the bullet hasn't been made that would get me."

The Philippines were invaded in the fall of 1944. Woodman was in Noumea, New Caledonia. In January of 1945, he boarded the troopship USS PRESIDENT JACKSON. The destination was Lingayen Gulf. The night before the Lingayen invasion, January 7, Woodman noticed that there wasn't a ship to be seen in the Gulf. "But at 5 o'clock the next morning the Gulf was loaded with ships. You could almost step from ship to ship." The troops disembarked climbing down nets onto Higgins boats. (Invented by Andrew Higgins, twenty-one thousand of these wooden boats would be built during World War II). Woodman said that they stayed in these Higgins boats all day going back and forth from ship to shore helping to unload soldiers and equipment. Woodman said he was a Corporal and had no insignia and was actually an agent of the Treasury Department but no one knew it. At midnight they boarded the ship again. Headquarters unit including the generals hit the beach on the second day. Tokyo Rose was broadcasting before the invasion and trying to weaken their morale. Her voice boomed over the radio extending a welcome to the 25th Infantry Division. Woodman pointed out that the tide was high in Lingayen Gulf that day. "The boat officer, an Ensign, didn't know anything and he must not have known too much about automatic pistols. The one he carried was loaded with rust. The enlisted man – the boatswain or coxswain, did a good job driving the boat," Woodman remarked.

"After landing we slept on the sand. They didn't know what to do with us at first," Woodman said. He said he eventually did get assigned to counter intelligence work. His first contact with the enemy was at Binalonan, a town supposedly in American control. He was at a crossroads when he saw U.S.tanks and he heard 25 caliber Japanese machine guns. A bullet fired from about 200 yards struck a tree near him. "I worried about being a coward. 'Why are they shooting at me? I said to myself. I'm not mad at anyone,' Woodman recalled. There was a tank nearby and we got into a culvert by it for protection.

That day at Binalonan we were sitting around and an infantry rifleman was checking the scope on his rifle. He was looking through it and he apparently spotted a Japanese sniper and shot him. The sniper had tied himself in a tree waiting to shoot some American officer. "The Japanese often left snipers back after the main body of troops had retreated, hoping to kill the officers or any other soldiers they could before losing their own lives," Woodman exclaimed.

Even though it had been over fifty years, Woodman recalled several interesting sidelights. He said the Nisei (American-Japanese) acted as interpreters and we had to protect them from the Filipinos who regarded the Nisei as "enemies." Woodman also said if the troops needed equipment or supplies they would be taken from a Filipino and paid for them or a receipt would be issued. "I was sent out to get a typewriter which I obtained from this Filipino woman and I wonder if she ever got it back." He also told how spies (American and Filipino) would radio to the U.S. ships and submarines to let our troops know Japanese positions. These spies would come into contact with us and we would give them meals and they would be on their way.

In March of 1945 someone in headquarters had called Corporal Woodman and said to him, "Got any water? Get a glass of water and sit down. You are to be at the University of Michigan Law School at Ann Arbor, Michigan to attend Officer Candidate's School in one week."

He returned to the United States and spent thirteen long and difficult weeks in OCS school. "Even the son of the Governor of Texas flunked out," Woodman exclaimed with a serious expression. "But, we enjoyed it. At breakfast we had our own chow line and we enjoyed being waited on at the tables. At the other meals we often sat down with the students who were attending the law school."

After completing Officer Candidate School in June of 1945, Woodman was commissioned a second lieutenant and assigned to the Judge Advocate General Department at Camp Edwards, Massachusetts. As a Judge advocate, he became very familiar with the <u>Uniform Code of Military Justice.</u> He prosecuted and defended army deserters. He acted as Trial Counsel (prosecutor) and Defense Attorney in special courts-martial. Also, while at Camp Edwards, he worked on many special courts-martial. The military has three levels of courts-martial, which are as follows: Summary, Special and General. There were times while serving as Judge Advocate when Woodman felt like he was walking a tight rope. Since he was defending soldiers as well as prosecuting them, it created situations when he expressed opinions that were sometimes contrary to court members and his superiors. This was a constant concern. He certainly did not want to get himself court-martialed. A dishonorable discharge would have ended his legal careers so he had to be careful.

In one case, Woodman recalled, a soldier had a "yellow ticket"- a dishonorable discharge. He was discharged and then was drafted again and restored to duty and later accused of desertion from duty. He had been in an accident with a truck and while walking down the street one-day he met a girl who took him home. She said she was his wife and he lived some time with her. The soldier got a job washing dishes in Philadelphia. He was picked up and was to be tried for desertion since he had been away from duty for over six months. He claimed to have forgotten who he was and didn't remember being in the Army. A psychiatrist administered sodium pentathol (truth serum) to him to determine if he were really amnesiac. The result of the test showed that the accused had no memory of being in the Army. The weekend before the trial, Life magazine came out with an article on the truth serum and so the whole court was knowledgeable about it.

The Trial Counsel, a colonel, would not accept amnesia as a defense and said the accused was over six months away from his duty station and was guilty of desertion. Desertion is a more serious offense than absence without leave (AWOL) and was a capital offense. "After calling my expert witness – a medical doctor, my client was acquitted. The colonel was also the officer who periodically evaluated my performance. The general at Boston Headquarters was upset with the verdict and sent a skin letter (a letter of reprimand) to each member of the court," Woodman added.

Continuing with his recollections, Woodman related the following:

> *...I remember another case of a master sergeant that was framed by a captain who didn't like him and had him reduced to a private.*

So he took off to the oil fields and after he was apprehended he was charged with desertion. He had been away for a year and a day (over the statute of limitations for that offense). To prove desertion, intent to desert must be proved. Woodman, acting as defense attorney, had to show that the master sergeant intended to return to duty, but the court convicted the sergeant. Being the last case of the day, the court adjourned to the officer's club for the "happy hour." At the Club, Woodman asked the court members why they debated so long arriving at the verdict. They said that they were not discussing the case – They were discussing "you", (Woodman). "We discussed whether we should have charged you with contempt of court after you asked the question – 'Doesn't the court know the difference between AWOL and desertion?' Woodman remarked that maybe he was a little strong but was trying the case the best he could. They told him that he had better not do that again.

Woodman said that he and the former state senator and majority leader of the senate, Warren Anderson of Binghamton, New York, tried most of the cases together in the Judge Advocate General's Department while at Camp Edwards. "The role of Judge Advocate was a unique experience that broadened my legal experience," he added.

Woodman recalled that most of the time while in the Army, he did investigatory work and did serve some time in the combat areas. He remembers being shot at once or twice and he did receive a battle star for the invasion of the Philippines.

First Lieutenant Richard Woodman was discharged in April of 1946 and returned to Waterville to resume his career as an attorney and partner in the Fuess and Woodman firm (presently known as Woodman and Getman).

He resides in Waterville and at age 97 still continues to practice law as a partner in the Woodman and Getman firm.

27

John Youngs

TANK DESTROYER BATTALION

To combat the powerful tank, the tank destroyer was developed by the British and American armies. Mounted on tank frames, the heavily armed vehicle was faster than a tank and moved along on wheels or a caterpillar track. The M-3 carried a 105 mm gun, which had a range of seven miles and a speed of 35 miles an hour. (Cole 23).

John Youngs of Waterville was assigned to the 9th Army, 84th Infantry Division, 638th Tank Destroyer Battalion, during the last few months of World War II in the European Theater of Operations.

* * * *

Youngs was an altar boy during much of World War II. And after the older altar boys graduated from school, they either enlisted or were drafted into the service. The author, also an altar boy at the time, recalls the boyhood games and picking up potatoes on the old Cleary farm with "Father John/Aggie" Youngs.

After graduation in 1944, the 17-year-old Youngs left Waterville for basic training at Camp Hood, Texas. "I was only 5' 5" and 125 pounds, he said. After 17 weeks of basic and eight weeks of advanced infantry training, his body was transformed. He claims that when he finished training, he was 5' 10" and he weighed 205 pounds. "The food was good, "Youngs laughed.

When asked to describe his most memorable experiences, Youngs replied:

> *...Never having slept even one night away from home, the trip to Fort Dix, the first base before going to Camp Hood, was really something, for example, in New York City while having to change trains. At Fort Dix, I walked up to the gate and asked some soldiers, 'Where do I report'? He replied, 'Stay with your group.' I said — 'I am the group.' So I started my Army career.*

After basic training, Youngs was assigned to a tank destroyer battalion and explained that he did not fit in with the "old guys" at first. "I was known by the name, 'Hey there!' rather than 'Jack,' he remarked with another big laugh.

Youngs boarded a Coast Guard manned troop transport, the USS WAKEFIELD in New York, and left for Europe. He arrived in England in January of 1945.

Youngs explained that during his time with the 638th Tank Destroyer Battalion, he was assigned as a loader and gunner on a M-18 tank destroyer. He said that the M-18 had no top and most of the crew stood on the vehicle and were not completely covered. Only the driver and assistant driver were actually sheltered. There was a five-man crew and the tank commander was a sergeant. He stood on a type of platform and manned a .50 caliber machine gun that rotated 360°.

Recalling a humorous incident, Youngs said that one time, at dusk,

> *...I backed a tank destroyer inside a barn. The sergeant said, 'There are no friends in front of us, so keep on your toes.' The "old guys" went off to sleep and left 'Hey you, there,' on guard. It was dark and I heard noises and somebody going through a fence. I didn't dare to move. If I couldn't see them, they couldn't see me. After a while about three or four more came through the fence. Then there was nothing. I did guard duty all night - too afraid to move. In the morning I saw a cow in front of me – reaching through the fence. I never told anyone of the incident...*

The 84th Infantry Division crossed the Rhine River on April 1, 1945. Youngs recalled that one night on watch duty near the Rhine River, there was a line of parked tank destroyers in a field. He received an order to fire the 76 mm gun.

> *...I fired and soon there was another order -'on two- close five' I was number two and I had never heard of such an order. I looked around and I think the other guns were pointed in every direction but to the rear. I figured that the first round must have been okay so I left mine aimed as before. After the shot was fired, a voice wanted to know who was on number two. 'I replied 'Private. Youngs, sir.' The voice said – 'Well dammit; it was a replacement who got it right. Now you old guys – get on the ball.'*

Youngs said that he served in Belgium, Holland, and Germany and received two battle stars. His unit advanced to the Elbe River in May of 1945, where U. S. troops waited for the Russians advancing from the East. After the Germans surrendered, his unit was the first combat unit to return from Europe, which explains why he was one of the first to return home.

Youngs traveled to Camp Lucky Strike in LeHavre, France, and boarded a ship for the trip back to the United States. Granted a furlough, he went home to Waterville.

He pointed out that his late brother, "Chesty," who had been wounded while driving a tank in Patton's Third Army, also made it home early. A shell hit his brother's tank and "Chesty" was thrown from the tank and landed behind a fence. He was then shot in the hip by an enemy infantryman. The lieutenant in the tank had been killed.

Youngs was home on "V-J Day. "It was a happy day and what a day that was," he recalled. Youngs told how "Mike" Jannone and Albert Tarbox were carrying a washtub and dishpan and led a parade up Stafford Avenue over to Bacon Street and returning to the Ye Olde American Hotel. (The author recalls a celebration bonfire near the old mill on the corner of Putnam and Conger Streets).

After his furlough, Youngs reported to Fort Benning, Georgia and was discharged several months later in April of 1946.

Returning home, Youngs worked in construction and for the village of Waterville, retiring in 1988.

28

Leo Zweifel

PARACHUTE INFANTRY

The twentieth century saw the introduction of varied methods of warfare and the unique use of infantry personnel. Surely, one of the most dangerous was the use of parachute infantrymen. This most hazardous type of duty was voluntary and courageous. These brave men went into battle - sometimes filled with terror - with a strong feeling that they would not survive the engagement. Jumping from transport aircraft, sometimes as low as 500 feet, they participated in many battles, including campaigns in Africa, Sicily, Italy, France, Holland, and Germany. Heavily armed, these "paratroopers" acted as the vanguard in allied invasions and often dropped behind enemy lines. The 82nd and 101st Airborne Divisions led by General Matthew Ridgeway and General Maxwell Taylor respectively, are two of the more famous of the airborne units, which fought in Europe. The mission of the airborne divisions at Normandy on June 6, 1944 was to occupy the Germans by causing diversions and keeping them from moving against the invading allied troops that would come ashore.

Parachute Infantry Divisions were used primarily in Europe. The use of paratroopers was not practical in the island-hopping campaigns of the Pacific.

The late Leo Zweifel of Bridgewater and Waterville, New York, was assigned to the 82nd Airborne Division. He fought in several campaigns and was decorated with the army's third highest medal, the Distinguished Service Medal, and also received the Purple Heart with an Oak Leaf Cluster for wounds in action. The Distinguished Service Medal, which was instituted in 1918, is awarded for exceptional meritorious service in a duty of great responsibility.

His commendation reads as follows:

81mm Mortar Platoon
2nd Battalion
505 Parachute Infantry Regiment

OUTSTANDING PERFORMANCE OF DUTY

For meritorious service in action on 6 October 1943, at Arnone, Italy. This platoon was given a mission to cover the withdrawal

of "F" Company from the town and support the left flank of the Battalion in the face of over-whelming enemy counter-attack and concentrated artillery fire. It maintained its position on the right flank and stopped the hostile force, estimated at one battalion. With utter disregard for its own safety, this 81mm mortar platoon successfully accomplished its task in the face of heavy artillery, automatic weapon and rifle fire, and blocked a numerically superior enemy group from its objective.

/s/ M. B. Ridgeway, Major General, US Army.

****

Like so many other young men Leo Zweifel worked on a farm before graduating from Bridgewater Central School in 1942.

His widow, Althea Browne of Waterville, has supplied the author with much of the following information. He enlisted in the Army on November 6, 1942 and volunteered to become a paratrooper. He was eventually assigned to the 82nd Airborne Division, 505th Infantry Regiment - 2nd Battalion. As a member of the parachute infantry division he made jumps from airplanes into enemy territory. The weapons he fired or helped load were the BMR Carbine Machine Guns, heavy and light mortar, bazooka and 57mm and 75 mm howitzers. He served in Africa, Sicily, Italy, Belgium, Ireland, England, France, Luxembourg, and Germany and saw action in the Sicily, Italy, Normandy, the Battle of the Bulge, and the Rhineland.

Prior to the invasion of Normandy when Zweifel was stationed in Northern Ireland, a clipping from a local newspaper included a picture of Private Leo Zweifel of Bridgewater and his friend, Staff Sergeant Walter Will of West Winfield. Will's parents had informed the newspaper that the picture was sent home and the article indicated that the two had met in London, England on January 16, 1944. Will and Zweifel had been in North Africa and Sicily but were not able to get together. In Sicily, Will went to Zweifel's outfit but learned that he was in the base hospital in North Africa with malaria and two cracked ribs. The article also pointed out that Will had won the Silver Star for gallantry in action in North Africa. Later, Will was posthumously awarded the Medal of Honor for heroism in Germany. (See chapter on Walter J. Will).

The following is taken from another newspaper account about Zweifel's combat experience in Normandy:

...For eight days paratrooper Leo Zweifel, 20, of Bridgewater, NY, directed the fire of a powerful 88mm mortar from forward

positions subjected to intense enemy fire in a Normandy battle area where he had dropped on "D" Day. On the 9th day he was relieved. From the time his plane passed the coast of Normandy until its arrival at the jumping zone, the Nazis threw everything they had up into the sky, from tracers to heavy ack-ack. It was a rugged experience diving into a mess of hot lead, said this veteran of the Sicilian and Salerno campaigns. We were fighting the minute we hit the ground. Snipers knocked off a lot of our boys, but we'd get their measure after the first days's scrapping. My job was to direct the fire of a mortar squad and we blew pillboxes well entrenched in woods, sky high. In all, my squad fired more than a thousand mortar shells. The fighting was the worst I've ever been in. It went without a break day and night. The Nazis did everything they could to wipe us out, but they didn't succeed and we captured and held roads, bridges and a small village until infantrymen came up to consolidate the positions. I'm a lucky guy to be able to take a real rest. (Name and date of newspaper unknown)

In D-Day, June 6, 1944, Stephen Ambrose mentions the 505th Infantry regiment several times and he describes what it was like for Zweifel and his unit to jump into a sky full of tracer bullets. He wrote that four men in the 505th refused to jump. (202). Their terror was so great that they chose to take the humiliating consequences rather than jump into the "hot lead" described by Zweifel in the newspaper account above.

Althea Browne said that Zweifel had told her that after jumping from the plane he saw a paratrooper friend, who was also descending toward the ground, cut in half by deadly enemy machine gun bullets.

Following Normandy, Zweifel fought in the Ardennes campaign, the Battle of the "Bulge," and in the Rhineland.

He was discharged on September 22, 1945 and worked at Remington Arms in Ilion, New York.

He passed away January 1969.

B-17E FLYING FORTRESS
(National Archives)

Part II
The Army Air Forces

CPL FREDERICK BARNES

29

Frederick S. Barnes

ARMY AND AIR FORCE- CAREER MAN

Frederick S. Barnes was born in Buffalo, NY. With a Canadian mother, he claims to have dual citizenship. His father was an Englishman and moved with the family back to Canada while in high school. Barnes said that he received some military training in the Royal Canadian Air Force cadet program. He learned the British style rifle drill. Prior to entering the service Barnes was a carpenter apprentice in St. Catherine, Ontario.

* * * *

"Though my brother was in the Canadian Army, I finally decided that I wanted to take advantage of my dual citizenship. In 1944, my father drove me back across the border so I could enlist in the American Army," Barnes related. His father did not have the necessary papers to re-enter the United States, so he stayed in Canada.

At the age of seventeen, Barnes entered the Army reserves in Buffalo on December 18, 1944 and was called to active duty with the infantry March 10, 1945. "That's all that was left since everything else was filled. I then went to Fort Dix, NJ for processing."

"From Fort Dix, I went to Camp Croft, SC. My entire previous manual of arms and military training had to be unlearned—the drill sergeant had a field day with me for at least a week," Barnes recalled. "I had difficulty marching since marching in Canada was different." As mentioned above, Barnes had learned the British style in Canada. "They carry their weapons in a different way swinging their arms when marching. Also, in Canada we wore boots with hobnail cleats, whereas Americans have rubber heel shoes," be added. Barnes received training in different weapons. During basic training, a tragic incident occurred when two men lost their lives due to defective mortars, while undergoing 81mm mortar and rifle training at Camp Croft, South Carolina. Barnes was there for 17 weeks, which included advanced training.

Barnes's most interesting memory was of a certain 'unnamed' bad marcher who didn't fare well with machine gun fire. With laughter, Barnes related: "I didn't do too well firing the machine gun, so a friend suggested that I go up there and punch holes in the target with a pencil. They found out what he had done and was ordered to do forty pushups with a full field pack. Also, he was assigned to moving the targets on the rifle range-moving them up and down in between firing so the targets could be checked. The heat on the range was so bad that I passed out -the sun got to me."

Frederick Barnes received six additional weeks advance training at Fort Meade, Maryland. He then rode a train to California for tank training. Of his varied training and assignments, Barnes explained that he "was a casual all of the time and never assigned to a unit." Following the tank training, Barnes boarded a Victory ship, the USS ADMIRAL C.F. HUGHES; a Coast Guard manned ship, to sail across the Pacific. "We were berthed four decks down and the bunks were stacked four high," Barnes said.

After 26 days at sea, the Victory ship docked on the island of Mindanao in the Philippines. "We were scheduled for an invasion of Japan and...were immediately engrossed in training. We were anchored off the Philippines around the middle of August 1945. The dropping of the A-bombs brought an end to the war so our mission was ended. The Black Hawk division was still on the ship that was filled with troops...I was still a casual with no unit."

At this point in the war, Barnes explains he "ended up on Luzon...From Manila, we boarded a train [with] many coal cars. We were on our way to a Japanese POW camp at San Fernando [known as Base M]. It was the first time I had the experience of falling asleep in a sitting position with a rifle in my lap. Along the way, I saw a lot of jungle and Japanese prisoners on their way to the POW camp and Filipino kids drinking coconut milk and riding water buffaloes. After 24 hours I arrived at the Japanese camp at San Fernando where many Japanese were incarcerated." Upon arrival there, Fred Barnes noticed that "the harbor was loaded with sunken ships and it was there that I became ill and needed an appendectomy." Following the hospital stay, he was assigned to headquarters and performed administrative work.

On this work, Barnes explained that:

> *... I was given the choice of two assignments; one of them was the job of courier with my own jeep to transfer correspondence, documents, mail to other organizations. The assignment was to be the base Sergeant Major's (SGM) clerk. The SGM was a Master Sergeant with extensive combat time. He had accumulated enough points to return back to the states, plus he was suffering from jungle rot. I was on the job for about 60 days when the SGM received his orders to return to the states. I was a basic infantryman (specifically 81mm mortar), and since I had no experience in administrative work, I had started a self-taught*

typing course. The SGM came to advise me that I would take his place in three days because he would be on board the next ship back to the states. He pointed to the desk, shook my hand and advised me "It's now yours." He turned his back and walked off. I never saw him again. Completely dazed, I asked myself—what the hell do I do now?. Here I am, a PFC (private first class– a green recruit), and now forced to assume the job as sergeant major.... On December 28, 1945, I was given my Corporal Stripes—it was my 19th birthday.

This manpower switch mentioned above was widespread throughout the United States Army in the Western pacific, according to Fred Barnes.

...Experienced personnel needed to fill jobs were in great demand. The point system to return stateside was being lowered every week. GIs reading their point numbers on the bulletin board were heading to ships regardless of the military needs—'I've done my job, I'm going home—I've got the points' was the general attitude. As a result the higher headquarters devised a plan called the "red apple" bill. I believe this bill was designed to stop the flow of manpower out of the western pacific and other related areas. It was an excellent bill for the soldiers that wanted to make the services a career. This bill allowed me to, in effect, to change services out of the ground army to the Army Air Corps (future air force). It also allowed me to keep my rank—I was promoted to SGT in Jan 1946 only 30 days after making CPL.

An interesting provision of the bill allowed anyone who re-enlisted to switch to any branch of the service you wanted and keep your rank. I could have gone into the Navy, Coast Guard or Marines but would have had to attend basic training again—not something I wanted to do.

The other aspect of the "Red Apple" bill, was really interesting because it promised you a way to get home even more quickly— they offered 90 days leave without charge to those who signed onto the "Red Apple" bill and immediate shipment home en route to the new service or assignment—what a deal: same rank, new job, maybe new service and 90 days uncharged leave at home—Many soldiers in the Philippines couldn't wait to put their signatures on the line. Ten days after I signed, word came down that only the first 30 days were free and that the other 60 would be charged over the period of the enlistment.

On January 21, 1946, I received my orders to return stateside to First Air Force at Mitchell Field, NY to be further assigned to Fort Slocum, NY the new headquarters of the 1st Air Force. I was given assignment to the Inspector Generals office. The first day on the base, I went to the Base Exchange and purchased new brass insignias, patches and a new Air Force overseas hat. Then I headed to the tailor shop for some special sewing. I told the seamstress that I wanted some uniform changes. She stated that I would have to wait till tomorrow. I told her that would be too long and that I would sit and wait. She shrugged and said, 'Give them to me'. I marched proudly back to the office with my new Air force hat, with my new AF patches on my uniform—all thanks to the "Red Apple bill

Before retiring from the Air Force, Barnes served three tours at Thule, Greenland with an aviation engineering unit between 1946 and 1948. Other duty stations Barnes was at afterwards included a European posting for thirteen years.

In recollection of his service years, Barnes said, "when I retired after 33 years, I never regretted any of it and still look fondly on the entire time." After retirement he obtained a degree in social work and was employed for the Office of the Aging and the New York State Department of Veterans Affairs.

Frederick Barnes' late wife, Iris, is featured in the Navy section of this book.

30

Joseph Beha

COMMUNICATIONS

The Army Air Forces of World War II was made up of several organizations including support units, which helped the combat commands function efficiently. Army Airways Communications was one of these support groups.

Airways Communications included all types of communications between ground and aircraft. This included the use of VHF (Very High Frequency) radios that would send out signals for aircraft. In addition to the radio, the Teletype would also be used for messages, which were in code (cryptographic). It also ran control towers and direction finding equipment for lost aircraft.

Joseph Beha of Waterville served at one of four radio stations located in Brazil during World War II. His duties included the repairing of radios, serving as a radio operator, working with direction finding of aircraft, and operating a Teletype machine. He was attached to the 156th Army Airways Communication System Squadron.

* * * *

After graduation from Waterville Central School in 1940, Joseph Beha worked for Bissell's Hardware Store in Waterville, General Motors in Rochester and the Carborundrum Company at Niagara Falls. He had a disagreement with his boss and decided to quit his job and enlist into the Army Air Corps. His boss said, "You can't quit. You have been deferred." Beha informed his boss that he would go home until his classification for the draft was changed. He went to Rome, NY to sign up and the Recruiting Center told him he could not sign up. "I told them I would go home until I could sign up," Beha said. They told him that they would put him on the next draft list.

Beha was drafted and sent to Camp Upton, Long Island where he was placed in an old barracks, stating that there was no basic training at Upton.

From Camp Upton he went to Atlantic City and stayed in a hotel on the Boardwalk. In Atlantic City he took a series of tests and received almost a perfect score in math, which indicated that his IQ was 154. He was transferred to Amherst College for a year to study meteorology. There were about 280 in the school when it started and each quarter several would be dropped. "We had about 140 graduate after two years in an accelerated program which included basic training," Beha explained. While at Amherst, Beha said that he played the flute and piccolo in the cadet band, was captain of the soccer team, and played on the football team. "Navy was the only team that beat us," he said proudly. During this time I met a teacher, Leonie Don Carlos, of the Amherst School system. We announced our engagement at the Military Ball, which was part of the graduation festivities of the Meteorology Program.

After completing the school Beha was told that there was no longer a need for meteorologists so he was shipped to Durham, New Hampshire for ASTP Engineering (Army Specialized Training Program), which lasted three to four months. Since the Army also had sufficient engineering personnel, Beha was transferred to Greensboro, North Carolina. After a month he was shipped to Selfridge Field, Michigan to learn Radio Repair, Radio Operation and Direction Finding. At Selfridge he was made Acting Staff Sergeant and put in charge of a group from Selfridge to Miami. They then flew to Brazil and divided into four groups and each group was assigned to one of the following stations: Ascension Island, Bahia, Fontaleza, and Natal, Brazil. Beha was attached to Natal Station as a Direction Finder, and he later worked as a Teletype Operator. He described how a plane would call in and ask for help – for a location. We would have the plane send out a solid note- a long dash or a series of long dashes. Then the four stations would get the direction from that. The center station, Natal, would then locate where the plane was, Beha explained.

> *...On one occasion I had a guy ask me for a location. It was a little overcast with high clouds but clear underneath, good visibility almost anytime of the year. I told him to drop down through the clouds and land. Well, he had two engines out and just after I told him to drop through the clouds and land, he said his third engine had just quit. He said, 'I see the runway!' I said it is all clear. Go ahead and land. He came around and landed and as he was running down the runway, his fourth engine on the B17 had quit. It was close. That was the kind of stuff we ran into.*

Beha described another occasion when there was a signal.

> *...I tried to trace it at my station and everything pointed toward New Orleans and I alerted other networks up through and they sent me their bearings on this signal – an S.O.S. so I reported that somewhere 50 to 100 miles south of New Orleans that a plane was in distress. I received word back that there was no plane in that*

vicinity. Two or three hours later we got a report from that area that a plane had strayed off course and went down. It may have been the plane that had sent the SOS message. We didn't know if there were any survivors.

Beha tells of President Roosevelt stopping off at Natal.

...One time, we received a Teletype message, which was all in crypto (cryptographic code). Since it was in crypto, I did not know what was in the message. We never did find out until later that President Roosevelt went through Natal enroute to the Yalta Conference. His plane did land at Natal and also came through the Natal area on the way back.

Beha said that the weather in the Natal area was very consistent. "For three months it would rain day and night from December through February, then we would have hot sun from June through August, then rain again in December. Beha said his biggest danger was malaria and one-third of the base contracted the disease.

He said his highest rank was acting Staff Sergeant and he was in charge of a shift but his actual rank was Corporal and he was attached to the Army Air Forces Communications System.

Beha recalled that he was in Natal when the Japanese surrendered on August 14, 1945. "What a happy day that was for us since we had been scheduled to go to the Pacific. When V-J day arrived we were very happy. I have heard of so many people who have criticized President Truman, but when V-J Day arrived, we were elated," Beha emphasized with laughter.

One day Beha received a Teletype message stating that someone was needed for duty in Panama as soon as possible. "The fastest way to Panama was to go to Miami then back to Panama. I went to the First Sergeant and said. 'I'd like to take advantage of this and go to Panama.' The sergeant said 'OK.'" Beha received Orders for Panama the following day to take the next plane leaving Natal. As he gave Beha the Orders, the sergeant said, 'you know when you get to the States you'll have to sign to go over again."(To Panama). "I said, 'Oh, I will?' The sergeant said, "You knew that. Good luck, Joe," Beha explained that "If you have been out of the country for over a year, you have to sign again to go overseas."

Beha said it was Thanksgiving of 1945 and the war was over. In Miami he was asked to sign in order to go to Panama. He told the officer," I don't sign anything but my check, sir," Beha replied.

Consequently, Beha did not go to Panama and he was given 45 days leave to go home on furlough.

Corporal Joseph Beha was discharged from the Army Air Force in Miami on January 29, 1946. He returned home and obtained an Associate Degree in electronics. He worked for 28 years at General Electric in electronics designing computers that guided missiles used in the British–Argentine Falkland Islands War and the Persian Gulf War.

Joseph Beha passed away March 19, 2011.

31

Farron Benjamin

TOP SECRET DUTY

As work on the development of the atomic bomb progressed during World War II, two major problems would arise. One problem was whether the U.S. would use the atomic bomb once it was perfected. The second problem was to develop a plan to deliver it to the enemy successfully.

With the surrender of the Nazis on May 8, 1945, the Japanese were in retreat but fighting desperately. It was predicted that the war against Japan would last another 18 months and the invasion of the Japanese mainland was scheduled for November 1, 1945.

Soldiers, sailors and airmen were in the process of being transferred to the Pacific Theater of Operations and it was predicted that there would be a million casualties. The Japanese would fight stubbornly as the home islands were invaded. Japanese Vice Admiral Takijiro Onishi, the founder of the Kamikaze forces, said that Japan was ready to sacrifice 20 million men (Pashall 50-51).

Plans had been underway since mid-1944 to meet the second problem – the successful delivery of the atomic bomb. The 509th Composite Group, commanded by Colonel Paul Tibbets, was given this task.

Farron Benjamin of West Edmeston, New York, was assigned to the 509th Composite Group as a member of the 1027th Air Material Squadron. As a member of the 1027th, he trained with the 509th Composite Group for about a year before the first atomic bomb was dropped on Japan.

* * * *

Farron Benjamin was born in Burlington Flats, New York and attended school at Edmeston. Before entering the service on March 23, 1943, he did carpentry work and worked at Savage Arms in Utica.

At Miami Beach he was placed into the Army Air force and after completing basic training, was transferred to Camp Lee, Virginia, and then to Camp Kearns, Utah for about a year.

About the middle of 1944, he was transferred to Wendover Field, Utah where he was assigned to the 509th Composite Group – also referred to as the First Atomic Bomb Group. Benjamin explained that getting into the outfit required an extensive background investigation. Back home his mother thought that he had done something bad, since the investigation involved the contacting of neighbors.

The Group had five B-29's and there were almost 1800 men in the Group, which was made up of five squadrons. In the 509ᵗʰ Composite Group Pictorial Album, Benjamin pointed out the various squadrons, which made up the Group, and a photograph of Wendover Field. He indicated that he was assigned to the 1027ᵗʰ Air Material Squadron and he said his main duty was loading and unloading conventional bombs on B-29's. "The Bomb Squadron would have practice bombing runs from Wendover to Battista Field in Cuba, using conventional bombs that I helped load. In addition to his Air Material Squadron, other squadrons in the Group included the following: Headquarters, Ordnance, 393ʳᵈ Bomb Squadron, Engineering, and the 1395ᵗʰ Military Police," Benjamin explained.

When Wendover Field was established in 1940, the town of Wendover had a population of only 103 and is located near the Nevada state line. The hotel that was built there was called the Stateline Hotel. One-half of the hotel was in Utah and one-half was located in Nevada. Benjamin recalled that when Bob Hope visited, he referred to Wendover Field as "Leftover" and "Tobacco Road with slot machines." Today, he added, Wendover is a city with several hotels and is built on the Nevada Side.

Benjamin recalled that as they were leaving Wendover Field in late May of 1945 to go overseas, he observed a sign which had been set up at the Field earlier. Still looking at the Group book Benjamin showed a photo of the sign, which read – 'What you hear here, see here, and when you leave here, let it stay here.' "It was the most secret thing that was ever done. Nobody, anywhere, knew what was coming," Benjamin explained.

Colonel Paul Tibbets was the Group Commander and he was the pilot of the "Enola Gay" that carried the atomic bomb to Hiroshima.

> *…Before we went overseas, he got us all together and said that we probably wouldn't be over there more than six months. Of course, no one believed him. We didn't know what he had. And of course, he was the only one in the unit who knew. He didn't tell us where we were going. Even the bombardier didn't know until the plane was airborne. During the flight, Tibbets climbed through a big pipe back to the bombardier to tell him about the bomb. We did get back to the states exactly six months after we had left. He really knew what he was doing, I guess.*

Benjamin was at Wendover Field about a year, and his wife Dorothy, who had accompanied him almost everywhere, was with him.

"Before the Group left the States, I remember Tibbets saying that we had a big bomb. He didn't tell us what it was – just that we had a big bomb," Benjamin explained with a laugh.

From Wendover Field the 509th traveled to Seattle, Washington by train and boarded a ship to Tinian Island in the Marianas by way of Hawaii. The Marines had taken over the island July 24, 1944 and the island would be used to launch B29's against Japan.

The 509th arrived at Tinian and made preparations for the August 6 mission to Hiroshima and the August 9 mission to Nagasaki. The two atomic bombs on Tinian were named "Little Boy," and "Fat Man." The Atomic Age was about to begin and Private First Class Farron Benjamin was in the midst of one of the greatest historic events of the 20th century.

Benjamin said that Colonel Paul Tibbets took "Little Boy" on the "Enola Gay" and another plane took "Fat Man" to Nagasaki August 9, 1945. He also explained that the bombs were armed in the air after take-off. Once airborne, three blue pins were taken out of the bombs and three red pins inserted. Also, when the "Enola Gay" returned that night the base went on high alert, as there was a report that the Japanese might make a counter-attack. "We were put all over the island with guns and ammunition. The Japanese sent out planes for an attack on Tinian but they never made it, Benjamin said.

"As the "Enola Gay" took off that morning I was out there and Colonel Tibbets waved. The ocean is located at the end of the runway and he needed the entire length of it to takeoff. Tibbets later said that after the plane left the runway that morning, it began to drop before he got any altitude," Benjamin explained.

"When the 'Enola Gay' returned from the Hiroshima mission, Tibbets called everybody to his headquarters and we had quite a celebration. We had all the food we could eat and beer and Coke and Pepsi. We celebrated that day. When he got up to give us a talk," Tibbets said, 'I saw a city and then I didn't,'" Benjamin explained.

Another of Benjamin's memories is that when the Group arrived at Tinian the base personnel had made fun of them. In the 509th Composite Group Pictorial Album, there are some humorous poems. Here is an excerpt of one, which was written by a clerk in Base Operations.

…Into the air the secret rode.
Where they are going – nobody knows.
Tomorrow they'll return again but well—
We'll never know where they have been. —

Don't ask us about results, as such,
Unless you want to get us in Dutch.
But take it from the one sure of the score –
The 509th is winning the war (no page number).

The two atomic bombs dropped on Japan, "Little Boy" on Hiroshima, and "Fat Man" on Nagasaki brought the war to a sudden halt August 14, 1945. "A third bomb was on its way to Tinian. However, since the Japanese finally surrendered, the third "Bomb" did not reach its destination and it was returned to the United States," Benjamin said.

Turning to face the wall and to the reunion pictures of 1999 in Washington, D.C., he pointed out Colonel Tibbets who was wearing glasses and had his arms folded in the photograph. "He was 85 years old then," Benjamin remarked. "And he was a very outspoken man," Dorothy Benjamin added. At a reunion in Dayton, Ohio, there was a lady there who asked Tibbets if it were necessary to drop the bomb. "If there hadn't been a Pearl Harbor, there wouldn't have been a Hiroshima," Tibbets replied. Benjamin said there were a lot of people there feeling sorry for the Japanese and were objecting to putting the "Enola Gay" in the Smithsonian Institute.

"We saved a lot of lives by dropping the bomb," Benjamin remarked as he pointed out his picture in the reunion photograph of 1999. There were only 79 out of 1800 of us left that year. Dorothy had an operation in 2000 so I did not attend that reunion. I'm going in 2001 because it probably will be the last because there are so few of us left."

After the war, Private First Class Farron Benjamin returned home and worked as a self-employed building contractor.

32

Melvin Brewer

RADIO REPAIRMAN

The less glamorous duties of Air Force personnel are those performed by the ground crew. Combat aircrew members have been highly appreciative of the ground crew who are sometimes ignored or forgotten by the general public.

These ground crew members are the mechanics, electricians, metal workers, landing gear specialists, radiomen, air control men, ordnance handlers, fuel personnel, meteorologists, and others. They are the support personnel, operating in the rear areas, who make it possible for the planes to fly. Without their efforts, the countless bombing missions and fighter plane sorties would not have been successful.

The following account is about former Technical Sergeant Melvin Brewer who was an Army Air Force radioman who installed and repaired ground radios and radios in the fighter planes.

****

Melvin Brewer was born in Beverly, New Jersey and moved to Waterville to live with his aunt and uncle in 1940. He worked as a shipping clerk in the textile mill before being drafted into the Army Air Forces on August 30, 1942.

His basic training was at Atlantic City, New Jersey and he remembers marching on the sandy beaches near the steel pier and even marching on the Boardwalk. Following basic training, he attended radio school for twelve weeks at Truax Field in Wisconsin. His first day there was spent digging ditches for plumbing facilities. "We lived in tarpaper shacks," he said.

Brewer gained experience working on radios in planes at Richmond Air Base. At Richmond the pilots engaged in flight training including night flying, and his job was to install and repair radios in P-41's.

From Richmond Brewer went to Camp Springs Army Air Base that is now called Andrews Air Force Base, and was assigned to the ground crew working as a radioman.

On November 23, 1943, he boarded the Queen Elizabeth and crossed the Atlantic in six days. "We rolled a lot from the heavy sea since the ship made many turns in an effort to avoid possible submarines," Brewer related. He explained that in the mess hall the trays would slide all over the place. The guys got seasick and he ate only candy bars and cookies during the voyage. "I gave up on eating in the mess hall," Brewer exclaimed with a laugh.

Brewer arrived in England on November 29, 1943 and he went by train to his first base at Bottisham, a Royal Air Force Base that only had one runway. He went up the hill from there to Saffron Walden. He said that they were up so high that he could see the buzz bombs launched by the Germans going through the valley below. They were located near Cambridge, which is about fifty miles from London. The P-47's were arriving almost every day.

While stationed in England, he was attached to the Eighth Air Force, 361st Fighter Group, and 374th Fighter Squadron. The planes were P-51 Mustangs which made attacks on the mainland of Europe.

The squadron traveled to Southampton by train and the troops crossed the channel on the British troopship, "ANTENOR," on February 6, 1945. Two days later the troops left for LeHavre, France. They marched for two miles with full field equipment and boarded a train of French 40'x 8' boxcars and went to a marshalling area called Twenty Grand. They arrived at Brugellette about February 15, 1945 (Gotts 126). "We were stationed between Mons and Ath, located at Brugelette, and acted as support for the planes. We operated in rear areas and I recall that after the Battle of the Bulge and after the Rhine was crossed, all of our planes, the B-17 and B-24 bombers were put into the air. Our fighters were on the ground waiting for the bombers, and then the fighters would take off and escort the bombers on their way to targets in Germany," Brewer recalled.

The squadron was ordered back to England but the pilots, enjoying the favorable flying weather on the continent, which permitted more flying time, did not wish to return to England and the bad weather.

The squadron returned to Saffron Walden, England and was located there when the war with Germany ended on May 8th. While in England, Brewer explained that he was still assigned to working on radios but was still entitled to battle stars. He summarized the record of his squadron.

...We got six battle stars for being in the area of our planes in combat. Our fighter planes went into battle areas while we were back in England, but we got credit for battle stars. Our squadron had engaged in 441 missions between January 21 and April 20, 1945 and one hundred and eight aircraft were lost. We operated from bases in England, France, and Belgium in support of the air offensive taking place over Nazi-occupied Europe supporting

the land and airborne operations in Holland, at Bastogne, the Ardennes, and at the crossing of the Rhine.

The Groups' pilots shot down 226 enemy aircraft in the air and 105 on the ground (Gotts 126).

Technical Sergeant Melvin Brewer returned to the United States on a Liberty ship. He was discharged on October 27, 1945, returned home, and was employed at various jobs including Deputy County Clerk and Court Clerk for Oneida County Court and State Supreme Court.

He passed away October 17, 2002.

33

John Gallagher

B-17 FORTRESS PILOT

The Boeing Aircraft Company designed and constructed the B-17 heavy bombers in 1934. Few were manufactured until the United States entered World War II. From 1935 to 1945 over 12,000 were built and almost 5,000 were lost during the war (B-17 1-2).

The bomber was almost 75 feet long with a wingspan of over 100 feet and it weighed over thirty tons when fully loaded. It was powered with four Wright Cyclone nine cylinder engines. Each engine had 1200 horsepower at takeoff and could carry over 3500 gallons of gasoline. Since the B-17 was used primarily for daylight bombing, it required considerable firepower. The plane carried thirteen .50 caliber machine guns, which included a tail gun, top and bottom ball turrets, and one waist gun firing from the mid-section on each side of the fuselage. The navigator and radio operator also operated chin and cheek guns. Because of all of this firepower, a Seattle reporter named the B-17 a "flying fortress". (And the label remained to be used synonymously for the B-17). Their bomb bays could carry over 17,000 pounds of bombs (short range) (B-17 1-2).

The B-17 carried a crew of ten men flying as a team frequently dodging heavy flak from anti-aircraft guns from the ground and engaging in deadly combat with enemy fighter planes.

John "Jack" Gallagher of Sangerfield, New York flew 35 missions as a B-17 "Flying Fortress" pilot in the 15thAir Force.

****

Gallagher, the son of a Sangerfield dairy farmer, left home and the farm to become a pilot of the most widely used bomber in World War II. As a freshman at Alfred University, he enlisted into the Army Air Corps Reserve Program and was ordered to, "Stay in college until we call you!"

The call came in 1943 to report for basic training at Atlantic City, New Jersey. After receiving primary and advanced flight training at various locations around the country, which included training in multi-engine planes, he was commissioned as a second lieutenant in March of 1944. The following months involved B-17 training in Tampa where a skeleton crew was picked up.

The remainder of the crew (the gunners) was picked up at Savanna, Georgia and after combat training; the crewmembers proceeded to Hampton Roads, Virginia to board a transport for the European Theater of Operations. The transport arrived in September at the harbor of Naples, Italy, which Gallagher observed was filled with sunken ships. The railroad station had recently been blown up.

In September of 1944, the twenty-one year old Lieutenant Gallagher (the average age of the B-17 pilot was 21) reported for duty with the 20th Bomber Squadron, of the 2nd Bomb Group of the 15th Air Force in Italy.

In Italy Gallagher flew out of Amendola near Foggia on the Adriatic coast, which was headquarters for the fifteenth Air Force under General Nathan Twining.

Gallagher's squadron participated in daylight raids over Romania, Hungary, Poland, Austria, Czechoslovakia, and East Germany. The object of each mission was to destroy oil refineries or means of transportation at Linz and Vienna, Austria, and Munich, Germany. Some of the targets were heavily defended.

On Christmas Day in 1944, Gallagher must have had many thoughts of home and farm and the hills of central New York as he prepared for the all out effort to destroy the huge synthetic oil refinery in Brux, Czechoslovakia - the last oil refinery of the Germans.

Following the briefing, the crew boarded the bomber and made final preparations for take-off. The thirty-ton fortress, heavily laden with bombs, thundered down the runway lifting slowly into the air. In the early hours of Christmas morning, as the huge formation of 1,000 B-17's and B-24's -the whole 15th Air Force, headed out over the dark waters of the Adriatic bound for their all important target in Brux. (Gallagher stated that the average number of planes on a mission was about 140). The cruising altitude was 25-30,000 feet. In the book, Bloody Skies by Melvin McGuire and Robert Hadley, Sergeant McGuire, the bombardier on the Christmas mission, relates how he liked flying with Gallagher stating that "Lieutenant Gallagher was an excellent pilot." (362).

Gallagher explained that the crews wore heated flying suits and oxygen masks. At 25,000 -30,000 feet, the temperature was a very cold 50-60 degrees below zero. Without the mask, crewmembers would be unconscious in a minute - dead in three to five minutes. Escape and evasion kits were carried in the flight suits to be used on the ground to avoid capture by the enemy. As the planes approached the target, interceptor planes attacked. As the B-17's got closer to the target and the enemy fighters had returned to base, anti-aircraft ("ack-ack") guns were directed at the bombers. Anti-aircraft guns often made direct hits on planes and created dangerous flak areas (shrapnel from exploding shells). Also, tinfoil referred to as chaff, would be released from the plane to combat flak.

"The raid was not as tough as anticipated," Gallagher recalled. The Nazi Air Force (Luftwaffe) had become weakened by the end of 1944 and attacks by fighters were not as threatening. He explained an incident that hastened the collapse of the Luftwaffe.

The Germans had planned a secret mission to eliminate the 9th Air Force (Tactical or fighter group) and had massed their fighter planes in an attempt to wipe out the 9th Tactical Air Force in a pre-dawn raid. The air battle took place on January 1, 1945 in France. The mission was so secret that the Germans had never told their own anti-aircraft groups about it and as a result actually ended up shooting down some of their own fighters. Four hundred German planes and 300 allied planes were lost. These losses practically eliminated the Luftwaffe.

On a December 1944 mission to attack the rail center at Linz, Austria, the Nazis were moving equipment to the "Bulge" front in Belgium. At the time of the Battle of the Bulge, "the flights were concentrating on transportation targets including bridges at Linz and we destroyed a lot of Nazi equipment," Gallagher related. He reported that destroying this railhead stopped the Nazis in moving much of their equipment. He added that during the raid, the sky was filled with an unexpected mobile flak attack from the German 88mm guns mounted on railroad flat cars. This long ranged anti-aircraft gun was very destructive and was one of the most feared guns of the war (Wheal, Taylor and Pope 154). The B-17 could take a lot of punishment and still return to base provided it did not receive a direct hit from the ground. "Luckily, we always returned from our missions but sometimes the plane got shot up a bit," Gallagher added. Luftwaffe fighter planes attacked the B-17's and American P-51's and the twin fuselage P-38's would help protect the heavy bombers. The World War II fighter plane could not carry enough fuel, and therefore, could accompany the bombers only part of the way toward the target. At the end of the war, fighters carried drop-tanks with extra fuel to extend their range, and provided protection for a greater part of the mission.

The British had designed the jet aircraft engine but only the Nazi Luftwaffe utilized the jet plane during the war. Lieutenant Gallagher's largest encounter with the jets took place in March and early April of 1945, two months before V-E day in a raid over Germany. "They raised hell with us," commented Gallagher. "As we approached the target, a Nazi jet, -a Messerschmitt Me-262, flying at 550 mph, was sighted by Warren McKane, the top turret gunner. He yelled that jets were attacking and the turret could not be turned fast enough to take a bead on the jets," Gallagher said. The B-17 turrets did not have the rapidity needed for jet defense. Gallagher pointed out that the German jet pilots had been told not to sacrifice their jets. Since the range of the jets was short, they had strict orders from the Nazi high command to make only one pass against the bombers. However, on this particular day, one persistent jet pilot, apparently hoping for an easy kill, decided to make one more pass. This turned out to be fatal for the jet. It made a pass to the rear and looped over the B-17. As it did, the gunners sighted their .50 calibers and shot down the jet making an historic kill. "It was the first jet shot down from a bomber formation," said Gallagher.

Another memorable experience was that the B-17, a daylight bomber, obtained more fighter protection and Gallagher recalls being told that the famed Tuskegee squadron of P-51's had escorted them at times. He did not know this until later that these black airmen had been part of their escort.

No crewmembers died on these 35 missions but some crewmembers did receive shrapnel wounds and the planes Gallagher flew did sustain a few holes. Some landings did get a little "hairy" because of engine problems and there were a couple of shaky returns flying over the Alps. The worst thing of all was flying in bad weather, especially since the formations were so tight, according to Gallagher.

On the 6th of May 1945, Gallagher was on a ship passing Gibraltar and getting ready to go to the Pacific, but the Germans surrendered on May 7th. He was discharged as a First Lieutenant on July 4, 1945. His time in the Army Air Force had ended. I had an opportunity to get out and I took it. I had had it." He had won several air medals and the Distinguished Flying Cross. Gallagher modestly says, "For what - I don't know. I give a lot of credit to all the support groups. We were lucky to get back."

What was the best thing Gallagher liked about the flying fortress? Gallagher responded. "It could take a lot of punishment and we would fly at a higher altitude than the B-24 Liberator. We usually flew 5,000 feet higher. The Nazi's preferred attacking B-24's since B-24 formations were not tight. If there were a choice, the Nazis would attack the B-24's." His only criticism of the B-17 was that it was "too slow."

After discharge from the Army Air Forces, Gallagher returned to the family dairy farm in Sangerfield, which he continued to operate for many years. He passed away July 5, 2005.

34

Richard Hilsinger

B17 FLIGHT ENGINEER

The Flight Engineer on a B-17 advises the pilot regarding landing gear and other mechanical problems and during emergencies the Flight Engineer could be asked to assist the pilot and co-pilot in flying the plane. There have been occasions when a flight engineer has had to manually release a bomb or bombs that have not released properly. Flight Engineers have been responsible on more than one occasion, for saving the aircraft from disaster. The regular duties of the Flight Engineer on a B-17 are limited during combat as well as the mechanical tasks that he is able to perform. His main duty during a combat bombing mission is to man the top gun turret and protect the aircraft and crew from enemy fighter aircraft. (Hilsinger E-Mail).

Richard "Dick" Hilsinger was originally from Waterville and flew thirty-three missions as a flight engineer and top turret gunner on a B-17 in the Eighth Air Force during World War II.

* * * *

Hilsinger graduated from Waterville Central School in 1940 and worked for a while in the old textile mill and in construction. After enlisting in the Army Air Force on June 30, 1942, he went to Fort Dix, New Jersey and then to Miami Beach, Florida for basic training. Hilsinger said that basic training on a field in Florida in July was unbearable, but the trainees did get to stay in a hotel during the training.

Following basic training, he received training as an aircraft mechanic which included specialist training on Wright aircraft engines. After working as an aircraft mechanic in Arkansas, he applied for and received instruction in aerial gunnery in Florida.

Hilsinger was then assigned to a B-17 flying fortress crew and on one training flight in Louisiana the plane got lost because all of the directional equipment was not operational. They wandered about most of the night looking for a place to land until the plane almost ran out of fuel, but an airport was spotted and the plane landed. The B-17 was out of fuel and only one of the four engines was running as the plane rolled to a stop on the runway. "Someone had to be looking out for us that night," Hilsinger recalled.

It was early spring of 1944 and Hilsinger boarded a ship transporting him to England. He said the ship was loaded with troops and very crowded. "It was terrible crossing the Atlantic with a constant threat of German submarines," he stated.

Fifteen days later the ship arrived in England and Hilsinger was assigned to a heavy bomber group attached to the Eighth Air Force. "The Eighth Air Force is considered by historians as the Air Force responsible for breaking the back of the German Luftwaffe in the spring of 1944" (O'Neill xiv).

Technical Sergeant Richard "Dick" Hilsinger was stationed at Rattlesden, a small town near Ipswich, England, and he was always with the same crew of ten men and they always flew the B-17, which was assigned to them. It was named "Fuddy Duddy." Hilsinger flew as a flight engineer and Top Turret Gunner. He said his main duty was to assist the pilot in any way that he could.

> *…I used to stand just behind the pilot when we were landing and he would move his right earphone off his ear so he could hear me call off the speed of the aircraft as we approached for landing. That allowed him to concentrate on the landing without having to look down at the instrument panel to maintain his landing speed. My pilot used to let me fly the plane in formation at times just to give me experience in case it was needed. His plan was to allow me to sit in the co-pilot's seat and actually get the feel of landing the aircraft if it ever became necessary to sub for the co-pilot. I never got that opportunity since none of our landings were ever routine.*

Hilsinger said that he flew thirty-three missions over Germany and "everyone of them was hell." He explained that the Germans did their very best to shoot them down with their anti-aircraft guns. The flak from the AA guns at times was treacherous. It was very thick and was capable of causing severe damage and direct hits would knock planes out of the sky. The German fighters, the single and double-engine Messerschmitts, Fockewulfs and Junkers, tried to knock the planes down in an effort to stop the B-17's from bombing the cities. The B-17's did have fighter escorts for part of the mission. Fighter planes flying as escorts were P-38's, P-47's, and finally the P-51's, which had a greater range and could stay with the bombers for a longer time before returning to base.

"We were fortunate that only one of our crew members was wounded and he recovered after months in the hospital. He is alive and well today. There are five members of our crew who are still alive today and we keep in touch," Hilsinger said.

Hilsinger said that his bombing missions over Germany included bombing such cities as Berlin, Munich, Leipzig, Hanover, Bremen, Kiel, Stuttgart, and Mannheim, St Lo on the French coast, and many other cities of Europe.

In addition to anti-aircraft fire and fighter planes, "We had to fear mid-air collisions, the weather, running out of fuel and, of course, a safe landing on return to base," Hilsinger added.

When taking off. the planes would have to reach a certain altitude and formation slot within a set time or risk mid-air collision. There were hundreds of bombers and fighter planes on a mission. The formation would have a high element following the lead element above, and to the left, and the low element would follow below and on the right (O'Neill p.25) Bombs were sometimes dropped from the higher element planes, narrowly missing and sometimes striking a plane flying at the lower altitude.

Hilsinger recalled a very frightening incident, which occurred when his plane was approaching a target.

> *... I looked straight up from my position in the top turret into the open bomb bay of an aircraft above us. I called desperately to my pilot on the intercom to make him aware of it. He in turn got on the radio and called the aircraft above us. I watched that aircraft as it slowly slid to our right and as the bombs dropped, one of them just nicked our right wing tip. We were extremely lucky that day and I hate to think what would have happened if I had not seen it and alerted our pilot. When you are flying in formation there is extreme turbulence from the prop wash of the planes ahead of you as well as the concussion of the exploding anti-aircraft shells all around you. There were mid-air collisions for the same reason (Hilsinger E-Mail).*

Hilsinger said that about a month after he returned to the States, his old plane, "Fuddy Duddy," was involved in a mid-air collision over Germany and all but two crew members in the two aircraft were killed. The two surviving crewmembers were the navigator and bombardier on "Fuddy Duddy" and they were in the nose of the aircraft when the collision took place. They are both still living. The B-17 named "Fuddy Duddy" at the Warplane Museum in Elmira was named after Hilsinger's old plane, "Fuddy Duddy."

Richard Hilsinger said that while in England he was able to locate his brother Fred.

...I got him to my air base (Ipswich) and through my pilot finagled a ride for him in our B-17 on a "trumped up" test flight. I arranged for my pilot to give him a ride he wouldn't soon forget. Fred got to experience "weightlessness" long before the astronauts did. I'm sure Fred remembers this.

Hilsinger returned to the United States in November of 1944, prior to V-E Day. On V-J Day he was in a hospital at Patterson Field in Ohio recovering from what the Army doctors termed as "severe combat fatigue."

Technical Sergeant Richard Hilsinger was fortunate to have survived thirty-three bombing missions. He said that it was a war we really did not want but when Pearl Harbor was bombed, "I for one, was ready, willing, and able. It became a very necessary war at that point and it was hoped that it would be a war that would end future world wars. I still have those hopes even though things appear very shaky at times," Hilsinger declared.

For gallantry and meritorious service, Hilsinger received the Distinguished Flying Cross, and an Air Medal with three oak leaf clusters.

He was discharged on September 20, 1945 and was employed at various jobs, which included working for General Motors for twenty-eight years as a maintenance electrician.

He passed away April 14, 2008

35

Andrew Mondo

B-24 NAVIGATOR

The B-24 carried a crew of ten men, which included a navigator. The navigator on the B-24 heavy bomber had to keep track of his plane's position on the way to its bombing target and help guide the plane back to its home base safely.

The air navigator performs about the same work as a ship's navigator but has less time to do it since the plane is traveling faster than ships. The B-24 navigator took a difficult four-month course, which included training in celestial navigation that required considerable night flying. The trainees would fix on three stars using an octant that had eight lenses. Normally, daylight navigation involved dead reckoning utilizing the compass and charts and pilotage (observing landmarks on the ground).

Andrew Mondo of Utica, New York, was a navigator and first lieutenant on a B-24 Liberator in the European Theater of Operations. He flew 35 missions over Yugoslavia, Germany, and other countries of Europe.

* * * *

Mondo worked for two years at the Savage Arms defense plant and enrolled as a freshman at Clarkson College. Though defense plant work made him exempt from the draft, he joined the Enlisted Reserve Corps at Clarkson, and was called to active duty in March of 1943 when he was 20 years old.

Following basic training at Miami Beach, he attended Radio Operator's School at Scott Field, Illinois. Interested in becoming a pilot, he was enrolled in flight training at Hondo, Texas. There he became known as - "Mondo From Hondo." In flight training, Mondo flew Piper Cubs and the spins would cause him to become ill. He would hold his head outside the plane and his vomit would cover the outside, which he later had to wash off. Consequently, he decided to give up his desire to be a pilot and switched to navigator training. "You don't do spins in a B-24," he laughed.

Navigation school was a four-month course at Santa Anna, California. A twin-engine plane was used with a pilot and navigator-instructor in front and three students in back. He said the highlight of the course was learning celestial navigation since it was such a novelty to them. They would fly at night and using an octant that had eight lenses, the navigator would fix on three stars, which are ideally 120 degrees apart. The navigator would then stand up and look through the clear astrodome in the plane and measure the angle between the stars and the horizon. Then three lines would be drawn and where the lines intersected would be the aircraft position on the map. "We seldom got an exact intersection but a small triangle. That would be close enough to estimate within 50 miles. He said that during the training they would always fly a three-leg trip and each student navigator played the lead for one leg of the trip and when we came back down each student would have to report and be evaluated," Mondo explained.

Mondo, commissioned a second lieutenant, was then transferred to Boise, Idaho where B-24 crews were assigned for extensive training, and in 1944, he was assigned to the 15th Air Force 304th Bombardment Wing, 455th Bombardment Group.

From Boise, Idaho, Mondo rode in a troop train to the east coast. The destination was unknown other than it was the ETO – European Theater of Operations. He boarded a ship and eventually found out that it was bound for Naples, Italy.

In Italy, assigned to the 15th AF, Mondo's Group flew out of San Giovanni Air Field. The bombing targets were in northern Italy, Austria, Germany, and Czechoslovakia. Mondo explained that on the missions there were four squadrons with seven planes in each squadron and one lead plane – the leader. The lead plane carried the lead navigator and lead bombardier. He said that he participated in 35 missions and every one counted as one whether it was an easy mission to northern Italy or a long mission to other parts of Europe. Earlier in the war some missions counted as two. "I bombed my 'paisans,' and I was aware of that, too," Mondo pointed out. He explained that as the war was drawing to a close:

> *…We were fortunate in that enemy fighters did not hit us as we returned from our missions. However, the enemy was retreating and they were taking their anti-aircraft guns with them as they fell back. Thus, we were receiving heavy anti-aircraft fire and we were flying through great amounts of flak. It was the worst anti-aircraft of the war and we did get a lot of holes in our plane. The closest hole was about the size of an apple about three feet from me.*

Describing a mission, Mondo said that when the plane reached the IP, the initial point, which was not directly toward the target, but about twenty-five miles from it, they turned all of the planes toward the target. The formation was tightened so that all of the bombs would drop together on the lead bombardier's drop. This tightening up also would provide more concentrated firepower in case of attack by fighter planes. The last plane in the formation had the toughest position since it had to keep up with the rest of the group. Flying in formation, the pilot and co-pilot would take turns flying the plane to better observe the other planes. This would depend on the position of the plane in the formation.

Mondo stated that the squadron never lost a plane on a mission. At the start of one mission, Mondo recalled, "We lost a crew who had lived in a tent next to us. The plane was taking off one day and as it was rolling down the runway attempting to take off when something went wrong. They tried to stop but it was going too fast, and it went off the end of the runway into a ditch and blew up and they were all killed."

Mondo said that the B-24 was a flying boxcar. "Whatever merits it might have had, beauty was not one of them. It was just an ugly aircraft. I remember being disappointed when I was assigned to B-24's instead of B-17's. But it did the job for us," Mondo exclaimed. He said there were three oxygen stations on the bomber. One station supplied the flight deck, where the pilot, co-pilot, radio operator and flight engineer were located; one was in the nose where the navigator and nose gunner were stationed, and the third station was in the tail section, which supplied the waist gunner, tail gunner, and the belly turret gunner. He said the navigator's quarters were very limited and the facilities for the navigator were not too desirable. Mondo further described the B-24 and the bomb load as follows:

> …The B-24 had a high wing and was noisy. We regularly cruised at 28,000 feet and cruising speed was about 160 miles per hour, which is not very fast compared with today. The early models had no nose turret and when the nose turret models came out, there was a lot of air leakage and I really had to hang on to the maps so the wind would not blow them away. Our standard bomb load consisted of ten 500-pound bombs but a few times we carried three 2,000-pound bombs and less often, we carried fragmentation bombs ("frags"), which were anti-personnel weapons. The bombardier has a little control box in the glass nose of the airplane, which he sets up to; control the distance between bomb hits on the ground target. This setting varies from target to target and is part of the preflight briefing data. There is a little propeller on each bomb and on the way down the propeller spins and that is what arms the bomb so that it will explode on contact with the target. When the plane is loaded with bombs,

little wires go from the structure of the plane through the little
holes in the propellers so the propellers do not turn while they are
in the airplane. When the bombs drop, they pull free from the
wires and now the propellers are free to spin.

Mondo also recalled what was his most memorable mission. This was only the second mission for the crew, but they did have an experienced co-pilot who was flying his thirty-fifth and last mission. They left their base in Italy and were on a bombing mission deep inside Germany. They were flying at 28,000 feet when the flight deck lost oxygen. They were out of air. The plane had to leave the formation of twenty-eight planes and get down to an altitude of 10,000 feet, the highest at which you can live without oxygen masks: Mondo's account of the mission follows:

…We were all alone and my job was to navigate the plane back
'home.' Suddenly, the tail gunner was on the radio. 'There are
six fighters behind us,' shouted the gunner. We were scared. Here
it is only our second mission and we are going to get shot down.
Shortly, the gunner called, 'The fighters have split into two groups
of three and each are coming at us from both sides.' Now, we
were sure that our luck had run out. But, they turned out to be
friendly P-38's. The leader pulled along side and shouted over
the radio, laughing, 'Hey, what you boys doing up here all by yo-
selves?' It was a black outfit. The famous 'Tuskegee Airmen'. They
flew with us awhile and we were quite relieved. The leader of the
Tuskegee group got on the radio and said, 'we're going down and
see if we can raise a little hell. Call if you need us and we'll come
right back up.' The P-38's then all peeled off – a beautiful sight.
Heading back to our base in Italy, we felt, at first, that it would
be best to get rid of the bomb load in the Adriatic Sea. You never
brought the bombs back to the base and you never landed with
them. But the pilot said, 'Let's not waste them.' I said that we were
still over enemy territory – over Yugoslavia. The bombardier was
told to see if he could find any target. We had no bombsight since
the Group always depended on the lead bombardier in the lead
plane in the formation. Our bombardier saw a target and then
stuck his toe near the glass of the nose and sighted down his leg.
With no bombsight he used his leg to sight. All of the bombs were
dropped. After the bombs were dropped the tail gunner called on
the radio and said he saw red, blue, green, and yellow smoke from
one of the bomb hits. A week later the <u>Stars and Stripes</u> Army

newspaper had a story about a lone B-24, returning to base after being forced to leave its mission, had blown up a chemical plant in Yugoslavia.

First Lieutenant Andrew Mondo earned four Air Medals (one medal and three oak leaf clusters). The Group received two Presidential Unit Citations.

After 35 missions, Mondo was ordered to Naples, Italy. While waiting for a ship to take him home, the Germans surrendered on May 7, 1945.

After boarding the MARIPOSA, he left Naples and endured a stormy and unpleasant trip across the Atlantic. Though the war in Europe was over, the ship engaged in routine zigzag maneuvers to avoid possible submarines, which contributed to the rough ride back to New York. "Thinking back, it all seemed pretty awful," he remarked.

He was discharged in October of 1945 and came home to Utica and graduated from Clarkson College as a mechanical engineer. He retired after 34 years at General Electric.

36

Arthur Roberts

C-47 RADIO OPERATOR

The pilot, co-pilot, flight engineer (mechanic and crew chief), and radio operator made up the crew of the World War II C-47 transport plane. Military transports, bombers, and even some fighter planes were assigned radio operators as crewmembers. On the C-47 transport (civilian DC-3), nicknamed "Gooney Bird," the radio operator often acted as the navigator. There were no guns on the twin-engine transport and when flying as a squadron, the lead ship would have a navigator assigned as a crewmember.

The radio operator maintained and operated the radio on board and was responsible for making contacts for weather reports and would also call for the ETA (Estimated Time of Arrival). He had general communication with the pilot and often did some navigation if his plane were the lead ship. Toward the end of the war the radio operator was also doing radar navigation. There were usually three or four radios on board with at least one voice and one Morse code radio.

* * * *

Arthur J. Roberts, formerly of Waterville, served as a radio operator on a C-47 during World War II. Leaving the family dairy farm, which was located just north of Waterville, he enlisted into the Army at the age of 24 and was subsequently assigned to the Army Air Forces.

After basic training at Keesler Air Base in Mississippi, he requested mechanics school. Roberts was interested in becoming a mechanic but he did not wish to be stationed any longer at Keesler so he requested radio school. The radio school was operated by Trans World Airlines at Kansas, Missouri and was three more months in length.. From there he was transferred to Sedalia, Missouri where the plane crews and the Group were setup. He was assigned to a crew in the 32nd Troop Carrier Squadron of the 314th Group.

In May of 1943, Roberts boarded his C-47 at West Palm Beach, Florida, and left the States for North Africa by way of the southern route, (Trinidad, Puerto Rico, South America, and Ascension Island). The plane landed at Accra, the capital of the former Gold Coast in West Africa. He then flew on to Dakar in what is now Senegal and on to Berguent, French Morocco in North

Africa. Roberts said he arrived a day after the North African campaign ended. Roberts recalled what he referred to as a "scary" experience. "When we got to Africa, we were flying in a sand storm. Our plane was able to communicate with the Commanding Officer in the lead ship but the CO could only talk to the rest of the squadron through us. I never found out why he could not communicate with other planes in the squadron. Perhaps it was because his plane and mine had an older and different type radio."

He related some memories of North Africa and C-47 missions to Sicily. Attached to the 12th Air Force, his squadron transported paratroopers for drops over Sicily. On July 9, 1943, the first night of the invasion of Sicily, Roberts' plane was down waiting for an engine and since one of the other radio operators was unable to fly, Roberts flew as a substitute and he remembered that on that mission a young Colonel pulled his plane off to the side and ended up in the wrong location for the paratrooper drop. We pulled off and went to where we were supposed to be and our squadron was the only one that dropped the paratroopers where they were designated to land, Roberts explained.

However, on the second night, the radio operator was able to take his own flight and Roberts did not fly the second night of the invasion. He did describe an unfortunate and tragic incident that occurred when several American planes carrying paratroopers were shot down by "friendly" fire. He said the cause of this was probably due to the fact that the Germans had been bombing the convoy off and on during the day and then returned about the same time that the American planes were in the same area. Though there had been warnings given to watch for American planes, the Navy kept shooting. Roberts claimed that this "friendly" fire shot down forty planes and some of those planes were full of paratroopers.* He said that no planes in his Group were shot down.

Roberts remembered another interesting story pertaining to the second night of the invasion of Sicily. A paratrooper captain had been dropped from one of the squadron planes, and when he landed, he suffered a broken leg when he hit the ground. He then sent someone to get him a horse that he rode to compensate for his broken leg.

In another story, Roberts said he also had heard that his squadron commanding officer, a pilot, had been shot in the wrist while flying that same night. His wrist was just hanging by a tendon. The pilot instructed the co-pilot to cut it off but the co-pilot refused to do it and told him to hang in there 'till we get back.' Later, the medics did save the pilot's wrist and after

---

* This same incident was mentioned in the Joseph Billings chapter.

the war he was able to go back to his job as a pilot at Eastern Airlines and he even became Chief Pilot.

Roberts recalled that a plane in his Group had carried Leo Zweifel, a paratrooper in the 505th Parachute Infantry, from Bridgewater and Waterville. While carrying paratroopers over Sicily, "One of the planes in our squadron that was flying as wingman was shot down," he explained sadly.

Roberts said that when he was in Kairouan in North Africa, he saw his brother Bill who was in Bizerte. "My plane was out for an engine change and I wasn't able to fly. So I asked for a couple of days off to go and see my brother). I hitched a ride to Bizerte and went to the Red Cross and after they located him, we spent a couple of days together."

In recalling some of his other memorable experiences, Roberts said that one operation while carrying paratroopers over Italy, two men didn't jump. On the transport, the pilot used red and green lights to signal the paratroopers when to jump from the aircraft. The pilot had turned the green light off before all the troops left the plane. The plane had to return to the drop zone so they could join their buddies on the ground.

With one of his grins, Roberts related one of his humorous memories that caused some frightening moments.

...We used to practice what is called dead-stick. Both engines would be shut down and then the pilot would let the plane glide and it would glide quite a ways. One day we had some new pilots and the older pilots were giving transition training. I used to sit up between the pilots to see what was going on. The pilot, feeling mischievous, decided to play a little trick. There are switches that control the fuel for each engine. He turned to me and winked and he made a gesture to tie his shoe. While he was doing this, he turned the gas off and an engine quit. The new guy then reached up to turn the map switch (like a car key) on to feather the prop but mistakenly turned the wrong switch off. Now, both engines were off and there were now some fast movements made to get the engines restarted. Since both engines were off, the "Wobble Pump" (similar to a booster pump to allow the gas to flow faster) had to be used to make the gas come out faster.

Roberts recalled a time when his plane narrowly escaped an accident:

...While in Africa, I was at Berguent and Kairouan and one time the starter wasn't working in one engine. To remedy this we had this big long crank that required two men to get the flywheel

going to restart the engine. We had landed at one place and were taxiing over with one engine, the trim tabs were turned to push the rudder control over to one side to make it easier to taxi. We were going down the runway and the pilots forgot to put the trim tab back in place on the rudder, so instead of going straight down the runway we were going from side to side and we almost ran into a house. We just missed it. At the time, I was in the radio area and the crew chief came back and I noticed that the sweat was running right off him.

From Sicily, Roberts transported supplies to the mainland of Italy at Bari, Naples, and Salerno. On one occasion, after unloading cargo in Italy, his C-47 was on a mission to pick up the wounded in litter racks. However, they were ordered to leave the area quickly since the Germans had just strafed the area making it too dangerous to take on the wounded. While in Italy he visited and enjoyed the Isle of Capri, which was one of the places the troops could visit for rest and recreation.

Roberts remembered spending Thanksgiving of 1943 in Castelvetrano, Sicily. One of the jobs was loading the C-47 with turkeys and transporting them from Naples to various bases in Africa. "When the reefer ship came in with a load of turkeys, the whole squadron would load up the planes with the turkeys and fly them to bases in Italy and Africa. However, we did save some of the turkeys and placed some of them into a truck and kept them for ourselves. The food in the mess hall was usually lousy," he added.

In explaining other transport activities, Roberts said that if a squadron were being transferred they would move their equipment. He remembered that in Palermo, Sicily, he saw Bob Hope and Frances Langford and had talked to them, but had not been able to see them perform. They were waiting to board a plane to another base. He also mentioned that his plane once took Ingrid Bergman, who was traveling alone for the USO, to Germany. After the war, his squadron also carried USO troops.

Christmas of 1943 was spent in Sicily. Due to the weather all planes were grounded, but his plane was ordered to fly because a Lieutenant Colonel wanted a "buddy" to be transported someplace. The pilot, crew chief and Roberts had to fly regardless of the bad weather. Once on detached service in Sardinia, a general needed some peanuts. "We had to fly a plane from Sardinia to Africa to get the peanuts," Roberts explained with a laugh.

Roberts said his plane was a real "clunker" and there was something wrong with it. When he arrived in England, "They wanted to take me off from the old plane and I objected. They made me go to a new plane and as it turned out, the old plane that I had been ordered off, ended up being shot down during the invasion. Boy, was I lucky, Roberts said with emphasis. "They never did find the radioman of that plane," Roberts explained.

"Our main job was carrying supplies and we dropped paratroopers some of the time. We flew every day – almost 80 hours a month. On the night before D-Day in Normandy, June 6, 1944, three flights (one from each of the three squadrons in the Group) were needed to carry paratroopers. Cards were cut to determine which flight would be assigned from each squadron. Roberts said he didn't have to fly, but on the night of D-Day plus one, his plane did fly with a load of supplies. "The flak was coming up like crazy and my plane got shot full of holes, he described. We got the daylights shot out of us and we took eleven hits. The only serious damage was that it took out the rear tire. It went flat as the plane landed," he explained.

Right after D-Day, Roberts was allowed to come home for 30 days. He came home on a slow boat convoy and returned on a fast boat – the USS WEST POINT. "I got back in September – just in time for "Market Garden" and I got another air medal for that mission. We carried paratroopers to and dropped them in the Netherlands to capture roads and bridges from the Germans." The main objective was the bridge at Arnhem, Netherlands. "Market" was the code name for the airborne operation and "Garden" was the code name for the land operation. (Wheal, Pope and Taylor 30). Roberts recalled that,

> ···*We carried a lot of Polish troops and you know the white star on the American planes? We liked to watch the Polish troops write their long names all over the white star on the C-47 before boarding. Later, we carried everything such as gas for Patton's tanks and also transported the wounded. Twice we had nurses with us for medical evacuation. After the war we carried displaced persons from Paris, France to Russia and displaced persons from Russia to Paris – displaced persons that belonged in France. We also used to tow gliders and we towed one in Germany crossing the Rhine River.*

During the North African campaign, Ernie Pyle, the war correspondent said, "the DC-3, known in the Army as the C-47, is the workingest airplane in existence, I suppose" (Pyle 289).

Roberts concluded his memories by pointing out that he had participated in seven campaigns including Sicily, Italy, Normandy, Central Europe, the Rhineland and Air Offensive Europe and received five air medals and the Distinguished Unit Badge with one oak leaf cluster. Attending a reunion in 2000 at Dayton, Ohio, he said that sixteen in his squadron were there including the pilot of his C-47. He said that when he saw his former crew chief at the reunion, the guy said. 'Here's the man that kept the airplane flying.' Roberts explained that he was often called upon to do mechanical work on the plane.

On V-J Day Roberts was at Camp Lucky Strike in LeHavre, France waiting to come home. He boarded a plane in Scotland as a passenger to come home. Since Iceland was fogged in, the plane had to return to Scotland before proceeding later to New York.

Staff Sergeant Arthur J. Roberts was discharged at Fort Dix in September of 1945. He returned to farming, worked for General Electric and SUNY Morrisville in the Buildings and Grounds Department..

He passed away January 9, 2008.

37

Kenneth Roberts

FIGHTER SQUADRON CREW CHIEF

The fighter plane squadrons of World War II provided ground support for land and sea forces, flew coastal patrol, and flew escort for the heavy bombers. The more famous fighter planes of the Army Air Forces were the P-38 Lightening, P-39 Airacobra, P-40 Warhawk/Tomahawk, P-47 Thunderbolt, and the P-51 Mustang. In the early days of World War II, the United States had few of these fighter planes in England that were manned by Americans.

Kenneth Roberts of Chadwicks, New York was an aircraft mechanic and crew chief that worked on aircraft engines and was responsible for keeping fighter planes in the air and operating safely and effectively. For most of World War II, his squadron flew British Spitfires until they were replaced by the more effective P-51 Mustang. The British Spitfire had an "elliptical wing," which reduced the drag and increased speed. Over 20, 000 were manufactured during World War II (World 1).

* * * *

Eight days after the attack on Pearl Harbor, on December 15, 1941, Kenneth Roberts of Chadwicks, New York, left his job as shipping clerk at the Willowvale Bleachery, and enlisted into the Army Air Corps (changed to Army Air Forces in 1942). Following basic training at Jefferson Barracks, Missouri, he attended aircraft mechanic school at Casey Jones School of Aeronautics in New York City. He graduated from the school as a qualified Crew Chief in June of 1942.

At Grenier Field in Manchester, New Hampshire he was assigned to the 52nd Fighter Group, 2nd Squadron as a Crew Chief. "I didn't see any planes while I was there because the squadron was preparing to go overseas," he said.

On August 4, 1942, Roberts boarded the USS MONTEREY, a converted ocean liner. On the next day, as he was leaving New York harbor, he recalled viewing the Statue of Liberty through a porthole. After a few days aboard ship, he arrived in Glasgow, Scotland and then was ferried across the Irish Sea to Belfast, Ireland. Roberts explained that while the 52nd Group was in the

States they had the P-39 Airacobra. Its range was very limited so the whole Group, pilots, mechanics and materiel went to England with no airplanes and there was no way to get our planes over. While they were in Ireland, Roberts further pointed out that the Royal Air Force brought in British "Spitfire" fighter planes. He said the American pilots trained with Spitfires for about three weeks. It was necessary for the Crew Chief and mechanics to train for three weeks so that they would be qualified to work on this type of aircraft.

The "Spitfire" was an entirely different aircraft. Since the P-39's were short range, America didn't use them but they were part of the lend-lease to Russia. "Spitfires" were used by our pilots who thought that they were great – a beautiful, beautiful plane. Though limited in range, it flew better than the P-39 and it was very acrobatic with four machine guns — two in each wing. The British used a 7mm shell, which is equivalent to a .30 caliber bullet. The 7mm did not have much range but was effective if the plane had a classy pilot and could get in real close to his opponent. The British proved this when the "Spitfires" defeated the Nazi Luftwaffe.

During August of 1942, the squadron trained by making short trips to France but did not actually engage in combat with the Germans. The pilots, under British supervision, were learning formations and practicing take-offs and landings

"My squadron was separate from the RAF. I worked as Crew Chief on the "Spitfires." The "Spitfire" had a liquid inline Merlin Rolls Royce engine and was similar to the P-39 in operation since the P-39 also had an inline Allison engine. The Merlin Rolls Royce engine was a lot more powerful than the P-39's," he described.

In November 1942, the Group boarded the British ship DONOTER CASTLE and sailed to North Africa and tied up at a dock in the harbor of Oran, Algeria. After leaving the ship they marched 12 miles to an airfield and Roberts said that within a couple of days their pilots, flying from England by way of Gibraltar, landed with 27 "Spitfires." Some of the pilots were ferried in on C-47's. The squadron then flew along the coastal areas patrolling Mediterranean shipping and did engage in some aerial combat. The planes were equipped with external fuel tanks, which gave them more range.

Around February 1943, the Group moved east toward Tunisia and the Kasserine Pass where the ground troops experienced their first sighting of an enemy plane. This was at Telepe 1 and since the field was under fire, they were told by radio to leave. They loaded everything on flatbeds and moved to Biskra, an oasis village located right in the desert where there was a huge airfield with B-17's and "Spitfires." The Group was now attached to the 12th Air Force.

From Biskra, they moved further north to Telepe 2 where they stayed until the end of the war in Africa. "Our planes were flying all the while, -10-12 hours a day. The planes did a lot of strafing of the German Afrika Corps as they were being driven out of Africa. The fighting ended in May or June 1943 and after the Germans were out of Africa, we moved to Tunis where we enjoyed six weeks of R&R," he said.

In July of 1943, still on R&R in Tunis, "we saw some C-47's pulling gliders, and the scuttlebutt was that something was going on. At the time we didn't know that Sicily was about to be invaded. We had no idea until one day we were told to get our gear packed," he explained.

"We boarded LCI's (Landing Ship, Infantry); the deck was only 12" above the water. They had steel pipes sticking up with cable all around and the water would slosh up on our feet. That was a nervous time. The LCI was not very wide," Roberts described.

Landing at Palermo, Sicily after the actual invasion, Roberts said that he stayed there for about six weeks as a Crew Chief on the "Spitfire."

In September of 1943, Roberts went on to Corsica where he was still attached to the 12th Air Force. Throughout the winter of 43-44 in Corsica the Nazis bombed the island. While in Corsica, the first P-51's, three of them, arrived. Roberts described the thrill he experienced when they appeared.

...It was about the time that we were scheduled to go to Italy. When the P-51's came in, we went bananas. I had never heard anything about 51's. When I saw one of those guys come across buzzing the field and chandelle up for a landing I said to myself, 'Holy shit! Look at that!' He must have been going 400 miles an hour and when he pulled that sucker up he almost inverted. He then put his gear down and came around and came in hotter than hell. You could hear the squeak as the tires hit the runway. As he left the plane all of the Crew Chiefs rolled out there. The pilot said, 'I just came in from Africa and I wanted to show you guys a pretty good flying machine.' All of our pilots had their jaws to their knees as the P-51 pilot was talking. We couldn't wait to get the cowling off and look at the engine. After a half hour the guy took off, but before he left he said that all of the "Spitfires" would soon be replaced with P-51's. We shipped off to Bari, Italy before the 51's arrived. At Bari, we were then attached to the 15th Air Force and our squadron finally received the "Mustangs."

The Crew Chiefs had a challenging time when the "Mustangs" came in since they had Allison engines and were considered inferior to the "Spitfire" Merlin Rolls Royce engines. The British discovered that the Rolls Royce engine could be put in the P-51 with a few cowling changes. Roberts said that Rolls Royce people in England, through Roosevelt and Churchill, made a deal with the Packard Company who was building the Allison engine. The Packard Company received the plans for the Rolls Royce engine so Packard then put an American Rolls Royce engine in the P-51. The engine for the 51 became the Rolls Royce. The P-51 was a fine aircraft but the Allison engine was inferior to the Rolls Royce and with a Rolls Royce installed in the P-51, it became more efficient at high altitude and the modified model was known as the P-51D. The P-51 now had a more powerful engine with a bulbous canopy. Roberts also explained that the P-51D, with its American made Rolls engine, also had a built in supercharger, which increased power considerably in emergencies.

Roberts then explained how the P-51 was such an improvement over the "Spitfires." He said that the "Spits" had only 30-40 minutes flight time and after it took off, it took 25 minutes to reach 30,000 feet and by that time they were almost out of fuel. "It was a beautiful machine but lacked power at high altitude. With the P-51D's that our pilots now had, they had a six-hour flight time and with drop fuel tanks in the wing they could get to 30,000 feet in five minutes."

Our "Mustangs" were now the flying escort for B-24's and B-17's. They were scoring many victories. As the 5th Army moved north, the Group moved from one airfield to another. The last place was Madna where the squadron flew escort there until V-E Day.

From Madna the Group went to Naples and boarded the USS GRANT – a transport that brought them back to the states to Fort Patrick Henry, Virginia in June of 1945. Sergeant Kenneth Roberts was there about a week and everyone thought they were on the way to the Pacific. However, the war ended and he was discharged in1945.

Roberts said that he and his Group received twelve battle stars for the various campaigns in the European-African-Middle East Theater of Operations in which they had participated.

He worked for the New York Telephone Company for 28years until retirement.

He passed away September 16, 2002.

38

John Ryder:

B-24 TAIL GUNNER

Lewis Smith:

B-24 NOSE GUNNER

Consolidated Aircraft, North American Aviation, Douglas, and the Ford Motor Company manufactured eighteen thousand B-24 "Liberators" during World War II. Equipped with four Pratt and Whitney R1830 engines, each having fourteen cylinders and 1200 horsepower (B-24D 1).

Though there is more than one version of the origin of the name "Liberator," Martin Bowman in his book <u>B-24 Liberator 1939-45,</u> writes that it is generally believed that the British selected the name. The "Liberator" had several sharp contrasts to the B-17 "Flying Fortress." The B-24 had a twin tail and the fuselage was more box-like than the B-17, equipped with a front wheel landing gear that allowed its tail to balance off the ground when taking off or landing. The B-24 was 66 feet long with a 110-foot wingspan and could carry 8,000 pounds of bombs and at first they were armed with only .30 caliber hand held Browning guns. Later, they were equipped with .50 caliber guns. The B-24 had a greater range and more speed than the B-17 and carried a greater bomb load, about 2,000 pounds more than the B-17. Compared to the B-17, the B-24 was easier to maintain and had more working space than the B17 (Ryder and Smith).

It was 1939, and World War II had begun with Hitler's invasion of Poland. John (Jack) Ryder was working in the old Waterville Knitting Mill where the new village hall is now located.

* * * *

Lewis Smith of Washington Mills, New York, lived just a few miles from Waterville and had never met Jack Ryder. A world war would bring them

- 179 -

together as crewmembers on the same B-24 heavy bomber – one a tail gunner and the other a nose gunner.

They were both assigned to the 13th Air Force - known as the "Jungle Air Force" in the South Pacific. Made up of two B-24 Groups of four squadrons each, the 13th Air Force was quite small compared with the 8th or 15th Air Forces of Europe. Consequently, the "Jungle Air Force" received little recognition because in the Pacific the Navy was in control. Later the 13th joined the 5th Air Force and anything that MacArthur wrote would give credit to the 5th Air Force and not the 13th. However, the 13th Air Force did get two unit citations. The following account describes some of Ryder and Smith's experiences while flying 50 missions battling the Japanese fighter planes and anti-aircraft flak over various islands of the South Pacific. Smith's log indicated 465 combat flying hours plus many hours flying sea service and rescue.

On October 6, 1942, after the U.S. had entered World War II, John "Jack" Ryder enlisted in the Army Air Corps. He had already spent a year in the New York State Militia and trained at the armory on the Parkway in Utica. Drilling with the State Militia convinced Ryder that he didn't want to join the Marines. So, along with friends Vincent Ford and Richard Dunster, he joined the Army Air Forces.

Ryder had taken some flying lessons before enlisting, but poor eyesight prevented him from entering flight training. Reading the eye chart with his left eye allowed him to qualify later for aerial gunnery school.

He completed his basic training at Atlantic City, New Jersey, and by December of 1942 was attending aerial gunnery school at Fort Myers, Florida. It was at gunnery school that Lewis Smith met Jack Ryder. Smith said that from his hometown, he followed the same route as Ryder from Fort Dix to Fort Myers. "I was out drilling one day, Smith said, and I asked this guy where he was from. "He said something like 'New York State or New York' and I said whereabouts? Jack said, 'Waterville' and I said, 'I'm from Washington Mills,' Smith replied to Ryder. Jack and I have been friends ever since."

Ryder recalled that at gunnery school several trainees "washed out" of the course. Some were fearful of flying, but it was no problem for him since he had taken flying lessons. "At Fort Myers, Florida, we flew in AT6's behind the pilot and fired 30 caliber guns. The kids were scared of flying, and after we finished with the targets, some of us would ask the pilots to do some rolls. I loved it, but the kids didn't and they got sick," Ryder grinned mischievously.

At gunnery school, the men worked with all kinds of guns from the BB gun to .50 caliber guns. The school was four weeks long but Smith said that he had "flunked out." He said that he failed to get the required number of hits on the target. He said that flying in a trainer, an AT6, they would fire .30 caliber tracer bullets at a target towed by another plane. "I didn't get enough hits to graduate with my class. I did the extra week and graduated December 20, 1942, and advanced to Sergeant," Smith explained. Later, Smith pointed out, that two schools, gunnery school plus one other, would be required before being advanced to sergeant and every crewmember was required to attend gunnery school.

After graduation, Smith and Ryder were on a troop train bound for Lowry Field in Denver, Colorado to attend armaments school. Armaments school included instruction in taking care of all of the .50 caliber guns and when they were assigned to the same crew, Smith and Ryder took care of all of those guns on the plane so they wouldn't malfunction. "We kept them in top shape," Smith said. Ryder added that armaments school involved much ground-based practice, but during the armaments school, Ryder and Smith did not see one another since they were in different sections.

Smith said that he started as a tail gunner while he was in training. (It was later determined that more firepower was needed in the nose of the B-24 so a modification was made to add a nose turret which became his new location on the airplane).

From Lowry, Ryder then traveled to Tucson, Arizona in the spring of 1943 and it was at Tucson that Ryder and Smith met up again. Smith said that he had been assigned to a crew but their plane needed one more aerial gunner. "I hadn't seen Jack since December 1942 and one day I went into the Orderly Room. I saw Jack and I said, 'What are you doing here?' He said, 'I'm waiting to get on a crew. "You are? We need one more on our crew. Let me go talk to the pilot." The pilot did manage to add Ryder to the same plane as Smith. "Jack was from Waterville, New York and the co-pilot was from Waterville, Maine." Smith added.

In May of 1943, the two B-24 gunners journeyed to Blythe, California. "We were right in the desert and was it hot there. The wind blew and the sand flew and it was not a place for bombers," Smith explained.

In the middle of July of 1943, they picked up a new B-24 at Lincoln, Nebraska. They then flew to California and across the Pacific to Hickam Field in Hawaii arriving there in August. They were at Hickam Field for 18 days and that is where the consolidated turret was taken out of the tail of the B-24 and placed in the nose to give the front of the plane more protection. In September, Smith said they flew over various islands of the South Pacific such as Christmas Island, Samoa and Nandi and finally, after four days, they reached Espiritu Santo where their operations base was located. The crew was assigned to the 307th Bomb Group, 372nd Bomb Squadron, and 13th Air Force.

Smith remembered that they lost a lot of planes due to the violent storms in the South Pacific. Ryder recalled that on a bombing mission to Truk Island,

"We were at 20,000 feet in a terrible storm and losing air speed and altitude. The pilot had to put the nose down to increase air speed and altitude." Smith said that their worst enemy was the weather. "Storms came up fast."

Ryder said that their plane was nicknamed "Nipponese Sunset." (Smith remembered only a number for the plane -the 788). Their early bombing missions included Henderson Field at Guadalcanal, the Solomon Islands and the Admiralty Islands. The mission usually included twenty-four planes – twelve in each squadron. The B-24 was equipped with .30 caliber guns in the nose but later carried only the heavier .40 and 50 -caliber variety. These guns were located in a tail turret, top and bottom turret, waist gunner, and the nose turret. The B-24 cruised at 8,000 to 18,000 feet but did fly as high as 36,000. The B-24 had difficulty gliding because of the wing shape. The B-17 had a wider wing.

"I remember that on my first mission, Smith recalled with a laugh, that, at first, they took all of us new crewmembers and mixed us in with veteran combat crews. We took off one day from Guadalcanal and were flying around getting into formation, and I had commented mistakenly to other crewmembers that we were already over enemy territory. We hadn't even left Guadalcanal yet and we were just off the shore, he explained with another laugh.

Smith also explained that some of the Group would be in combat for six weeks and some would be back in Guadalcanal either for training or doing sea service and rescue duty. He said that he flew 50 missions and everyone was with his friend Jack Ryder. These missions did not include all of the flying they did in sea service and rescue.

The B-24 carried 4500 gallons of 100-octane gasoline, a few 500-pound bombs and a 1,000-pound bomb. On one take-off at Munda Point, after becoming airborne, the odor of gas was detected because the ground crew forgot to connect the safety wire seal on the gas cap. From the tail turret, Ryder could see the fuel flowing along the fuselage carried by the slipstream (stream of air pushed back by the propellers). The pilot made a made a hasty turn and landed the plane.

Ryder related how they also carried 10 to 20 anti-personnel bombs that generated fierce fires after exploding. The bomb, (probably a Napalm bomb) was constructed with a rubber material and a steel propeller.

...When they explode, they cause a fire that burns and burns and fragments of the hot rubber would stick on buildings and set the building on fire. We hated to carry them because we were afraid of them. One of our planes, which were carrying these rubber bombs, got hit with 'ack ack' (anti-aircraft guns). It set off one

of these rubber bombs. The waist gunner was so scared of it he jumped out the open window where the gun was located—no parachute. Fortunately, for the rest of the crew, the slipstream effect put out the flame. At 200 miles an hour there is a lot of pressure from the slipstream.

"One trick the Japanese would try is that they would fly over our formation with their 'Betties', a plane that looked like our C-47, and drop phosphorus bombs attached to little parachutes. They would hit our planes and set them on fire," Ryder recalled.

When asked what his toughest mission was, he answered, "It was Rabaul, New Britain. Rabaul was so pretty we felt guilty bombing it." He said that the "ack-ack" fire was heavy and the Japanese fighter planes were tough. "We used P-40's to escort our bombers, but they could accompany us only so far," he added.

During World War II, Truk Island, located in the Pacific and held by the Japanese, was a virtual fortress. It was considered invincible. Ryder recalled that he participated in a night mission to bomb Truk. Smith remarked that they did a lot of night flying. "They were long flights. We would take off at 6 P.M. and return at 6 A.M. Flying at night I would look out from the nose and see a star. I thought it, was a plane," he laughed.

His 50th mission was a dangerous daylight raid over Yap Island with no fighter escort. The weather was stormy, and the formation had to break up temporarily. The Japanese were flying their newest aircraft, the "Tojo." Ryder explained that because of normal prop wash, the B-24's do not fly close or wing tip-to-wing tip. From the ground it would look like this but actually the formation was set up in a step-like fashion – each plane flying a little above the other.

...I spotted a Japanese plane turning toward us and I hollered, 'Pilot from Tail— Up!' The 'Liberator' rose sharply in an evasive maneuver to avoid striking two 'Liberators' flying on a collision course below us. I could see one B-24 steering to the right and another one was on my right, which had been shot full of holes along the length of the fuselage. The pilot was apparently dead or unconscious and the plane veered and tipped over and slammed into the one on the left. We were at about 20 to 25,000 feet and if we had not pulled up quickly we would have gone down tangled with the two planes as they circled down, leveled off and hit the water –about 20 feet apart. Two smoke piles. We had forty planes in our attack on Yap Island, which was out of range for our P-40

fighter escort. Arriving at Yap we dropped incendiary bombs to mark the area. The incendiaries would hit the water and blink and some hit land-causing fires, which lit up the area for our bombers. At this time, we were flying silvery aluminum planes, which were easily spotted. Our plane was the lead plane. The bombs were released, and the planes returned to base.

Ryder explained how happy they were after they returned from their 50th mission. This meant they could go back to the States. After landing, he recalled that after the plane was parked, the crew looked over to another parking area and there was a ground crew gathered that was waiting for their plane to return. "Their plane did not make it back. Leaving the plane we kissed the ground. Our plane was back safely." Ryder praised the ground crews for the outstanding job they did as support forces. They performed all kinds of service including kitchen work (KP).

He remembered that one time he participated in flying a sea search. Their plane did a figure eight over the sea as they searched for John F. Kennedy's PT109 which had been cut in half by a Japanese destroyer.

One of his fond remembrances was in a crowded cafeteria in Auckland, New Zealand. He and a friend were seated at a square table and a waitress asked if two nurses on rest leave could sit with them. "They were lieutenants, and we were enlisted men. Officers and enlisted are not supposed to fraternize. They were just young kids and had been on duty for a long time and were on rest leave from Okinawa. One was from Rochester, New York, and we had a good time talking to them."

Ryder said that he never received a scratch and never aborted a mission. He and Lew (Smith) earned an Air Medal with eight oak leaf clusters and three battle stars -The Bismarck Archipelago, the Japanese Mandates, and New Guinea.

Lewis Smith received orders to fly back to the United States and at Denver; he was assigned to instructor duty in armaments school. Later, he was a machine gun instructor on the B-29 Super fortress. He was discharged at Lowry Field on September 18, 1945 and returned to Washington Mills where he worked at various jobs and operated the Citgo service station until he retired in 1981.

Staff Sergeant Ryder wasn't lucky enough to obtain a flight back to the States. He requested passenger status on an auxiliary aircraft carrier USS CASABLANCA in August 1944. The ship sailed from the Admiralty Islands in the South Pacific and it took 30 days to reach the States.

On V-J Day, he was stationed at Westover Air Force Base as an instructor in K3 and K4 computing gun sights. He was discharged August 31, 1945 and returned to Waterville to work in the mill. He was later employed for Monroe Business Machines as a serviceman for 30 years. John Ryder passed away April 10, 2006.

39

George Tucker

"FLYING THE "HUMP"

One of the most precarious places for airplanes to fly during World War II was from the Brahmaputra Valley in India to Kunming, China. It was considered by many to be the most dangerous route to fly during the war, because of the mountains that reached about 15,000 feet. Nicknamed the "Hump" by the Allies, the C-4, C-46 and other transport planes carried thousands of tons of arms and supplies (Wheal, Pope and Taylor 223). And, sometimes personnel were transported as in the case of truck drivers returning from convoys to Kunming, China in 1945. The danger was not only the rugged mountains and enemy aircraft but also the inclement weather where the planes sometimes went into a spin if caught in an updraft. Flying into clouds sometimes led to planes running into mountain peaks. Because of the numerous crashes, the route has sometimes been called the "aluminum trail" (Wheal, Pope and Taylor 223-224).

For eighteen months, these remarkable pilots and crews worked twelve hours a day seven days a week to keep the Chinese supplied. They flew in rickety non-pressurized transports with oxygen only for the pilots, dodging mountain peaks and Japanese fighters... Much was owed to the men who "flew the Hump... (Leckie 549).

One of these C-47 crew members who "flew the Hump" as a C-47 Radio Operator was George Tucker, who was born in McDonough and later moved to Oriskany Falls, NY.

* * * *

Born in the rural hamlet of McDonough in Chenango County, George Tucker worked at the Bell Aircraft defense plant in Buffalo before he was drafted into the Army Air Forces in September of 1942. He was 21 years old.

He was inducted in Buffalo and was then transferred to Atlantic City, New Jersey for basic training. "It did seem different to do my training in Atlantic City," he said. I stayed in one of the large hotels, but we were up at 4:30 and went five miles to the drill field and drilled ten hours a day. The training lasted ten weeks.

From Atlantic City, Tucker was transferred to Scott Field, Ill where he attended CW Radio School. Tucker stated that it involved learning the Morse code and general training as a radio operator and instruction in air traffic control. He said that it was intensive training to qualify as a control tower operator.

On November 19, 1943, Tucker traveled to southern California for shipment overseas to India. After boarding the USS URUGUAY, the long 34-day voyage to India commenced and stops were made at New Zealand, Tasmania, and Australia. Their destination was Calcutta but since the Japanese were bombing in the vicinity of Calcutta, the ship went around the southern tip of India to Bombay. "It really was an experience going across India. We rode for a while on the train – then walked awhile and got on the train at another point and continued our trip. Arriving at Shillong in northeastern India in the province of Assam, I was assigned to the 98th Air Drome unit." Shillong, located near Cherrapunji, one of the world's rainiest areas in the world, was headquarters for the Air Forces and the troops stayed in Bashas. Tucker showed the author a picture of a Basha, a thatch roof 60 x 16 native hut that could house 16 people.

Tucker's first assignment was with air to ground communications and radio and communications between different Air Force stations. Flying as a radio operator, he made several sorties between India and China. "I made several trips over the "Hump" to Chungking, China. This was during 1943-44 and we were flying in supplies to the Chinese army that was fighting the Japanese," he explained. "Flying over the 'Hump" was an experience. There were reports of Japanese Zero fighter planes that sometimes were a threat. Japanese planes on one of the sorties shot down two men who had been assigned to our Basha. At first, our C-47's didn't have guns. Later we put .50 caliber guns on the plane and kept our fingers crossed that we didn't see any Zeroes. It wasn't the safest place to fly.

He said that one of his most memorable experiences was traveling to China by truck convoy over the Ledo-Burma road. He said that the whole 98th Air Drome unit was transported from Shillong to Kunming, China. He recalled that it was in the spring of 1945 and six months later the unit was back in India.

The war had ended and the unit went to Calcutta and boarded a Kaiser built liberty ship, the S.S. Brooke. "A lot of happy GI's were going home, Tucker beamed. "We had spent almost two years and three months in the CBI Theater of Operations and I liked the people there. On board the ship, there were over 3,000 personnel including 38 civilians," he added.

The ship left December 8, 1945. "We made a stop at Colombo, Ceylon (Sri Lanka), and I remember going through a real bad storm in the North

188 | ★ *Louis C. Langone*

Atlantic. The ship pitched and rolled for two days but I didn't get sick," Tucker pointed out proudly.

After three years and three months of World War II Army life, Sergeant George Tucker was discharged at Fort Dix on January 6, 1946. "It was a great experience for me and I was thankful that I came back to the United States safely," Tucker said.

After his discharge, Tucker and his brother took over their family store in McDonough and also operated stores in South Otselic, Georgetown, and Smyrna. He later moved to Oriskany Falls, NY where he established a grocery store, hardware store, laundromat, and restaurant. A few years ago, the Oriskany Falls community showed their gratitude for his many contributions to the community, including a gazebo in the park, by holding a George Tucker Day and, for one day, renaming the village – Tucker Falls.

After retiring he lived above the hardware store located adjacent to another former business – the Big M Market.

He passed away May 20, 2008.

40

Helen Voll

WOMENS ARMY CORPS

TECH.SGT HELEN VOLL

Among the many revolutionary changes resulting from World War II are the improved status of women and the role of women in the military. During the War women actually served in the Army and the Navy whereas women who volunteered during World War I worked as civilians only.

In 1941, it became evident that there was a significant manpower shortage and that there would be a need for women to serve in the armed forces. This would make it possible to release men for combat and sea duty. Women could fill such non-combatant billets in administrative, communications, mechanical, and other fields. A congresswoman from Massachusetts, Edith Nourse Rogers, had a meeting with Chief of Staff General George C. Marshall. She said she was going to introduce a bill into Congress to set up a Women's Army Corps, which would be a part of the Army and provide to women the same benefits that men receive. At first, the Army objected. However, it was agreed to set up a "Women's Army Auxiliary Corps (WAAC) to work with the Army, but men would not be commanded by women. After the attack on Pearl Harbor, it was not long before the bill, which Congresswoman Rogers introduced, was approved and signed by President Franklin D. Roosevelt (Bellafaire 1).

The first director of the WAAC was Oveta Culp Hobby and she was given the rank of major. The Corps would be trained in non-combatant jobs and "free a man for combat."

"The gaps our women fill are in those non combatant jobs where women's hands and women's hearts fit naturally," said Hobby (Bellafaire 2).

Fort Des Moines was the first training site for the WAAC. To be a member of the Corps, women had to be between 21-45 years old, at least 5' tall and weigh 100 pounds or more (Bellafaire 4).

The Women's Auxiliary Army Corps became known as the Women's Army Corps in 1943 and grew to about 100,000 by 1945.

Though many women serving overseas found conditions to be extremely difficult, the WAC performed well and it was evident that they were contributing much toward winning the war. General Eisenhower, who at first was opposed to women in uniform, changed his view after seeing women in Great Britain operate anti-aircraft guns. "From the day they (women soldiers) first reached us, their reputation as an efficient, effective corps continued to grow. Toward the end of the war, the most stubborn die-hards had become convinced and demanded them in increasing numbers" (QTD. In Jones 242).

Albert Speer, Hitler's weapons production chief made the following comment on American women's contribution to the war effort: "How wise you were to bring your women into the military and into your labor force. Had we done that initially, as you did it, it could well have affected the whole course of the war. We would have found out, as you did, that women are equally effective, and for some skills, superior to males" (QTD. In Jones 243).

Helen Voll of Waterville was a World War II member of the Women's Army Auxiliary Corps, which later was called the Women's Army Corps (WAC).

✳ ✳ ✳ ✳

Prior to World War II, Helen Voll lived in Utica. After graduating from high school she taught horseback riding at Lakeview Lodge at Big Moose,

New York. A <u>Utica Daily Press</u> news clipping of August 1943 highlighted her horseback riding experience. She said that she had learned riding from a trooper and her blacksmith father, and that she had won several trophies in competitive riding

Voll was 21 in October of 1942 when she enlisted into the Women's Army Auxiliary Corps and was sent to Fort Des Moines in Iowa for her basic training. At Fort Des Moines, she had to wear male enlisted clothing since there were not enough female uniforms. Fort Des Moines was an old cavalry post with beautiful parade grounds. The officers were mainly men and would ride horses in all of the formal parades.

After basic training, she was assigned to the Army Air Force as a first sergeant and transferred to New York City. From 1943 until the Air Force became a separate branch of service in 1947, many WAC's were assigned to the Army Air Force. During World War II over 40,000 "Air WACS" served in the U.S. and overseas.

Voll said that she was stationed in New York City for four months between December 1942 and March 1943. From the Collingwood Hotel on 34th Street, she underwent training as an aircraft spotter of airplanes. Her duties consisted of spotting aircraft coming in from the east coast which were picked up on radar and then plotted on a map.

After leaving New York City, Voll went to Camp Polk, Louisiana for overseas training and from there was transferred to Blackland Air Force Base at Waco, Texas. There she took over as acting first sergeant of the WAAC squad and served as the WAAC supervisor. She supervised 100-150 personnel, which included cooks, photographers, and mechanics.

"We had our own mess hall and I had to supervise the cooks. I had a few discipline problems, too. There were these two redheads who were twins and were often in trouble. I couldn't always tell them apart and was never sure which one did it," she recalled.

Voll showed the author a Waco Star newspaper article dated August 17, 1943, which reported that in her spare time at Blackland, she performed in a rodeo doing trick roping, trick and show riding including headstands, and also bronco busting.

Voll also recalled how women were not fully accepted as part of the military. She said she remembers when she was stationed at Camp Polk people on the street would spit at them, because they didn't figure the military was a place for women. Some men objected to women in the military and the replacement of men with women for other duties such as administrative. When she attended administrative school in Cheyenne, Wyoming, there were only twelve other enlisted personnel in the class. In some places women

192 | ★ *Louis C. Langone*

could not go off the base alone. They would travel in groups of three or four for their protection.

Technical Sergeant Voll said that she was assigned Temporary Additional Duty (TAD) to Pampa Air Force Base in January of 1945 to activate a squadron of WAC. Pampa Air Force Base had a flight school where cadets earned their "wings."

The commanding officer, a colonel was a West Point graduate and strongly felt that a person had to prove his worth. This became a serious challenge for Voll, since the Colonel did not want women at his base. "I had to convince the Colonel that women should be at Pampa.and when it was finally decided to have women at Pampa, Voll explained, the colonel requested that I be the First Sergeant of the squadron. I got kids right out of basic training including a second lieutenant," Voll explained.

"The first afternoon that the squadron was scheduled to assemble for Retreat (lowering of the colors), the Colonel called me into his office and gave me my first sergeant's stripes at four o'clock. He said to have them on by five o'clock for the Retreat. I had little time to do this but I had some girls who could sew so they took my shirt and I told them that I wanted the shirt back in a half-hour. At the Retreat I brought them to attention and did an about face, and who was in front of me – the Colonel. Under his breath he said, 'Congratulations, Sergeant, I see you made it.' After that, I had no more problems with the Colonel. He was a real die-hard. Believe me!" Voll emphasized with a smile.

On V-J day, Voll was at Pampa Air Force Base in Texas. Several months later she was discharged from Fort Dix in November of 1945

Sergeant Voll enjoyed the military and traveling all over the United States and meeting people from all over the world and seeing how other people live. She also learned, she added, "that people were not quite ready to accept women in the military even though they were volunteers. Women were more than willing to give their lives for what they believed."

After the war, she attended a two-year business college. Voll also enlisted in the regular Air Force in March 1949 and recalled during the Korean War. In November 1952, she was promoted to Master Sergeant.

Voll was stationed at Headquarters, U.S. Air Force, Bolling Air Force Base, Washington, and D.C. She later attended administrative school in Cheyenne and later served at Stewart Air Force Base in Newburgh, New York. She was later transferred to the 32nd Air Division at Hancock Field, Syracuse, NY and during that assignment was named First Sergeant of the Women and Assistant Sergeant Major of the Division.

Following discharge, she went to work for the New York Electric and Gas Corporation.

Additional Photos

SGT. "EBB" BELFIELD AND ARMY BUDDY-NORMANDY

SGT.LEE HUFF

HITLER'S HOME
(Courtesy of Sewell Morgan)

DEATH CAMP-1945 – GERMANY
(Courtesy of Robert Treen, Jr.)

WALTER WILL GRAVE MARGRATEN, THE NETHERLANDS
(Courtesy of Walter J. Will)

SM 3 KENNETH SLITER

T-5 (CPL) ROBERT TREEN- 1942

CPL. GEORGE TUCKER

FIRST CONVOY OVER THE LEDO ROAD-U.S. SIGNAL CORPS
(Files Of Charles Thompson Family —Photo Enhanced By David Hazelden)

CONVOY CARRYING SUPPLIES TO EASTERN
FRONT- U.S. SIGNAL CORPS

GMC SYLVESTER PUCCIO

FIRST LIEUT. MARGARET CLEARY-ARMY NURSE CORPS
(Courtesy o f John Cleary)

GERMAN JET-1945-ARGONNE FOREST
(Courtesy of Robert Treen)

THE WASP, YORKTOWN, HORNET, HANCOCK AND TICONDEROGA
AIRCRAFT CARRIERS AT ULITHI ATOLL,
(Courtesy of National Archives)

Part III
The Navy and Coast Guard

PHARMACIST 3/C IRIS BARNES
(Courtesy of Frederick Barnes)

41

Iris Barnes

WAVE MEDIC

The history of women in the U.S. Navy dates back to World War I when enlisted women served as Yeomen performing clerical work. Between the two world wars a small number of women did serve as Navy nurses, but were not commissioned as officers.

However, on July 30, 1942, an Act of Congress signed by President Franklin Roosevelt, established the WAVES (Women Accepted for Volunteer Emergency Service) program, reestablishing women in Naval duty stations. WAVES was considered a wartime necessity by relieving men from certain position in order to perform combat duty. Needless to say, the women were not greatly accepted in 1942 by their male counterparts.

The first WAVES director, Mildred McAffee, was sworn in as a Naval Reserve Lieutenant Commander- the first female commissioned officer of the U. S. Navy. Within a year of the program's creation, 27,000 women were serving in the Navy. Significantly over and above their prior clerical positions, Naval service women now worked in medical care, ground aviation (air traffic controllers), photography, mechanics, intelligence, communications, science, as well as the legal arena in the Judge Advocate General Corps.

Many female personnel remained in the Navy into the postwar era. WAVES lasted as a program until 1972, when the Navy integrated women into mainstream service. (www.history.navy/mil.).

The following narrative is about a former WAVE service member, Iris Barnes, who served as a pharmacist and hospital worker during World War II.

* * * *

Iris Glazier Barnes was born in Niagara Falls, New York. Before entering the Navy she trained as a laboratory technician. People were needed to work in this field of the war industry. Iris Barnes also worked in a high explosive TNT factory for a year. Barnes subsequently was employed at the Atchison Graphite Company in Modeltown, New York. At the time, Atchison was known as the "Lake Ontario Ordnance Works." As a lab technician at Atchison, Barnes recalled making graphite used to make big plates which, in turn, was used in the creation of the atomic pile for the first atomic bomb.

On July 6, 1944, Barnes celebrated her 20th birthday. The following day, a navy recruiter met her on the front steps of her house where she had been scheduled to meet with him. In less than three months, Barnes signed a contract to enlist into the WAVES.

Iris Barnes completed boot camp training at Hunter College, Bronx, NY. Of this time period, Barnes relates: "I went down to New York on the Empire State Express train of the New York Central. The WAVES boot camp was six weeks long and I was far from home. I was from a small town but I had the opportunity to see the eastern half of the United States and meet so many people from all over. While [at boot camp], we were reviewed by President Franklin Roosevelt." Barnes remembered taking a battery of assessment tests during her training; "the Navy said I had a lot of language skills," and wanted her to be a cryptographer. Instead, Barnes chose hospital work.

Assigned to Bethesda Naval Hospital, Iris Barnes received six weeks of intensive hospital training with patients. At the end of 1944, Barnes was asked where she wanted to be stationed. Stating no preference, she was transferred to the Quantico Naval Hospital Wave Detachment at the Marine Corps base at Quantico, Virginia. There, she cared for Marine patients who returned from the South Pacific in need of long term care. When asked by the author if she remembered any particular experiences, she replied, "I passed out meds… It was an interesting experience. One thing that struck me was when I was passing out meds to Marines in the brig. There was a small brig attached to the hospital. Some marines would get drunk and smash things and end up in the brig. Passing out meds with a marine guard with a 45 on his hip was quite an experience. But they were wonderful patients. They never complained no matter what we did to them."

Iris Barnes was discharged as a Pharmacist Mate 3rd Class on October 23, 1945. After the war, she went to secretarial school then worked as a secretary. She married Frederick S. Barnes in 1952 (featured in an earlier chapter of this book).

Iris Barnes passed away October 23, 2008.

42

Rear Admiral Willis C. Barnes

U. S. NAVAL ACADEMY

Located on the Severn River in the quaint and historic city of Annapolis, Maryland, the U.S. Naval Academy was founded in 1845 by then Secretary of State, George Bancroft. During the War Between the States, 1861-65, the Naval Academy was located at Newport, Rhode Island.

Twelve hundred candidates are appointed each year taking various courses including naval engineering. The midshipmen spend their summers training at sea or pursuing some other aspect of Navy life and after four years they earn a BS degree in one of 18 majors. Eight of these majors are in engineering. Commissioned as ensigns in the Navy or second lieutenants in the Marine Corps, they are obligated to serve five years on active duty (Naval 1).

The following is about Willis C. Barnes who was originally from Utica, New York, graduated from the Naval Academy and served 33 years in the Navy, rising to the rank of rear admiral.

* * * *

Prior to World War II, Willis Barnes attended Hamilton College from 1939-41. He received an appointment to the Naval Academy in June of 1941 and graduated as an ensign in June of 1944. Because of the war the coursework at Annapolis was accelerated and a degree was granted after three years.

Ensign Barnes' first duty after graduation was the USS WOOLSEY, a destroyer of the Benson class that weighed 1630 tons, which he referred to as a "classic tin can," loaded with armament. Capable of doing a fast 36 knots, the WOOLSEY was named after LT Melancthon Taylor Woolsey who had built a brig, the ONEIDA, in Oswego and commanded it in battle on Lake Ontario in the War of 1812. He retired as a Commodore and is buried in Forest Hills Cemetery in Utica.

It had taken Ensign Barnes several weeks to find the WOOLSEY, which was off the coast of France in September of 1944. The ship had just participated in the invasion of southern France. When Barnes found the WOOLSEY, it was providing fire support (shore bombardment) for the troops advancing eastward along the coast. "It was the only thing resembling combat that I experienced. Sometimes the enemy shot back, but fortunately they were not too good at it. Floating mines and suicide boats were about the only other hazard we faced," he explained."

From southern France, the WOOLSEY sailed to Naples, Italy. "On Christmas Day I went ashore in Naples," Admiral Barnes recalled. "On New Years Eve, I had the duty and after my mid-watch, I turned in, and one of the men was partying and brought the movie star Danny Kaye and the Brooklyn Dodger's manager Leo Durocher aboard. Not interested in joining the party, I stayed in bed," he said with a grin.

The destroyer then steamed on to Oran in North Africa and then home to Brooklyn Navy Yard for alterations and repairs in preparation for a convoy run to England. Near Gibraltar, the ships were ordered to do plane guard for President Roosevelt. His plane was on the way to the Yalta Conference in southern Russia. The ships were to provide plane guard in case the president's plane went down. About 100 miles off the Azores Islands, we were in the roughest seas that I had ever been in. From trough to crest the waves were 50 feet. Waves came almost over the bridge;" Barnes described.

"We were halfway to England in a convoy on V-E Day in May 1945. The WOOLSEY returned to Brooklyn Naval Shipyard where the vessel was to get ready for action in the western Pacific. More guns were placed on the ship in preparation for Japanese suicide planes. Brooklyn was homeport for the WOOLSEY.

On the way to the Pacific, a stop was made at Guantanamo, Cuba and then the ship traveled through the Panama Canal. Lieutenant Junior Grade Barnes arrived at Pearl Harbor in the Hawaiian Islands on V-J Day.

"We arrived at Sasebo, Japan, to inspect some Japanese ships for demilitarization. I'll never forget the degree to which the city was devastated – virtually flattened, although it had not been atom-bombed," Barnes solemnly explained.

In December of 1945, the WOOLSEY arrived in Charleston, South Carolina. Barnes helped to put the ship out of commission, and he was detached in March 1946 with orders to another destroyer in the Pacific, which was to participate in the atom-bomb tests at Bikini Island in the Pacific. He served as Chief Engineer and Senior Watch Officer until March 1948, including a six-month tour on the China Station, just before the final collapse of the regime under the communist assault. During this period, he married Marjorie Loftus of Waterville and later they raised three children: Barbara, Thomas, and David.

Barnes' next duty and first command was a minesweeper, and he said that it was the best duty that he ever had for one year. "It was a good little ship that bounced up and down and floated like a cork," he described. There were about thirty men assigned to the minesweeper, and his most memorable experience aboard it was when he was in a hurricane.

His next assignment was postgraduate work at the Massachusetts Institute of Technology. He spent three years doing postgraduate work at MIT majoring in naval architecture and marine engineering, specializing in nuclear engineering and nuclear propulsion. "I had always wanted to get into nuclear propulsion," he said. After completing the graduate work, he was then designated an EDO – Engineering Duty Only – and assigned to the naval shipyards, fleet maintenance and research activities.

He did a tour of duty at the Brooklyn Naval Shipyard from 1952-54 as assistant ship superintendent for construction of the USS SARATOGA. He was next assigned to Washington, D.C., from 1954-59 working under Admiral Hyman Rickover in the nuclear propulsion program. When asked what it was like to work for Admiral Rickover, Barnes replied, "There never was a dull moment." He became director of the advanced development division for the conceptual design of nuclear propulsion plants for the USS NARWAHL, the world's first natural circulation reactor, and the USS BAINBRIDGE, the first nuclear powered destroyer.

Following his duty in Washington, D.C. he was assigned to the Knolls Atomic Power Lab in Niskayuna, (a suburb of Schenectady, New York), where 2,000 engineers and scientists designed nuclear propulsion plants. General Electric had operated the lab for the Atomic Energy Commission for which Barnes worked. The AEC operated two proto-type reactors at West Milton, New York, located twenty miles north of Niskayuna. "I did that for five years – from 1959-64," he said.

From 1964-67, he was out of nuclear propulsion and was assigned as repair superintendent at the Norfolk Naval Shipyard where he was very busy, sometimes working on five different aircraft carriers at one time.

From 1967-70, Captain Barnes was assigned to the staff of the Commander-in-Chief of the Atlantic Fleet. As Deputy Commander of Fleet Maintenance at Norfolk, Virginia, his assignment was to keep the ships of the Atlantic Fleet in operating conditions.

From 1970-72, he served as Commander of the Mare Island Naval Shipyard in California. "It was a great assignment but tough, since there were many problems," Barnes pointed out. Before he had arrived, a nuclear submarine which was 95% completed had sunk alongside one of the piers while the Secretary of the Navy was dining with the Navy League across the river. The reactor had not yet been installed, but the ship was refloated in a hurry. The propulsion plant had to be almost completely rebuilt.

In 1972 Willis Barnes was promoted to rear admiral. He was assigned as the Fleet Maintenance Officer in Norfolk, Virginia. In 1974, Rear Admiral

Barnes was transferred to Washington, DC, as Commander of the Naval Ship Engineering Center, responsible for all ship design and engineering for the Navy.

He retired in 1977, after 33 years in the Navy. Admiral Barnes was then employed in a technical services company (ORI, INC.), an operations research group in Silver Spring, Maryland.

The author asked Admiral Barnes if he had any comments to make about World War II. In his quiet and reserved manner, the retired admiral replied:

"One of the few good things about it is that it established an incredible bond of friendship and brotherhood among those who fought together, phenomena visible today in the reunions still being held of former military units and in organizations like the American Legion. In attending WOOLSEY reunions, I always sense that for most of those shipmates, their experiences in the Navy were some of the most meaningful things they ever did." Admiral Barnes lived in Waterville and Virginia for many years. He passed away in 2008.

43

Charles D. Browne

SUBMARINER

The attack on Pearl Harbor saw the virtual destruction of the Pacific surface fleet. The submarine base was not damaged and many of the submarines were not at the base on that historic day in December of 1941. Consequently, they were thus free to patrol the Pacific and become the main offensive weapon for several months.

The U.S. Naval Institute publication, "The U.S. Submarine Operations in World War II," relates the outstanding work and courage of our submarines during World War II. In the Pacific, American submarines sank over five million tons of Japanese merchant shipping and naval vessels. The U.S. lost 52 submarines (48 in combat) and 3505 submariners lost their lives. Almost 1700 war patrols caused more than one-half of Japan's losses (Roscoe, Voge, et al. foreword and 7).

During World War II, there were 314 submarines in commission and volunteers manned them. Submarine service was more dangerous than any other sea duty, and for every surface sailor killed in action – six submariners lost their lives. (Roscoe, Voge, et al. 493).

"The willingness to face this danger, and lose their submarine if necessary, and the voluntary aspect is shown in the following words by Lieutenant Commander Dudley W. (Mush) Morton, commander of the USS WAHOO (SS238) 1942-43:

> *"This submarine is expendable. We will take every precaution, but our mission is to sink enemy shipping.... now if anyone doesn't want to go along with these conditions, just see the yeoman. I am giving him verbal authority now to transfer any who is not a volunteer"*
>
> *(QTD. In Lowder VIII).*

The development of the submarine has made large strides since the submarine warfare of World War I, which was used so effectively by the German U-boats. Submarine service has been referred to as the "Silent Service," because the Navy concealed information about submarines and submarine operations from December 1941 to August 15, 1945 when World War II ended (Lowder V).

World War II submarines were about 311 feet in length and had a 27'

Beam. They were smaller than the nuclear attack subs. The USS LOS ANGELES attack sub is about 360' long with a displacement of 6900 tons. The USS OHIO, a Trident nuclear ballistic missile submarine, measures 560 meters with a displacement of 18,750 tons and is considerably larger than the submarines of the world war era (Sharpe 794).

Submarine service was not for those who found it difficult to conform to very cramped quarters. Claustrophobia would disqualify one for this duty. It was often uncomfortable to live in these confined spaces for a lengthy period.

Charles E. Browne was a World War II submariner who resided in Waterville before enlisting into the Navy.

* * * *

It was September 1947, and the author, sixteen years of age at the time, remembers that sad evening when he and his father and mother, walked two houses down the street to attend calling hours for Chief Petty Officer Charles D. Browne. He was an uncle of some boyhood neighbor friends and had died as a result of a tragic automobile accident near Key West, Florida.

Chief Yeoman Charles D. Browne had participated in many daring missions as a crewmember on the submarine USS JACK. He had enlisted in the Navy shortly after graduation from Waterville Central School in 1939 and after boot camp was assigned to the Atlantic Submarine Force and later served in the Caribbean and Pacific.

Browne was assigned to the R-12 and R-1 submarines before being assigned to the USS JACK, which was commissioned in 1943.

The book <u>U.S. Submarine Operations in World War II</u> mentions that the JACK was equipped with the most modern equipment including new radar devices, new supersonic gear, and an ice cream machine. Browne made the first five war patrols on the USS JACK. On the very first patrol in Japanese waters, the JACK sank 16,000 tons of Japanese shipping. In the fall of 1943, on its second patrol, it was assigned to Fremantle, Australia as part of the Southwest Pacific Force. On February 19, 1944, in the sea-lane connecting Singapore and Okinawa, some Japanese tankers, were spotted moving in two columns. The JACK sank four of them in one day (Roscoe 332-333).

On the 23rd, 24th and 25th of February 1944, three more Japanese oilers were sunk. The USS JACK did a total of nine war patrols and on the eighth, since most of the Japanese shipping had been sunk, was assigned lifeguard duty for the aircraft carrier strikes and bomber missions being launched against the mainland (Roscoe 334).

The *Waterville Times* of February 28, 1946 gives an account of the awarding of the Presidential Unit Citation to the USS JACK for war service in the Pacific. The citation reads:

> *...The USS JACK received the award for extraordinary heroism in action during her first war patrol south of Honshu, her third in the South China Sea and her fifth in the area off the west coast of Luzon. 'In bold defiance of anti-submarine measures, the JACK sought her prey over wide areas and penetrated heavy escort screens in order to make contact with her targets and strike fiercely at strongly protected convoys. Severely bombed during her first war patrol, she was blown to the surface close to an enemy destroyer and with a 25 degree angle, lost depth control and plunged deep in the midst of a barrage of depth charges from the escort. With her battle damages repaired, JACK returned to the attack several days later to sink a 6,700-ton freighter and again escaped destruction under the pounding of vicious counter-attacks. Continuously harassed by severe depth charging throughout the third and fifth patrols, the JACK blasted at the enemy from all sides and sent to the bottom of the Pacific 102,800 tons of vital shipping with an additional 18,000 tons damaged** *(Waterville 1)*

Another *Waterville Times* article dated April 4, 1946, reported that Browne was one of several recipients of a Commendation Medal for meritorious service in the Pacific.

On March 27, 1946, on board the USS POACHER, Rear Admiral John. J. Brown, USN, Commandant of the Portsmouth Naval Base, Portsmouth, New Hampshire, presented the awards and the citation reads as follows:

> *...The Commander-in-Chief, United States Pacific Fleet takes pleasure in commending Charles D.Browne, Chief Yeoman, USN, for services set forth in the following:*

Citation:

> *...For meritorious conduct in action in the performance of his duties in the USS JACK during the First War Patrol of that vessel in the area south of Honshu from 5 June to 15 July 1943.*

---

*   U.S. Submarine Operations in World War II states that the JACK sank 15 ships sinking a total of 76,687 – ranking 9th highest of all submarines(Roscoe 525).

As a member of the crew, his exceptional skill and proficiency at his battle station materially assisted his Commanding Officer in conducting successful torpedo attacks which resulted in sinking and damaging a total of more than 30,000 tons of enemy shipping. His calm manner and devotion to duty contributed to the success of his vessel in evading severe enemy counter measures. His conduct throughout was an inspiration to all with whom he served and in keeping with the highest traditions of the United States Naval Service." C.W. Nimitz, Fleet Admiral, U.S. Navy signed the citation (Chief 1)

Brown's last duty station was on board the former German submarine, U-3008, at the Key West Submarine Base. In the October 2, 1947 issue of the *Waterville Times*, it was reported that on Sunday September 14, 1947, Browne was on duty supervising the preparation of the submarine for an approaching hurricane. At the end of the day, he and two other chief petty officers left the base and were returning home. At the Bahia Honda viaduct on the overseas highway, a moving van without lights had stopped at a curve in the road to help a motorist whose car had stalled. Witnesses said the car in which Browne was a passenger, had been traveling at a moderate rate of speed. However, it apparently did not see the moving van and struck it in the rear. All three men were injured but Browne had sustained a severe brain injury (Military 1).

Chief Yeoman Charles D. Browne, who had survived several precarious combat submarine experiences, died a week later on September 21, 1947 in the Key West Naval Hospital at the age of 26. His body was returned to Waterville and was buried in St. Bernard's cemetery.

44

Clayton Greig Farrall

AMMUNITION SHIP FIREMAN

FIREMAN 1/C CLAYTON FARRALL- USS FIREDRAKE(AE-14)

One of the most dangerous duties in the Navy was serving as a crew member aboard an ammunition ship. Ammunition ships transported ammunition for Navy ships and aircraft. They also transported ammunition from one weapons station to another. During World War II, former merchant ships were retrofitted into ammunition ships, armed, and manned with Navy crews. (www.en.citizendium. org) Ammunition ships had the hull letters AE and their names were suggestive of fire, explosives, and volcanoes. Over the years several ammunition ships have suffered disasters vividly illustrating the danger and anxiety of serving aboard an ammunition ship. The most famous disaster occurred on November 10, 1944 when the USS HOOD (AE-11), was anchored in 35 feet of water on Manus Island in the Admiralty islands. The USS HOOD, formerly the MARCO POLO, a merchant cargo ship, exploded and killed almost the entire crew of 350 men. The only survivors were one officer and five enlisted men who left the ship just before the explosion which left a trench in the ocean floor extending a thousand feet. A piece of the hull 16 x 10 feet was found later, but no other remains were located.

Of eight ammunition ships in existence today, seven are operated by the

Military Sealift Command with a civilian master and crew. One is manned by
the Navy with a commanding officer.(www.usmilitary/about)
    The following account is about Fireman First Class Clayton Farrall who served
on an ammunition ship USS FIREDRAKE (AE-14) from 1944 to 1946.

* * * *

Clayton Farrall was born in Cambridge, Massachusetts and grew up in Utica,
New York enlisting when he was seventeen years old. After completing a
series of special examinations to finish high school, Farrall entered the Navy
on April 15, 1944.

    Farrall recalled that a group of about twenty new servicemen were
transported together by train for basic training; "Every one but me was
Army, and I being Navy, was put on the wrong car of the train. "They must
have thought I was part of the Army contingent." After the train stopped
and everyone but Farrall and the conductor got off, he told the conductor
he was supposed to go to Great Lakes, Illinois. "Finally, the conductor got
me headed in the right direction on the correct train to Great Lakes," Farrall
added. After Farrall finished boot camp, military aptitude testing indicated
he could go to fireman's school. At the time, Clayton Farrall did not know
a fireman in the Navy did not fight fires. Actually, a Navy fireman worked
below decks on boilers and with boiler tenders. Farrall explained that "[he]
would check the gauges for the water level and keep the water at a safe level.
I was not happy with my Navy career after that. After Fireman training
school –I hated it-, I was assigned to the initial crew to USS FIREDRAKE
(AE14) an ammunition ship. It was a newly commissioned Liberty ship with
six anti-aircraft guns."The USS FIREDRAKE's mission was to transport
ammunition to warships such as DD's Cruisers- and Aircraft carriers engaged
in recapturing strategic Pacific islands from the Japanese.

    Farrall said that in accomplishing this mission, the FIREDRAKE traveled
in a semi-circular route, which involved an initial trip to the battle zone
where ammunition was transferred from the FIREDRAKE to the various
warships. A warship tied up alongside the FIREDRAKE and large cranes
unloaded the ammunition from the cargo holds. "This required some skill
since the ships would continue sailing during the transfer," Farrall said.
After unloading the ammunition, the FIREDRAKE proceeded to a location
far from the battle zone (Okinawa), then reloaded and proceeded to Leyte
Gulf to repeat the same process. The large cargo of ammunition made the
FIREDRAKE a floating time bomb. Farrall explained that a direct hit would
cause a high impact explosion destroying ships and property in the area, sure
to kill hundreds of personnel. Because of this danger, the FIREDRAKE never

traveled in convoy and was not allowed to dock in port. When involved in an invasion the ship had to anchor far from other ships once the unloading of ammunition was completed.

Farrall said that USS FIREDRAKE's involvement in the invasion of Okinawa was the more memorable of two in which it participated. Since the Japanese Navy had become weakened by February 1945, it resorted to Kamikaze planes for defense. The Kamikaze plane was essentially a flying bomb with pilot, whose sole mission was to destroy a ship. These planes inflicted heavy damage on U.S. ships. Farrall said that during the Okinawa invasion, of the hit 221 U.S. ships hit and fifty-one sunk, the majority of these were by Kamikaze attacks.

Consequently, the FIREDRAKE crew was understandably stressed during the Okinawa invasion. Since the supply of ammunition was vital to the invasion, two smoke ships were assigned to protect the FIREDRAKE during kamikaze attacks. If an attack occurred while underway, the smoke ships laid down a smoke screen for disguise protection. Though generally effective, Farrall related that "sometimes the smoke ships were caught by surprise and the FIREDRAKE was left unprotected. We did have anti-aircraft [guns] on the ship but they were not overly effective."

The crew of the FIREDRAKE was much larger than the average Liberty Ship given the need of more personnel to handle the rapid unloading of ammunition at sea. With the continual threat of Kamikaze attacks, speed was essential in loading the ships. A large group of men worked in the holds. Farrall and the galley staff helped. When a large ship such as an aircraft carrier was along side, a contingent from that ship was also sent over to help. "The AE13, an ammunition ship that we had replaced [had been] hit and blew up... [T]here were no survivors. I also saw the TICONDEROGA get hit by a kamikaze plane. We were lucky and came through the invasions untouched but we had some close calls." Farrall also recalled the following incidents:

> *....I remembers four different times when the planes came very close to the ship. Twice they ignored our ship and flew on to attack other ships. Another time the plane approaching our ship was on fire and the pilot couldn't control it and he missed the ship by 75 feet. Another time a plane had an excellent chance of hitting our ship and our guns had a difficult time getting an accurate line on the plane. But a destroyer appeared and shot down the kamikaze, which was making a run on the FIREDRAKE*

An interesting conclusion to this account is that many years later, long after the end of World War II, the crews of a number of the ships started having reunions. At one such event, some of the former crew members visited the hotel bar where they happened to meet other men having a similar destroyer reunion. In the course of exchanging war stories, an amazing coincidence emerged. The destroyer ex-crew members served on the destroyer that had shot down a Kamikaze plane and one of the ammunition ship crewmembers at the bar had actually been part of the anti-aircraft crew that manned the anti-aircraft guns. Naturally, the destroyer crew members didn't pay for their drinks for the rest of the evening.

Farrall also recalled other activities he and his fellow crew member pursued while serving on the FIREDRAKE. Overall, he was not happy stationed in the fire room of the ship and needed something to keep him entertained:

>*...I came from a farm and I never worked in confined areas such as below deck on a ship. I hated it! I went to the officer-in-charge of the division and requested a transfer to the deck division. He didn't like that so he said no one gets transferred. He had to provide a certain number to the mess area. 'I'm taking you off duty as a Fireman and sending you for permanent duty in the spud locker,' the division officer said. He was joined by another crew member, John Gryalsky, who had also incurred the wrath of his division officer. We peeled potatoes and brought supplies from the food locker to the galley and when we had to load ammunition, we went below to help load the ammo. We peeled a large amount of potatoes every day with a special machine and the timer was set so that no skin was left on the potatoes. With this time setting over half of the potato disappeared by the time all of the skin was gone. I considered this a terrible waste so after some experimenting with the timer, I found a setting that left only a few patches of skin but improved the size of the potato. Thinking that the chief cook would be pleased with this I ran off a load with the new timer setting and sent them to the galley and waited for the chief cook's reaction. There was a reaction but one I did not expect. The chief cook a huge man about 300 pounds, came charging into the spud locker and grabbed the both of us. He shouted in a loud voice. "What happened to the potatoes? Don't send potatoes like that!" he said. He said he was returning the potatoes and that they had better come back with no skin. He also said that all future potatoes would be skinless or that we would be very soon.*

Shortly after the above incident recalled by Farrall, the FIREDRAKE was temporarily removed from battle and assigned to a remote Pacific island for necessary repairs and refurbishing. Ship personnel were informed that there would be an inspection by members of the fleet admiral's staff to insure that the ship was ready to return to the battle zone. Meals were modified to give the galley staff extra time to do the necessary cleaning and refurbishing. Farrall recalled that he and his shipmate, Grywalsky, used this extra time to paint the spud locker; "[W]hen the captain came around he noticed that we had painted the kitchen and polished everything. He was amazed and we received a high mark. There was a special compliment to the chief cook and after that our relations with the chief cook improved.

Farrall further explained that a small ship such as his had limited space for recreational activities. Card games and shooting dice were the major forms of leisure and sailors regularly waged larges sums of money. "I made one attempt at shooting dice and after losing a fair amount of money, I decided that gambling was not for me," he recounted.

The FIREDRAKE arrived in Ulithi March 1, 1945 and a part of the invasion of Okinawa on April 7 when it regularly loaded ammunition aboard ships until November 1 that same year. The only crew opportunity for liberty was at Ulithi. He said this rudimentary form of 'shore leave' consisted of breaking up the crews into sections and sending each section via boat "to go off to one of the small God-forsaken islands. A six pack of beer was given to each sailor and they would drink beer, swim and play various sports. They would wander around the area and visit booths set up by natives to sell clothes, beads and other trinkets to the sailors. The area was policed by the Navy shore patrol and the boats would come back to pick up the sailors later the same day." Farrall added that FIREDRAKE crewmen were each allowed two liberty trips to the islands during this time.

On August 14, 1945 when the Japanese surrendered, Farrall said that he had been at sea and his ship had just pulled into port that day. All of the ships that night set off flares celebrating the end of the war.

The FIREDRAKE left for the east coast of the United States in November 1945 reaching the Panama Canal on December 5th. There, it anchored at Colon on the Atlantic side of the Canal. Farrall recounted that "[t]hat is where the crew had its first real liberty in a civilized area since leaving for service in the invasion of Okinawa... Most of the men returned from liberty, but about twenty were missing. The commander detached the more sober members of the crew, including myself, to accompany the Shore Patrol to go ashore again to search for these men. The majority was located, with the exception of one or two, and the ship left Panama without them."

The FIREDRAKE ultimately anchored in Orange, Texas and decommissioned in 1946. She was recommissoned March 19, 1971 and eventually sold for civilian use. Farrall explained that after several months at Orange, Texas, he left with a large group of men for Lido Beach, Long Island.

Near the end of the trip the train suddenly stopped and one of the conductors informed us that our train line was on strike and all service is discontinued. The train crew did not realize that they were dealing with a large group of men who had been away from home for a long time and were longing to return. The group was angry and wanted to get the train moving again so they approached the conductor... The conductor, realizing the impending danger, decided to call management. Management, realizing the bad publicity that would result from interfering with our returning home, quickly authorized the movement of the train and made sure the tracks was clear to Lido Beach.

Fireman Clayton Farrall was discharged from the Navy on May 18, 1946. After college, Farrall was employed as a school psychologist. After receiving his PhD, he became a professor at State University of New York at Potsdam and retired in 1987.

He presently lives in New Hartford New York.

45

Gerald Furner

MINE SWEEPER

COXSWAIN 3/C GERALD FURNER and
SHIPFITTER 3/C ANTHONY LANGONE
(Courtesy of Jeanette Doyle)

The mission of the Minesweeper, a mine warfare vessel, is to detect, sweep and clear the area of underwater mines so that ships can travel safely. The 1995-6 <u>Jane's Fighting Ships</u> *describes a minesweeper of the Avenger class as about 200 feet long, has an oak structure, and carries a crew of 45. The vessels are identified mainly by a number but are named after birds such as the ostrich and seagull (Sharpe 831).*

According to the Merchant Marine internet website, during World War II there were several types of mines including magnetic, acoustic, and pressure activated mines. The latter responded to changes in the water pressure. Also, there were combination type mines such as pressure-magnetic, and magnetic-acoustic mines (Merchant Marine).

Gerald Furner of Waterville, New York served on a Minesweeper YMS-403.

* * * *

Prior to World War II, Gerald Furner was in high school and had worked at various jobs including highway construction on Route 20 in Sangerfield during the summer of 1942, when he was 16 years old. He remembered picking up potatoes on the Jack Cleary farm on Route 12 for $.03 a bushel and the happy times he enjoyed with the neighborhood kids. One time, playing touch football behind the Catholic Church, during one of those happy times, he suffered a broken collarbone. In November of 1942, at age 17, Furner enlisted in the Navy and went off to "boot camp" training at Sampson Naval Training Center, south of Geneva, New York

Following boot camp, he attended Mine Warfare School in Yorktown, Virginia. Training on World War I minesweepers, he studied all types of mines – contact, magnetic, and sound, and minesweeping equipment. He also attended gunnery school at Dam Neck, Virginia, receiving training in operating 20 mm anti-aircraft guns.

Furner became a Coxswain, which is comparable to a Boatswain Mate in today's Navy and in June of 1943, he went aboard the minesweeper, YMS 403. He said that the vessel was a small wooden ship with a crew of 28 enlisted men and four officers. Furner showed the author a picture of his ship and pointed out the sonic hammer on the bow that created underwater sounds to detonate the sound mines. The ship carried about 1,500 feet of cable that had electrodes, which sent current through the water exploding the magnetic mines. Also, the contact mines filled with air and explosives were anchored in the water with a cable. This cable would move and cutters on the cable would cut the cable that anchored the mine. In explaining contact mines, Furner said that a cable with two square shaped water kites was released from the ship to sweep for the contact mines. One kite, the depressor, would keep the cable submerged about 20 feet. The cable, which extended from the depressor kite, had cutters for cutting the mine cable. The other kite, the paravane, would keep the cable away from the ship while it was being manipulated to cut the mine cable. The paravane kite also had a float extending from it to mark its location. After the mine cable was cut, the mine would float to the top and sailors on the ship, armed with rifles, would shoot at the mines and detonate them. "It was pretty safe sweeping for mines," Furner added. The ship swept for mines along the east coast of the United States for a year and one-half but never found a mine. "We would go out for about three and one-half days and then come in to refuel at Tompkinsville on Staten Island. We also picked up supplies and water."

In March of 1945, the YMS 403 left for the South Pacific and Okinawa. The ship stopped at Miami, Mexico, Nicaragua and then traveled through the Panama Canal and on to San Diego. Furner displayed some letters written by his close friend, the late Anthony Langone, and one of the author's brothers. Langone was serving on the LST 988, and had written some letters to Furner in 1945. In one of the letters, Langone writes of his thrill in going through the Panama Canal: "Hi, Jerry, we left Cuba and Panama a while back. It sure is interesting to go through the Panama Canal. I'm sure I won't forget it and neither will you when you go through it."

From San Diego to Pearl Harbor, the ship ran short of fuel so re-fueling at sea was necessary. Stops were also made at Eniwetok to pick up mail and then at Guam before reaching Okinawa. The trip to Okinawa took three months. "We anchored in Buckner's Bay off the island in June of 1945. There were kamikaze attacks about five miles away but they never got near our ship and I did see a ship get hit. We were busy putting up smoke screens for protection from possible Kamikaze attacks, and the whole harbor looked like a big cloud," Furner recalled.

In August of 1945, as the war was ending, his ship was sweeping for mines in the East China Sea and in the Inland Sea near Kobe, Japan, one magnetic mine was swept. He indicated that the mines had been laid earlier in the war by American minelayers, and that the minesweepers had swept hundreds of mines.

"The crew went wild when word was received about the end of the war," he remembered. Furner pointed out that his ship was scheduled to participate in the invasion of Japan in November of 1945, but the atomic bombs brought the war to a sudden end.

YMS 403 docked in Japan and the crew enjoyed the times they went ashore on "Liberty". "The Japanese beer was great and the people seemed very intelligent and it was very exciting to witness a different culture," Furner explained.

Coxswain Third Class Gerald Furner returned to the United States and was discharged in March of 1946.

Reminiscing about the war and its causes, Furner said, "Many millions of people died because of greed, aggression, and materialism. It ought to be replaced with love of God and neighbors."

After the war, Furner worked for three years on the former DL&W railroad replacing ties and rails from North Brookfield to Utica. He also worked as a carpenter for 35 years on various construction jobs from Niagara Falls to Albany.

He retired in 1987.

46

Robert Hughes

CRUISER SAILOR

Sleek cruisers replaced the frigates of the early Navy and over the years have served in various ways such as anti-aircraft defense, escorts for aircraft carriers, and supporting amphibious landings. Equipped with 5-8" guns, missiles, and the phalanx system, their mission today is to destroy surface ships, submarines, airplanes and missiles. Cruisers of the Ticonderoga class have a crew of about 500 men, are 567 feet in length and are armed with AEGIS surface to air missiles. Some of the missiles are nuclear powered (Sharpe 810).

The USS CANBERRA (CA-70), a World War II cruiser of the Baltimore class, was 673' 5" long with a beam of 70' 10". It could travel about 33 knots per hour and was commissioned October 14, 1943 in Boston, MA (Hansen 1). Robert "Cap" Hughes of Waterville served aboard the CANBERRA from January 1944 until the end of the war. Hughes and the ship received seven battle stars for engaging in some of the fiercest and most crucial battles of World War II. On Friday the 13th, 1944 while preparing for landings at Leyte Gulf off the Philippine Islands, the Japanese torpedoed his ship and twenty-three shipmates lost their lives.

* * * *

Robert "Cap" Hughes attended Waterville Central School and at age 17, left school and thinking that he knew it all, enlisted into the Navy on February 5, 1943. He traveled to Sampson Naval Training Center for "boot camp." Hughes recalled with a grin some of the humorous stories from "boot camp." As every former navy man knows, there are boot camp stories that circulate to frighten the young and innocent. There were stories that foot long square needles were being used for inoculations. If you complained, they would threaten to use fishhooks for needles.

Following "boot camp" Hughes was transferred to the Naval Training Center at Newport, Rhode Island for gunnery school. Gunnery school lasted several weeks and instruction was on 5", 8", and 20mm and 40mm guns. The 40mm had four barrels, two and two, Hughes described. "Two would go off and alternate with the other two." The 40's were nicknamed "pom-pom" guns because of the sounds the 40's made as they were fired. "After I got aboard ship, I manned a 40mm (two quads) located on the superstructure on the starboard side. I controlled the firing and aiming or direction of the fire and my battle station was referred to as Pointer," Hughes added.

In January 1944, Hughes traveled to Boston and stayed at the old Fargo Building in South Boston. Prior to boarding the USS CANBERRA (CA-70), a heavy cruiser which was named after an Australian ship the HMAS CANBERRA, which was lost in the battle of the Savo Islands in August of 1942. The ship went on a shakedown cruise and many sailors got seasick.

The CANBERRA left Boston on January 14, 1944. "Leaving Boston and seeing the setting sun – you wonder if you will ever see it going down again. It is a sinking feeling," Hughes said reflecting on his departure from Boston.

The cruiser sailed down the Atlantic coast and into the Caribbean and through the Panama Canal. Hughes remarked on how the Canal was a tremendous sight, and after a stop in San Diego, the ship set out across the Pacific for the Hawaiian Islands. At Honolulu, the CANBERRA joined the Sixth Fleet and later the Seventh Fleet. "As we were cruising around looking for Japanese, there were some enemy reconnaissance planes spotted. The Navy knew they were there and did not want to start shooting since it would give away our location. The engines were stopped and the Japanese dropped flares which lit up the sky as bright as day. Then all of our ships released smoke creating a smoke screen. When the flares dropped it made the area look even blacker. We were lucky they didn't see the ship," Hughes explained.

Hughes said that he learned that a friend from Waterville that he grew up with was also serving on the USS CANBERRA. His name was Earl Salm who lived in Sangerfield, before World War II. Hughes said that one night in Hawaii one-half of the crew had an overnight pass. The next day Hughes saw someone with a bunch of T-shirts with grass-skirts. It caught his attention since they were made in Utica. He found out that the guy with the T-shirts was Earl Salm. Salm was assigned to the First division and was a seaman quartered in the bow of the ship. Hughes was quartered amidships close to his battle station. Not only had Salm served with Hughes aboard the CANBERRA, but also had lived next door to him in recent years. "A quirk of fate," Hughes remarked with a smile.

The CANBERRA joined Task Force 58 in February 1944, participating in the Battle of Eniwetok. Hughes said that the cruiser pounded the beach with five and eight-inch shells, and gunner's mates and other crewmembers manning the guns wore earmuffs to protect their eardrums. "The five-inch made a big "bang" sound and the eight-inch made a "boom" sound, which was easier on the ears," he added.

The CANBERRA engaged in raids on the Palau Islands, Yap, Ulithi,

Truk, and other islands between March 30 and April 1, 1944. Following those raids, the CANBERRA also took part in the Marianas operation and the Battle of the Philippine Sea (Hansen 1).

On October 2, 1944, the CANBERRA joined Admiral Halsey's Task Force 38 for an air strike on Okinawa and Formosa. On October 13, about 90 miles off Formosa, the CANBERRA was hit with an aerial torpedo. "Struck below her armor belt in the engineering spaces, the torpedo blew a jagged hole in her side and killed 23 of her crew instantly. Some 4,500 tons of water flooded the fire room and the engine rooms" (Hansen 2). Hughes remembered being told that when they were to encounter the Japanese fleet the formation of the Group was set up so that the CANBERRA was often used as bait. The enemy would want to sink a cruiser. Thus we were used as bait and torpedoed," Hughes stated.

Hughes was on the starboard side at his battle station. The ship was under battle conditions and the hatches and compartments had been secured to preserve watertight integrity. Hughes was manning the 40mm on the superstructure when the ship was hit on the opposite side from him. In his quiet and articulate manner, Hughes described the incident.

> *...I heard the explosion and it was scary. It seemed like a "Jolly Green Giant" had picked the ship up, shook it, and then put it back into the water. The CANBERRA is 673 feet long. For one torpedo to do this was hard to believe. I wondered how far is the ship going down? We then checked to see if our lifejackets were on securely. Everything had gone out – we had no power, no engine power, no propulsion, and no sound powered phones. We were dead in the water.*

Divers investigated underwater to estimate the damage. After checking the size of the hole, it was decided that the bodies of the sailors were not to be removed until the ship was in dry dock, a floating dry-dock. Hughes said that after the ship was torpedoed, it was towed by another vessel until the seagoing tug arrived. A Japanese reconnaissance plane was seen patrolling around a couple of days after the CANBERRA was hit and Hughes explained that it was scary because he felt like the ship was a sitting duck ready to be hit again by the enemy. "We couldn't have been hit in a more vulnerable spot. The torpedo had knocked out everything," Hughes described.

"When we reached the floating dry dock, temporary repairs were made and a burial at sea ceremony was conducted. The ceremony is one of the saddest memories a person can have. Even today, when Taps is blown, it hits me hard and I hate to hear Taps because of what it reminds me," Hughes explained sadly.

According to the Dictionary of American Naval Fighting Ships, both the CANBERRA and the HOUSTON (CA-81), which was hit on October 14, were escorted by the task force and towed by the WICHITA (CA45). Admiral Halsey nicknamed the group "Bait Division 1" and it would be used to lure the Japanese into the open, but the Japanese became suspicious and did not fall into the trap. The CANBERRA was towed to Manus for temporary repairs (Hansen 2).

In describing the battles in which the ship was involved, Hughes explained that shelling the beaches to soften things up for the landings was the main duty of the CANBERRA prior to and during the invasion.

In September of 1944, "We went through a terrible typhoon and there were many seasick sailors and even though everything had been secured, we heard dishes breaking. I saw a DD (destroyer) in the hurricane, and I saw how it would go up and down in the water because of the typhoon. When the bow went down in the water you could see the exposed screw up in the air at the stern of the destroyer.

One night, when he was on watch on the fantail, Hughes experienced one of his frightening memories. He noticed a carrier approaching very close to the CANBERRA and he wondered if he should call the Bridge to warn of a possible collision. Luckily, the carrier went to starboard preventing the collision. "I don't know if it was one of the ships that was off from its designated course. There was no collision and I never reported it," Hughes explained.

The CANBERRA left for the Boston Navy Yard for permanent repairs in February of 1945 and after arriving in Boston, Hughes was admitted into the Chelsea Naval Hospital for a leg injury. Following his stay in the hospital, he was ready for transfer to a new duty station. Since he had accumulated extensive sea duty, he had his choice of any naval base in the United States, so he chose San Diego where he worked in a Naval Radio and Sound Laboratory.

He hitched a ride all the way to San Diego and said people treated him nicely. He said that he spent more time in the hospital at San Diego and later worked at the Naval Radio and Sound Laboratory.

Seaman First Class Robert Hughes was discharged on January 17, 1946. His stay in the Navy was over and once again he hitchhiked across the country. This time he was headed home.

He returned to Waterville and was employed at several jobs and was retired from the New York State Electric and Gas Co. in February 1990 after thirty-one plus years with the company.

He passed away October 16, 2001.

47

Milton Jannone:

NAVAL OFFICER CANDIDATE SCHOOL

During World War II the military and naval academies and Reserve Officer Training Corps programs in our colleges were not able to meet the demand for officers. Therefore, other programs were employed to meet this need. The most well known of these programs is the Officer Candidate School (OCS)- a training program of 90 days that led to the labeling of these graduates as "Ninety Day Wonders." And wonders they were – as most performed superbly as commissioned officers in our armed forces.

One of the graduates of Naval Officer Candidate School was Milton Jannone of Clinton, New York who was originally from Waterville.

* * * *

Prior to entering the Navy in July of 1943, at the age of 22, Jannone attended Hamilton College in Clinton where he excelled as a football halfback. He was featured in a "Saturday Evening Post" article of the early 1940's, which relates some of his achievements on the gridiron. Since he had attended a small college, "Mercury Milt," who had never played football in high school, was described as a "Little All America."

Forest Evashevski, Jannone's coach at Hamilton, later coached at Iowa University and in 1943 was coaching a military team called the Iowa Sea Hawks. The team provided good publicity for naval aviation and Evashevski wanted Jannone to come to New York City. "I was the only person there in New York, when I arrived, and I was met by a Navy captain and a lieutenant commander," Jannone said.

He was in New York to determine whether he had the physical requirements for flight training and eventually, for playing football for a Naval aviation team, the Iowa Sea Hawks. "I decided that I did not want this so I applied for Officer Candidate School," he said.

In the summer of 1943, Jannone left for Chicago for OCS school, which was located on Michigan Avenue. He said that he was glad he selected OCS because it was in Chicago where he had met his wife, Mary.

"After 30 days of OCS we were allowed liberty." He chuckled as he recalled a humorous incident. The officer candidates were required to wear the white sailor "Dixie Cup" hats with a navy blue circular stripe, which were similar to what midshipmen at the naval academy wore. Jannone said that "the guys would come down from the Great Lakes Naval Training Center on a Liberty pass, and all of the enlisted men had the same white caps, but their hats had no blue ring. The girls would ask the sailors from Great Lakes, whose hats did not have the blue stripes why the men from OCS had the blue stripe. They told the girls that we all had a venereal disease and that was why we had to wear white hats with blue stripes," Jannone explained with a big laugh.

Commissioned as an ensign upon graduation from Officer Candidate's School, Jannone was transferred to small craft and navigation school at Little Creek, Virginia that was located adjacent to the amphibious base at Little Creek.

After a month of this training at Little Creek, he traveled to Brooklyn Naval Shipyard and boarded the USS STANTON (DE-247), a destroyer escort. Jannone was assigned as Radar Officer with General Quarter's duty in Combat Information Center (CIC).

Jannone recalled the following:

…We were on convoy duty on a cruise to Africa and the German Air Force attacked us. I could only hear the fighter planes but couldn't spot them on the radar. It wasn't very comfortable. I learned afterward that there was a torpedo coming toward our ship but one of the lookouts had spotted it. Our captain immediately turned the ship sharply toward the oncoming torpedo to avoid being hit. This maneuver made it possible for the torpedo to miss the STANTON, but the same torpedo succeeded in striking one of the other ships that had a convoy position next to us.

The Dictionary of American Naval Fighting Ships, Vol. 6, records the following about the incident:

…The STANTON escorted convoys and as a unit in Task Force 65, was part of a 60-ship convoy from Norfolk to Bizerte. (Jannone indicated that the convoy was from New York City to Bizerte.) Just before midnight two dozen Dornier 217's and JU's 88's attacked us off Algeria on April 11, 1944. The STANTON shot at a plane crossing the bow and later had a stick of bombs fall close aboard. The USS HOLDER (DE-401) was torpedoed on the port side by one of the low flying planes. No merchant ships were hit.

The convoy reached Bizerte the next day and then returned to New York City (Mooney 605).

Jannone said that this was all he could relate about his combat career and that he was on the ship for about a year. "They wanted me to stay aboard for a North Atlantic run but I knew enough about the North Atlantic, and it was close to winter. They gave me a choice of staying aboard or going to small craft training in Miami. I took a ten-day leave and went to Chicago and was married and from there I took a train to Miami," he explained. At the small craft school, the classrooms were small and very hot. It was very uncomfortable since this was before the days of widespread air conditioners. Having to wear the World War II officer working gray uniform to class with neckties caused additional discomfort, he added.

Jannone indicated that during his time in the Navy while waiting for ship assignments, he attended fire fighting training schools at Brooklyn Naval Shipyard and at Norfolk, Virginia. He also explained that one of his shore assignments was duty as an inspector of merchant ships where he inspected "Handy Billy's,"(Portable pumps) and other fire equipment.

After the school in Miami, he was transferred to Norfolk for duty aboard a sub-chaser. "This was a wooden ship with iron men and I served on it until the end of the war. On the sub-chaser, we patrolled the shores of the Atlantic and about this time, in 1945, the war was almost over and I was in Boston on V-E Day. The homeport for the ship was Norfolk.

Lieutenant Junior-Grade Milton Jannone was released from active duty on March 5, 1946. He received one battle star in the European, Africa, and Middle East Theater of Operations in reference to the USS STANTON being attacked by a submarine and German aircraft while it was in convoy.

Returning home, Jannone taught school at Waterville Central School and later was a professor and coordinator of social sciences at Mohawk Valley Community College. He retired in 1985. A few years ago, he was inducted into the Greater Utica Sports Hall of Fame.

He passed away March 19, 2008.

48

Francis R. Kelley

SIGNALMAN

Communications between ships is essential for the survival of the ship, the fleet, or a mission. The messages exchanged can be by voice or Morse code, Teletype, semaphore flags, or computers. The job of the signalman is to send and receive various colorful flags, which denote letters of the alphabet and also certain conditions aboard ship. The signalman also operates the large lights on the flying bridge to send messages using the Morse code – one flash for a dot and two flashes for a dash.

Francis Kelley of Waterville served as a Signalman on board a destroyer escort (DE) and an attack transport (APA) during World War II. On board the attack transport, he was assigned to the 12ᵗʰ Beach Battalion.

* * * *

Francis Kelley enlisted in the Navy in 1943 at the age of seventeen and was sent to the Sampson Naval Training Center for "boot camp" training. When asked if he had any memorable experiences of boot camp, he replied, "I missed a watch and got hell for that plus four hours of extra duty working in the bowling alley." Also, in the drill hall he saw Willie Pep, a professional prizefighter and featherweight champion of the world. Kelley would get ice cream for him and Pep would always give him some.

Kelley said that Sampson had a great football team in 1943 and played the West Point Army team when Blanchard and Davis were star backfield men for Army. He was happy that "boot camp" had ended, and he then spent sixteen more weeks at Sampson, attending Signalman school.

Upon completion of the school, he was assigned to a destroyer escort, the USS HOWARD F. CLARK that was located at the Boston Naval Shipyard.

The Navy used destroyer escorts because they were not as expensive to operate as an ocean escort to counter the submarine threat. They could achieve the mission of the larger destroyer by attacking surface ships with guns and torpedoes and also act as a scout ship for the fleet. The Frigates in today's Navy have replaced the destroyer escort vessels (Destroyers 1).

The USS CLARK then went on a shakedown cruise to Bermuda. After leaving Bermuda, the sonar picked up a submarine and pursued it and dropped quite a few depth charges. "We were all very excited and chased it for about three days. On the cruise, the ship went aground on a spur and another DE came along and pulled us off," Kelley explained with a laugh. He said DE's could go 30 knots an hour, but going aground bent the screw and left the CLARK with only half speed. Kelley said that in Bermuda he toured a captured Italian submarine.

The CLARK was on anti-submarine patrol and on one trip from Boston, Massachusetts, the ship covered about half of the Atlantic looking for German submarines. Kelley said that by 1944 the enemy submarines were less of a threat and that his ship made only one contact. The DE left the convoy and chased it until the British took over. He said that he saw many mines and the Gunner's Mates exploded the mines with rifle shots.

Returning to Boston, the ship sustained damage as a result of running into the dock. Several officers and men on the Bridge wondered why a right rudder order was not given as the ship was allowed to continue straight ahead and ended up hitting the dock.

While in Boston, Kelley was allowed to go home for the weekend and was involved in an automobile accident caused by the driver falling asleep. He had to spend two weeks in Rhodes Hospital in the Town of New Hartford and from Rhodes was transferred to the naval hospital at Chelsea, Massachusetts.

From Chelsea, Kelley then went to Fort Pierce, Florida where volunteers were needed for a Beach Battalion, which would be organized after completing amphibious warfare training. Included in the training was firing a carbine and he carried a pack and shovel for digging foxholes and also had patrol craft training. One time, he was on a Coast Guard cutter and he was required to jump off the ship and drift in with the current. He was assigned to the 12th Beach Battalion, which had 25-30 men in a company. They had weapons inspection and the one with the best performance received $2 bills and could go ashore in Miami. Company A won it every week and each member received $2 bills. At Fort Pierce, Kelley saw Hank Gardner from Waterville who was also a Signalman and an instructor in the school.

Kelley then traveled to Pascagoula Shipyard, Mississippi and he boarded the attack transport USS HANOVER (APA 116) as part of the 12th Beach Battalion. Aboard ship he had the same duties as the crewmembers. The ship was loaded with beer, tanks, and troops and got underway on May 6, 1944, sailing through the Caribbean and the Panama Canal and into the Pacific to Pearl Harbor, Hawaii, engaging in training operations along the way. They arrived in Pearl Harbor May 24 and unloaded troops and participated in underway training operations in Hawaiian waters until June 6.

At Pearl Harbor, the 12th Beach Battalion engaged in maneuvers on the island. "It was very hot and we would get in LCVP's (Landing Craft Vehicles and Personnel) and the sea was rough and we boarded the LCVP from a net dropped over the side. It was kind of dangerous as we went in toward the beach. When we got there, the ramp of the LCVP was dropped and we got off and the water was up to our shoulders," Kelley recalled. On the beach a command post was established and radios were set up for communications.

"On board ship we had a covered light that was used for ship-to-ship communications and special binoculars were needed to see the light. It was used especially in convoys. Every hour on the hour we would look for a signal," Kelley said.

The author interviewed Kenneth Sliter, a World War II Navy signalman from Lowville, New York, who explained that some of the visual communication was absolutely necessary when the radio could not be used. In using the semaphore flags, "you had to be fast in running up the flags," Sliter said. The duty was extra hazardous in heavy seas as the signalman waved the semaphore flags or operated the large blinking light on the uppermost deck of the ship. Ashore, the gear that was used was cumbersome and heavy and sometimes broke down. The blinker light had to be mounted on a tripod. While in the Pacific, Sliter added that during a typhoon, he was on the flying (signal) bridge and there was a destroyer on one side of the ship and a destroyer escort on the other. He said the sea was so rough that the signalmen had to ask for IMI (repeat your last letter groups). "We could receive our messages by blinking lights."

The <u>Dictionary of American Naval Fighting Ships, Volume 3</u>, states that after leaving Hawaii on July 1, 1945, the HANOVER continued its course across the Pacific and on July 14, reached Eniwetok Atoll, an important Pacific staging area, preparing for the invasion of Japan (Johnson and Roberts 238).

On July 17, the HANOVER was bound for Ulithi and traveled in a convoy bound for Okinawa and reached there on August 12, two days before V-J Day. At Okinawa, the HANOVER unloaded replacement troops and planned on taking part in the occupation of Japan after hostilities ended (Johnson and Roberts 238).

The Japanese, probably from the mainland of Japan, were flying around and tried to land at the airstrip on Okinawa at night. A smoke screen was used to conceal the HANOVER. There were still Kamikaze attacks, and explosions caused by planes hitting the ships could be heard. One Kamikaze plane took the stack out of a ship and part of the plane was sticking out of it. Kelley spent most of the time aboard ship, but the Beach Battalion did go ashore on Okinawa for a while.

The HANOVER traveled to Tientsin and Tsingtao, China, and Chinchow, Manchuria (Johnson and Roberts 238). Kelley said he walked part of the Great Wall of China and that he also visited Hong Kong where he enjoyed a rickshaw ride. "You could ride all day for a dollar," he said with a laugh. His ship was transporting Chinese troops and he remembered that one or two of the Chinese officers could speak English. The Chinese would set up a tripod on deck and put a kettle on it and cook fish and rice. On the trip two or three of the Chinese died from dysentery. They were then put in a bag and buried at sea.

In early September the HANOVER was loaded with troops and sailed for Jinsen, Korea. Kelley also recalled the frightening experience of going through a typhoon off Okinawa in mid-September. The ship was returning from Korea and was forced to stand out to sea and ride it out (Johnson and Roberts 238).

Kelley recalled that one time the HANOVER was carrying troops from China and was on the way to Korea but the ship was being fired on and was unable to drop off troops. They turned around and returned to China.

Kelley said that he saw Don Dunster, another friend from Waterville. He was stationed on an attack cargo ship (AKA). Kelley went aboard the AKA to get supplies and he didn't know that Dunster was assigned to the ship. Dunster yelled "Kelley." He noticed Kelley's name on his shirt and Kelley said that after he returned to his ship, he asked the Captain if he could get a ride on the Captain's Gig to go over to Dunster's ship. An officer was on the Gig and wanted to go directly to shore but Kelley told the officer that the Captain told him the Coxswain could stop off at the AKA to let Kelley off to visit Dunster. The Gig, on its return trip, stopped at the AKA to pick up supplies and Kelley.

SM3 Kelley was on his way home in December of 1945. His ship was assigned to the "Magic Carpet" fleet to transport American troops home from the Pacific. They loaded up with Marines in Manila and headed back across the Pacific to Portland, Oregon. From there he boarded a troop train across the country to New York and Lido Beach, New York, where he was discharged from the Navy on December 30, 1945.

He returned home and worked at Eastern Rock, now Hansons, as an equipment operator.

Francis Kelley passed away November 19, 2001.

49

GEORGE LIM

NAVAL OFFICER

ENSIGN GEORGE LIM

Many Americans in the nineteenth and early twentieth centuries feared the immigration of the Chinese into the United States. This fear manifested itself through widespread discrimination. The Chinese Exclusion Act of 1882, a prime example of this prejudice, allowed no quota for Chinese to immigrate into this country. However, in 1943, that Act was abolished thereby making it possible for Chinese who had entered the country to become naturalized citizens.

The needs of the United States during World War II certainly brought about a significant change in the governmental attitude toward Chinese-Americans. Starting in 1940, they were drafted into the armed services. If Chinese draftees could not speak English, they would be sent to language school to learn. Since understanding English was a requirement for military service, Chinese soldiers would not be allowed to serve if they didn't speak the language. (Lim-Interview)

The Chinese-Americans wanted to fight on behalf of the United States in order to win the war and to ensure the survival of China. They served in combat, as interpreters, intelligence personnel, and in administrative and legal affairs. K. Scott Wong, in his book <u>Americans First: Chinese Americans and the Second World War</u>, writes that twelve to fifteen thousand Chinese-Americans served in World War II. Of particular note is the number of Chinese from New York City drafted into the war; forty percent of the city's population at that time. This "shaped the social position of Chinese-Americans."(Sampan website-2)

Iris Chang, in her book, <u>The Chinese in America,</u> reveals that "Unlike African-Americans and Japanese-Americans whom all branches of the military segregated from whites, the Chinese were partially integrated in the United States armed services." However, that integration was not without incident, objection, or prejudice.

There were definitely Chinese-American heroes of World War II. Among them, was the late Gordon P. Chung-Hoon who was born in Honolulu and attended the Naval Academy in 1934. He won the Navy Cross and Silver Star for gallantry and heroism. (Chang, p. 230). "To the men of our generation, World War II was the most important event of our times. We felt we could make it in American society." (Chang, quoting journalist Charles Leong, p. 227). " The war took them out of the ghettos and put them into uniform and sent them overseas where they became a part of patriotic America and went into combat against the enemy.(Id).

Dr. George Lim, served during World War II as a naval officer in the areas of naval aviation and legal affairs. After the war ended, he also served in Naval intelligence mainland China.

(Interview with George Lim, October 2, 2009).

* * * *

George Lim, whose parents immigrated to the United States from the Canton region of southern China, was born in the back of a Chinese laundry in Brooklyn, New York. After graduating from high school in June 1941, Lim enrolled in Brooklyn College. He was still a new freshman a few months later, when in December of that year the Japanese attacked Pearl Harbor. The following January, 1942, Lim attempted to enlist into the Navy in January of 1942. He was just sixteen years old. A Navy representative happened to be visiting Brooklyn College at that time regarding the Navy officer V-5 program. Because of his Chinese extraction he could only be a mess boy in the Navy and therefore not eligible for a commission as an officer. The Navy representative told him that policy may change, but in January, 1942, Lim was not eligible for an officer's commission

Later that same year, Lim applied to the Army Air Corps, which required a physical exam. Since he was still only seventeen then, he needed his father's permission. With 20-20 vision in one eye, but only 20-30 in the other, the Air Corps did not accept Lim. However, in 1943, the Navy V-12 and Army ASTP programs started up. Now a sophomore at Community College of New York enrolled in civil engineering, the Navy declared Lim an 'engineer.' Accepted into the V-12 program, the Navy sent Lim to engineering school at MIT at Cambridge, Massachusetts.

Lim was sworn into the Navy on December 15, 1943 and reported to MIT in March of 1944. The Navy V-12 program stated that an engineer is allowed eight college semesters and he already had two at Brooklyn College and three at CCNY. The MIT-run V-12 program was only three semesters. This would otherwise have ranked him as a junior, but when he arrived at MIT, Lim was considered only a sophomore. Within the next year, George Lim completed a specialty in aeronautical engineering.

Thereafter, in February of 1945, he was ordered to report to Cornell University for a 120-day Midshipman school. Lim graduated July 7, 1945 and was commissioned an ensign with the designator ALUSNR-Aeronautical Engineer. For this new position, Lim ordered a blue uniform and was surprised when told that he could have ordered a green uniform. It is interesting to note though, that the 'aviation green' uniform of Lim's time is no longer a required uniform for naval aviation officers of today.

Upon his ensign's commissioning, Lim went home on leave for two weeks. His new military address would be "FPO (Fleet Post Office) Pacific," but at the time, Lim did not know what his exact duty destination would be. Making his way from home to that region, Lim took a train from Brooklyn, that headed to upstate New York and, from there, traveled across the country to San Francisco. When he reached that city, Lim checked into an elegant hotel overlooking San Francisco bay used mainly by Navy personnel.

The comfort of that hotel would become a memory once Lim boarded the transport ship that would take him to Hawaii. That "baby aircraft carrier," as Lim described it, originally manufactured by Henry Kaiser, had been converted to a transport vessel. It had a liberty ship hull that was transfigured into an escort carrier which transported officers. "We were stacked five deep and I was the second form the top and could only have 60 second showers with treated sea water. [One...] night the smell of diesel oil made me sea sick [and] I had to go topside to the open deck and it was a beautiful August night on the way to Pearl Harbor in the Hawaiian Islands." (Lim Interview) That night Lim refers to was August 6, 1945, the date the U.S. had dropped the atomic bomb on Hiroshima.

...By the time that we pulled into Pearl Harbor there were flares and turned on searchlights. The second atomic bomb may have been dropped and the war was over I thought.

My first duty station was Kaneohe, Naval Air Station on the east side of Oahu at a CASU. I thought "What was that!?" It meant the Carrier Aircraft Service Unit, and I asked to explain my duties. I was told that I was an aeronautical engineer and would serve as a torpedo bomber officer. I said "tell me what I have to do" [Lim recounts with a laugh]." They said, "Don't worry –ask a Chief Petty Officer, he will tell you everything."

After being assigned to quarters, Lim went down to his duty station and asked what he had to do. It was explained to him that he was in a Carrier Aircraft Service Unit and every two to four weeks the unit gets two squadrons. In one squadron there are torpedo bombers and the other is made up of fighter planes.

The combat planes did come in and the pilots and crews got two weeks rest in town. We updated the planes [including] changes in the tail hook, navigation gear, the wings, or landing gear. By the time the planes [left CASU] they [were] updated for the latest specifications. In the meantime, while they [were] here, the pilots [had] night landing training; touch and go landings. They would come in one at a time- 18 planes in the air while 18 would land on the runway with a landing signal officer directing the touch and go landings. There were 18 fighters and 18 torpedo bombers. The landings would start about 8 o'clock and go to midnight... I thought 'that's terrific.' One night while I was out there they took off and only 17 planes landed. One was missing. No one saw him come in but the plane was down. They saw the pilot floating in the water with his life jacket and he was rescued. I was impressed with this wartime training. "I got to fly in the turret gunner's seats on TBM's on dive bombing and torpedo bombing missions.

I learned that I was probably the first Chinese-American midshipman to be commissioned in the Naval Reserves. But in Hawaii, I met a Chinese-American who had graduated in South Carolina and was a Navy Ensign. His name was George Chan and he had a direct commission. He had not gone to midshipman school. He wanted me to meet his family; [they were] Chinese-

Hawaiian. I went to meet [them] and everyone had black tie and tails [on.] Caviar and steak were served – a very well-to-do family... His father-in-law owned a meat packing business in Hawaii.

Within 60 days after I had arrived, CASU was decommissioned and I was put on a list of 150 officers [Lim was 149th] on the list to go home in October of 1945. So I went to Pearl Harbor and said that I would like to go to mainland China. I was told that I could go but not as an aeronautical engineer, but would be transferred to naval surface forces. I said OK and was assigned to CUB 19 [cub stands for baby lion; LION refers to a larger supply unit] in Tsingtao (Qingtao), China. At that time, it was a city of 100,000 and now it has a population of 7 million. My duty was to be a supply officer in the unit.

Lim was in Tsingtao from October 1945 to February 1946 as a supply officer. Assigned to living quarters with four other officers, in one building, Lim and the others were assigned a Chinese man as a houseboy.

We received some California oranges and the houseboy asked how they arrived in China. We said that they arrived by ship. The houseboy said he was not going to eat it but would take it to his family. He asked how could the Japanese defeat a country that was able to send an orange way across the ocean. He was very proud to meet Americans.

The author makes this side note about the creative use by the Chinese of the United Nations Ration Relief Aid supplies which the U.S. troops disseminated during the post-war relief effort there. Since the Chinese do not as a regular practice eat bread, they made beer from the UNRRA wheat. As for the tropical butter (which does not need refrigeration) sent by the U.N., the Chinese used that for axle grease. On this non-standard use of supplies, George Lim remarked that "relief aid needs to have a cultural sense."

Lim's LION supply unit would have been part of the invasion of Kyoto in November of 1945 if the atomic bombs had not suddenly ended the war. Supplies had arrived for the invasion. No longer needed for that purpose, a box of library books was now to be turned over to the Chinese Nationalists under the supervision of the U.S.Sixth Marine Division. "We were not allowed to leave the city and at night the marines were shooting at the Chinese communists that had surrounded the marines. The marines were holding the city, waiting for the Kuomintang (Nationalists) to arrive in the city." (Lim interview).

In 1946, CUB 19 was being disbanded. There was a one star Commodore there serving as SOPA (Senior Officer Present Afloat). "They wanted me to be their flag secretary to SOPA, but I was transferred to Shanghai for 12 months. I was the Officer-in-Charge of the security unit and our main job was guarding warehouses. There were many Chinese coolies working for the Navy. Movie projectors were missing and Washington. DC was concerned so we were contacted in China. Films were being shown with 16mm projectors and probably using those stolen from NOB (Naval Operating Base) in Shanghai," Lim recalled. Lim investigated the matter and successfully recovered the projectors. "A store operated by a white Russian had the missing movie projectors, Two persons were arrested. They had bought them from two sailors and both were later tried."

The summer of 1946, Lim was assigned to the Shanghai Naval Forces Legal Office. The Legal Office asked that Ensign Lim report one day in Chinese coolie clothes as a disguise for special duty that night to monitor a Chinese civilian bar. Lim was to be part of an investigation into a report that an American merchant seaman had reportedly assaulted a Chinese civilian.

Lim had the same assignment for two nights which led to his reassignment as Investigative Officer for the Legal Office in courts-martial and other disciplinary hearings. Another of his cases involved helping to prosecute Navy brig inmates for trying to overcome their guards. Such an act qualified for a general court-martial for the capital offense of mutiny. In considering this time, Lim recalls that "much of my wartime Navy experience was invaluable to my later capabilities as a practicing orthopedic surgeon, a military reservist, and as an activist in organized medicine through state and national orthopedic surgery and medical organizations such as the American Medical Association, and the Board of Directors of a medical liability insurance company."

> *...During the summer of 1946, I was able to visit my ancestral village near the city of Toishan in Kwangtung province in south China. I spoke the local dialect fluently and got to meet many Chinese relatives. I found my name in the local schoolhouse as a donor in 1927 to its new construction. I found that I still "owned a one family dwelling" as a direct descendant of my father, a former owner.*

While Lim was in Shanghai in 1946, his father in New York City died. Lim took a non-stop flight to San Francisco, but did not make it home to New York City it in time for the funeral. He then had to return to San Francisco to be discharged in 1947 before returning home again to New York. After his discharge, Lim returned to school at MIT. Though he was recalled to the service in 1950 during the Korean War, the Navy told him to stay in medical school and he became an orthopedic surgeon. In 1966 the Navy discharged him again. Lim then joined the Army Reserve where he completed an accumulated thirty years of military service. His final year was in the Army National Guard medical corps.

George Lim retired in 1991 as a Colonel. He now lives in New Hartford, New York with his wife Beverly.

50

Winfred Michel

USS CALLAWAY

Amphibious warfare ships included the large attack or assault transports, the APA's that carried troops, supplies, and equipment into the beachheads. Each APA, over 455 feet in length, carried 22 landing craft, many of which were LCVP's – Higgins boats.

Assault troops and members of the beach battalion would climb over the sides of the APA and then step carefully and apprehensively down the cargo net draped down the side of the transport. The book, The Beach Boys – A Narrative History of the First Beach Battalion, Major W.D. Vey, USMC, and Lieutenant Commander O. J. Elliot, described the hazards involved in the transfer of troops from the ship to the landing craft when Sicily was invaded in 1943.

...Going down the spaghetti-like cargo nets from the transport, the landing craft is rocking in the water and the frightened soldier is trying to get a firm hold on the boat with his feet. He waits for the boat to come back up on the next rise as he tries all over again to get his footing. Compounding the situation was the roll and pitch of the transport that terrorized the troops. Sometimes a soldier would be crushed between the transport ship and the landing craft as both, (ship and boat) gyrated in the churning seas (17).

Until 1967, the Coast Guard was part of the Treasury Department, but during World War II, it was under the jurisdiction of the Navy Department. As part of the Navy during the war years, the Coast Guard manned 802 cutters, 351 Navy ships and craft and 288 Army vessels. Almost 2,000 Coast Guardsmen died during the war, one-third of that number were killed in action (Scheina 1).

Coast Guardsmen manned many of the attack transports and one that participated in several battles in the Asiatic-Pacific Theater of Operations was the USS CALLAWAY (APA-35). Former Coast Guardsman, Winfred Michel, of Bainbridge and Waterville, New York served aboard the USS CALLAWAY and was one of four crewmembers assigned to an LCVP landing craft, which carried troops and supplies during several Pacific campaigns.

* * * *

Michel had attended Bainbridge Central School and worked on his cousin's farm and was seventeen years old when he decided to enlist into the Coast Guard on March 8, 1943. After completing his "boot camp" training at Manhattan Beach in Brooklyn, he was assigned to the navy attack transport, USS CALLAWAY (APA-35), on September 10, 1943.

According to the <u>Dictionary of American Naval Fighting Ships</u>, Volume 2, the CALLAWAY sailed to the Pacific Ocean. At San Diego, there was training with Marines to prepare for the first of five-assault landings (Mooney 16).

Seaman Michel, trained to operate a .30 caliber machine gun, was part of a four-man crew on board LCVP's that carried troops and supplies to the beachhead. He also was assigned as part of the beach battalion crew unloading and handling supplies. While aboard ship, he was assigned to the Deck division.

The CALLAWAY joined Task Force 53 in Hawaii and sailed to the Central Pacific. On January 31, 1944, still seventeen years old, Michel participated in the invasion of Kwajalein in the Marshall Islands. Going into the beach on a Higgins boat, he described it with one word – "terrible." After landing at Kwajalein, Michel became part of the shore party and took orders from the marines. He stayed there a few hours unloading supplies and standing guard duty before returning to his ship. Fortunately, Kwajalein was taken with only a few lives lost. More than 4,000 Japanese were killed. On March 20 they invaded Emirau Island.

"We had Carlson's Raiders on board a couple of times. Carlson had just brought back Japanese prisoners and was at a staff meeting on board the ship," Michel explained. Michel explained how he worked about 16-18 hours in the shore party and that Emirau Island was needed as a base for fighter planes.

Following the invasions of Kwajalein and Emirau Islands, the USS CALLAWAY participated in the invasion of Eniwetok atoll in the northwestern part of the Marshall Islands. Since Kwajalein had been conquered so easily, the Task Force Commander suggested (and received approval by Admiral Nimitz) for an immediate attack on Eniwetok (Richardson 142).

Michel's next campaign was the invasion of Saipan, June 15-24, 1944.

...We went into the beach again. My mother was watching the news of the day in a newsreel at the movies and she told someone in the family that she saw me in the newsreel. While on the beach at Saipan we had to dig in so I dug a foxhole. Four of us from our landing craft stayed there a couple of days. Our ship had pulled out and we found it later at a different anchorage.

Michel said he had spent his 18th birthday on one of the islands and said the average age of the crew was 22. The next campaign was the Southern Palau operation that took place between September 17-October 14, 1944.

Following Palau the ship returned to Manus and New Guinea to prepare for the Leyte landings in the Philippines, which took place October 22, 1944 and November 24, 1944, and the Lingayen landings of January 8 and 9, 1945. It was at Leyte that the ship was under heavy air attacks, and the CALLAWAY had to fight off enemy airplanes while unloading troops (Mooney 16).

Michel is mentioned in a Coast Guard public relations press release in 1944, where he describes how a Japanese plane at the Lingayen Gulf invasion hit his ship. "The bomb hit the Flying Bridge and we lost one-half of our power but we were still able to maintain 16-18 knots," Michel recalled. Twenty-three shipmates were killed but "the ship continued into Lingayen Gulf to unload the liberators of Manila during nineteen attack-ridden hours." The release goes on to say that "the ship received its first attack ten days before the invasion and the gunners succeeded in downing the lone Japanese raider. Attacks continued periodically during the slow journey to Lingayen and the fatalities occurred during a raid 24 hours before the beachhead was established." Michel said he watched a dogfight between some Navy Hellcats and three Japanese Zeros. Sadly, Michel described the Callaway being struck by a bomb.

> *…The day before we hit Luzon a Japanese plane swooped in from astern and dropped a bomb that missed by only 60 feet. The pilot strafed our port side, swung across the bow and came back for another try. By this time we were throwing a lot of lead at him. After a few seconds we took the hit. It was pretty awful. It was the first time any of our boys had been killed even though our ship had been through six other invasions. The gun crews did a great job. They stuck in there and they got him, too.*

Tearfully, Michel recalled how they buried 23 at sea the first night, and transferred several others to a hospital ship. One crewmember, who was on fire, had jumped overboard and was picked up by a destroyer,. He was sent back to our ship by breeches buoy set up between our ship and the 'tin can'.

The <u>Dictionary of American fighting Ships</u>, records the following about the suicide plane hit:

> *…. As the invasion force sailed north for the Lingayen assault, desperate Japanese kamikaze attacks were launched in a determined effort to break up the landings, and on January 8,*

1945, a suicide plane broke through heavy antiaircraft fire to crash on the starboard wing of CALLAWAY'S Bridge. Cool and skillful work against resulting fires kept material damage to a minimum, but 29 of CALLAWAY's crew were killed and 22 wounded. Temporary repairs at Ulithi put her back in action by early February, when she carried Marine reinforcements from Guam to Iwo Jima, and wounded back from Iwo Jima to Guam, arriving on 8 March (Mooney 17).

Michel's public relations release goes on as follows: "We got into the Gulf the next morning (January 9) at Blue Beach and we were busy unloading for nineteen hours. There were some raids and hits on other ships, but we were busy and did not pay much attention. We had three more raids as we left the Gulf. It was a busy day," Michel concluded.

The public relations release concluded by pointing out that the USS CALLAWAY was in every major Pacific invasion of 1944. The Coast Guard vessel carried an U.S. Navy flagstaff and some of the casualties were Navy personnel.

From January 31, 1944 to March 5, 1945, Michel participated in the following battles or operations: Marshall Islands, Emirau Island, Eniwetok, Saipan, the Palau Islands, Leyte, and Lingayen Gulf in the Philippine Islands, and Iwo Jima.

Michel's last invasion was Iwo Jima, the next to the last major battle of World War II. "I didn't get off the ship at Iwo Jima. A 'Big Bertha' shell did get close to our ship one day. We changed anchorage and didn't get ashore at Iwo."

On the long voyage home across the Pacific, his ship reached San Francisco on June 16, 1945. For the sailors, anxious to get home, experienced a great feeling as the ship passed under the Golden Gate Bridge. He was home on leave when, on August 14, the Japanese had surrendered. The USS CALLAWAY returned to Pearl Harbor and loaded occupation troops and then sailed to disembark them in Japan. Two more trips across the Pacific were made carrying troops back home in late 1945 and 1946.

Michel also has a letter dated November 10, 1950 from the Commandant of the Coast Guard. It stated that the USS CALLAWAY had been awarded the Navy Unit Commendation "for exceptionally meritorious service in action against enemy Japanese aircraft, submarines and mines in the Pacific Campaign." The letter listed the various operations in which the Callaway had participated – from Kwajalein to Iwo Jima. Michel had participated in nine operations and had been awarded seven battle stars.

Seaman First Class Winfred Michel was discharged on March 16, 1946 and returned home to Bainbridge, New York. Married to the author's sister, Nancy, he moved to Waterville, where he became employed as a railroad trackman and then to Oswego, New York to accept a position as section foreman.

After retirement from railroad work, he moved to Florida. He passed away April 30, 2007.

51

Fred Moon

NAVY MEDIC

War always necessitates the extreme need for medical personnel. During World War II thousands of doctors were drafted and many nurses volunteered to join the Army and Navy. To assist these professional medical personnel, enlisted personnel were trained as medical corpsmen. In the Navy, these enlisted men were referred to as, hospital corpsmen, pharmacist mates, and as "Doc.". Today they are known as hospital corpsmen. The U.S. Navy Hospital Corps, the only enlisted corps in the Navy, was established in 1898. More than one-half of all Navy enlisted personnel who have been awarded the Medal of Honor are hospital corpsmen (Kahler 1).

Whether army or navy, they came to be known as - the medics. Since the Marine Corps comes under the authority and jurisdiction of the Department of the Navy, navy medics were not only assigned to hospitals ashore, to submarines, auxiliary ships and warships, and hospital ships, but also assigned to the Fleet Marine Force to serve marine corps personnel during battle campaigns ashore. Smaller vessels had no doctors assigned and no female nurses served aboard naval vessels (other than hospital ships) during World War II. On these smaller vessels, the only medical personnel assigned were the enlisted hospital men or pharmacist mates. On every battlefront in every far-flung theater of operations, and on every naval vessel, these dedicated medical corpsmen have cared for the sick, the injured and those wounded in battle. Much has been written of their brave exploits.

* * * *

Fred Moon of Waterville was a Navy medic who served in military hospitals and also saw duty in the Pacific on board an attack transport.

Before enlisting into the Navy in 1943, seventeen-year-old Fred Moon lived in the village of Oriskany Falls, which is located four miles from Waterville, where he presently lives. Moon was one of many central New York enlistees who did their "boot" or basic training at the Sampson Naval Training Center in the Finger Lakes region of New York State.

Moon's first duty station after "boot camp" was at the Brooklyn Naval Hospital. Next, he attended medical corpsman school at St. Albans Hospital in Maryland and was then transferred to Lido Beach, Long Island and assigned to SNAG (Special Naval Assignment Group) and waited for shipment overseas.

In January of 1944, Moon boarded the English ship HMS AQUATANIA with 350-hospital corpsmen, 100 nurses, and fifty doctors for the voyage across the Atlantic. One section of the AQUATANIA ballroom was set aside for the hospital and Moon stated that on the trip only fifty minutes a day were allowed for outside exercise. He said that during one of the fifty-minute exercise periods, he noticed a German reconnaissance plane flying over the ship taking pictures. "On board the AQUATANIA, we ate breakfast at noon and dinner at midnight. And, we also ate a lot of lamb stew," he added.

It took five days to cross the Atlantic and then the AQUATANIA docked at Glasgow, Scotland. He then traveled to Netley, a small town located near Southhampton, England.

Moon was assigned to the Queen Victoria hospital, which was located in Netley, England. Queen Victoria had once resided in the building before it had been converted into a hospital. Built in 1856, for the wounded of the Crimean war, it was known as the Great Military Hospital. The work of the famous nurse, Florence Nightingale, influenced Queen Victoria to have this building made into a hospital. The wounded from the battle of Normandy would be brought into the hospital for treatment. Moon said that the hospital was over one-fourth of a mile long and three stories high with 100 wards. There were over 400 medical corpsmen, 50 doctors, and about 10 nurses at the hospital.

During his stay in England, Moon said that a practice invasion landing took place in April 1944. Few people knew that this occurred until a few years ago. These practices were designed as a rehearsal for the landing on Utah beach scheduled for June 6, 1944 and the exercise was to invade a beach at Slapton Sands in England. Several amphibious ships that were packed with thousands of soldiers participated. The rehearsal, which came to be known by the code name "Exercise Tiger," turned out to be a disaster where, some claim, cost the lives of about 1,000 personnel. The practice evolved into actual combat in the English Channel when fast German E-boats, (PT boats) sank or damaged several of the invading amphibious vessels, that were used in the mock invasion. The official figure that was later released was that 749 American lives were lost. Moon stated that many wounded from this disaster were brought to his hospital to be treated. He and others were told that this was to remain a secret and if any of them talked about this incident they would be tried for treason and shot.*

Two months after Normandy, Moon boarded a Coast Guard vessel for the

* See chapter on Steven Sadlon entitled "Exercise Tiger."

USA. Upon arrival in the USA, he traveled by train for San Diego, California, where he was assigned to the USS BLADEN (APA-63), an attack transport, which carried troops for amphibious landings.

The BLADEN headed out over the Pacific (usually smoother than the Atlantic), for Hawaii and then to Saipan, located in the Marianas, for maneuvers. This was preparation for the invasion of Iwo Jima scheduled for February 1945.

During the Iwo Jima invasion, the wounded were brought aboard the BLADEN. The hospital ward was set up behind the officer's wardroom and during the invasions emergency stations for the wounded were set up in the mess hall. "One time when the doctors gave us a break from working on the wounded, I went outside the hospital area with binoculars in hand. Using the binoculars, I happened to see the raising of the flag on Mount Suribachi. I went back inside and said, 'they must have taken the island - they're raising the flag.'" Little did Moon realize on that day in February that he had just witnessed (from a distance) - a scene, which would become one of the most memorable in world history.

The next invasion for the USS BLADEN was Okinawa, the last battle of World War II. This took place on April 1, 1945. Moon said that the BLADEN was engaged in a mock attempt to invade the island to deceive the Japanese. "We went through the movements to attack by going almost to the shore and then we backed up. The actual invasion took place on the opposite side of the location of our ship. Since it was the first of April, we called it an April fool's joke," Moon explained.

After the third day of the battle, the ship backed up and dropped the troops from landing craft. Moon related the following:

> *...A Japanese suicide submarine missed the bow of our ship and struck the ship next to ours. We were there for two more days and then took some of the wounded back to Guam. On our way we got into the fierce 1945 typhoon and things were really rough as we sailed through high waves. A magazine type rack on the wall in the sick bay held glass bottles, which were smashed into pieces because of the rough sea. Tincture of Violet was spilled and it was very tough to clean up.*

Moon displayed a magazine rack in his barbershop that his son made for him in shop class. It is almost an exact duplicate of the rack, which contained the chemicals and medicines on board his ship.

"We were on our way to Seattle to pick up troops to transport to the Pacific islands in preparation for the invasion of Japan. On the way to Seattle, we heard of the dropping of the atomic bomb on Hiroshima," he recalled. Since the war ended within a few days, Moon's ship was ordered to deliver these troops to Osaka, Japan.

Moon arrived in San Francisco in November of 1945. "As we entered San Francisco Bay, we were happy to see a large banner strung up at Alcatraz Island which read 'Welcome Home, Boys.'"

The war was over and Hospitalman First Class Moon was discharged from Lido Beach, Long Island in 1946.

After he was discharged, he turned down an opportunity to become a nurse and worked in the Utica Knitting Mill and at Sherill Community Plate before becoming a barber.

Semi-retired, he lives in Waterville.

52

Francis Moyer

USS ASTORIA (CL-90)

The USS ASTORIA (CL-90) was 610 feet long and her speed was 31.6 knots. The ship was commissioned in Philadelphia on May 17, 1944. Her mission was to bombard the shore prior to invasions and provide support for the carriers while their planes supported troop landings. (Mooney 439).

Seaman First Class Francis C. Moyer served on board the ASTORIA and since he passed away in 1992, the following account is based on an interview with his widow, Bertha Moyer of Vernon, New York, and his personal journal from May 1944 to April 23, 1945, and an April 12, 1945 letter written to his mother, Clara Moyer. Moyer served in the Pacific Theater of Operations and was awarded six battle stars.

****

Moyer was born in Albany, New York and had lived in Canajoharie and Yorkville. He attended Whitesboro Central School before enlisting February 22, 1944 into the Navy. After "boot camp" training at Sampson Naval Training Center and further duty at the Newport Naval Training Center, Newport, Rhode Island, he boarded the ASTORIA in Philadelphia.

On June 6, 1944, the ship left for the Caribbean on a shakedown cruise and then returned to Philadelphia.

In September of 1944, the light cruiser was on the way to war in the Pacific. The warship traveled through the Panama Canal and sailed on to Pearl Harbor. Moyer noted in his diary on October 31 – "From there we were drilled until we couldn't stand it any longer. We had contact with enemy aircraft twice." The ship arrived at Ulithi Island in November.

Moyer noted in his journal that on the 27th of November the ASTORIA left Ulithi and the next day formed Task Force 38 of the Third Fleet, a carrier task force under the command of Admiral William "Bull" Halsey. The carrier task force was made up of four battleships, two AA cruisers, 44 destroyers, and 14 carriers, eight light cruisers, and four heavy cruisers." The task force was headed for Luzon in the Philippine Islands and took part in the invasion of Luzon.

Moyer's journal further stated, "We had to bombard airfields. Three days of bombardment destroyed 750 Japanese planes as opposed to 50-75 American planes lost."

Returning to Ulithi around December 16-17, the task force encountered a typhoon. "No one was allowed to go topside since nine or ten men had been lost off the side. We had drifted 150 miles off course during the storm. Three destroyers were lost and we later picked up survivors," he noted in his journal.

In other campaigns prior to the invasion of Iwo Jima, Moyer's journal includes the following:

On December 30, 1944, the ASTORIA left Ulithi with a smaller task force of 34 ships –29 destroyers, six carriers, two battleships, and six cruisers. On New Years Eve "We are about to go into battle so the Captain comes up with the bright idea of 'Holy Stoning' the quarterdeck."(Scrubbing and cleaning the teakwood deck with pumice stone).

On New Years Day 1945, the ASTORIA combined with another task force. "The Commander of the 3rd Fleet said that 'we had a good old year' and wished the Fleet a Happy New Year and added –'keep the bastards dying.' Moyer's diary also noted that on January 3, 1945 they were 60 miles off Formosa and carrier planes were launched to bomb Formosa and on the return trip, a convoy of Japanese vessels were attacked and several cargo ships were sunk. On January 4, the task force shot down three enemy planes and entered a minefield. "The Japanese had tried several times to sink us but have failed."

"On January 5, we are 80 miles off Luzon and carrier planes are bombing Luzon." Throughout January, the crew is often on alert off the Philippines and in the China Sea.

" On January 15, carrier planes are bombing Hong Kong and on January 18 weather conditions are bad and the ship is pitching and rolling like hell. So far we've hit about 30^0 rolls," Moyer's diary notes.

On February 3 Moyer wrote that the crew stood Captain's inspection. "He told us that the next time we leave Ulithi that 'we were going right up and look into Jap's eyes.' The ship got underway again on February 10. Scuttlebutt said that we were going to volcanic islands south of Japan."

On February 16, the ASTORIA was 78 miles off Japan and the carriers launched 2,000 planes to bomb Tokyo. Moyer's journal described the sinking of some Japanese picket boats.

…Our destroyers sunk two picket boats just ahead of us. I saw one blow up – what a sight! One of the destroyers picked up eight Jap survivors and put them on the BUNKER HILL. Later, two more

picket boats were sunk and three Japanese survivors were picked up. One 17-year-old Japanese survivor said he thought we were the Japanese fleet. He never thought the Americans could get this close to their homeland. I saw a few of the Japs that were killed aboard the picket boats float by our ship – they were not very pleasant to look at (one's head was blown clear off).

Moyer noted that on February 19, the invasion of Iwo Jima had commenced.

...We are to protect the carrier planes while they go in and soften up the shore batteries. By 1020, our forces had advanced 200 yards. Our planes are landing within 300 feet of our troops so to weaken the Jap strongholds. On February 20 I got a letter from my mother. We are bombarding the island. I have had no sleep for 24 hours."

Almost two months after the Iwo Jima battle began, Seaman First Class Moyer wrote home to his mother describing this bombardment. Portions of this letter, which was dated April 12, 1945, are quoted below:

Dear Honey,
Permission has been granted that we may write you a little about our part in the campaign for Iwo Jima. We were for two days participating in the naval bombardment of the island. It was a sight never to be forgotten... All of our ship's bombardment was done just off of Mt. Surabachi on the western side of the island. It is said that this volcanic rock received a greater concentration of ship, troop, and plane bombardment per square inch than any other area in the history of warfare; even after this great concentration of fire, at night from the deck of our ship, this area seemed to be dotted with flashes from Jap machine gun fire. They were really dug in deep. Pillboxes, caves and revetments seemed to be everyplace...

On February 27, Moyer recorded the following in his journal:

...Tom Cardinal, a buddie of mine from Herkimer, and I were talking over the good old times we've had in the good old Mohawk Valley. It makes you homesick as all hell to talk about the things that are thousands of miles away. Everyday scuttlebutt gets

around of when we're going back to the States. None of it's the actual dope but it makes you feel good to think that one of those great days you will be flying the homeward bound pennant...

Moyer's account describes a navy plane crashing near his cruiser on March 1, 1945.

...Not much doing today. All we did was lay around topside. We were watching the carrier planes land on the ESSEX when one of the planes had to make a crash landing in the water. Boy, when those babies come down they really make a splash. The pilot was thrown clear of the plane and was picked up later.

On March 19, the crew is awakened at 0330 for GQ (battle stations), which lasted all day, and two Japanese planes were shot down. Moyer describes the USS FRANKLIN, a famous aircraft carrier of World War II being hit. He said that it took a 500-pound bomb in the superstructure and came down in the engine room before it exploded. He noted that the crew abandoned ship and destroyers picked up most of the crew.

The <u>Dictionary of American Fighting Ships</u>, Volume 2, notes that a single plane dropped two bombs that struck the FRANKLIN, one struck the flight deck at centerline and the second hit aft. Seven hundred and twenty-four were killed and 265 were wounded. Many of the crew was blown overboard when hit by the bombs. One hundred and six officers and 604 enlisted volunteered to stay aboard and did manage to save the ship. A chaplain, Joseph T. O'Callahan, USNR, was awarded the Medal of Honor for his heroic acts in organizing and directing fire and rescue parties (Mooney 443-444).

On April 1, the Okinawa invasion began and on the 6th, the ASTORIA attacked three times during the day and the gunners were able to shoot down one enemy plane. On April 12, Moyer noted that the Captain announced that President Roosevelt had died. "Quite a shock to everyone." His last entry in his personal diary was dated April 23, 1945. "Rigged for fueling, starboard side. Expect to re-provision and rearm today."

On V-J Day, August 14, the ASTORIA was patrolling off Honshu, the main island of Japan with Task Force 58. On September 3 she was ordered back to the States and arrived at San Pedro, CA.

Seaman First Class Francis C. Moyer and the USS ASTORIA were awarded six battle stars - five for Asiatic-Pacific campaigns and one for the Philippine Liberation.

He was discharged from the Navy on May 4, 1946 and returned home, residing in Clarks Mills and Vernon. He worked as a trucker and retired in 1987.

He passed away March 11, 1992.

53

William Northrop

USS WASP

Since three aircraft carriers of the U.S. Pacific fleet were away from Pearl Harbor on December, 1941, this made it possible, within six months, to launch a successful offensive against the Japanese. The carriers, floating airfields, are nicknamed "flattops" because of the flat wide decks. They became the most vital ships during the war. The carriers travel into battle escorted by cruisers and destroyers and the group is referred to as a "carrier task force." The aircraft carrier has a flight deck with an island structure, a hangar deck, various repair shops, as well as living quarters. Aircraft Carriers today, such as the USS ENTERPRISE, are over a thousand feet in length and carry a crew and carrier air group, which together number over 5,000 men and women. During World War II, carriers had over 2,500 men aboard including the air group.

Carrier planes took part in all of the major battles of the Pacific Theater of Operations during World War II and one of the more famous carriers was the 872 foot USS WASP (CV 18)- "The Stinger." Since the American Revolution there have been ten WASPS. The eighth WASP was sunk in the Battle of the Coral Sea in 1942. The ninth WASP, - "The Stinger," was of the Essex class and was commissioned in November of 1943 and would forge a blazing page in the annals of naval warfare (Mooney, vol. 8, 148). The USS WASP participated in eight battles in the Pacific; survived 30-suicide plane attacks, and was at the Battle of Leyte Gulf when the Japanese initiated its first Kamikaze attack. A few days before World War II ended, the WASP was given credit for shooting down the last of the Kamikaze planes (Newton and Morris 2).

One of the WASP's crewmembers, William Northrop, graduated from Waterville Central School in 1943 and performed all of his wartime duty aboard "the Stinger." In about a year after finishing high school, his ship would be engaged in one of the greatest air battles in history — the Battle of the Philippine Sea in the Western Pacific.

* * * *

It was the summer of 1943; Northrop left Waterville for several weeks of training at the Sampson Naval Training Center. He was eighteen when he enlisted on June 28, 1943.

After "boot camp", Northrop was assigned to the WASP. The keel had been laid in Quincy, Massachusetts in March of 1942 and it was to be named the ORISKANY. It was renamed the WASP and commissioned in Boston where Northrop boarded the ship. Eleanor Roosevelt was the sponsor.

There were 2600 personnel on board, which included the air group, an F6F Grumman fighter squadron, a TBM -Torpedo Bomber Squadron (George Bush was in a TBM squadron), and an SB2C Dive-Bomber squadron).

After a shakedown cruise to South America, the WASP returned to Boston and by April was in Hawaii. Following training exercises, the ship sailed to the Marshall Islands and became part of Task Group 58.6, attached to Admiral Marc Mitcher's Fast Carrier Task Force. The ship participated in air strikes on Marcus and Wake Islands (Mooney 149).

The Japanese were fighting desperately to save their vast Pacific Empire. The WASP's assignment was to help capture and occupy Saipan, Tinian, and Guam. In June, the WASP was engaged in its first battle, the Battle of the Philippine Sea. The ship's location was west of Guam and off the coast of Saipan. The Task Force was protecting the Mariana's landings. Northrop said that a "Turkey Shoot" took place in the Marianas.. Carrier aircraft met the Japanese in aerial dogfights and so many enemy planes were shot down that one pilot called it a "Turkey Shoot" and since then it has been referred to as the "Marianas Turkey Shoot." The date was June 19, 1945.

> *...I remember that day. The ships were being bombed and strafed by Japanese planes. We shot down so many planes and the WASP shot down six. My General Quarters (Battle) station was Pointer on a 40mm located on the island structure. A pointer is a sight setter, separate from the 40mm gun but controls the actual mount. The main job is to keep a lead on the attacking plane.*

Task Force 58 destroyed over 400 Japanese planes over the two-day period. Following the "Turkey Shoot" (The Battle of the Philippine Sea), there were air strikes on Iwo Jima in July. From Iwo Jima, the WASP went on to Guam and Palau to meet other units in preparation for the September 15 invasion of the Palau Islands (Mooney 149, 151).

In September, the Third Fleet struck Mindanao and the Visayas (a group of islands in the central part of the Philippines). The planes were launched from pitching and rolling decks of the ships in very heavy seas. The gunners of the ship were given much credit for holding off the Japanese planes. One

American pilot said it looked as if the WASP were "ringed with fire" and said that he would not want to attack it (Newton and Morris 1).

The next major battle for the WASP was the Battle of Leyte Gulf in October of 1944. The Third Fleet led by Admiral William Halsey included Task Force 38, the Fast Carrier Force led by Vice Admiral Marc Mitscher also included Task Force One (TG38.1) commanded by Vice Admiral John S. McCain. His flagship was the WASP and Northrop pointed out that McCain was the grandfather of Senator John McCain of Arizona and LT John Roosevelt, the president's son, was also a Supply Officer on the WASP.

Northrop said that the WASP was to support General MacArthur's troops that were invading Leyte in the Philippines on October 20 and to launch air attacks against the Japanese ships.

The Japanese had become more desperate after the disastrous loss of over 400 of their planes and of their losses of surface vessels and troops. Almost every night there were enemy attacks on the WASP. The Battle of Leyte Gulf saw the first of the Kamikaze or suicide pilots, which were attacking the ships. "It was a whole different war when they came in," Northrop declared.

In October and November, the WASP proceeded to the Luzon and Lingayen Gulf area where several air strikes were made against Luzon. Air strikes were also made on Formosa and Okinawa.

In December, off the Philippines, a devastating and very powerful Typhoon Cobra with winds up to 100 miles per hour created a nightmare experience for the Third Fleet. Northrop said that the seas were very heavy and the WASP, as part of Task Force 38, was refueling destroyers and had to cast off. He said that three destroyers had sunk and that there were only five survivors. He said that they rolled over so far that the stacks took in water and they couldn't steam and they capsized. The destroyers were the HULL, SPENCE, and MONAGHAN (Miller 887).

Following the typhoon, the WASP carrier planes hit Formosa, the Ryukus and the China coast in early January of 1945. They also raided the Tokyo Bay area and Northrop said Indo-China was also hit with air strikes (Mooney 151).

The next campaign was Iwo Jima and Northrop stated that there were several air strikes made on Iwo supporting the invading forces, which landed on February 20, 1945. He said the WASP was under heavy attack by the Japanese in their effort to sink the carriers. There were many Kamikaze attacks made on the ship as the bloody battle on the island was taking place. The Air Group made more raids on Japan. After Iwo Jima, the WASP went to Ulithi Island for refueling, re-arming and some rest and recreation (R&R).

With sadness in his voice, Northrop described a suicide plane that dropped a 500-pound bomb on the WASP. On 19 March 1945 while traveling north to launch air strikes against Kyushu and Honshu in Japan, a suicide plane made a direct hit on the ship. He showed me the book entitled "The Wasp" (history of the WASP) which included pictures showing the hole caused by the bomb going through the flight deck. "The bomb went through the flight deck, the hangar deck below, and fell between the second and third decks and it blew out the galley and laundry," he described. One hundred and three died and 300 were wounded. The bomb caused considerable damage to the ship but the air strikes continued after the fires were extinguished. Northrop said sometimes the suicide pilot, in an effort to hit more than one ship, would drop a bomb on one ship and then attempt to crash directly into another. "We were attacked many times by suicide planes since they were first used at Leyte Gulf. I can't even remember the number of times –maybe 30," he mentioned, as his expressions suggested, that this was a block of time that he would prefer not to remember or discuss.

The Kamikaze pilot was doomed to die whether he crashed into the ship or the sea (Miller 923). Admiral Mitcher had said, "One thing is certain; there are no experienced Kamikaze pilots"(QTD. in Miller 923).

Northrop described the incident which killed over 100 of his shipmates. He pointed to an "In Memoriam" page in the book about his ship's history, The Wasp, which listed those crewmembers who died as a result of the bomb. At the bottom of the page the author noticed the words of the beautiful "Navy Hymn"- taken from the poem- "Eternal Father, Strong to Save," written by William Whiting in 1860 and found in many hymnal books (Ferris and Wheeler)

"The middle of March was considered the busiest week in flattop history. In seven days fourteen planes were shot down, a Japanese battleship and other ships were hit, the WASP was under constant attack by enemy planes from shore and the WASP's guns fired 10,000 rounds of ammunition."(Newton and Morris 2).

The next major battle began on April 1, 1945, the battle of Okinawa. More Kamikaze attacks took place and the carrier air group made strikes on Okinawa.

Following Okinawa, the WASP returned to the United States to the Puget Sound Navy Yard at Bremerton, Washington for repairs. By July 11, it was back in the forward areas after a stop at Pearl Harbor. The "Stinger" joined the Third Fleet and the Task Force led by Vice Admiral John S. McCain. The ship made an attack on Yokosuka Naval Base near Tokyo.

What would be considered the last Kamikaze plane of the War attacked the WASP on August 9. A Hellcat pilot crippled the plane, which then headed for the ship. Gunners on the ship hit it and on its way down missed the ship but some debris landed on the flight deck. On August 15, two Japanese attacked after the cease-fire but were shot down. "The last planes to be shot down on the day which the "Cease-firing" order was given" (Newton and Morris 2).

The WASP was hit by another typhoon on August 25 and battled gusts that hit 78 knots. Northrop showed a picture of the ship's damage - 30' of her forward light deck had been pushed in from the force of the waves. The planes had to be launched off a short deck.

On August 27, 1945, Halsey's Third Fleet went into Japan for the occupation of the big Japanese Naval Base at Yokosuka. The WASP was also in on many mercy missions carrying food and medicine to prisoners of war (Newton and Morris 2).

Northrop said that the WASP returned to Boston on Navy Day, October 27, 1945. Her next mission was temporary duty as part of "Operation Magic Carpet," where she was to be used as a troop transport. In Brooklyn Naval Shipyard, changes were made, to berth 5,500 enlisted troops and 400 officers to be transported back from Europe in November 1945. "We ran into another storm in the Atlantic," Northrop recalled.

First Class Petty Officer Northrop went home to Waterville for a visit but he decided to stay in the Navy. There were jobs in the knitting mill in Sherburne, New York but that did not interest him so he re-enlisted and continued to serve aboard the WASP until February 1947. He said that his wife, ever loyal to the Navy, wanted him to make the service a career.

As a yeoman, Northrop's professional duties while he was in the Navy were administrative. He said his happiest time was when he became a Chief Petty Officer. He was eventually promoted to Chief Warrant Officer 3(CWO3), a commissioned officer. His duty stations included much more sea duty aboard a destroyer tender, USS HAMEL; several destroyers; and another aircraft carrier, USS TARAWA, where he served as the Personnel Officer.

Other duty stations included the USS JOSEPH P.KENNEDY, JR., Chief Yeoman to the Naval Attaché in Paris, France, Personnel Officer at the Officer Candidate School in Newport, Rhode Island; Administrative Officer in London, England and Bremerhaven, Germany; and Order Writing Officer at the Naval Training Center at Bainbridge, Maryland.

In 1969, after 26 years in the Navy, and after traveling to 25 countries, he retired at Bainbridge.

Chief Warrant Officer 3 Northrop earned 15 medals and he said that he is most proud of the Asiatic-Pacific medal with eight battle stars. He earned an additional battle star while aboard the destroyer KENNEDY during the Korean War.

When asked to describe some of his feelings while in combat and while he was in the Navy, Northrop replied:

...There was no place to run. I wasn't scared at the time. We just wanted to get the enemy planes shot down. Afterwards, we realized what had just happened and we would be shook up. We all became like a family and in later years we rarely discussed it, since all of us had a friend who had lost his life.

After retiring from the Navy, Northrop moved to North East, Maryland and worked for several years in Elkton, for the Philadelphia Electric Power Company.

He passed away September 20, 2004.

54

Robert Pierson

NAVY ARMED GUARD

Most of the ships of the Merchant Marine fleet are privately owned and are normally manned by civilians. The fleet is made up of cargo and passenger vessels and bears the label S.S. before the ship's name on the bow. Navy ships bear the label U.S.S. before the ship's name or numeral.

During World War II the government had the power to lease privately owned merchant ships to carry troops and supplies. These merchant ships included the Liberty ships, more than half, constructed by the late industrialist, Henry J. Kaiser. Enemy submarines sank about 200 Liberty ships that were transporting men and materiel. Victory ships later supplemented the Liberty class (Merchant 1).

In the book Sailing on Friday, John A. Butler points out that 6,380 merchant seamen lost their lives between December 7, 1941 and August 14, 1945. Eleven thousand were wounded and 604 were taken prisoner. He further stated, "The American Merchant Marine suffered a greater percentage of war related deaths than the sum of the nation's military forces (193).

According to the Merchant Marine Shipping Administration, U. S. Merchant Marine, 1,554 merchant ships were sunk in wartime conditions during World War II. Seven hundred and thirty-three were over 1,000 gross tons (Merchant Marine Website).

The Navy implemented the convoy system (also used in World War I), which permitted more merchant vessels to complete their mission without being torpedoed by enemy submarines. Warships such as the destroyer escort and escort aircraft carriers were built especially for the purpose of providing protection to ships in convoy carrying troops and supplies.

An example of the consequences of merchant ships not staying together in convoy to their destination is Convoy PQ-17. This was a merchant ship convoy that left in June1942 from Iceland and bound for the North Russian port of Archangel. Fearful of an attack by Germany's new battleship, the Tirpitz, which had been reported in the area, the convoy was forced to disperse to reduce losses if the "Tirpitz" attacked. The Tirpitz never appeared but the scattered ships became easy targets for the enemy bombers and submarines. Over seventy-five per cent of all of the U.S. merchant ships were lost in this convoy alone and it was World War II's worst convoy disaster (Convoy 1).

Robert Pierson of North Brookfield and Waterville, New York served aboard two merchant ships during World War II as a member of the Navy armed guard, which provided merchant ships some defense capability at sea.

* * * *

Following graduation from high school, Pierson left the farm and joined the Navy on June 24, 1943. He completed six weeks of "boot camp" at Sampson Naval Training Center. At Sampson, Pierson recalled, "I learned the 'Navy Way' and how to say 'Yes Sir and No, Sir.' I didn't know anything about the sea. I was a farm boy accustomed only to grass and I couldn't swim. In "boot camp", he was made to jump from fifteen feet into ten feet of water and an instructor would extend a long pole from the side of the pool. He was then told to swim and not grab the pole. The pole would go down and back up and the instructor would not allow him to grab the pole. "I said to hell with that and made it to the side of the pool and was really scared, mad, and ready to fight."

Following "boot camp", he had four weeks of gunnery school at Camp Shelton, Virginia. He was then assigned, as a member of the Armed Guard to serve as a gunner and his first ship assignment was the S.S. WOODROW WILSON. He was one of 27 gunners, which made up the armed guard of the ship, which carried a crew of 87 merchant mariners.

One of 2,800 Liberty ships manufactured during World War II, the S.S. WILSON could carry 11,000 tons of war cargo – the equivalent of three hundred railroad cars (Prados 9).

Pierson mentioned that on his first trip there were 132 ships in the convoy. Destroyer Escorts and escort carriers were in the convoy to protect the merchant ships. And, on this first trip across the Atlantic, Pierson related, he had no life jacket available and he couldn't swim (not all sailors can swim). There were five cargo holds filled with ammunition, food, and general supplies. "We were headed to England and North Africa and the trip was rough and made much rougher when we had zigzag drills." (The zigzag maneuver involved short sharp turns to avoid being torpedoed by submarines.)

His ship traveled in convoy completing six trips across the Atlantic bound for various ports in the British Isles and France. The convoy often followed the northern route in the sub-arctic area to avoid submarines and it took 21 days to cross the ocean. "On the northern route we had to secure the watches on the bow, since everything froze up. We weren't able to walk the catwalk to the bow so we had to stand our watches amidships. We saw icebergs and had to wear our foul weather gear and I also remember being seasick the first three days of the trip," Pierson described.

On one trip across the Atlantic to Europe, German aircraft had sunk two of the ships in convoy. "We had General Quarters (battle stations) drills morning and night and stations would be manned whenever German aircraft appeared. We had eight 20mm guns on the Bridge, four 50mm guns on the stern and three 50mm guns on the bow," Pierson said.

Seaman Pierson arrived at Normandy in June 1944 nine days after D-Day. Cargo was unloaded at Royal Albert Dock, London, Normandy, and Cherbourg. They made shuttle runs from England to France and there were some aerial attacks by the Germans off the beachhead and the ship could not get to the docks. "We were firing at mines that the Germans had dropped in the area. We would fire at the mines with rifles to make them explode. We did see considerable action in France and I did receive two battle stars, he described." While in Europe, Pierson said that he also had the opportunity to visit Cardiff, Wales, and Scotland.

His ship was rammed twice. The first time was when his ship was approaching England. "Another ship hit us on the port side and the gun tub was damaged but there were no injuries. This put us in dry dock for repairs," he said. "In New York, we were hit again and this time the damage was below decks, so we loaded up with ballast to prevent tipping and took off across the Atlantic."

On board ship the armed guard stood a 24-hour watch looking for subs and torpedoes. The merchant marine crew ran the ship and had the mess men do the cooking. "They waited on us and we ate off plates rather than metal trays (used in enlisted mess in Navy). We were served two kinds of meat every day. During action, we had sandwiches and always lots of coffee. There was a separate mess for the merchant marine and the navy personnel and we got along well," Pierson related. When asked why he had to change ships after 17 months, Pierson stated that the reason was to prevent familiarity. After the seventeen months on board the WILSON, he had 30 days leave and went home.

While he was at the Brooklyn Navy Yard (the Armed Guard Center), he happened to notice the big blackboard with ship listings. With tears in his eyes and voice cracking, Pierson told of the sad information he read from the blackboard. His former ship, the SS WILSON had been sunk in the Red Sea and all hands went down with the ship. Eighty-seven merchantmen and 27 armed guard of the Navy.

Seaman First Class Pierson was now assigned to the SS TIDEWATER ASSOCIATION – a merchant tanker, on which he served for the next six months. The ship picked up oil in Venezuela and Ecuador in South America and then traveled to British Columbia and unloaded the oil. He then traveled to Pearl Harbor and said that he was not engaged in combat while in the Pacific. Pierson added that the Pacific Ocean was very calm compared to the Atlantic.

While in Honolulu, Pierson visited Stuart Cowen of Stockwell, who was in the naval hospital recovering from the multiple bullet wounds he had received at the Battle of Tarawa. He said that Stuart was in good shape at that time and he also saw him later after he was released from the hospital. Stuart was very surprised to see him and asked him, "Where did you come from?"

In early 1946, Seaman First Class Pierson was transferred to the USS BEN FRANKLIN, an aircraft carrier. He served on board the BEN FRANKLIN for three months until his discharge at Lido Beach, New York on March 5, 1946.

Happy that the war was over, he returned home and worked at several jobs. He retired from Oneida Limited and presently resides in Florida.

55

Calvin Southwick

ARMED GUARD-RADIO OPERATOR

RM3 CALVIN SOUTHWICK(Courtesy of family)

This account and the preceding chapter portray the Navy armed guard who served aboard merchant marine ships that transported cargo and troops during World War II.

After graduating from high school in Glens Falls, New York in 1942, eighteen year old Calvin "Cal" Southwick joined the Navy on January 20, 1943. Of his choice, Southwick recalled "I walked down to the Navy recruiting office to join the Navy. [My] dad had been in World War I and to quote him, "I horsed a pack all over France for a year." Dad was instrumental in my joining the Navy." Southwick was assigned to Sampson Naval Station on Seneca Lake, south of Geneva, New York for basic training. One of his memories from that station was of drilling and marching in the frigid months of January, February, and March 1943. The average temperature was thirty-six degrees below zero. Not only was it a bitter cold winter but the heating system failed three times.

Following boot camp Southwick attended radio and signal school at Sampson Naval Station. He was then assigned to the Armed Guard Center at the Brooklyn Navy Yard. The duties of an armed guard on a merchant ship were to "maintain the firing of the guns and manning the signal flags and standing radio watches to supplement the radio operator so that the radios could be manned 24 hours a day." (LIVE -Project Liberty p.22). While waiting for a ship assignment, Southwick was assigned to guard duty.

The first ship to which he was assigned was the S.S.WILLARD, a Liberty ship. Over 2700 Liberty ships were built during World War II. The armed guard retinue for the S.S. Willard was made up of twelve navy men. The commanding officer was LTJG John Shepard. Shepherd became a Hollywood actor after the war and was known as Shepherd Strudwick. This author recalls seeing Strudwick in several movies. The S.S. WILLARD had been converted to a cargo and troop ship. Southwick recalled serving on the ship for four months. We transported cargo and troops to North Africa (Oran), Palermo, Sicily, Naples and Anzio in Italy taking on troops at Anzio and unloading replacements." Southwick added "traveling in convoy helped a lot and there were no submarine scares. In Oran, Algeria I tried to use my school boy French but it was not too good." When asked by this author about the rough seas he experienced, Southwick said "the worst was once coming back from Gibraltar on board the WILLARD; the ship would pitch from bow to stern, back and forth, back and forth. When we got to the Chesapeake Bay we started rolling side to side and actually did a 45° roll. I tied my chair to the desk and the typewriter fell to the deck. Typewriters were scarce and somebody asked if the typewriter was okay."

About the duties of the armed guard unit on board, Southwick explained that "[he] didn't man the guns. Other members of the Armed Guard did that. On board the ship we had a 3", 5", and 20MM guns. My job on the ship was as a code signal operator. I worked in the radio shack sending and receiving messages by Morse Code." Southwick worked in the radio shack unless anchored out or was tied up to a pier. In convoy, radio silence was maintained unless they were under attack.

After serving on the WILLARD, Southwick was assigned to the SS TULLAHOMA, a brand new tanker, in September or October 1943. After degaussing [degaussing is a procedure whereby a steel cable is placed on ship to prevent explosion of magnetic mines] the ship followed the inland waterways to Texas to join a convoy bound for Bristol, England then returning back to Norfolk, VA. The tanker transported oil and gasoline. Once again, there were no submarine scares. Southwick served about two months on the tanker and then went back to the armed guard center in Brooklyn, NY.

In 1944, the Armed Guard was disbanded and Southwick was transferred to Treasure Island, CA. There, he reported for duty on the SS AMERICAN MANUFACTURE, a brand new C-3 motorized vessel. Impressed with the speed of this new ship, Southwick approached an old Chief and asked him how fast the AMERICAN could go. The Chief spit into the ocean and then replied, "about eighteen knots." Compared to the SS WILLARD, his prior ship that traveled at about eight knots, his new vessel was more than twice as fast.

After his assignment at Treasure Island, California with the SS AMERICAN MANUFACTURE, Southwick was transferred in August 1945 to the amphibious Navy, and placed on the USS HARRY LEE, an APA [attack transport vessel] where he remained until discharged from the service. Southwick recalled that he "traveled in convoys to Ulithi in the central Pacific, and made two trips to Mindanao in the Philippines, as part of the Magic Carpet runs bringing troops back to the States from the Pacific." He was aboard the LEE for about 6-8 months before being discharged from the Navy.

Radioman Third Class Calvin Southwick concluded his account of his World War II experience with the following interesting story:

> *...At one time during the war, our ship was docked in Naples, Italy. The Radio shack was shut down and I was walking on the dock and I saw a Red Cross shack and coffee and doughnuts were being served. While enjoying the coffee and doughnuts, the gal behind the counter said that she could read my fortune. She got my age correct and said that I would be safe, return home and live to be at least 45. Years later, when I turned 45, I developed spinal cancer. At that time there was no known recovery. However, I did have surgery and survived the cancer and returned to work. I should have got the name of that Red Cross nurse so I could remind her of that prediction of 45 years of age. To me, that was just a miracle that I did recover.*

On V-E Day, Southwick said that he was in Italy. Then, in August, 1945 when the Japanese surrendered, Southwick was in the Philippines. He was discharged at Lido Beach, Long Island, New York on February 20, 1946.

After returning home, Southwick attended St. Lawrence University. Following graduation, he worked in the insurance field, eventually owning and operating his own insurance agency in Ilion, New York. Southwick retired in 1988. As the Red Cross nurse had predicted during the war; Southwick did return home safely and lived for many years beyond age 45. Calvin Southwick passed away January 27, 2009.

Part IV
Prisoners Of War

CAPTURED JAPANESE PHOTO SHOWING AMERICAN PRISONERS
CARRYING ILL FELLOW SOLDIERS. MAY 1942.
(Natonal Archives)

56

Richard Cowen

BATAAN DEATH MARCH

Throughout history there have been many incredible and shameful accounts of "man's inhumanity towards man." Few have had the magnitude of cruelty and barbarism as exemplified by the Japanese treatment of American and Filipino prisoners of war —preceding, during, and following the infamous Death March on the Bataan Peninsula during World War II.

Had it not been for World War II, the Bataan peninsula in the Philippine Islands might still be a little known place on the map of Asia. It was there in Manila Bay in April of 1942 on the island of Luzon in the Philippine Islands, that 78,100 American and Filipino troops surrendered to the Japanese.

Though there had been stories about Japanese atrocities in 1942, it was not until mid-1943 that the leaders learned with great shock about the Bataan Death March. Three American officers had escaped from a prisoner of war camp in the southern Philippines and informed General Douglas MacArthur in Brisbane, Australia. However, it would be another six months before the American public would be made aware of this since it was originally thought that if this information were revealed, the Japanese would have retaliated with further brutality (Falk 204-6).

Many prisoners were moved to Japan and the survivors of the prisoner of war camps would spend over three years as captives of the Japanese.

How many died during the Death March? The records are not clear. General Edward P. King, Jr., Commander of the Luzon Force, and his Personnel Officer, Colonel Floyd Marshall, mentioned in their official reports that about 9,300 prisoners reached Camp O'Donnell by the end of May 1942. It is believed that 600 to 650 Americans died on the 70 mile Death March between Balanga in Southern Bataan and the destination—Camp O'Donnell. Filipino losses are more uncertain. Many Filipinos were massacred even before the Death March began, but it is estimated that 5,000 to 10,000 Filipinos died during the March (Falk 196-198).

Richard Cowen of Waterville was one of the survivors of the Death March and imprisoned over three years at Camp O'Donnell, Davao (located on the island of Mindanao, Philippine Islands), and at camps in Japan.

* * * *

Prior to World War II, Cowen had lived in the hamlet of Stockwell near Waterville and at one time had worked on the Grand Coulee dam in the state of Washington. At Spokane on January 20, 1940, he enlisted into the Army Air Corps. Since Cowen died several years ago, his daughter, Elizabeth Kane, has provided the author with her father's handwritten recollections, which were written after his experience as a prisoner of war of the Japanese during World War II.

In April of 1940, at Fort McDonough, California, Cowen boarded the USS GRANT for transportation to the Philippine Islands. After the long journey across the Pacific, he arrived in the Philippines on May 20, 1940 and was assigned as a mechanic in the 3rd Pursuit Squadron at Nichols Field.

Cowen did not enjoy his days in the pre-WWII Army. In a letter to his family in April of 1941, he expressed his dissatisfaction with the Army and mentioned that he did not know when war would begin, but that it was not far off and was glad to be in the Philippine Islands. "I like the Islands - but God damn the Army. I am going to see if I can get a discharge here and look around a bit," he wrote." He also indicated that Americans (civilians) and their families had been asked to move out. He speculated that the first war would be with Japan and then Germany.

He mentioned that in July of 1941, the 3rd Pursuit Squadron was moved to Clark Field and later moved to Iba Zambolies in October of 1941. Iba Zambolies was a dirt strip, which bordered the China Sea.

Cowen further described how on the morning of December 8, 1941 Japanese bombers had attacked the airfield on two different passes. One time the Japanese Zeroes strafed them and they lost about a third of their personnel. Most of the P-40's were in the air and about five had been destroyed on the ground.

After attending to the wounded and the dead, Cowen and others of his unit were trucked to Manila and Nichols Field. Rifles and combat gear were then issued and the troops took up positions around Manila.

It was Christmas Day, 1941, Cowen was on the Bataan Peninsula holding off the Japanese invading forces and on January 15, he was engaged in beach defense duty attempting to stop the Japanese from invading.

By February 1, the food supply was short and they were eating monkeys and horsemeat. By the middle of March, the troops were living off the land eating roots and fruits.

"I had my first attack of malaria around the first of February. I took quinine most of the time until the surrender. It was about the 10th of March when I began to swell up from fluids and by the first of April, I couldn't wear shoes and only a few of my clothes," Cowen had recorded in his account.

As the Japanese invasion of the Philippines progressed, the American troops were forced up the side of a mountain. On the morning of April 11, 1942, the American troops were ordered by headquarters at Corregidor to surrender to the Japanese at Cabcaben Air Field. Those who couldn't walk had to be carried.

> *...We were herded like animals in the hot sun with no food and very little water. Several bodies lie all around. Some were buried but most were not. The Japs were drunk with joy and pride and they had to show us who were boss. Several Americans died from disease and starvation and several others were bayoneted and clubbed to death just for entertainment. One American was carrying some Japanese money in his pocket. This called for a big celebration. Later that afternoon the Americans had to gather around and watch a Jap cut his head off. Then several Japs ran yelling and screaming as they bayoneted the body. The head was placed on a long pole and it was carried by a bunch of Japs to make sure that we all knew they were our superiors.*

Cowen further described the "March" as follows:

> *...I was on the march off Bataan for sixteen days. I was fed once. There were bodies all along the road. Some bodies were piled around the artesian wells where they had been shot and killed when they broke ranks to get water. I saw men who were too weak to walk buried alive. Others went crazy and ran and screamed - they were clubbed to death or bayoneted.*

Cowen was unable to wear shoes because his feet swelled and he wore only a G-string for clothing. Arriving at Camp McDonnell, which was a former Filipino army training camp, the prisoners received very little to eat and stood in line for 24 hours a day to get a drink.

About May 20, 1942, a large group was removed from the camp to the south of Manila. "Our job, he wrote, was to help replace a bridge that had been blown up by Americans as they retreated to Bataan. "There were 150 of us when we arrived and we were housed in an old theater. I had taken a pair of coveralls off a dead man and I wore these at night to keep warm,"

The prisoners, including Cowen, were placed in three groups of 50 and each person had an armband with a number on it. Each group had a different number and Cowen's number 16 was in the pink group and they were told if anyone escaped the rest of that group would be shot.

> *...On June 11, Filipino guerillas came in to liberate us but all of us were too sick and weak. The Japs, headquartered in a schoolhouse about a quarter of a mile away came in with all guns blazing. We took cover on the dirt floor because the shells were coming in through the steel sides of our building. Afterwards, the Japs came in and did a recount - one man had gone. We were then marched to their headquarters. We knew somebody was going to be shot.*

The Japanese counted out forty-nine and Cowen was included in the count. There were about 120 Americans in Cowen's group who were still alive. Thirty had died and ten of the remaining 120 were too weak to march to headquarters.

The Japanese then decided to pick out ten men that slept closest to the escapees. Cowen was number five or six in the group of ten that was called out of ranks.

> *...A Jap got up on a box and said that originally all 49 would be shot but 'we are going to be very good to you. We are only going to shoot these ten men.' We were marched up a little path to a spot that looked like a picnic ground...we had our backs to a side hill facing the firing squad. Beyond the firing squad were the rest of the Americans forced to witness this. The Japs had to make a big ceremony of this. During the ceremony a high ranking Jap appeared and after a long discussion and after several had passed out from the heat and strain, the ten were allowed to return to ranks...*

It was learned that the man who escaped was from the green group and his number had been seventeen. Cowen's recollections of the horrific execution continues:

> *...The Japs then called for numbers eighteen, sixteen, nineteen, and fifteen and so on until they had ten and they were shot. They didn't all die from the first volley. The Japs had to reload several times and tried to shoot them in the heads. This went on for ten minutes before the Japs were convinced they were dead. As the firing squad started to march away two of those who had been shot pulled themselves up and said, 'you got to give it to me again.*

You haven't got me yet.' All the riflemen turned, reloaded and blasted him. Then another man raised his head up and said, 'you haven't got me neither.' Then all ten riflemen turned on them, too. In one group there were two brothers and one had to watch the other being shot.

About twenty of them including Cowen were taken out of ranks and told to pick up the bodies and pile them near the road. The bodies were then covered with lumber since they were going to be cremated. When they were about to light the fire a guard came and called for Cowen and asked him if he were out of the 3rd Pursuit Squadron. Cowen told him 'Yes.' The guard said, 'Follow me!'...The Japanese questioned him and Cowen soon found out why he was asked the question. "The man who escaped was out of the 3rd Pursuit Squadron. I was the only one left. They thought I had something so do with the one who had escaped. When I couldn't give them an answer they started beating on me. They used an old broomstick."

Cowen recorded how he was struck on the back, head and arm and noted that it was very painful. He went to his knees and they twisted his arm and then tied him to a table and left the room. When they came back they untied him and told him they had made a mistake (Cowen did not know what mistake was made). They then brought him rice and boiled meat and told him to eat as much as he wanted. His arm had gone numb and he ate with his left hand - no spoon or fork. As he was walked back they told him not to say anything about their talk or the beating. He wrote that the feeling did come back to his arm and hand that evening, but the pain had been the worst he had ever experienced.

The following day the malaria returned. He had high fever and drank more and more water causing the swelling to become worse. "My stomach was so big it looked like it was going to blow out. My eyes ran constantly. I knew that if too much fluid went to my head or brain I would die like I saw others. They would go out of their heads, talk constantly or scream for three or four days before they died," Cowen described.

A Filipino doctor was permitted to come in and he administered medicine that relieved the swelling, which Cowen said was called wet beri beri and the pain in the hands and feet was called dry beri beri. Cowen was also given quinine, which controlled the malaria for another month.

In July of 1942, Cowen was trucked to Cabanatuan. He was there until the end of September working on a burial detail.

"The hospital conditions were terrible. I made up my mind that I would never be carried in or out of there." Ten to sixty bodies a day were carried out from the hospital to a graveyard and a few inches of dirt or mud covered their bodies.

After leaving Cabanatuan at the end of September 1942, Cowen was taken to Bilibid Manila. At that time, he weighed 128 pounds. There he went aboard an inter-island boat. His mind went blank and he was told that he had said mean things to all on board and even tried to cause fights. On the first evening he had refused to eat rice. Around midnight, he started to scream and yell and the others tried to hold him down but he didn't calm down until daybreak. The Japanese wanted to throw him overboard but the other prisoners pleaded with them to not do that. They told the guards that Cowen was close to death and should be allowed to die before throwing him overboard. Cowen was in a coma for the next seven days. The Japanese let him have some canned milk and crackers.

About the 15th of October he arrived at Davao, Mindanao that is located in the southern Philippines. He then weighed 93 pounds and was 72 and one-half inches tall. He was not only extremely underweight and weak but he had several bruises from the convulsions he had on the boat. The doctors told him later that the malaria had caused the convulsions.

Cowen said that the conditions at Davao were the best he had experienced. They received better food, quarters and a few clothes but remained barefooted with no shoes. He was able to go on work details again but the pain in his arm had returned. He had more malaria at Davao but was eventually able to use the arm again.

He was placed in a group of ten and some of the group had escaped. No one remaining in the group was shot for this, but some were punished.

Cowen did receive three shipments of Red Cross packages and he said that these helped a great deal. He received shoes and a woolen sweater from home, but the Japanese took the sweater away from him.

About the middle of April 1944, seven hundred of the two thousand held at Davao were taken from the group to a place to build an airstrip. Cowen was considered too weak and skinny to do the work.

After the war, Cowen learned that an American submarine had torpedoed the ship taking the 700 men north and there were only 83 survivors. Some went down with the ship and others were shot or bayoneted as they tried to swim ashore.

On June 6, 1944, the rest of the group left Davao. For the next 104 days they were on a ship bound for Japan. There was little food and many physical beatings. Cowen arrived in Japan on September 2, 1944 and worked in a smelter that had electric furnaces that melted down scrap iron from the USA. They were not supplied protective glasses for their eyes and the hot metal burned their eyes. When they tried to sleep, it felt like some one was pouring sand in their eyes. This camp was at Osaka and since many died from exposure; men were given some clothes and footwear. "It was a rough winter and starting about March 1945 we endured several B-29 air raids," Cowen noted.

Around July 1, 1945 some of the troops were moved to Toyama. Cowen had a recurrence of malaria and his feet started to swell again and he had to go barefoot. "I was just about "done-in" by the time the war was over." They were not told for several days after V-J Day that the war had ended.

Richard Cowen wrote the following letter on September 2, 1945 from Toyama, Japan:

...Dear Folks, The great day has come. I am free. The news came to us slow and gradual. We were not sure until August 22nd. You will never know the suffering and torture we have been through. I am ashamed of my appearance. In fact a press reporter was here tonite (sic) and took some pictures. I ran away because I didn't want anyone to see me. - Richard. P.S. Tuffey died early in concentration. (Francis Tuffey was from Sangerfield, NY).

Of the 33,021 American military captured by the Japanese during World War II, 12,526 died in captivity. (Pixler 1).

Cowen was flown to San Francisco and he arrived at the former Rhodes Hospital, which was located in Utica, New York, on September 22, 1945. He was then sent to Moore General Hospital at Asheville, North Carolina. There he was treated for four different kinds of internal parasites, malaria, and malnutrition.

He left the hospital on June 25, 1946 and was discharged at Fort Dix on June 28, 1946. He re-enlisted and after a furlough, returned to duty at Griffis Air Force Base, Rome, New York, on December 6, 1946 where he was assigned as an aircraft mechanic.

Shortly after the war, Cowen, his father and mother, and brother William were invited to sit on the speaker's stand at Skaneateles, New York, honoring the homecoming of General Jonathan "Skinny" Wainwright, who succeeded General Douglas MacArthur at Bataan. Wainwright had also been a prisoner of war of the Japanese after the fall of Bataan.

Cowen married Frances M. Gragen, who served in the Army Nurse Corps for three years in the Asiatic-Pacific Theater. She was assigned as a General Duty Nurse in Hawaii and the southern Philippines.

While in the Air Force, Master Sergeant Richard Cowen also served as a recruiter and retired on February 29, 1960 after twenty years in the Army Air Corps, Army Air Forces and the U.S. Air Force. After his military experience,

Cowen worked as a real estate broker in the Waterville area for many years. He passed away in 1988.

57

Eugene Excell

TANK DRIVER/ESCAPE IN ITALY

The tank, developed by the British during World War I, saw limited use toward the end of the war and brought about the end of trench warfare.

During World War II, American tanks such as the Grants and the Shermans were inferior to the German and Russian tanks in armor and protection. However, the Sherman M-4 was more reliable, more serviceable, and more cost effective than those of Germany or Russia. The M3A5, a medium tank, was used until 1944. It had a six-man crew with one 75mm gun, one 37mm gun, four 7.62mm machine guns, and three 30-caliber machine guns. It weighed over 32 tons with a speed of about 25 miles an hour (Quick 481).

Eugene Excell of Earlville was an M3 medium tank driver. He was wounded at Kasserine Pass in North Africa and taken prisoner, escaped from an Italian Prisoner of War camp, and hid behind enemy lines living with Italian families until he was able to locate the allies.

****

Excell was raised in East Hamilton, New York and lived in Brookfield, New York when he enlisted into the Army on February 11, 1941, at the age of 28. He was the first in the area to enlist. Before enlisting, he worked as a barber and was in charge of a maintenance crew with the New York State Department of Transportation

At Fort Knox, Kentucky, he attended Armored Force School and was a gun instructor on all tank weapons. Excell was then attached to the First Armored Division, 13th Armored Regiment, company "I". He was asked by his commanding officer if he wanted to attend Officer Candidate School. His Sergeant, who was also asked, chose not to accept, so Excell decided that he would not accept either.

From Fort Knox, the Division went to Fort Dix and to New York City where he boarded the QUEEN MARY for Ireland. The ship traveled in convoy and while approaching England, it was decided to unload the troops onto a lighter ship in the English Channel since the water was not deep enough for the big ocean liner to dock in Northern Ireland.

...In the Channel I said 'what happened? I can't hear a thing.' There was a sub scare and we had shut down all of the engines, and hoped they wouldn't find us. On the radio the next morning, we had heard that the QUEEN MARY had been sunk. I said, 'How the hell can that be, I'm on the QUEEN MARY and if they sank us, I wouldn't be here looking at the coast of England.'

After the troops were loaded on to the lighter ship, the QUEEN MARY went on to Ireland and docked. From Ireland, they eventually traveled to England and then engaged in training in tanks and gunnery. Excell's main job was tank driver of company command tanks. Also, he added with a laugh, "I used my experience as a barber to cut hair in the company."

As tank driver, he steered the tank and operated a machine gun, which had trigger controls on the steering levers. The full tank crew consisted of seven men including a radio operator. The ammunition was stored inside the tank and he said the medium tanks took fifteen gallons of oil and used ninety-two-octane gas. The tanks had a 37mm turret machine gun and a 75mm cannon. The 75mm was on a Sponson, which is the platform on the side of the tank next to the hatch. Excell said the 37mm was like a shotgun as it sprayed shot.

Boarding a ship in England, Excell headed out for Africa. While traveling in convoy in the Mediterranean, one of the British transports was torpedoed. The ship was carrying English women but they got off safely on to another ship and then the ship was purposely sunk by gunfire from another English ship.

The troops of the First Armored Division went ashore at Oran meeting much more resistance than was met at Casablanca in the earlier invasion of Africa. The Oran invasion in November 1942 was primarily a British Naval Force and there was tough resistance from the Vichy French Navy. The First Armored Division supported the First Infantry Division and the invasion was a surprise to the Germans who had expected it to take place in Europe (Pictorial 161).

"In North Africa we were engaged in battle at Station Synod. I was being referred to as the 'Demon'," Excell said with a laugh. This started because a guy in Company E in the 13th Armored Regiment was talking with an officer and he asked him if Excell was all right. The officer said, "We don't call him 'Excell' anymore. We call him the "Demon." Excell was nicknamed 'Demon' because of an incident when he was firing the machine gun and he was told that he had aimed his machine gun in an area and killed very many of the enemy.

Excell's first major action was at Kasserine Pass in Tunisia. It was February of 1943 and the Nazis launched their last major offensive in North Africa at Kasserine Pass in Tunisia. There was bitter fighting as the seasoned 21st German Panzer Division battled the Americans. One-half of the tanks of the First Armored Division were knocked out of action. Eventually, reinforcements drove Field Marshal Rommel back through the Pass (Pictorial 177).

Excell describes the battle of the Kasserine Pass and circumstances leading to his being wounded and captured by the enemy.

> *...The Germans got in on us and zeroed in. This was a terrible battle for the Americans. The Germans blew my tank up. No one in the tank was killed. Two men were hit and wounded by machine gun fire after they got out of the tank. When I got out I could hear the bullets whistling over my head. If I had raised my head it would have been goodbye. Luckily, the Germans couldn't depress the muzzle of the machine gun low enough to hit anything near the ground. Tracer bullets were used and we could see the tracers since it was early morning and still dark. Tracers were used and fired from the tanks to help in aiming. We were all huddled up in some cactus. The Germans came up and one could speak a few words of English. He saw my leg and said you are wounded. There were other wounded there also. A medic came up and picked us up in a captured American half-track. The doctor checked my leg and I could remember his saying something like "rota". Maybe it meant broken. I was taken to a hospital. All the time in the hospital in Tunisia I had no crutches. The latrine was a room about the size of a living room. The concrete floor had holes in it to be used as toilets. Imagine squatting and hitting the hole with no railings to hang onto.*

From the hospital he was taken to an Italian Prisoner of War camp in southern Italy. There was a big concrete wall with guards and Excell said that he could see Mt. Vesuvius from the prison camp and while at the camp an earthquake occurred which knocked down a few buildings.

> *...There's a funny feeling you get when that earth gets knocked around. One of our guys was Italian and had gone to America and was drafted into the U.S. Army. He was also taken as a prisoner and his folks lived about 2-3 miles from the POW camp. He knew the language well and spoke to the guards and after talking to one of the guards, he found out that his own brother*

*was one of the guards. The guard went to the commandant and
said, 'My brother is a prisoner here.'*

The Commandant was skeptical and came down to where the prisoners
were to see if this were true. The Commandant did allow the prisoner to see
his parents.

Excell pointed out that the prisoners were treated well.

> *...The Prisoner of War camp was almost like going home. They
> received Canadian, American, English, and Indian Red Cross
> parcels. The parcels had cigarettes, biscuits, canned corned beef,
> and crackers. The Canadians had the best packages. Believe it
> or not they had one pound of real butter in the packages. The
> American and British parcels were fair but I didn't like the
> Indian parcels because of the spices they use.*

Seven of them did manage to escape from the prison and spent a whole
year behind German lines (Excell is not sure how long he was a prisoner). Italy
had surrendered in 1943 and Excell was hiding from the Germans. During
that time the Italians were sheltering Excell. He had lived with six different
Italian families and he related how he liked the Italians and that they had
saved his life. Italians would come and bring him food. "We ate lots of pasta
and polenta and I loved the bread," he said with a big grin. The father in one
family named Frachetti, treated Excell like a brother and "I loved him like a
brother. They even changed my name to 'Luigi,'" Excell recalled excitedly.

One day an Italian came to the house and said, 'Inglese!' The English
were marching up the Adriatic coast. Excel described how he and his friends
finally made contact with friendly forces:

> *...We were walking across Italy to the coast. The first person we
> saw was someone who appeared to be an English Army captain.
> He had an English uniform but he couldn't speak English and we
> couldn't understand him. There were 15-20 soldiers coming down
> the road and one of them could speak a little English. We found
> out that they were Polish soldiers with English uniforms. One
> Pole had learned a little Italian and was trying to buy a chicken
> from a farmer and when he finished talking with the Italian
> farmer, I asked him if he could speak English. The Americans had
> earlier sent paratroopers to look for us with plans to get us out
> on an LST. We ran into them (the paratroopers) behind German*

lines one time and we were supposed to meet them at a certain place- but this fell through.

The Polish soldiers trucked them to the suburbs of Foggia where there were British troops. A woman with a blue bag with a red cross on it was there. "I didn't know whether she was International Red Cross or which country she was from. I got a razor, razor blades, toothbrush, toothpaste, and two packs of cigarettes - one pack of Old Gold and one pack of Chesterfields. I still have them in my dresser drawer," Excell said with a smile.

They were flown to Africa by the British on a C-47 and stayed there in a few months before boarding a British ship, the "MARIPOSA," bound for New York. He was sent to Fort Dix and Camp Upton on Long Island and given new uniforms and a 30-day furlough. He went to Penn Station and then Grand Central for the train trip home.

After his furlough he reported to Fort Buckner, North Carolina where he was reclassified and sent to Fort Dix.

At Fort Dix there was a German Prisoner of War camp and Excell asked the First Sergeant for some work to do. He was sent to the Motor Pool and was issued a pistol and ordered to transport Germans to their work site. The Sergeant didn't know that I had been a prisoner of war and said if he had known that, he wouldn't have given me that job. The Germans had considerable freedom at the camp and appeared to enjoy being a prisoner.

T-4 (Sergeant Technician) Eugene Excell went to Fort Devens, Massachusetts and was discharged on December 5, 1944. After returning home he became a self-employed barber and painter.

He passed away December 17, 2001

58

Nelson Pardee

BALL TURRETT GUNNER/
THE "BLACK MARCH"

Much of the world is familiar with the Bataan Death March but very little is known about another death march which has been named "The Black March."

During World War II, American, British, and some Canadian airmen who had been captured by the Germans were imprisoned in camps called Stalag-Luft (Air). Stalag-Luft IV was located in Poland where several thousand prisoners were held. In early 1945, as the Russians were approaching Stalag-Luft IV, the prisoners were ordered westward across Germany.

The prisoners trudged along through the rain and the snow of a severe winter for about 600 miles. They had little food and rest, sleeping on the ground or in barns, and sometimes on feces left by those marching ahead. The "March" lasted about three months and along the way, some prisoners who could not keep up were shot. Several hundred Americans would die before the "March" ended in April of 1945 (Turbak 32,34).

Nelson Pardee of Ilion, NY, a member of the famous 100th Bomb Group, Eighth Air Force, was a Ball Turret Gunner on a B-17 and on his fifth mission was credited with shooting down a German Fockewulf fighter plane (FW-109). He had flown on nine bombing missions over Berlin. No other crew of the 100th had that many missions over Berlin. On his 26th mission, German fighter planes hit his plane and he had to parachute out of his aircraft. He became a prisoner in Stalag Luft IV for nine months and then marched for 86 days in the little known "Black March" across Germany.

* * * *

On the day after his 18th birthday, Pardee enlisted into the Army Air Forces. After basic training at Atlantic City he attended aerial gunnery school for six weeks at Fort Myers, Florida. On one training exercise in gunnery school, Pardee recalled that while firing from our plane, one of the guys, in the process of operating the gun, experienced a malfunctioning of the linkage into the shoot where the ammunition is fed. (The Shoot has to be hit with one's hand where the links go down into the shoot in order to free the links.) The pilot called back and said, 'Hit the shoot! The guy, thinking he meant 'CHUTE,' panicked and parachuted out of the plane. "He did not graduate from gunnery school," Pardee added.

Pardee was assigned as a Ball Turret Gunner in a B-17G. The Ball Turret Gunner is located on the bottom of the fuselage in a very precarious position, especially if the plane is forced to crash land. The Ball Turret could rotate 360° as opposed to the Top Turret, which has a cut-off spot preventing it from turning beyond a certain point. This is to prevent the Top Turret Gunner from shooting off the tail of his own plane.

Pardee flew across the ocean and arrived in England in February of 1944. He was stationed at Thorpe Abbotts, which is located about 20 miles south of Norwich, England. He was in the 3350th Squadron of the 100th Bomb Group, Eighth Air Force. Pardee joined a Group that was earlier nicknamed the "Bloody Hundredth," since it had suffered such heavy losses from June through October of 1943. The 100th would fly 306 missions from June 25, 1943 to April 20, 1945 and would win two presidential citations. (Crosby 1-2).

The nineteen-year-old Sergeant Pardee flew 25 combat missions over Germany. Nine of these were over Berlin. He said that he had participated in the first daylight raid over Berlin on March 4, 1944. Thirty-one planes succeeded in bombing Berlin. The rest of the planes had been recalled before the target was reached. "The flak was real heavy. The planes carried bales of tinfoil (chaff) that was released to confuse the enemy radar. This would make it more difficult for the anti-craft gunners to set the correct range," he said. After the mission, General James Doolittle, Commander of the Eighth Air Force, had a celebration party for everyone at the Officer's Club. Generals Doolittle, Curtis LeMay, and Karl Spaatz attended.

On March 6, 1944, there was a maximum effort raid over Berlin as 600 planes bombed the capital of Germany. Pardee explained that a bombing raid over Berlin took 9.5 hours round trip and that he had logged 242.2 combat hours. After 13 missions, a crewmember could go to "Flak House," to calm the nerves. (A place to rest and relax and wear civilian clothes.) Pardee refused to go to "Flak House." He chose to go to London, instead. "I had a good time there," he said.

Pardee recalled the day, May 24, 1944, when Luftwaffe fighter planes hit his B-17.

> *...The fighter had been shooting at us for 20 minutes. It was my 26th mission and we were over Berlin flying at about 26,000 feet. I had been over Berlin 12 other times. I was in the Ball Turret and*

my heated suit was off and I was freezing. The Flight Engineer switched with me and I went up to the top. I found out later at one of our reunions that he had his leg blown off. He told me that while having lunch, during the noon hour at work, he would sit down and pound a nail in his wooden leg. He then would hang his POW cap on it.

Pardee describes in detail what occurred after his plane was hit:

…Three engines were on fire and we were ordered by the pilot to bail out. People have asked me, 'How did you react? This was the first time I ever had to bail out. You remember what you did in training— it flashes through your mind and you have to act fast in order to get out of the plane. Everyone bailed out. Since our aircraft had been hit so badly, we had to drop our bombs and we did hit our target. I went back to the bomb bay doors, released the bomb bay, and jumped from there. (I was told later by Mike Foley, a guy I saw recently, that on the May 24 mission, the Germans had knocked down nine of our planes in the Group). I floated down to the ground and what entered my mind was not whether I was going to live or die, but how long was I going to be here (in Germany). While I was floating to the ground I had no fear of being killed. Another fellow, Graham, landed near me and I didn't know at first who it was. I went over to him and saw that he had flak wound in his leg and was bleeding like a stuck pig. I took this first aid pack off my parachute and put a tourniquet around his leg and packed the leg. I had a 45 automatic with three full clips in my flying suit. We were not supposed to carry one but if they were going to kill me I wanted to take a few with me. So after landing, Graham kept telling me to 'Get rid of that .45.' I said, 'No.' I want to wait and see who captures me because he had heard how prisoners were being pitch forked by civilians. I said rather than let this happen I would wait to see if the military picked us up. So when I landed in this field close to this other guy, Graham, we saw these kids (did not know at time they were kids). They made this big circle around us and were closing in. They knew where we had landed and there must have been hundreds of them. They got up close and they had these rusty old shotguns. They searched us and you should have seen the kids go for the Chicklet (candy coated) gum they found on us. The Air Force stocked our uniforms with Chicklets. I have told many people – 'If

only the chicklets had been a laxative, I could have walked away from there.' Then they closed in and two Gestapo agents with a car picked us. The little car they drove burned charcoal. They came over to us and while I am holding on to the wounded Graham, one of the Gestapo agents said to me, 'You Schwein!' And he hits me. I said you son-of-a-bitch! Graham says, 'Jesus, don't – You'll get us killed.' I think I got hit, rather than Graham, since I was not wounded. I did have a slight wound from shrapnel and later received the Purple Heart. They took us into a chicken coop and the Luftwaffe interrogators came and then took us to town. I threw my gun into the brush after I found out that they weren't going to kill us. I remember this little fellow who found the .45 that I had thrown into the brush. The little guy kept pointing it at me saying it was mine. He was finally told to put the gun down.

Pardee said that everyone was required to go through interrogation by German intelligence in what was called the Dulag-Luft. Robert Doyle in the <u>American Legion</u> article entitled "Forgotten Warriors, Voices from Captivity," wrote the following: "The harshest treatment took place in the Dulag-Luft which was a transient camp for fliers captured by the Germans. The camp was operated by the Air Force Intelligence Service."(Doyle 44).

Pardee explains the interrogation and trip to Stalag Luft-IV:

...We got in there and they tried to make out who was on the crew together. There were six of us left outside. They came out and said, 'We have all the crews made up and we now have six pursuit pilots knocked down.' I didn't have my dog tags with me and, looking at me, he said – 'You six are the pursuit pilots.' They were pretty rough on pursuit pilots whose duties included extensive strafing of ground equipment and personnel. One of our men said, 'I don't want to be classified that way.' I said,' Just give them your name, rank, and service number.' That was all that we did. They offered us American cigarettes and they tried to get information from us. If they did not get any information you were put into solitary confinement. If they think they can get information they will keep you longer. We were only in solitary a few hours and then we were loaded into crowded railroad cars and transported to a prison camp. While on the train, Americans bombed and strafed the trains and the Germans just left us there during the raids. Except for an empty pail to relieve ourselves, we had no facilities. The pail would fill and as the train moved

and lurched, the contents of the pail would slosh around. It was like a cattle car. We just had to tolerate this because we had no choice. We got to Camp Stalag-Luft IV in Groscrow, Poland and were imprisoned there for nine months.

Pardee explained that all of the other camps without LUFT in the name were for those who were not airmen. Officers went to one place and enlisted to another. After nine months, the prisoners were getting reports on the radio from BBC of positions of the front lines. As the Russians got closer, Pardee said, the Germans evacuated the camp, and moved the prisoners in February, in the middle of a snowy winter with only one blanket provided to each prisoner.

...They wanted to keep us as hostages to rebuild their cities. So we walked all the way across Germany the last three months of the war. We slept in barns and fields, scrounged for food, found potatoes and turnips in the fields. We would tie the arms of our undershirts and load them with potatoes and turnips and put them on our backs, because maybe at the next farm we might not find anything. At night we would cook them up. We were always under guard until we reached British lines and were liberated. There were 12,000 prisoners in our camp with one compound of British. The rest were all Americans. We marched along and as the front lines moved we moved. There were no physical beatings but we had to keep up.

Gary Turbak noted in his VFW article that there were about 6,000-9,000 prisoners in Stalag IV-Luft and that when the "March" began on February 6, the number in the march was 6,000, minus the sick and wounded"(31).

Recalling more details of the "March," Pardee said that he was determined not to give up and to keep going and he described how the prisoners finally reached the British lines.

...The guards had dogs in back of us and if anyone lagged behind, they would nudge the guys with bayonets or the dogs would nip at the legs. My idea from the start was "survival of the fittest" – had to keep yourself in shape. I had no problem since I was only 20 years old. The officers were not in as good shape. After a couple of days they had trouble keeping up. The officers had received more Red Cross packages and received better treatment than us while they were in their separate facility at Stalag IV. Maybe that is

why they were softer and had trouble keeping up. Finally, we reached British lines and a half-track pulled up. The Germans still had their guns and the British said 'Get those guns!' I said to a guy next to me, 'If you get a gun you will have to carry it. Don't be a fool. Don't take it!' Some of our guys grabbed guns and began shooting into the air. I was more afraid of them than when the Germans had the guns. The German Wehrmacht guards were mainly old guys in their 40's and 50's and were tired of the war, and they gave up their guns without a problem. There weren't many young Germans left. They had been cleaned out and the old Home Guard was all that was left. The British grabbed the guns and had us walk about 20 kilometers a day. We had already walked 600 miles across Germany in three months all the way to the Rhine River. This has since been referred to as the "Black March." The British said to march a couple of days and then there would be transportation. The transportation was slow in arriving and as we walked we would take a bicycle and a civilian would come out and yell at us.

The troops got deloused and given a British uniform. It was late April and they went into Brussels and stayed there a couple of days before their arrival at Camp Lucky Strike in LeHavre, France to await a ship home. There, they were given cocoa and eggnog to help make up for their lost weight. While waiting there, Pardee decided that he wanted to visit Paris where he enjoyed the "Follies." "Quite a place," he recalled.

Technical Sergeant Nelson Pardee had been a prisoner at Stalag IV for nine months and then ordered to march across Germany. Counting the three months of the "March" his total time in captivity was about one year. He said he had previously frozen his feet as a B-17 crewmember and then forced to march over fields in the snow and rain with only one blanket. He said he would have to remove his shoes and turn them upside down so they wouldn't fill with water.

Pardee spoke of another POW from nearby Frankfort, New York who was in his camp. His name is Dominick Green and he was moved into Stalag- Luft IV from another camp located at Barth in Poland. This created more crowded conditions and so another bunk was placed on top and some slept on the floor. It raised the number from 20-30. Pardee said that Green has told him that he still feels his wounds. Myles Sinnott of Ilion was also a prisoner with him.

Sinnot, a flight engineer and top turret gunner, was in the 305th Bomb Group, 364th Squadron. He was on his fifth mission flying over Germany on September 3, 1944, when a barrage of shells hit his B-17 and shrapnel injured his arm. Three engines of his plane shut down and the plane was on fire. "The pilot told us to abandon ship immediately so we had to jump. I hit the ground and couldn't breathe. A German was standing behind me and I was then a POW," he said.

Sinnot related his experience in the POW camp.

> *...At least five times a day we had to look up and see the lousy swastika flag and that was just to rub your nose in it. The food was lousy and we called it 'shit,' he described. "The meat consisted of any dead animal that was killed by bombing raids and the animals were never bled out. The meat was cooked with rutabagas grown in human manure. The rutabagas were slimy and stunk. If you were caught throwing it away you wouldn't get any bread. The drinking water was always contaminated due to manure piled by the well.*

Sinnot said that he joined Pardee's camp on September 13, 1944 after being locked in a boxcar overnight. "Nelson was in Stalag IV, Lager A. I was in Lager D. My radio operator was in D after I left and he was liberated by the Russians."

He, also, was a part of the "Black March," and walked from Poland across Germany to Hamburg then southeast to Bittenfeld, Germany. The 104th-106th Infantry Regiments of General Patton's Third Army liberated him in April of 1945.

Sinnott also told of the famous Nazi "Flying Circus." Hermann Goering, leader of the Luftwaffe and World War I pilot had also been a member of the group. "The pilots were all "Aces," and they flew out of the area of Holly, Germany. The noses of their planes, FW109 and 190's were painted like a checkerboard and when you saw them, you knew you were in for a fight," Sinnott described.

Pardee mentioned that some of his "buddies" have returned to where Stalag Luft IV is located in Groscrow, Poland. He said there is only a stone there that marks the site. "I have had no interest in going back to see a stone." He also added that he has not gone back to visit his old base at Thorpe Abbotts, either. There is a British museum there for the 100th Bomb Group, maintained by the British but financed by the 100th.

Before leaving, Pardee showed the author a certificate indicating his membership in the "Caterpillar Club" for successfully bailing out of his plane after it was hit. He has a pin with a caterpillar that he wears on his POW cap. He also displayed his "Short Snorter," a dollar bill, and a silver certificate, signed by Generals Doolittle, Curtis LeMay, and General Spaatz. These were awarded for having flown the ocean and a requirement for membership was a signature by a current member. Pardee mentioned that it was at the party celebrating the first daylight raid over Berlin that he was able to obtain the signatures.

The 100th Bomb Group had earned two presidential citations. He had earned an Air Medal with four oak leaf clusters and the Purple Heart.

Pardee arrived back in the United States on June 2, 1945. Since he had been a prisoner of war, he was re-assigned close to home at Plattsburg Air Force Base, New York. There was no room at Griffiss Air Force Base at Rome, New York, which was located closer to Pardee's home in Ilion. Discharged in October 1945 at Plattsburg, he returned home, worked for Kelsey-Hayes, and retired after 35 years of service.

59

Nicholas Sango

ESCAPE IN GERMANY

Nicholas Sango of Deansboro, NY passed away in 1994. The following account is based on information provided by his wife, Nancy Roberts Sango.

Nicholas Sango graduated from West Winfield Central School in West Winfield, New York in June of 1942 and enlisted into the Army Air Forces in December of 1942 at the age of 18.

After training at Goldsboro, North Carolina and Buckingham Air Field at Fort Myers, Florida and other military bases, he flew overseas in April of 1944 and became a member of the Eighth Air Force. Staff Sergeant Sango flew as a Flight Engineer on a B-17.

Nancy, located in the Lorraine section of France, is about 175 miles from Paris, and was the target of Sango's first mission. It was after the target was bombed and the plane had started back to their base in England, that the plane developed engine trouble, and the crew was forced to bail out of the aircraft. As Sango and some others were descending toward earth, it appeared that they would land right inside a Nazi prison compound. He and another crewmember narrowly missed landing inside the POW camp in France. After landing, the gates were opened for them and they were escorted inside.

Sango was a prisoner in Stalag-Luft VI and throughout 1944, Sango and the other prisoners were moved around and marched all over Germany in the opposite direction from which the allied forces were attacking the Nazis. Food was scarce and the lines of the march were long, and the POW's would get out of line and scrounge at the barns of the farms along the way in search of food. One farm contained several bags of dried peas and the prisoners took this and prepared soup one night over their campfire.

Nancy Sango continued her account of her late husband's ordeal as a prisoner:

As the march continued across Germany, the police dogs nipped at their legs and goaded the sick and injured that were not keeping up with the rest.[*]

---

[*] Information on this march that has been provided by Nancy Sango is similar to the "Black March" in the chapter on Nelson Pardee. However, Sango's group was marching in an eastward direction from France.

As they were marching in the vicinity of Bavaria, Sango and his buddies were gathering firewood and were picking up sticks of wood. As they picked up wood they wandered into a forest and kept right on walking as they attempted to escape. They kept right on walking into the forest. Nick said that he heard the click of a guard's rifle, as the guard attempted to shoot his rifle. Sango had said that he wasn't sure if the rifle had misfired or that the guard had decided to let them go since the war was almost over. It was April 1945 and it would be another month before the Nazis surrendered.

After the escape, they went into a village and found someone who obtained an old horse and wagon and the three of them entered a village. They were very hungry. They noticed a meat market that was located in a house. One of the three prisoners, who had earlier managed to obtain a gun, waved it at the lady inside the house and demanded something to eat. The lady cooked them some very greasy sausage but they were not particular, since they hadn't eaten very much in the past several months. Nancy Sango said that her husband suffered terrible heartburn after eating the sausage stating that Nick always felt that this caused him to suffer a lifetime of troublesome heartburn.

Eventually, the three escapees managed to get to the British lines and they were then provided with medical care and food.

Nicholas Sango returned to the United States to Denver, Colorado where he recuperated from his ordeal as a prisoner of war. He had lost much weight and had to spend several months in a rehabilitation center in Denver where he was evaluated physically and mentally.

Staff Sergeant Nicholas Sango was discharged in September of 1945, after thirty-three months of military service. He married the former Nancy Roberts and lived in Deansboro and worked as a mechanical engineer at Griffis Air Force Base. He retired from there in 1978 and passed away in 1994 at the age of 70.

60

John S. Taibi

PRISONER OF WAR

CPL JOHN S. TAIBI
(Courtesy of John Taibi)

The following account is from the personal diary of the late John Salvatore Taibi, a prisoner of war during the latter months of World War II. An interview with Taibi's son, John, from Munnsville, New York, also provided information for this chapter.

* * * *

John S. Taibi entered the Army November 11, 1942. He went to Camp

Funston, Kansas for basic training. After which, Taibi endured desert training at Camp Ibis, California and further practice maneuvers at Camp Polk, Louisiana. Following this, he went to Camp Kilmer, New Jersey, an embarkation port for transport overseas, in August 1944. Just before heading out, Taibi married Margaret Orlicky.

On August 28, 1944 he boarded the English liner, Queen Mary in New York City. A few days later, after docking in Scotland, Taibi traveled to Camp Fargo, England, before finally crossing the English Channel and landing in France in early November.

After being on the defense for several months, the Nazis surprised the allies with a counter-offensive attack. Unfortunately for Taibi, less than two months after entering the fray, he was captured in the Ardennes –during the Battle of the Bulge December 18, 1944. Seized in Magaret, Belgium and taken to Limburg, Germany, Taibi was imprisoned in Stalag IV B. He remained incarcerated there between December 18, 1944 and April 13, 1945. While a prisoner, John S. Taibi kept a journal of daily events describing the inhumane and agonizing treatment of himself and fellow prisoners. Taibi wrote that "practically the whole battery was captured and held in a cold barn writing that the Germans made quite a catch. They marched us three miles all along the front lines and all day to a cold barn. We were packed in like sardines- no sleep and no food."

Taibi was imprisoned for four months and his diary states that he and two of his army friends, Master Sergeant Davis and Buccini (Buck) managed to stay together all of the time that they were prisoners. After their capture and original placement in Stalag IV, located in Bitburg, Germany, Taibi and 160 others walked or rode in railroad boxcars to just beyond the Elbe River at Braunschweig, Germany. General Eisenhower had ordered American troops to halt their advance at the Elbe River to avoid collision with Russian troops coming in from the east. The Russians were then able to invade and conquer Berlin before the Americans arrived. The prisoners of war were liberated by American troops on April 13, 1945, twenty-four days before V- E Day.

During the arduous long march across much of Germany, Taibi relates in his lengthy journal the inhumane treatment the prisoners endured, such as bitter cold weather, sickness, and constant hunger. Also, the Nazi guards periodically beat and shot prisoners. Taibi recorded witnessing prisoners, desperate for food, engaging in fights to steal food from each other in order to stay alive.

Day after day they marched several kilometers across Germany. As the Allied forces advanced from the west, the Nazi captors marched their prisoners farther and farther away. At the same time, the Russians were closing in from the east.

A prisoner's daily rations were meager – ½ or ¾ of a loaf of bread to last for days and skilley- a thin watery soup. They would scavenge for onions and sugar beets in the fields, without the guards' consent. Seldom did they enjoy meat or other protein. Prisoners sold their jewelry and cigarettes to the German guards for food. As the fortunes of war changed on a national level, the individual soldiers still suffered. The cigarettes they sold, according to Taibi's notes, were equal to a month's pay for the German captors. Colds and dysentery were prevalent and made all the more common because of malnourishment. Rarely did prisoners get the opportunity to change clothes. Instead, frequent delousing was used to combat lice. Red Cross packages sometimes came. These included highly appreciated socks, Taibi recorded. They walked through many villages nude. The names of these locations are noted in the journal. He often wrote of home and future plans. John S. Taibi was liberated by American troops at Braunschweig, Germany on April 13, 1945.

Below are excerpts from Taibi's journal. Some entries are shortened for reader understanding.

...Dec. 18 - Captured at Magaret, Belgium- 11 p.m. Practically the whole battery...held in a cold barn. Hope other Bat [battalion] made out all right. Marched us 3 miles long the front lines......

Dec. 19 A small slice of bread issued- Everyone hungry, men picked up frozen food and raided sugar beets [stock]. Interrogated and name taken. Given some soup and coffee. Slept in a cold bowling alley.

Dec.20 Marched us again.......They believe in long marches..... Taken out of the column to burn dead men and horses. Tough digging through slate. M/Sgt Davis and I and Salyes made to walk mined field- certainly aged some and sweated there. Plenty soup and bread.

Dec. 25 Christmas. A piece of bread and oleo. No church services- Bombed and strafed by our own bombers. Plenty casualties. Marched us at night.

Jan 1 New Year. Going to make these holidays up. Everyone talking food.

Jan-2-3 Resting and freezing in a tile warehouse in Werges near Limburg. Frozen feet. Men ailing with colds and dysentery. Red Cross packages arrived. P.P. [Indian]. Had some socks. Prevented frozen feet.

Jan.5 Left Limburg. Warehouse. Loaded on 40 and 8 Boxcars. (60 men) [built for 40]

Jan. 6-7-8-9 Five days [in boxcar] - Lived like pigs. No water-scooped snow for quenching thirst.

Jan. 10 Arrived at Stalag IV-Bathed and deloused-sauerkraut & spuds. Name taken for Geneva [Geneva Convention rules for Prisoners of War]. Met a good Britisher. Davis, Buck and I are still together.

Jan. 17 to Feb14 Left for Stalag VIII A at Gorlitz…Sleeping together on chicken… like roost … placed in barracks for 150 men -but we were 271. Went to mass regularly and confession. Russians-English- Belgians there.

Feb. 14 Left Stalag VIIIA. Gorlitz. Too close to Russian advance. Walked 20km. Miljewski died.

Feb 20 Still walking- Crossed Elbe River. Tea and skilley ¾ loaf of bread for three days. (Didn't last).

Mar. 14 Dunderstadt- Laid over in brick factory. No ration. Ate carrots and beets. Delousing and baths. Notice first lice.

Mar. 15 Man shot for __?____on roof. Men fought for soup. Guards used guns on the men……….No soup for days…..Hit man for trying to steal a blanket. Hand stiff. Bad sleep. Russians and French walked and stole all night. We three promise to be good home men. Like night time best for we always think of home. Drawing plans for building a house & future.

Mar. 16 ……Davis, Buck and I tried to cook spuds. We traded off for cigarettes. No fires. Cigarettes equal to German's month pay…..War news good. Hope for end-

Mar. 24 Men still talking food and recipes like housewives. All going into restaurant business. My cook will be my little Slovak. Don't believe I'll ever hear from home this way by traveling.

Mar. 17 St. Patrick's day – Asking for Commando [working parties]. Many are signing up. Not fed enough for working. Undecided yet. Much better food and clothing than at this filthy hole. Main talk- still food- never women. Promised double ration tomorrow.

Mar. 18 Same stinking hole. Human excrement all over the place………

Mar. 20 Volunteered for Commando. The three of us. Mainly to get a little more food and attention. Maybe a delousing. 4:30 – we three all set to leave tomorrow for Commando. Hurry out of this TB and lice house. Skilley [grass soup].

Mar. 22 Schweigerhausen Steffenburg. Sun beautiful. Everything in bloom. One man killed a frog and ate it raw.

Buck got 3 sugar beets, the dog close to his heels. Two fools tried to escape-broad daylight. One shot.

Mar. 24 Signed up for Commando. Laid out in sun and toasted day's ration of bread. Men still talking food. Must weigh about 170 now (skin and bones). Could use a change of underwear (6 weeks). Walked 2 km for skilley (carrot soup). Picked dandelions and cooked....

Apr. 9 Allies getting closer. May move tomorrow again. We prayed a plenty last night. It won't be long now. <u>*Home*</u> *and* <u>*Muggs.*</u>

Apr. 10 Near Konigslutter. Guards are much nicer now.

Apr. 11 Guns getting nearer. Living on straw in barn.

Apr 12 Horsingen. ......Liberation soon. Rumor is tomorrow. Made a meat and veg. Soup & I fried two potatoes in oleo <u>*AND A EGG*</u> *to go with it. Given to me by a Serb commando. All people are very happy that war is definitely near end (especially* <u>*soldiers*</u>*)....*

Apr.13 At Horsingen. Good and bad news today. Pres. Roosevelt died. We will be liberated in about an hour. We are completely surrounded.....12:30 -American recon car just showed up. Men are cheering and crying. If I wasn't writing I'd cry too. Even German guards are crying. Everyone is happy. Soon be able to write Muggs. Got autograph from Lt. Richard Cressy of Beverly, Mass. He was first American officer we've seen and our liberator. 4:20 – A GMC truck arrived and picked up the sick.......

All the PW's are stripped.-Delousing themselves, washing. Sorry looking bunch of men-underfed-almost skeleton in appearance.

Apr 16 Taken to prisoner of war release point awaiting a plane to take us to LeHavre for the states. The men today stripped German prisoners as they did us when we were captured. We were a bit easier on the bastards.... Seen my BN commander Col. Warner and Major Bookstrom. They fared much better than we enlisted men.

Apr. 20 Left by plane for LeHavre.

Following his liberation, Taibi once again enjoyed freedom, more food, and recreation. He wrote of attending a GI show. After his arrival at LeHavre, France, Taibi boarded the USS SEA ROBIN bound for New York's Lake

Placid Club. POWs stationed east of the Mississippi River were sent to Lake Placid Club to recuperate.

Corporal John Taibi was discharged from the Army in November 1945. He returned home and worked for the New York City Subway System for a short time, then for the U.S. Post Office department, which was later renamed the U.S. Postal Service. He retired in 1975.

Taibi's son recalled his father's reaction to his prisoner of war experience in later years; "Dad did not dwell much on his war experience. That is why, while we knew of the diary, he wouldn't let us see it until after he passed away."

Corporal John S. Taibi passed away June14, 1994. He is buried in the Veteran's Cemetery at Asheville, North Carolina.

Part V
Amphibious Warfare

AMPHIBIOUS MAN

You've heard plenty of the navy,
Or ships, both forward and aft,
But we'll bet a pretty penny,
You've heard least of landing craft.
...
They're loaded from the transports
In the middle of the night.
Sail around to rendezvous;
Can't even show a light
Find their way in darkness
And land upon the shore..........
Through bombs discharge their cargo
They go right back for more.

(Author unknown. Found among the personal effects of Thomas
R. Fisher, U.S. Navy Memorial Foundation Newsletter by Edward
Prados, September 1999).

61

Thomas Guidera

USS OBERON(AKA-34)

During World War II amphibious warfare was a major method of warfare used in the various invasions of North Africa and Europe. It was essential in the island hopping campaigns in the vast Pacific. This method of warfare utilized both sea and land to transport men, supplies and equipment to the beachhead.

The attack cargo ship was an essential element of World War II amphibious warfare. Attack transports (APA's) dispatched troops, but the attack cargo ships (AKA's) transported supplies, tanks, and troops. The USS OBERON (AKA-14), originally listed as AK-56, was 459 feet in length and was launched in March of 1942 in Brooklyn, New York. She received six battle stars and survived a kamikaze attack during World War II and also saw action during the Korean War. The Dictionary of American Naval Fighting Ships, Vol. V, states that in 1970, she was placed in the National Fleet in Olympia, Washington, and sold to the Marine Power (Mooney 130).

Thomas Guidera, of Utica served on the USS OBERON as a plank owner (original crewmember) from June 15, 1942 to about October 15, 1945.

* * * *

Following high school, Guidera enlisted in the Navy and completed boot camp at Sampson Naval Station in upstate New York It has been 56 years since Thomas Guidera boarded the USS OBERON in the Brooklyn Naval Shipyard. The gravel-voiced old ex-Boatswain Mate proudly described his brand new cargo vessel, which carried him to many well-known battles of World War II —from North Africa, the Mediterranean and on to the Pacific Ocean to Okinawa and Japan. Guidera displayed a framed photograph of the OBERON. He said that the picture was taken in Baltimore, Maryland and a portion of the caption reads as follows:

...USS OBERON (AKA-14) – 1942-1955. Six battle stars in WWII – Five during the Korean War. Participated in the invasion of North Africa in 1942 before transferring to the Pacific in early 1943. The ship traveled to the Solomon Islands, New

Hebrides Islands and on to Guadalcanal where fighting was still in progress. Returning to the Atlantic and the Mediterranean, the OBERON was in combat in Sicily in July of 1943, and Salerno Bay in Italy two months later. Following storm damage the attack cargo ship returned to action in 1944 for operations off Algeria, Italy and France. Back to the Pacific in 1945, the ship saw action off the Philippines and Okinawa....

Guidera said that his ship carried about 26 boats - the LCVP's and tank lighters (LCM's) that carried troops, tanks, and trucks to the beachheads.

In describing the booms aboard the AKA, he said that there was a middle boom and two booms located on each side of the ship. The booms were 50 feet long and 24" in diameter, and they could lift tank lighters, 35-ton tanks, ten wheeler trucks and weapon carriers. "We carried Sherman tanks which were the biggest that were used during the war. The booms could lift 40 tons and we carried everything from a toothpick to a tank including food and ammunition," he said proudly. "After the ships were unloaded, the landing craft were available to go and load troops from the transports and take them into the beach."

In further explaining the details of the photograph of his ship, he pointed to the three-inch guns on the bow that were later changed to 40mm guns. There was one five inch x 51 surface gun on the stern which was later replaced with a five-inch x 38 anti-aircraft gun. There were twelve 20mm guns on the flying bridge (the upper most deck where semaphore flags are flown).

From Brooklyn, the ship headed for Norfolk, Virginia and then across the Atlantic. The first battle for the OBERON would be in North Africa unloading supplies in French Morocco on D-Day, November 8, 1942.

There were air raids and a submarine attack but the unloading continued (Mooney 130). Following this, the OBERON returned to Norfolk and then set out for the Pacific carrying cargo to New Caledonia and the New Hebrides before returning to Norfolk again (Mooney 130).

The OBERON then crossed the Atlantic once more and the next invasion would be Sicily. Guidera recalled that in Sicily, an ammunition ship was torpedoed and the ship's history records this event as the outstanding incident of the battle. Guidera said it occurred about 200 yards from his ship. "We were at general quarters (battle stations) at the time and I was manning a 20mm on the flying bridge. I could see steel flying up, and Shrapnel injured two or three of our boys." Guidera said that while in Sicily in 1943, he visited some relatives including two aunts and five cousins.

The next operation was at Salerno Bay. Guidera said that they were kept busy with the anti-aircraft guns during that invasion.

The ship also did supply runs between Oran and Bizerte. It was in Oran, Algeria that he met his brother. "In Oran, he explained, we were training for future operations and the air attacks there were bad. The Luftwaffe surprised our convoy when we were underway for Bizerte."

On the first of December, the OBERON left with Army paratroopers for Northern Ireland. On the return trip, after unloading the paratroopers, the ship was caught in a storm and there were 25-foot waves causing damage to the deck. The plates on the deck are one-inch thick and about 20 feet of the deck had cracked and had to be welded. The ship was ordered back to Philadelphia for more permanent repairs.

In June of 1944, the ship returned to Naples and after practicing landings, participated in the August 15, 1944 invasion of southern France. One hundred and fifty-one soldiers and sailors and equipment were unloaded. On August 16, seven wounded American and five wounded German prisoners were taken aboard and the ship left for Mers El Kabir.

The OBERON returned to the United States on October 24 and then was reassigned to the Pacific. On Christmas Day, the ship got underway and traveled through the Panama Canal and it sailed on to Honolulu reaching Leyte in the Philippine Islands in February 1945, via Eniwetok, Pelieu and the Palau Islands (Mooney 130).

On April 1, the OBERON, while participating in the Okinawa invasion, had to postpone the unloading, and temporarily leave the area because of kamikaze attacks.

The squadron returned to the area by 7:00 that night and the squadron was attacked on the starboard side by the kamikaze and suicide planes hit four ships. The OBERON was not hit but was credited with shooting down one plane and perhaps two others that were not confirmed. The cargo and personnel were discharged rapidly and after the loading was completed on April 26, the OBERON left for Ulithi where the crew had their first liberty ashore in 97 days (Mooney 130).

The War Diary of the USS OBERON states the following: "May was a good month. The Germans surrendered on May 7. On the 13th of May, the ship sailed south to New Zealand, crossed the equator (second time) and reached Guadalcanal on the 20th and then on to the Philippine Islands."

The ship traveled on to Samar where the crew learned of the Japanese surrender. In Japan, Guidera left the OBERON and boarded an attack transport as a passenger and he was bound for the United States. "I can't remember the name of that ship, Guidera said, but I called it the USS MARMELADE. The chow lines were so long that I bought marmalade from the Ship's Store, bread from the mess hall and made marmalade sandwiches.

I did not want to wait in the long lines," he said "That is all I ate – morning, noon, and night."

BM3 Thomas Guidera received six battle stars and was a full-fledged "Shellback" for having crossed the equator. In fact, he had crossed it four times but only had to receive one "shellacking." Guidera remembered that the first time he crossed, on January 19, 1943, the Japanese dominated the Pacific.

He was discharged from the Navy in November of 1945 and returned to Utica. He then worked at various jobs before becoming a self employed home improvements contractor.

Thomas Guidera passed away February 16, 2010.

62

Edward Isley

LCT SAILOR

LCT's (Landing Craft, Tank) were also part of the amphibious force. The LCT was 105 feet long and 45 feet wide. They were transported to the invasion areas fastened to the top of an LST. The LCT could carry six tanks and six full sized army trucks. The crew of an LCT was made up of two officers and 12 enlisted men. There was a galley and supply section for ammunition and there were two gun tubs above the officer quarters.

Edward Isley, who was born in Oriskany Falls and moved to Waterville after World War II, served on board an LCT in the South Pacific.

* * * *

At age 16, Isley was working on Route 20 for the Dale Engineering Co., which is now known as the MWH Corporation. Still in school, his mother would not let him enlist when he became 17 years old so he went to work for General Cable in Rome in the foundry for a while.

Enlisting in the Navy in December of 1943, he traveled to the Sampson Naval Training Center for boot camp. Isley remembered that one day at Sampson it was snowing so hard and the visibility was so bad when they were marching, that one company of recruits ran right into another company.

Following "boot camp", he attended Motor Machinist's school at the Navy Pier on Lake Michigan in Chicago. The school was eight weeks long and after ten days leave, he reported to the Solomons, Maryland Amphibious Base which is located on the Chesapeake Bay. "It was ideal for landing craft training."

From Maryland, Isley boarded a troop train for New Orleans, Louisiana.

...That was something. I'll always remember that place (New Orleans) with the big signs on the lawns. 'Sailors and soldiers - be off the streets by eleven and stay off the lawns.' "I never forgot that. In New Orleans, while waiting for our LST, we would take the bus to visit the Lake Pontchartrain beach recreation area.

On the bus, a friend of mine tried to talk to these girls in the front and they turned around and said, 'We don't talk to damn Yankees.' Another time we were going out on the bus and the driver pulled over to the curb and stopped. We wondered why since we had not arrived to this beach yet. We were seated behind the side entrance exit. He came back and said, 'you guys have either to get up in front or we are going to stay right here. You have to sit forward of the door and the colored sit here.' "Both of us northerners didn't know anything about this.

At the port area, the men got aboard the LST and were mixed into the crew and assigned to a watch section. The next day they went to Gulfport, Mississippi and spent the night loading the ship with ammunition. Isley explained that LCT's were placed onto LST's for transport overseas where tanks from a Liberty ship were placed. The LCT's could carry six tanks— two in the back and four in the front. He said that the LCT's would go to the beach and tanks would then be driven off during the invasion. The LCT was used in various ways. One time, Isley recalled, his LCT traveled up a river through Manila carrying miscellaneous cargo.

Isley said that his LCT was placed on top of the LST at Gulfport, did a 180-degree turn, and headed for Panama. He thought that it was either May or June of 1944 when a stop was made at Coco Solo, located on the Atlantic side of the Canal Zone. After one day there, the LST went through the Canal with two other ships.

...On the watch bill I had been assigned as a Captain's Talker. Out of the 125 men on board, only twelve had been to sea before. I said to the boatswain mate, 'What the devil is a Captain's Talker?' Looking at the watch list he replied, 'you be on the Conn (the station where Captain or Officer of the Deck controls the ship) at noon (the day we were scheduled to go through the Canal) you keep your helmet and ear phones on. You will be in contact with all of the gun tubs. Every fifteen minutes you get the report from the gun tubs and repeat it to the Conn.' I had no experience but I did it with no problems. From the Conn I was looking down into the jungle as the ship was going through the Canal. I see all these guns sticking up. They must have been expecting some kind of air raid from the Germans.

After going through the Canal, the LST developed engine trouble from contaminated fuel. On the fourth day there were rough seas and the flat-bottomed LST was climbing up and going down huge waves. Isley was on scullery duty in the mess hall emptying trays in GI cans. Along came a Boatswain's Mate who thought Isley looked a little seasick. He told him 'Why don't you go to your rack (bed), I'll take over.' "I had a queasy stomach but I didn't throw up," he laughed.

The sea was rough and it looked as if they were not making much headway. They had been out for twenty-eight days. The ship was zigzagging to avoid submarines and Isley asked a friend on watch who had the wheel, what direction they were going. He said they were still going south. "I said that after two weeks we would hit the South Pole. The friend on watch disagreed saying that the ship was only doing ten miles an hour. After a thirty-day voyage we made it to Espiritu Santo in the South Pacific."

Isley described the manner in which the LCT is taken off the LST.

…There was a huge tanker anchored there and angled in a LIST position. (The tanker had shifted its ballast). The LST with our LCT aboard went alongside the tanker. We tied up to the tanker, which hooked on to the LCT. When the crane on the tanker lifted the LCT, it straightened the tanker upright and lowered us into the water. You should have seen the size of that crane. We were the first LCT that was ever lifted from an LST in the South Pacific. Isley pointed out that the old procedure for unloading an LCT was as follows: When an LCT was loaded on the larger LST, it was placed on large cross-timbers, and to unload the LCT, the LST would shift its ballast. This would place the LST into a sharp angle making it possible for the LCT to slide down the timbers into the water…

From Espiritu Santo, Isley said the LCT was cabled to a British merchant ship and towed to Manus in the Admiralty Islands. They were towed up the Slot between Guadalcanal and a couple of other islands.

At Manus there was a naval base that was still being built by the CB's (Construction Battalions). Isley located John Litz, a friend from back home. A letter from home informed him that Litz was at Manus. Litz was in the ship's service section working on a hut where ice cream and other items could be purchased. He was excited to see Isley and after jumping over something in his way, greeted him with a big hug. The two who were buddies in school got a six-pack of beer and went up to John's tent in the jungle.

From Manus the LCT went to Hollandia and then towed again in convoy to Leyte in the Philippines for the invasion. There was little resistance from the enemy at first but trouble developed as the troops moved inland. There was a big naval battle there. (The largest naval battle between surface ships of the war took place. The Japanese were making an attempt to divert Americans away from invading Leyte. This was to be the last engagement between battleships in World War II. (Wheal, Pope, and Taylor 276-7). Isley described the Leyte landing:

> *...The surf was six to eight feet high behind us and we were trying to discharge tanks. It was a pretty hairy deal. The Army engineers would hook cables to eyes on the sides of the LCT and then hook to the back of tanks and drive them right off with locked gears. This would hold us on the beach so we could discharge the tanks without getting into trouble like tearing off the ramp of the LCT. The ramp alone weighed ten ton. The surf was so high the waves would come right over the stern. The LCT's dropped everything they had. Even though it was towed to Leyte, the LCT had its own power—three engines when going into the beach. We stayed there several weeks bringing in tanks and trucks. We then went to the island of Luzon and there had not been much resistance there either. It was there that the Navy used some LCI's (troop carriers). When the Japanese retreated, some went north and others went toward Manila. The Navy got the LCI 's to go north along the Luzon coast to cut them off. However, the sea was very rough and the LCI 's rolled terribly and the attempt to cut the Japanese off was called off.*

Traveling from Luzon toward Subic Bay, Isley said that they were warned about mines in the area and to inform the minesweepers ahead if any mines were observed. With remarkable memory, he illustrates a detailed, vivid, and horrifying description of some of the events at Subic and Manila Bays.

> *...The Subic Bay Naval Station had been blown to pieces. We then headed toward Manila and three LCT's went into Manila Bay. Ten Navy planes were dropping bombs over a small island off Corregidor and we could see Japs shooting at our planes. The radioman picked up the pilots and he heard one pilot holler, 'Look out - those are our guys.'*
> *We anchored in Manila Bay a couple of miles off Manila. We sat there for five days and watched that city burn. As the Japanese retreated, they burned block after block. They burned everything. On the third night there I went aboard two PT boats that were*

there. I had earlier volunteered for PT boats or submarines but was put in the amphibious Navy.

One night I had the 12-4 watch and at about 3:45 I had gone to bed. At 4:30 the PT boats started up their engines. What a hell of a noise they make when they open up. They were going out to go after some Japanese troops who had gotten off the beach and they had made their way in canoes to some partially sunken ships in Manila Bay. The PT boats shot at the Japanese with 20mm guns. For the first time, I almost felt sorry for the Japanese.

Isley recalled that the next night it was very dark and quiet and he could hear splashing along side the ship and there was a fear that someone might be approaching the ship armed with grenades. "The sailors aboard carried side arms and were ordered to spray the water and all of sudden there was no splashing and we hear "God Bless America." being sung. A light was flashed on them and we saw six to eight Filipinos. The "Skipper" sent them away and told them to come back tomorrow."

Another time in Manila Bay when the area was being cleaned up of Japanese, they heard trucks coming down the road and music was being played on the loud speakers. The trucks were loaded with liberated American prisoners of war. They were placed aboard the LCT and taken to a transport in the Bay.

From Manila Bay, the LCT went to Corregidor with some material and Isley and two others had requested permission to go ashore.

We had been gone for about an hour climbing around looking at caves and where the American troops were in 1942 when Corregidor fell. About fifteen minutes after we got back to the ship an officer, a colonel, drove up in a jeep and wanted to know who was in charge. The "Skipper," an ensign, replied that he was in charge. The Colonel said, 'If I see any more of your men ashore without sidearms, your ass is in trouble.' The "Skipper" then told us, 'All right, no more going ashore.' We had been looking for souvenirs. A buddy found a World War I helmet that had been used at Corregidor in the early days of the war. He later lost that.

In the spring of 1945 in Manila, the LCT was making trips back and forth to Subic Bay and time was also spent painting and camouflaging the boat. Isley had an opportunity to see Fred Moon who was also from Oriskany Falls, and a corpsman on an APA (attack transport). He took an LCVP over to his ship and went aboard and saw him working in sickbay. Moon didn't immediately recognize him.

Isley recalled another interesting, but sad experience. He told of how he and some buddies went into a honky tonk on the Manila waterfront, and saw about ten soldiers who had been drinking and somewhat drunk and having a crying jag. They were the part of a company that tried to rid Rizal Stadium of Japanese snipers. The snipers had killed a lot of men in the company. MacArthur had wanted to prevent Rizal Stadium and the old walled city of Manila from being destroyed. Finally, MacArthur had to back off and allow the use of tanks to eliminate the snipers. "Seeing the soldiers cry gave us something to think about. This incident with the snipers had been kept quiet," Isley pointed out.

The LCT was hauling all sorts of cargo including large crates of cigarettes.

> *...A cruiser came in and we were assigned to it to take some of the sailors to a recreation area. There was to be a beach party and we took 100 men off the cruiser to an island where they played ball, poker and drank beer for three to four hours. They hadn't had liberty for eleven months. When we went back to get them they were so drunk that when they got back to the cruiser a cargo net had to be let down to the LCT and they were lifted up six at a time and then rolled out onto the deck. While others were waiting to be lifted, they would yell up to the officers swearing at them. I never forgot that*

In Manila on V-J Day, Isley said that there was a party that night. The 3" x 50mm gun was going off in the harbor and everyone was firing flares in the air with Very pistols.

From August to April of 1946, the LCT did a lot of hauling. Most of the crew had left and replacements arrived. Also, a directive was received which stated that a lot of Japanese ammunition dumps had to be taken out to sea. Isley describes the dangerous assignment and his apprehension and feelings:

> *...We would be on the beach at high tide and the Filipino stevedores would load us with 50 to 60 tons of the ammunition. With the tide high we would go out with the Filipino stevedores (all small people) and dump the ammo off the coast. We spent Thanksgiving, Christmas, and New Years up to March 1946 doing this. I got more gray hairs from this than all the while I had been in the Navy. We would go to the beach and play ball. The Army guys*

would come down with 500-pound bombs. The U.S. was afraid the "Huks", Philippine guerillas, would get the ammunition and cause an insurrection. We got stuck with that duty of getting rid of this ammunition and I got out of the Navy with an attitude.

He concluded his account by explaining that it was not possible to explode this ammunition ashore a little at a time.

Finally, the day arrived for going home. From Subic Bay, Isley was heading home on a victory ship loaded with about 900 men for the long trip across the Pacific. On the way the boiler sprung a leak that was repaired at Guam. A typhoon was also encountered. It took 22 days to reach the Golden Gate Bridge. In San Francisco by Easter Sunday, there was a one-day delay before docking because the fog was so thick. The crew could look up and see the Golden Gate Bridge over them, but could not see land until the fog lifted.

Boarding a troop train, he spent five days crossing the country to New York City and was discharged at Lido Beach, Long Island on April 23, 1946. Motor Machinist Mate Edward Isley received two battle stars and a Navy Commendation Medal.

After returning home, Isley attended college for about two years. He had joined the Naval Reserve and while working at Chicago Pneumatic, was recalled during the Korean War and served another twenty-three months in the Navy. Following his release from active duty, he was employed at the Bendix Corporation.

63

Alan Jamieson

BEACH BATTALION RADIOMAN

Beach Battalions were created during World War II as part of amphibious warfare. After the assault troops got ashore, they had to be supplied with weapons, food, ammunition, clothing, artillery, tank support and medical assistance. Controlling the distribution of the material across the beaches led to the establishment of Beach Battalions (Vey 12). The Beachmaster was the leader of the unit and each platoon was assigned a radioman, signalman, medical personnel, hydrographic specialists and boat repair experts. They went ashore in one or more of three or four assault waves and distributed equipment across the beach so that bombing or artillery would not destroy everything. Beach communications could be the difference between victory and defeat. Radios, signal lights and semaphore flags were used effectively (Vey and Elliott i and iii). Alan Jamieson of New Hartford, New York and a resident of Waterville for many years, was a member of a beach party during the battle of Okinawa as a Navy radioman attached to a communications unit.

****

After graduating from New Hartford Central School on his eighteenth birthday, Jamieson volunteered for induction into the service in August of 1943 and he chose the Navy. He was ordered to Sampson Naval Training Center and though "boot camp" was tough, Jamieson said that his choir experience made his training much more tolerable. "They came around and asked if anyone ever sang in a choir or if anyone had any training in singing. I said that I sang in a choir in church. They said, 'OK, step out.' All who stepped out were placed in a company that would sing in a choir. "We had a piano in the barracks and one guy would play the piano and we would sit around and sing. That was pretty good since "boot camp" wasn't the nicest thing going. We got out of KP by being in the choir," Jamieson related in his joyous manner.

Following boot camp, Jamieson attended radio school at Bedford Springs, Pennsylvania. The school was an actual navy base but was operated by the Keystone Schools and civilian instructors staffed it. Jamieson recalled that one old fellow who had been in the Merchant Marine was his instructor who said that he had been on three different ships that had been torpedoed and sunk. He said he finally decided that the Merchant Marine wasn't for him.

After completion of radioman school, he boarded a troop train for San Bruno, California near San Francisco. At San Bruno, the sailors slept in stables at a horse track and the building had been converted into a barracks. "Our room was a horse stable and the area had become a naval base." At San Bruno more training followed, and he was then transferred to Camp Pendleton, a Marine base, since he had been assigned to the amphibious forces. They were actually stationed at the naval base at Oceanside, California. but the sailors received amphibious training at Camp Pendleton. All of it was actually Camp Pendleton. "We always needled the Marines by telling them that they were just a part of us - the Navy. Once the Navy and the Marines marched in the Oceanside 4th of July parade. The Marines were always bragging but our little outfit, COM 42 beat them at marching that day."

Jamieson traveled overseas on the USS GENERAL HOWE (APA), an attack transport, manned by a Coast Guard crew. He said that the food was not too good and everyone was not feeling too well due to seasickness. "One night we had turkey and it was the best meal we had," he stated. However, the turkey was spoiled. All of them had to go to the sick bay and were instructed to vomit. Jamieson recalled with one of his big hearty laughs that one of them remarked, 'That's the best meal I had and I'm not going to throw it up.'

The communications unit to which Jamieson was attached did not do too much on the ship, and after six days they arrived at Hawaii and there was more training. It was 1944 and the stay in Hawaii was quite extensive. It was in Hawaii that Jamieson met his brother Bill who was stationed on board the USS SPERRY- a destroyer.

Jamieson boarded a troop transport and left Hawaii about the middle of February 1945. His memory of the Philippines is vague but it was a few months after the invasion of Luzon, when the ship arrived in the area. He said they did not get off the ship and did not do much there, but he felt that he was in the area of Mindanao and close enough to the combat area to earn one battle star.

On April 1, forty-six days after leaving Hawaii, the troop transport approached Okinawa. Jamieson explained that the troops went in from the China Sea and the Japanese were expecting the invasion to take place from the Pacific Ocean or eastern side of the island. The Japanese guns were pointing eastward and Jamieson said that it was a bloodless beachhead. After the troops landed, the Marines went right through taking the northern half of the island and secured the area. The Army, invading the southern half, had a more difficult time and their progress was slower.

Jamieson's communications unit went into the beach by landing craft where he acted as a radioman. "We had a voice radio and we had communication with the ship that would tell us when the troops would be coming in. We would relay the messages to the officers who would tell the ships where to direct the landing craft and we had a signal light on the beach and messages would be sent using a blinking light. I didn't operate that- but I could in an emergency," he asserted.

Jamieson gave a comical demonstration of distinguishing the dots and dashes of the Morse code in operating the flashing signal light. He made two quick forward movements with his fingers at the top of his right ear and quickly followed with a blinking of the eyes. The demonstration ended with a burst of laughter.

Kenneth Sliter, a former Navy signalman second class from Port Leyden, New York, had served in the 1st Beach Battalion and participated in the invasions at Salerno, Sicily, Anzio, and southern France. He also served in the Pacific and did duty ashore at Okinawa as part of communications. In an interview with the author, Sliter said that the beach battalions in the Pacific were referred to as Beach Parties. After the landing, the Beach Party would provide communication with ships. Sliter said that he also would contact ships from the beach with semaphore flags and the blinker light. For example, the message might be a request to send more jeeps. Sliter also explained that he performed signalman duties aboard the USS BINGHAM, as well as serving in the Beach Party. Also, some members of the Beach Party had to guard Japanese prisoners on Okinawa. He said the prisoners would be stripped naked while being searched for knives and then given fatigues to wear. The prisoners were then enclosed in a circle and later transported by small boats to the cruisers and other big ships.

Jamieson stated that there was an airfield behind their work area on the beach and one night an enemy "Betty" (a small bomber) had landed on the American airfield... "The Japanese got out and scattered. Now, the Japanese were in the area and I don't know what happened to them. There were just enough Japanese in the area so you couldn't sleep at night," Jamieson said.

The author asked Jamieson about suicide planes, which were such a frightening ordeal during the Battle of Okinawa. He answered by saying that they could look out from the beach area and see the suicide planes, and did actually see one hit a big ship. "We were about twenty yards inland and the big ships were way out and we could see all kinds of ships. The smaller amphibious vessels were on the beach unloading. The author mentioned that there were about 450,000 troops participating in the battle. Jamieson asked, "Were there that many there? "I thought I was all alone," he said with a huge laugh. "We were twenty year old kids and didn't know what the hell was going on. The things you do when you're young," he reminisced. "When we got a chance, we would grab a boat and go out to the different ships to visit. Once, an officer who saw us going out to the ships spotted us and he hollered to a petty officer to 'get that boat back!' The first class petty officer and the officer chewed us out. They said you guys are crazy."

"We had a jeep with a radio and would drive it back and forth on the beach area to our eating area. During air raids, the beach would be strafed and at first, it was quite often. We could see dogfights (aerial combat) going on in the air. Fortunately, no one in the outfit was injured. We lived in tents about a half-mile from where we worked on the beach," Jamieson explained.

The island was secured on June 22, 1945, Jamieson's birthday. He then went to Hawaii for training in preparation for the invasion of Japan. The war ended suddenly so Jamieson was ordered to Sasebo Harbor, Japan where he was engaged in the same kind of work with his communications outfit. In Sasebo, they lived in old Japanese barracks and were part of the occupation forces but he did not have to do very much. Sasebo was a busy harbor. He said the Japanese people treated him well and one time they walked into a shop and a Japanese man behind him said, "Hi fellows." Jamieson said the person had attended UCLA. He learned that many of the Japanese were very fluent in English.

In early 1946, Radioman Second Class Alan Jamieson boarded a ship and after a stopover in Hawaii, sailed on to Treasure Island, CA. He was discharged at Lido Beach, Long Island, in April 1946.

Returning home, Jamieson attended the Utica School of Commerce and since he had joined the Naval Reserve, he was recalled during the Korean War and served for fourteen months on board the USS HALE (DD) - a destroyer. "I was a Truman Trooper," he joked.

Alan Jamieson moved to Waterville, New York and worked in New Hartford as a mail carrier for the post office.

He passed away April 18, 2007.

64

Steven Sadlon

"EXERCISE TIGER"

In the weeks before D-Day June 6, 1944, a mock invasion was being planned as a dress rehearsal for the actual invasion of Normandy. "Exercise Tiger" was the code name and it was to take place during the latter part of April 1944. Three hundred ships and 30,000 men would be participating. On April 28, eight LST's (Landing Ship Tank) in the English Channel were headed toward Slapton Sands, England where the practice landing would take place. Unfortunately, this rehearsal failed in its purpose and caused the loss of 749 lives –581 soldiers and 198 sailors. (Tiger 1).

German E-boats (PT Boats) out of Cherbourg attacked the eight LST's. Two of the LST's were torpedoed and lost and one was crippled. There were more lives lost in this one practice exercise than the actual assault of Utah Beach on June 6 (Eckstam 1). For many years, very few people have had knowledge of this incident. To safeguard the secrecy of the planned invasion of Normandy, American leaders threatened courts-martial if any soldiers, sailors, or medical personnel revealed any information

The public became more aware of the disaster after a television program, ABC's 20/20, had a special report on "Exercise Tiger" in 1984.

In August of 1944, after the Normandy invasion, information of casualties was released to the <u>Stars and Stripes</u> newspaper. (Charles B. MacDonald, a former deputy chief historian at the Army's Center of Military History has written an article entitled, "Slapton Sands: The Cover-up That Never Was" in <u>ARMY</u> Magazine of June 1988. MacDonald wrote that the order of secrecy was never lifted for various reasons, but that there have been several accounts written since 1945 about the disaster. He writes that if anyone had taken time to investigate that, it would show clearly that there was no cover-up (MacDonald 64-67). Nevertheless, accusations of 'cover-up' still continue to be made, since the general public was totally unaware of "Exercise Tiger" until years after it occurred. ("Exercise Tiger" is also mentioned in the Fred Moon chapter of this book).*

---

* The Supreme Allied Command in Europe felt that information relating to "Exercise Tiger" should not be immediately released for fear of jeopardizing the June 6, 1944 Normandy invasion.

Steven Sadlon of Ilion, New York served aboard the LST 507, which was sunk during the exercise and he believes that there was a "cover up." He was one of the navy survivors and received the Purple Heart for the injuries he incurred.

✴ ✴ ✴ ✴

Enlisting into the Navy on January 12, 1943, he completed his "boot camp" at the Sampson Naval Training Center and then reported to the amphibious base at Solomons, Maryland and then was later transferred to Little Creek, Virginia. He boarded the LST 507 at Evansville, Indiana on the Mississippi River.

In April of 1944, Sadlon was in England when the allied powers decided to launch "Exercise Tiger." On April 28, informed that this was to be a dry run, the men and equipment were loaded onto LST 507. Shortly after midnight, the ship proceeded into the Channel. Sadlon described the tragic incident as follows:

> *...I was in the crew's quarters and I heard a rumble below our ship. It was a torpedo and it had gotten underneath the ship and did not explode but I could hear the noise of the torpedo. When I got to GQ (General Quarters), I went into the radio shack, my GQ station. A torpedo in the auxiliary engine room did hit us. I was just above it in the navigation division when the torpedo hit. I was in my chair when the explosion occurred and my head hit the overhead and the transformer went down and it was a good thing I wasn't in back of it, since transformers were as big as a refrigerator. I was knocked out and after I woke up I crawled out into the dark and into the Wheelhouse. The "Skipper" was giving a lot of commands and the ship was burning amidships. There were explosions and nine German E-boats were attacking the flotilla of eight LST's. I waited for orders, because being a radioman you got to see what you have to do. I pressed a lever and destroyed the codes since that was my job. After destroying the codes, I went down to the crew's quarters below deck in the fantail and got my revolver, so that if they picked me up, I might be able to defend myself. (I wasn't supposed to have a revolver but I kept one to carry ashore on liberty in London for protection). The tank deck was open and I looked in and it was all in flames and I heard the screams – just a horrible, horrible sight. They couldn't help themselves. They had been in the tank deck waiting for the landing and ready to unload. I got onto the fantail and*

all of these soldiers and sailors and my buddies were there. The signalman went into the water but got right back on the ship. He said, 'I'm not going into that water. It's too cold.' He had gone into the 48° water and I told him. 'You have two choices. Either you burn to death or you freeze to death. I'm going to take my chances of freezing to death because I don't want to burn to death because those flames are real close.' We just didn't have much time so I jumped in with the Assistant Navigator and several others. There was lots of diesel oil and flames in the water. We jumped in. But the soldiers – they just stayed there and didn't jump. After we jumped in, we scattered the flames with our hands and we got away from the ship. I was with the assistant navigator and I heard a drone and thinking it was a small boat, I cried out and screamed and said 'Help!' The assistant navigator said, 'Save your breath, it won't do you any good.' So I just quieted down and that is the last thing I remember. I passed right out.

Sadlon remembered that he had been placed on board another LST and laid out on a mess table in the crew's quarters located below deck in the stern of the ship. He said a pile of Army blankets covered him and he was shaking like a leaf.

...I said 'Where the heck am I?' The last place I was at was in the water. I had these tags attached to me, which said that I had morphine and blood plasma. One fellow came up to me and said 'you know, you are lucky. We picked you up and piled you with the dead.' He said that I was frothing at the mouth and he had pulled me out of the pile of the dead. That was the last I saw of him and I don't even know who saved me.

Sadlon added that when he attended an LST 507 re-union at Pittsburgh, Pennsylvania, one of the survivors of the sinking, the Communications Officer, "saw me and he thought he had seen a ghost." He said to me, 'I thought you were dead.' "He didn't think I survived the sinking and all these years thought that I had been listed as dead," Sadlon exclaimed. Sadlon further explained that the doctor on the LST 507, Lieutenant Eugene Eckstam, found out he was alive and started writing to him.

Sadlon said, "It burns me up that this was kept secret so long and the way we were treated. We were entitled to survivor's leave, but we were not permitted to have leave." There was fear that if the Germans had knowledge of the Slapton Sands disaster, it would affect the success of the Normandy invasion.

Sadlon explained that the American Admiral, Don Moon, Commander of Force U, and in charge of the operation, was supposed to arrange an escort in the Channel for the LST flotilla but that escort was not provided. The LST's left from Plymouth, England and were to participate in the practice invasion on to Slapton Sands in England. Sadlon said that before being confronted by the E-boats, their radar man had observed objects on the radar but thought it came from the promised escort. "After we were hit, ships were ordered not to stop for survivors," Sadlon added.

Captain John Doyle was the commanding officer of LST 515, the flagship of "Exercise Tiger." In addition to the flagship, the flotilla included LST's 496, 511, 531, 518, 499, 289, 507. Captain Doyle disregarded the Admiral's orders and did pick up survivors, Sadlon said.

>*...If it wasn't for Captain Doyle, I wouldn't be able to tell this story. Doyle went on against orders and he ended up losing command of his ship. He was up for court-martial and never promoted. All of the other LST's just left. They didn't stop to pick us up. That's what hurts, you know.*

Sadlon showed the author a picture of a memorial to Doyle. In Missoula, Montana, where Doyle is buried, there is monument, which bears the word "EVENT" centered at the top. Below his name, Captain H. Doyle, several words are inscribed as follows: "This monument is a tribute to Captain Doyle with the deepest respect from his crew of the LST 515 and the 100 men plus, as survivors of the sunken LST's 507 and 531."

From the hospital, Sadlon was assigned to a British Army base, and stayed in a rusty Quonset hut. He said that they were literally isolated and cast aside.

Sadlon displayed a large illustration that commemorates "Exercise Tiger." Two tanks are shown in the illustration – one tank is located at Slapton Sands (recovered from the English Channel), and the other tank is at New Bedford, MA. He also explained that a tree has been planted at Arlington National Cemetery in Virginia in memory of those who died during the practice exercise.

"We were later assigned to dangerous work parties unloading ammunition from two different ammunition ships, which were named NITRO and BAKER. Even during an air raid we had to unload 40 mm ammunition, silk bags and projectiles for battleships. My nerves were about shot, Sadlon recalled.

Sadlon was later assigned to the LST 500 and he remembered that prior to the invasion of Normandy, he was called to the Executive Officer's office and given his Purple Heart medal. The Executive Officer told him, 'You are not getting a ceremony.' Sadlon said that this was another example of attempts made to keep what happened off Slapton Sands a secret.

He described another sad incident that he witnessed.

>...*We took part in the Normandy invasion, anchored off Utah Beach. The LCVP's (Landing Craft Vehicles Personnel) were unloading men onto the beach and the tanks, trucks and 'Ducks' were also unloaded. A destroyer came alongside our ship and struck a mine. We could see the bodies of the destroyer sailors being picked up and placed on our ship.*

Sadlon returned to the USA and in Norfolk was assigned to the AF9, a navy refrigeration ship on which he served from 1944-46. He also served in the Asiatic-Pacific Theater of operations crossing the equator and earning the title of "Shellback."

Radioman Second Class Steven Sadlon had earned a battle star and the Purple Heart and was discharged from the Navy on March 15, 1946. He then joined the Naval Reserve and was recalled into the Navy during the Korean War. After release, he returned to Ilion and worked as a carpenter and managed his apartments and houses.

65

Edward Wazenkewitz

LST SAILOR

The LST (Landing, Ship Tank) was designed and used for the first time during World War II. This flat-bottomed vessel with a large door and ramp on the bow was the forerunner of various landing craft used in amphibious warfare of World War II in Africa, Italy, Normandy and the island hopping campaigns of the Pacific.

The initials LST have been translated by many as "LARGE SLOW TARGET." The author's brother, Tony, who served on the LST 988 (USS MINERAL COUNTY), used to say "it floated like a cork, couldn't be torpedoed (because of its flat bottom and shallow draft), but could be sunk by a shot from a .45 caliber pistol." He may have exaggerated a bit, but there are sailors that still believe this to be partially true. The author of "Large Slow Target," Melvin D. Barger said that a young Coast Guard officer once referred to it as the "weirdest ship afloat" (9).

John C. Niedermair, a civilian director for the preliminary design branch of the U.S. Bureau of Ships worked out the concept of the LST in about a half-hour on November 4, 1941 (Barger 13). It is said that when an LST captain had heard that the LST idea was worked out in a half-hour he said that after the problems he had experienced with LST's, he wished that Niedermair had spent an additional half-hour working it out. Niedermair's design became the basic pattern for all 1051 LST's that were built in World War II (Barger 13).

The World War II LST's were over 300 feet long and maximum speed was 10.8 knots an hour. They carried small craft topside and a hold full of tanks, vehicles, guns or cargo. Edward Wazenkewitz was a baker on the LST 384 that saw action in North Africa, Italy, and the Normandy invasion.

* * * *

Edward Wazenkewitz of Whitesboro was born in Yorkville, New York and before the war he worked in a bakery on Varick Street. He made an attempt to enlist on the day after Pearl Harbor at the age of 17 but he was turned down because he needed glasses. He tried again in July of 1942, with glasses, and was accepted.

Wazenkewitz went to the Naval Training Center in Newport, Rhode Island for "boot camp" from July to September and then to the Fargo Building in Boston where he attended cooks and bakers school. He recalled that he was in Boston when the famous Cocoanut Grove fire occurred in December of 1942.

After graduation from cooks and bakers school in December, he was given a choice of serving on PT boats or landing craft. He chose landing craft since he had heard it would be safer than PT boats and could not be torpedoed but the Germans made them liars because they did succeed in torpedoing LST's.

Wazenkewitz was transferred to Norfolk, Virginia after completing the school and went aboard the LST 384 on New Years Day. It was the second one to have been built on the east coast. He was the only baker on the ship and while at sea, had to work seven days a week baking bread, cakes, and pies. In port, the Navy was able to purchase baked goods.

His battle station was Pointer on a 20mm gun. "There were times when General Quarters (GQ), (battle stations), was sounded that I had bread in the oven and I would have to turn the stove off and go to GQ, and then come back and finish baking," he explained. "If I had not been a dumb 18-year-old at the time, I could have invented those "brown 'n serve rolls. I remember that the Army did do that. A couple of guys did that in the Army and I used to do the same aboard ship. I would half bake it, cook it, be on the gun for about an hour, and then come back and finish baking," Wazenkewitz said with a laugh.

After two months at Norfolk, the ship went to Bayonne, New Jersey, was degaussed and then headed toward Bermuda. A lot of time was spent there since they had struck a reef, which required a new shaft.

From Bermuda the LST 384 crossed the Atlantic bound for Oran, Algeria in North Africa in the spring of 1943. This was a few months after the "second front" was established in North Africa.

Wazenkewitz recalled, with a laugh, that when his ship arrived in Tunis, Tunisia, he and two of his friends were offered a tour of the city.

…We got into Tunis when the Germans were still there. A couple of us got off the ship and ran into a couple of Army guys who had a jeep. They asked us if we wanted to take a tour of Tunis and we said, 'Sure, why not?' We were riding along when there is a 'peeng' - 'peeng!' 'I said what the heck is that?' 'Oh,' one of the soldiers answered. 'There are still snipers in the city.' I said, 'Get us back to the ship!' No bullets came near us. All we heard was the sound.

The ship operated out of Bizerte and it was loaded with supplies and it participated in the invasion of Sicily. Prior to the invasion of Sicily, the ship was loaded with tanks, army personnel, trucks, amphibious trucks, (DUKWS, ("Ducks"), and mules. General Patton used mules in Sicily to carry ammunition and supplies through the mountains.

At the landing, while the invasion was in progress, the ship was strafed by German fighter planes. Following this, supply runs were made back and forth between Sicily and Bizerte until the invasion of Salerno.

At the invasion of Salerno on one of the trips into the beach, the ship lost her anchor and got beached for three days and Wazenkewitz said that during that time they were like sitting ducks. "The Germans would drop their bombs and take off, but we had two seagoing tugs that pulled us off the beachhead and we did have a lot of close calls and we lost about six or seven men due to the strafing by the German aircraft," he recalled.

The anchor was replaced in Bizerte and then the ship shuttled back and forth between Bizerte and Salerno transporting supplies.

During the invasion of Anzio, February of 1944, Wazenkewitz's ship couldn't get close enough to the beach, so pontoons that were on board were tied to the ship and used to unload vehicles and equipment. As the last Army jeep was leaving the ship, the Germans dropped a bomb and it hit the pontoons killing the soldiers in the jeep. About three or four men were killed. "The Germans had the big gun – a big 16" mounted on a railroad car that was being fired at us. We then carried German prisoners back to Naples.

The ship shuttled between Anzio and Pozzuoli, a suburb of Naples, transporting supplies. At Pozzuoli, as they were right in the channel, Wazenkewitz said that he saw Mount Vesuvius erupt. "What a sight that was! The flames were shooting out of it and lava was flowing down the mountainside. A super sight," Wazenkewitz described. While in Naples, the Germans had booby-trapped the post office and many people were killed.

The LST 384 left Italy and after stopping at Oran, set out for England to prepare for the invasion of Normandy. The training lasted about two months and LST 384 took the British Third Army into Sword Beach.

Wazenkewitz continued his account recalling his experience at the Normandy invasion.

...That was a piece of cake compared to Omaha Beach or the other beaches. We were being shot at but never got hit. We just shuttled back and forth until July. We were into dry-docking at Deptford, England, which is located outside of London. Train track was

being laid on the tank deck of the ship to carry locomotives and boxcars into France. LST 384 was the third ship outside from the pier and the loading never took place. A V-1 rocket hit us and it killed about eight sailors – most of the officers and the commanding officer. Most of us were then transferred to various bases. Wazenkewitz was transferred to Weymouth, south of London, working as a baker at a navy installation. The Navy had taken over a hotel there.

The ship was patched up and in October 1944, the LST was towed by a seagoing tug to Pier 42 in New York City. The trip across the Atlantic took thirty days. Before leaving England, the ship's oil stove was removed, since there was no power to operate the oil-burning stove. In its place, an English stove that burned soft coal was used to bake bread and cook the meals. In New York City all the equipment was replaced and new guns and parts were put on board.

LST 384 was in New York from October 1944 to January 1945 and then left for Norfolk, VA where he received orders for a Naval Air Station in Clinton, Oklahoma. In Oklahoma, they were drilled on survival in tornadoes. This new duty was, "as far from the sea that you can get, and I never saw a tornado. While stationed there, I married my wife on May 13, 1945 and still have the same woman," he exclaimed with grin.

Baker Second Class Edward Wazenkewitz was discharged in October of 1945 at Lido Beach, Long Island, New York.

Wazenkewitz returned home and worked in Allen's bakeshop on Genesee Street in Utica. He joined the reserves and was recalled during the Korean War and stationed at the Brooklyn Naval Shipyard. He said that he actually enlisted since he rejoined the regular Navy in 1955. His duty stations included the USS SARATOGA, USS INDEPENDENCE, and shore duty at Roosevelt Roads, San Juan, Puerto Rico, and two years at Groton, CT at the submarine base. Following those duties he was assigned to the USS GEORGE EASTMAN (YA-39), originally a "Liberty-type" ship before becoming an experimental ship. The vessel operated out of Hawaii and Wazenkewitz was never informed of the ship's mission, but he said that scientists did conduct experiments and the Russians used to follow the ship in the Pacific. He said that one job the ship was engaged in was staging birds and the missions may have also involved germ warfare. The missions have now been declassified and the Dictionary of American Fighting Ships, Vol. 3 states that the ship evaluated the detection of and shipboard protection against chemical, bacteriological, and nuclear warfare. Between 1966-7, the USS GEORGE EASTMAN operated as a research ship providing support for Department of Defense projects (Johnson and Roberts 76). Wazenkewitz' last duty station was the USS RAINIER (AE-

5), an ammunition ship. Chief Petty Officer Edward Wazenkewitz retired from the Navy in 1969 and became employed at various jobs including the old Oneida National Bank.

USS WEST VIRGINIA (BB-48)UNDER ATTACK AT PEARL HARBOR
(U.S. Army Photo)

Part VI
Pearl Harbor/Hickam Field

66

Louis Campese

USS PATTERSON (DD392)

There are few places in the world as well known to Americans as Pearl Harbor, and few historic events can stir the emotions as much as the surprise attack on Pearl Harbor. Other military installations located on the Island of Oahu in the Hawaiian Islands included: Army Air Force Bomber base at Hickam Field, Army Air Force Pursuit Base at Wheeler Field, Iwa Marine Air Base, Naval Air Station at Ford Island, Schofield Infantry Barracks which contained four infantry divisions, Bellows Field Air Base, Kaneohe Bay Naval Air Station, and the naval base at Pearl Harbor where most of the ships of the Pacific Fleet were moored. The ships including "Battleship Row" were berthed in various locations in the harbor. Though war with Japan appeared imminent, the American military leaders were confident that distance from Japan and the presence of so much military strength at Oahu, the Japanese leaders would decide to strike elsewhere.

Prior to December 7, 1941, Japan's imperialist policy was to create an East Asia Co-Prosperity Sphere with Japan in control. Since the United States opposed this policy, the Empire of Japan decided to destroy the Pacific Fleet and eventually force the United States to come to a favorable agreement on their expansion plans in Asia.

On December 7, 1941 at 0755 as many soldiers, sailors and airmen were still sleeping or engaged in Sunday routine, the surprise attack got underway. There were two separate air raids by Japanese airplanes, which bombed Pearl Harbor, Hickam Field, Wheeler Field, and other military installations on the Island. The planes also strafed aircraft and personnel on the ground for about two hours. Almost 2,500 were to die. The USS ARIZONA lost 1200 crewmembers, of which 1177 are still entombed aboard the ship.

The following two chapters relate the experiences of two survivors of that memorable day that President Franklin D. Roosevelt called "A Day of Infamy." The first account is of Chief Machinist Mate Louis Campese, who was stationed aboard the destroyer USS PATTERSON and narrowly escaped being struck by strafing from enemy aircraft on that Sunday morning. He later participated in every major battle in the Pacific Theater of Operations and was awarded seventeen battle stars for the many campaigns in which he and the USS PATTERSON had participated.

The second account is of Army Air Force Master Sergeant John Koenig who was stationed at Hickam Field and due to several quirks of fate escaped being one of the almost 2,500 deaths on December 7. He served as an aircraft mechanic, crew chief, and flight engineer, and following the attack went on many training missions in Hawaii and the United States.

John Koenig and Louis Campese did not know one another on December 7, 1941 but today both are members of the Central New York Pearl Harbor Survivors Association.

* * * *

Louis Campese of Utica dropped out of his senior year at Proctor High School and peddled milk for Belvedere Dairy before he enlisted for six years into the Navy on August 5, 1940.

After four weeks of "boot camp" at Newport, Rhode Island he reported to San Diego, California in September where he boarded the USS PATTERSON (DD-392). According to the <u>Dictionary of American Naval Fighting Ships,</u> volume 5, the PATTERSON was a 341 foot, three year old destroyer, equipped with four five inch, four 40mm, and eight 20mm guns. It also had 16 torpedo tubes and depth charge racks. The crew numbered about 230 (Mooney 230).

From San Diego the ship went to the Puget Sound Navy Yard and was equipped with degaussing gear. This was an insulated cable placed around the ship creating a magnetic field and it neutralizes the magnetic effect of the ship on magnetic mines.

The PATTERSON left for Pearl Harbor on December 6, 1940 and engaged in training exercises in Hawaii and the Midway Island area. This duty was to continue for the next year and one-half (Mooney 230).

On December 7, 1941 the USS PATTERSON was moored at East Loch at Pearl Harbor. Campese said that while in Hawaii there was some talk about Japan attacking Pearl Harbor but it wasn't much and no one really expected an attack. He said that there were no special alerts but the crew was informed to watch out for a possible attack. The water depth at Pearl is only 35 feet so the Japanese with their torpedo bombers had to modify their torpedoes since they normally go down about 70 feet before leveling off. This was another reason to think that Japan could not effectively use torpedo bombers against the ships at Pearl Harbor. Campese explained how the Japanese had practiced at an island with modified torpedoes and armor piercing bombs. The bombs would penetrate two or three decks before exploding.

Campese goes on to explain the major events of the morning of December 7. Using a map of Pearl Harbor, he points out the location of the PATTERSON in relation to the ARIZONA.

...Well, it was holiday routine since it was Sunday, and I was sleeping in. I had been out the night before and the boatswain came down and woke us up so I put on my shorts – that was the uniform of the day out there. I thought, 'why are they waking us up?' I went up on deck and we were over here in the area of East Loch across the way from the ARIZONA and had a good view of the ARIZONA there. When I looked at Ford Island it was all -aflame. Then I glanced over at the ARIZONA and she was blowing up. I was on deck and I saw the ARIZONA blow up and it kept on blowing up. I said something is wrong. About that time, the Chief Boatswain's Mate came running down the deck and said that the Japanese were attacking us. Only a few minutes had elapsed after I was awakened before the GQ had sounded. GQ sounded and I took one step and planes were circling over toward East Loch and they came over and strafed our ship missing me by about two feet. I was right outside the washroom amidships toward the stern. I was on my way to my battle station – number 4 magazine – a 5" x 38. I passed the ammunition through a scupper – a round hole out to the gun. We were firing at the Japanese planes. I also saw the battleship UTAH roll over.

Campese continued with his account by explaining that a ship cannot get underway with cold engines. The main engines must be warmed up and it normally takes about 45 minutes to almost an hour to accomplish this.

...So we had to just sit there and fire at the Japanese until we got the engines warmed. We did shoot one plane down that had hit the CURTIS – a seaplane tender, when the plane came down. The NEVADA, (pointing to the map of the harbor), came out this way toward the channel to leave the harbor and as it progressed, took some hits. She was beginning to sink, so the captain ran it on to the beach so it wouldn't block the channel. I saw this movement after as we were passing it. The PATTERSON left the channel during the second wave of the attack at about 0945 and the Japanese planes had dropped two bombs toward the ship, which were near misses. Other destroyers and two or three cruisers also got out of the channel and formed a small task force and stayed out about

three days. I didn't know what we were feeling at the time of the attack. We were too busy to think about it. Afterwards, we were all pretty mad about it. During the attack, we did not lose any crewmembers but we did lose crewmembers later in the war...

Campese concluded his narration describing what he remembered about the attack on Pearl Harbor. He said that the ship was loaded with ammunition, stores, and fuel. After joining with the SARATOGA, ENTERPRISE, and other ships, they then headed for Wake Island to help reinforce it. "We got close to Wake Island but Japanese planes got to Wake Island ahead of us and the plane off the cruiser saw that the harbor was loaded with Japanese ships so we turned around and came back to Pearl."

Following Pearl Harbor, Campese found himself involved in practically every major campaign of the Pacific Theater of Operations. In the Solomon Islands, in addition to Guadalcanal, the PATTERSON was right in the thick of battle. Campese remarked that on August 7 of 1942, the Battle of Savo Island in the Solomons was a "Son-of-A-Gun." His battle station was in the engine room. At Savo Island, according to Campese, it was a very dark night and there were squalls. The PATTERSON was the first to give the warnings of Japanese ships in the harbor and was firing at the enemy. The PATTERSON radioed the alarm. "Warning! Warning! Warning! Strange ships entering the harbor" (Mooney 230). Campese said that the PATTERSON was shelled and number three gun and a 300-pound depth charge were hit. Ten or twelve crewmembers were killed.

The HMAS CANBERRA, an Australian cruiser was being shelled and was hit by three torpedoes. It was decided to sink the heavily damaged and burning CANBERRA intentionally with friendly fire. Many seamen including about 100 wounded were taken aboard the PATTERSON and delivered to the transport BARNETT (Mooney 230). At Villa LaVella in the Solomons, there was a collision with the destroyer MC CALLA. The MC CALLA lost steering control and rammed the PATTERSON. Campese described the collision:

We backed down because we couldn't go forward and the bow, dangling to the side, finally fell off and was floating in the water. We had lost 52 feet of our bow and the Japanese later observed the bow floating and announced that they had sunk the DD-392. We lost four men. We had to wait for a floating dry dock and in the floating dry dock a stub nose bow was put on the ship, and we then went back to the States to Mare Island. When we got there the bow was already built and it was right there on the dock waiting.

They took pictures of the ship and then repaired it. We stayed in the States for 78 days and then went back to sea.

Returning to action, Campese participated in the invasion of Saipan and Tinian. At Saipan, the PATTERSON provided artillery support for the Marines and also shelled Palau Island prior to the invasion. The PATTERSON then went on to the Leyte and Lingayen Gulf invasions. The ship shelled the shore and shot star shells to provide illumination at night. "We also watched out for shore batteries," he explained.

"*And*, we were in typhoons. How can I forget that? Whew!" He emphasized with a laugh. The PATTERSON, patrolling as part of the Third Fleet off the Philippines, was caught in a terrific typhoon on December 1944. Three destroyers, MONAGHAN, HULL, and SPENCE, capsized and sank. (See chapter on William Northrop).

From his ship off Iwo Jima, Campese saw the raising of the first flag on Mount Suribachi. When asked about suicide planes attacking, he said, "Oh, we had suicide planes. Don't let anybody kid you. They attacked us earlier in the Philippines. When you heard the 20mm guns going off you knew the suicide planes were close," he added.

Campese was also in the last major battle of World War II – Okinawa. "The suicide planes were really bad here," he said. "The Japanese used to send out floating mines every night and take their chances of you hitting them and they were sinking one ship (picket ship) a day. The picket ship, on surveillance near Japan, would radio the ships of the fleet to see what Japanese planes were coming in to attack."

Campese made Chief Machinist Mate in 1943 and said that his watch duty consisted of four hours on and twelve hours off." When the Japanese surrendered on August 14, 1945, the PATTERSON was patrolling off the coast of Saipan.

When he was asked about his feelings of being in combat, Campese replied in his quiet manner. "I knew I had to be there. What could I do?"

He said when the ship arrived in San Diego to the same dock from which they had left; he recalled a band was playing welcoming them back to the States. The PATTERSON was going to New York to be decommissioned, and since Campese had more time left on his enlistment, he was transferred to the USS DIPHDA (AKA-59) and went to San Francisco and San Pedro. The ship was loaded with beer and whisky for the Philippines and asphalt for Tientsin, China.

After returning to the States, Campese was due to be discharged, so he boarded a troop train in charge of 200 men bound for Lido Beach, New York. He said that on the way he lost eight men who took off AWOL. After arrival at Lido Beach, he reported the eight men missing and was told, "Don't worry about them. When they come in we'll put them in the brig," Campese related with a laugh. He waited at Lido Beach for six weeks waiting for his six-year enlistment to expire. "But that six week wait for his discharge was a cake walk," he joked. "I was lucky during the war," he concluded. "I never got a scratch, but I drank a lot of booze."

Chief Petty Officer Louis Campese was discharged on August 7, 1946. He had received 17 battle stars for his campaigns: the Pearl Harbor star on the American Defense Ribbon, two on the Philippines Liberation ribbon, and fourteen other campaigns which include: Guadalcanal, Savo Island, Saipan, Tinian, Guam, Palau, Iwo Jima and Okinawa, on his Asiatic-Pacific ribbon. (A gold star on the ribbons represents five campaigns.)

After discharge, Campese returned home and attended school in Syracuse for refrigeration and air conditioning, and became a self-employed repairman.

He passed away April 14, 2010.

67

John Koenig

HICKAM FIELD

John Koenig graduated from West Winfield Central School in 1939. His father, a World War I veteran, encouraged Koenig to enlist. His Dad said, "I'm not telling you what to do, but I only suggest that you enlist in the service despite all the rhetoric of President Roosevelt saying that the U.S. would stay out of the war. I know we are going to be involved and I would hate to have you go over there as unprepared as I was." Heeding his father's advice, Koenig enlisted in the Army Air Corps on July 5, 1940.

He had been accepted at Cornell University and had to wait almost a year before he actually entered the service. He decided to postpone college and while waiting to enter the Air Corps, he took some extra courses during a postgraduate year at West Winfield Central School.

Koenig did some of his basic training at Fort Slocum, New York, a holding area, while awaiting a ship for transportation to the Hawaiian Islands. He had been given three choices on where to be located – Langley Field, Ohio, Panama, and Hickam Field in the Hawaiian Islands. It turned out that Langley Field and Panama were not actually choices since additional personnel were no longer required there.

The ship left New York Harbor and traveled through the Panama Canal and then up to Angel Island to San Francisco, California. After taking on more passengers, the ship then departed for Hickam Field on Oahu in the Hawaiian Islands.

After arrival, due to the exposure to the heat of the Islands while in his woolen clothing, Koenig acquired a severe rash, putting him in the hospital for a while. The United States was definitely unprepared for war. After a while the lighter and cooler khaki uniforms arrived which provided some relief.

Following basic training and aircraft mechanic school at Hickam Field, Koenig was assigned to various work details, since there were few aircraft and no extra crews were needed at that time.

...It was busy work. I wish I had a picture showing the big parade ground in front of the "White Majesty," the big barracks that

*could hold up to 3,000 troops. On the parade ground a whole
line of us were on our hands and knees going down the grounds
picking up cigarette butts. I thought, 'Good God,' I hope I could
do something better than this so I asked if there was another
school open. They said there was an automobile mechanic school
open but I had to transfer to the 481ˢᵗ aircraft ordnance unit.
That got me off the cigarette butt detail.*

Prior to December 7, Washington had advised the military that an attack
could come at various points in Southeast Asia and even Hawaii. The leaders
did not feel Japan could attack the Hawaiian Islands. For two weeks before
the attack, the troops had been placed on 24 hour alert. The ships had come
in and anchored on Friday. Koenig said they were working two 12-hour
shifts for two weeks. During that time no one could leave the base. However,
Koenig related, a question frequently asked is, 'Why was the 24 hour alert
called off?' The 24-hour alert was called off late Friday afternoon on Friday,
December 5 and many personnel were allowed to leave the base. Negotiations
in Washington between Secretary of State Cordell Hull and the Japanese
Ambassador Nomura were still going on and not going well. It is Koenig's
opinion that Washington may have lured the Japanese into attacking Pearl
Harbor. There are some who feel that President Roosevelt stationed most of
the Pacific fleet at Pearl Harbor to entice the Japanese into attacking so that
the United States would then enter the war against the axis powers. This was
never proved.

Koenig related how many people think that it was only the fleet that was
damaged or destroyed during the attack by Japan. He further explained that
articles are very misleading because the public is not informed of the fact
that it was not only Pearl Harbor but also military installations on the whole
Island of Oahu that were strafed and/or bombed: The Island of Oahu, the
main island of the archipelago, included Hickam Field, Schofield Barracks,
Wheeler Field, and the Naval Air Station at Kaneohe, Bellows Field, and the
anti-aircraft installations around the island. Also included were the Naval Air
Station at Ford Island and the Iwa Marine Air Base, which are located right
in Pearl Harbor. "Oahu in 1941 was the "Billion Dollar Fortress" and Pearl
Harbor was only one segment of the total destruction. However, most of the
casualties did occur at Pearl Harbor. There were a number of casualties that
did occur at Hickam Field, Wheeler Field and Bellows Field, particularly,"
Koenig said.

Koenig displayed a map of Hickam Field. He pointed out the PX (Post
Exchange), aircraft runway areas, aircraft hangars, aircraft repair depots, and
the mess hall in the middle of the "White Majesty," the 3000 man barracks.

He also indicated the two story wooden barracks that were being built at the time he was living there and the fence that separates Hickam field from Pearl Harbor.

On that Sunday morning, Koenig recalled:

>...*I walked across the parade ground to the mess hall. I was third from the door when the doors were closed. The mess hall usually closes at 0800. I was there at 0740. I couldn't help asking myself, why? Since I was not able to eat in the mess hall, I walked to the PX for a cup of coffee. When I reached for my billfold, I discovered that I didn't have it. Why? I had never forgotten my billfold before. So, I walked back to the barracks to get ready to go to church. The chapel was nearby. Someone who was still in bed said, 'Are you going to church? Wait and I will go with you.' While waiting, I heard the enemy aircraft. 'Who's up there!' I said. No planes are flying today. The wooden barracks had two stories with a ledge built above the first floor windows. I stood on the ledge and watched the planes fly over. Rushing to the other side of the barracks, we saw the first torpedoes being dropped on Pearl Harbor.*

With emotion, Koenig described the deadly attack further:

>...*We were all stunned and the next thing we knew there were bullets coming through the wooden barracks. After dropping their torpedoes, the planes came around and strafed the bombers on the ground and the few troops walking around. Thinking back I could have been injured or killed in several different locations. I came close to being inside the mess hall, which took a direct bomb hit and 35 soldiers were killed. I was unable to go to breakfast because the doors were closed early. The PX was blown up and I could have been in there if I had not forgotten my wallet. I could also have been in the chapel if I had not been asked by a friend to wait for him to go to church. My dear friend, Joe Nelles, the Chaplain's Assistant, was killed because he was inside the chapel when it blew up and he was blown apart.*

The Army Air Force losses from both Japanese attacks on December 7 were the greatest at Hickam Field where 121 were killed, 274 wounded, and 37 missing. The attacks began at 0755 and ended at 0920 hours.

Koenig continued his recollections as follows:

...We went to the bomb shelters and got six 100-pound bombs, put them on a bomb trailer and towed them to the flight line to load in a bomber. Here is another time that the angels must have been looking out for me. There was a 'cletrac' caterpillar parked on the outskirts of the airfield and normally the equipment such as the 'cletrac' would not be there, since all equipment is usually put away every night and especially for the weekend. As we approached the 'cletrac' with our load of bombs, the Japanese were ending their first attack. One of the Japanese pilots spotted Carl and me and was trying to hit us. We went from one side of the 'cletrac' to the other. The 'cletrac' saved us. All the pilot would have had to do was hit the load of bombs. We would have been gone for sure. Our mission was to find a plane that was not burning, or full of holes, without a flat tire, and with crews so we could unload our bombs. No one was available for directions, except two captains who told us to get off the runway because it was suicide to be out there. I recalled seeing two B-25 and two B-26 bombers that were parked at the very end of the parking ramp some two weeks prior to December 7. So in our exit attempt, we headed toward these four aircraft. These four aircraft had not been hit. There was a four-man crew by one of the B-25's. I asked the captain if he was willing to take off if his plane was loaded with bombs. His response was, 'Do you have ammunition for wing guns?' We only had bombs. After I explained the condition of the planes on the ramp. He finally agreed to have the plane loaded. He took off and was gone some 25 minutes or so. When they returned, one crewmember was bleeding slightly. For some strange reason the crew departed without saying a word. We didn't know at that time if they saw the Japanese fleet or whether they dropped the bombs in the ocean before returning. After departing, the crew got in a waiting command car and that was the last we saw or heard of them. Two or three weeks after the attack, there was a notice on the bulletin boards to report any heroic act that was not already recorded. Carl Weissman, who helped me with the bombs that day, and I, attempted to make a report. Officers listened to our story, but did not take any notes. For some strange reason, they didn't even seem interested. It seems as if they were told not to report any activity of the B-25's and B-26's because that would have revealed their presence at Hickam Field.

Koenig has been trying to verify, that those four bombers were on Hickam Field that day and that he and Carl Weissman loaded bombs in a B-25 that was the only bomber to take off during the attacks. He claims that the Air Force to this day has denied that the B-25's and B-26's were ever there.

> *...When I got home I went to Griffis Air Force Base and they tried to find information for me. To date, no records have been found of those planes. The Air Force said that General Allen who was a B-17 pilot at Hickam Field flew the only bomber that took off during the attack. But, Allen said that he did manage to take off, but it was after the second wave - after the entire attack had ended.*

(Koenig is still pursuing his quest to discover a record of the B-25's and B-26's.)

After the attack, Koenig and the 481st Ordnance moved out and bivouacked in tents to the ammunition dump. Koenig was with the ordnance unit for about a month and was then transferred to his original Headquarters Squadron Unit. At Headquarters, he was an aircraft mechanic, advanced to crew chief and then flight engineer and was training bomber crews.

> *...There were many rumors going around about the Japanese returning and it was pretty scary. Because of this a lot of flying was done at night. If we went down at night it was curtains. We could not send an S.O.S. since they didn't want us identified, which would indicate to the enemy that our side had sustained a loss. When we came in for a landing, it was on a wing and a prayer. We had to fly over Diamondhead in the dark using only a blinker light to identify us because the anti-aircraft gunners on the ground were trigger-happy right after the Japanese attack, and were always fearful of being a target. The training missions dealt with navigation, pilot and crew's training. We were flying B-24's at the time since all the B-17's were sent to Europe.*

After the attack, Koenig was transferred back to his original unit and assigned to an aircraft maintenance crew. As an aircraft mechanic, he also flew as a flight engineer and the pilot would, at times, let me fly co-pilot. "I had no flight training but as flight engineer I could start engines and taxi the plane on the ground."

One of his memorable events was flying as flight engineer on a B-18, which was an antiquated two-engine bomber. The B-18 was towing targets, and pursuit planes from Wheeler Field would shoot at the targets. After releasing the targets, the pilot of the B-18 would occasionally play tag with the pursuit planes. "It was pretty stupid to play tag going in and out of clouds," Koenig pointed out.

On another occasion, and it was during peacetime, Koenig said they were doing the "milk-run," to the big Island of Hawaii, picking up vegetables. He was in a B-17 and on the way back from the "milk-run," the pilot thought it would be nice to see if the plane could register 0 on the altimeter. "The tide was out a little and the pilot took the plane down right over the water, and if that plane had tipped a bit, one foot or another, the prop would have hit the water sending the whole plane into a spin and there would have been a court-martial," Koenig reported.

Koenig spent three years in Hawaii and in 1943 was transferred to Salt Lake City and then to the Air Force base at Tonopah, Nevada. At Tonopah, he was assigned as flight chief in charge of two sections consisting of 50 planes. His job was to keep these planes in shape and flying, and to train flight crews for the Pacific Theater of Operations. By the time the war ended, he was advanced to Master Sergeant.

Koenig recalled that two of his greatest thrills was having shaken hands with, and being a friend of former President Reagan, then Captain Ronald Reagan. He said that while he was at Tonopah Air Base in Nevada, he was selected to be in the Hollywood movie "God Is My Co-Pilot." He was transferred to the First Motion Picture Unit in Los Angeles in which Ronald Reagan was stationed. Reagan was assigned the task of forming a unit to film the whole African campaign comprising the tank battles between the German General Erwin Rommel and Field Marshall Viscount Montgomery of England. Captain Reagan wanted Koenig to be a member of the unit in addition to his being in the movie "God Is My Co-Pilot." Unfortunately, a new general was assigned to the Tonapah Air Base and his first command was that all servicemen on detached service were to report back to the base. Unfortunately, Koenig missed by one day being assigned permanently to the First Motion Picture Unit.

Koenig's second memorable thrill was meeting Captain Mitsuo Fuchida when attending Western Michigan University in Kalamazoo in the early 1950's. Captain Fuchida lead the air attack on the Island of Oahu on December 7. He was in the United States raising funds for the Fledging Wings in Japan, the equivalent to our Boy Scouts.

Master Sergeant John Koenig, survivor of the Japanese attack on Hickam Field, was discharged from the Army Air Forces on September 10, 1945. From Tonopah, he went to Los Angeles and then drove to Yakima, Washington. He then hitchhiked all of the way home to West Winfield, New York.

John Koenig is very forgiving to the former enemy but he said some survivors are not ready to forgive. He says that what makes many survivors angry is the criticism by the Japanese of the dropping of the atomic bombs on Japan. The reply of the survivors is: "If the Island of Oahu and the Pacific Fleet in Pearl Harbor had not been bombed, no atomic bomb would have been dropped on Japan." Koenig concluded by saying that he would like to remind all Americans that since the attack on that "Day of Infamy" was so humiliating and was the cause for so much loss of life and equipment, that we should always: "REMEMBER PEARL HARBOR – KEEP AMERICA ALERT."

After the war, Koenig graduated from college and eventually earned a doctorate degree. He has been an industrial arts public school teacher, college professor, and has worked for the Michigan and New Jersey Departments of Education.

He passed away in 2009.

68

Sylvester Puccio

USS WEST VIRGINIA (BB-48)

Commissioned on December 1, 1923, the USS WEST VIRGINIA, was a 624 foot long battleship.

In 1939, as Japan appeared to be an enemy of the United States, the U.S. Fleet was dispatched to Hawaii and throughout the Pacific. During that time "Wee Vee," as the West Virginia became known, engaged in training exercises, making trips back and forth between Pearl Harbor, Hawaii and San Diego, CA.

On December 7, 1941, the day of the Japanese surprise attack on Pear Harbor, the West Virginia moved out board of the USS TENNESSEE. The USS ARIZONA was behind her and the USS OKLAHOMA was ahead of her. This became known as the "Battleship Row."

The attack came in two different waves between 8:00 A.M. and 11:00A.M. The WEST VIRGINIA sustained seven aircraft torpedo and two bomb hits. Five torpedoes struck the port side and two bombs hit the superstructure. Before succumbing to a fatal shrapnel injury, the Captain gave an order to all personnel to abandon ship. The West Virginia sank into mud at the bottom of the harbor. Fortunately, the Navy successfully raised the ship and it went on to serve in several campaigns including the invasion of the Philippines Islands, the last great sea battle at Leyte Gulf, Iowa Jima, and Okinawa. (Dictionary of American Naval Fighting Ships, Vol. VIII, pp.. 222-3).

The Following account is about Shipfitter Chief Sylvester Puccio who served aboard the "Wee Vee" from 1939 to December 7, 1941 and survived the attack. As a member of a damage control group, he contributed greatly in preventing the ship from capsizing.

* * * *

Sylvester Puccio of Rome, New York did not complete high school. "School didn't work for me [he noted], but while I was in the Navy I received a high school diploma by taking correspondence courses through USAFI [United States Armed Forces Institute]… I remember what my math teacher, Mrs. Abbott, once told me, 'Be a go getter,' she said. She made an impression on me and I always remembered that. And every time I studied for an exam to be advanced in rate, I thought of those words."

Puccio joined the Navy at 18. After being sworn in at Albany, New York he was ordered to the Naval Recruit Training Center at Newport, Rhode Island for boot camp. Two months later, he left there as a Seaman Second Class and was placed on temporary duty training recruits. "You automatically are advanced to seaman second class from apprentice seaman on completion of boot camp," Puccio explained. After his temporary duty at Newport, he was temporarily assigned to the USS CONSTELLATION, a tall sailing ship at Boston, Massachusetts to await orders for California.

Upon arrival in Long Beach, California, Puccio boarded the USS WEST VIRGINIA as a crew member.

Aboard the ship he was assigned to the second division- the deck force. He chipped paint, swabbed decks and polished brass. At that time, a sailor in the Navy had two major duties- professional and military. Professional duties were mechanical and administrative tasks fundamental to ship operations. The military duties involved combat preparation and readiness to meet a potential enemy. "I didn't know what kind of work I wanted to do or 'strike' [Navy slang term referring to what kind of petty officer rating for which a sailor would strive]. I looked around the carpenter's shack and the metal shop and was assigned to the shipfitter's shop and began my training to become a shipfitter petty officer. Assigned to a petty officer first class, I now could learn a trade in welding and metal smith[sic]." Puccio said. He further explained that his military duty aboard the ship related to damage control, specifically, maintaining the water integrity of the ship by controlling water damage and flooding. "I earned my "crow" [Navy slang for the petty officer insignia worn on the arm of the blue uniform jumper - a white crow with red or gold chevrons] in nine months. I was a third class petty officer and I was so proud that I went right to the sail maker's shop and I had the tailor sew the "crow" on my undress blues. I really felt connected." Puccio recalled that while in the deck force as a seaman first class he was assigned a watch at the helm – steering the ship. "Here I am steering this huge battleship. My father wouldn't even let me drive his 1939 Buick. I was happy to be in the U.S. Navy."

The author then asked Puccio what he recalled about the attack by the Japanese on December 7, 1941. The following account relates his experience at Pearl Harbor on December 7 and December 8, 1941.

> *….Just before 8 A.M. that morning, a Fire and Rescue crew was called out to respond to a fire and I walked up the hatchway and saw smoke over at the 1010 dock. When colors were sounded by the bugler I stepped out of the hatch but I wasn't wearing a hat.*

When you go topside you must wear a hat or the master-at-arms will place you on report-that's regulation. I did stand at attention but could not see the flag being raised. Since I wasn't wearing a hat, I couldn't salute the colors. Thank God I wasn't wearing a hat or I wouldn't have seen an airplane flying low. Looking out of the corner of my eye I turned and saw the plane pass by the submarine base and was heading toward the ship. I thought it was an Army Air Force plane doing a mock raid. The plane dropped a torpedo and as it veered off, it let go with his machine guns to strafe. I then saw the rising sun on his wings. We had heard rumors that Japan might bring us into the war. I ran down the ladder to the shipfitters shop and yelled 'the Japanese are attacking!' One guy was about to say 'you're full of shi_!' And at that time the torpedo hit the port side. We went to general quarters (battle stations). I was in a compartment aft which was separate from the main repair party and my duty was to close the watertight doors, hatches and ventilators to maintain watertight integrity. I asked Roy Powers what should we do and he didn't know and I asked if we should get in touch with the main repair part forward. I felt the door to the main repair party for heat and then removed the brass catch on the door to smell for gas and smoke. I opened the door and saw petty officer Rucker. Rucker said- "Pooch!" 'I forgot my keys to the damage control locker up in the shop'. We had to get in to the locker to start the counter-flooding. There are counter flooding tanks throughout the ship. I saw this big brass lock and I knew I couldn't break it. I saw this cable reel that housed a large crank that was used to turn the reel. The crank was solid steel and shaped like a Z and it was hard to swing. I got to swinging and I knew that the hinges were welded so I attacked them. Finally the door to the locker came loose. I pulled the door open and tossed the crank to Rucker who opened the valve to the counter flooding tank. After Rucker started the counter flooding he yelled, 'We're okay now The ship is coming back to even keel.'" Rucker was a diver and said there was about ten feet of water below the keel. [The naval historian and author, Samuel Morison, wrote that the WEST VIRGINIA had a 28 degree list and that if it hadn't been for the counter flooding the ship would have sunk. The ship did settle into the mud but unlike the USS OKLAHOMA- it did not capsize and roll over.] Puccio said "we were on the third deck and Rucker and I then went topside. The second wave of the attack was going on. We went to the quarter deck where the order to abandon ship had been given by the Captain before he died. The captain had been hit by shrapnel. There were up to seven torpedo hits and bombs that were dropped and hit the ship. Later we found out that there had been nine torpedo hits.

Rucker said 'Pooch' stick with me but I said to Rucker 'I'm going over the side.' I couldn't go over the port side because of the damage so I went off the Starboard side. I went down the fender [a fender is a rectangular ball of line between ships moored along side another ship or between ships and deck, acts as a cushion as the ship drifts] line to the 16" high tension steel armor belt. I walked the armor belt and then got on the armor belt of the USS Tennessee (moored alongside). As I was climbing the Jacob ladder to board the Tennessee I looked up and saw bombs falling. They looked like balls. I said or thought to myself 'the sons of bitches are trying to kill me!' When I got aboard I was told that they would let me know if I was needed. I was later told after the second wave ended—about 11 o'clock or noon, to go to the administration building on Ford Island. On the way I saw in the distance that a Japanese plane had crashed in the water at the end of the runway. A marine with a bayonet in his mouth, swam out to the Jap who was dead and was bayoneting him. At the administration building I met Robert Adams, a shipmate from Binghamton. I couldn't remember a thing from about noon until that evening. That same night, at the administration building, we got on a ferry and crossed the channel and reported to the receiving station and then told to go to the arena (entertainment building) across the road to sack out. We were so tired we laid down on the mattress that was given to us. Then our division officer, Fred White, came in and he was asking for two volunteers to go back to the WEST VIRGINIA and fight oil fires from the USS ARIZONA and the fires were moving toward the West Virginia and that the fires had to be put out. Adams said- 'Don't volunteer Pooch!' So I didn't. Adams was older and I looked up to him. So our division officer, after asking three times said, 'I'll have to assign. Pooch and Adams, front and center.' He must have heard us. So we got on a motor launch and I had the bow hook and Adams was on the stern. We were out in the open channel and the over turned Oklahoma had an armed guard on the keel. Men were still trapped in the ship. The armed guard started shouting at us. Ducking down, I yelled, 'Boat Ahoy, WEST VIRGINIA'. They stopped their firing. I could have been the first to die of friendly fire. So we got to the WEST

VIRGINIA and put out fires in the executive officer's office and then went to the fantail to put out oil fires from the ARIZONA that were heading toward our ship. After that we went back to the Receiving Station and had breakfast, it was Monday, December 8. We went upstairs and FDR was talking on the radio asking Congress to declare war.

Within a week of doing salvage work we were sent to the submarine base to help them. The submarines were having a lot of trouble with 'duds.' We helped this young LTJG who had a method of improving the torpedoes. After that we were called back for more salvage work. We salvaged some AA [anti-aircraft] guns to use as shore batteries at Honolulu. There was a fear of an invasion of Hawaii. The second time that we were sent to the submarine base I could not get transferred back to the WEST VIRGINIA. At the sub base I had a bad case of dermatitis. I left the base in 1945 and was admitted to the hospital at the San Diego base.

I asked to go back to duty and was then assigned to New York-the first naval district I went aboard a dock ship- USS Camden that provided heat. I was also assigned to be in charge of the brig prisoners.

Following that duty assignment, Puccio was discharged from the Navy in 1945. After 26 days Puccio decided to reenlist and was sent to the receiving station in Brooklyn, NY and from there he was transferred to Annapolis, MD. He worked across from the Naval Academy on the Severn River. He was in charge of the training yacht and yawls used by the midshipmen.

Following subsequent duty assignments aboard the USS BLOCK ISLAND and the USS LITTLE ROCK, Chief Petty Officer Puccio decided to leave the Navy. He had accumulated eight years of naval service and was discharged in   1947. "I loved the Navy of that time," Puccio remarked.

After leaving the service Puccio was employed as a welder at Pettibone, Utica Structural Steel and he retired in 1986 from Rome Revere. He presently resides in Rome, NY.

Part VII
The Marine Corps

69

Donald Beha

CORSAIR PILOT

The Unites States Marine Corps is as old as the nation and dates back to 1775 when the American Revolution began. The Corps was established for land and sea operations or what later would be referred to as amphibious assault operations. Over this 227-year period of glorious Marine Corps history, the fleet marine forces have engaged in over 200 invasions living up to the motto of "semper fidelis,"- always faithful.

Under the jurisdiction of the Navy Department, the Corps is comprised of much more than amphibious infantry divisions, which are supported by their own tank and artillery units. They have served as security personnel on naval bases and on board the larger warships. Navy Corpsmen, doctors and nurses, who are often attached to the fleet marine force, provide medical services. The Marines have their own fighter-bomber planes and helicopters and often serve aboard aircraft carriers.

The Corsair fighter plane, used by the Navy and Marine Corps, flew off aircraft carriers and from land bases. It was an outstanding combat plane that was fast and powerful and was noted for its maneuverability. The Corsair F4U was manufactured by Vought and had a Pratt and Whitney 2300 horsepower engine with a wingspan of 41 feet. Maximum speed was 470 miles per hour and was armed with four 20 mm cannons and could carry two 1,000 bombs under the wing. It had an inverted gull wing (Taylor 252-3).

Donald Beha of Waterville, NY, was a Marine pilot who flew Corsairs in the Pacific Theater of Operation from Okinawa and other Pacific island airfields. Since he passed away on October 5, 1999, his daughter, Judy Santo and his brother, Joseph Beha, have provided much of the following information.

****

After graduation from Waterville Central School, Donald Beha left the farm to join the Marines in October of 1940. His family remembers Donald always saying that he joined the Marines "To get away from cows. Joining the Marines made my life easier – compared to farmers' hours"(Santo 1-2). In boot camp at Paris Island, South Carolina, Beha received normal combat training and was also the bugler who got the troops up in the morning.

When the war broke out in 1941, Corporal Beha was aboard ship off the coast of Ireland. He was assigned to the ship for fourteen months and while serving as an orderly for an admiral, he asked him if he would recommend him for fighter pilot training. The Admiral did recommend Beha, and after flight training at Pensacola, Florida, he was commissioned a second lieutenant in September of 1943.

After three months at Miami undergoing SBD dive-bomber training and fighter training at El Centro California, he was then assigned to fly F4U Corsair fighter planes in the Pacific Theater of Operations where he served in the Caroline Islands and later at Okinawa.

His brother, Joseph Beha, remembers that in correspondence with Donald between Brazil and the South Pacific, Joe feeling sorry about himself, would complain about the climate and weather in Brazil. "I would tell him it was so hot and muggy in Brazil." Don would write back and say, "You can be thankful that you have a bunk to sleep on. We lay in the mud in the South Pacific."

Flying from various Pacific islands including Okinawa, as close support for the infantry or over Japan, Beha flew his Corsair with its unique shaped wings as he engaged the Japanese in deadly combat. "I was here –and he was there – and then I knew I had him," Beha would say. His daughter, Judy Santo said, "that was Dad's "sign language" – one hand was his plane and the other was the other guy's as he described his aerial combat with an enemy aircraft.

One day, Beha and another pilot from his squadron (VMF-422) shot down a Japanese plane. As the Corsairs attacked, both fired simultaneously at the enemy plane. Neither pilot knew who did shoot the plane down so after they landed, they tossed a coin into the air and the winner of the toss received the credit. Beha lost the toss.

In one bombing mission with 11 other Corsairs, Beha was flying as wingman, the number two man. Flying under strict radio silence the squadron leader, Jeff DeBlanc, gave Beha a hand signal indicating that he was returning to base so Beha assumed squadron command. After dropping his bombs, Beha looked around for the other planes and thought that he was the only one who didn't get shot down. (After returning to base, Beha found out that the rest of the squadron had returned to base with the squadron leader since they had defective VT-fuses on the bombs. Beha had been left with only two other planes with him and during the bombing mission those two planes with him did not make it back.)

In reference to the above bombing mission, the following is an excerpt from a June 28, 1996 letter to Beha from his former squadron leader, Colonel Jeff DeBlanc, (Retired).

> *...I often reflect on the details of our flight with the VT-fuses. I didn't realize that you also dived with the bomb or did you? I remember flying under the aircraft of Stevenson and Landsberg to check the fuses and had ordered them to drop the bombs as I had ordered others to do. I even dropped my belly tanks along with the bomb. To this day I cannot understand why both of them went into the dive with the bomb attached. Both refused to drop before the dive as ordered (this they have the right to do since they are in command of their aircraft); however, I was going to give them hell upon our return to Ie Shima. After checking the linkage under each aircraft I told them to remain aloft and not dive. It was then I received a transmission from the Navy carrier pilots on the mission to hurry up and start the dive since they had a long distance to return to the carriers. In the next life Landsberg and Stevenson will have to answer to me!!...*

In a letter dated July 4, 1996, Beha replied:

> *...Now to my memory of the VT-fuses. My radio was out for this whole flight. You passed me the signal to take the lead. I didn't know why. I could see our primary target, so I started to dive at that time. No one followed me. I dropped my bombs on target, and then went after some machine guns. I headed out to sea and I was alone so I started back to Ie Shima. I didn't see anyone until I was in sight of the base.*

In another letter to DeBlanc dated May 17, 1997, Beha wrote:

> *...How many planes were with you coming back from Formosa after the fiasco when Lansberg and Stevenson and two others died when the faulty fused bombs blew up? As I remember, I didn't see anyone until I was in sight of Okinawa. I joined up with you just before we landed. After I dropped my bombs and checked for "secondary explosions," I used my rockets on some machine guns. Then I looked for anyone, didn't find them so I headed for Okinawa alone. In my memory most of my flying off Okinawa, - I was your wingman.*

Colonel Jefferson DeBlanc (Retired) of St. Martinsville, Louisiana, Beha's squadron commander, won the Medal of Honor for bravery in aerial combat over the skies of the Solomon Islands in 1943. President Harry Truman presented him the medal in 1945. ..."Protecting the fleet he shot down five Japanese planes." (QTD. in the Medal of Honor citation). Later in the war, he shot down four more and is listed as one of the combat aces of World War II credited with nine kills and three probable.*

Beha would tell the ground crew who took care of his plane that if you "do my plane right I'll take care of you." One time he went out to requisition supplies for the rest of the group. Beha said he "borrowed" a sergeant's uniform, put it on, and went to the Army supply depot. He returned with a crate marked, "aircraft engines." The contents of the crate were quite different since it held champagne and steaks. Later, the crate disappeared over a cliff to destroy the "evidence."

On one occasion, a few days before the Japanese surrendered, he took off from an island for a fighter sweep over Japan when he saw a mushroom shaped cloud in the distance. He found out later that it was the atomic bomb being dropped by a B-29. His brother, Joe, told the author that in one letter, Donald had written that after dropping his bombs he had turned his plane around and was headed back to his base when he sighted the mushroom shape in the sky. He also wrote that it was the worst explosion he had ever seen. Unknown to Donald Beha at the time, the mushroom cloud was the result of an atomic bomb. His squadron leader, Jeff DeBlanc, later said that he (Beha) should have received the Congressional Medal of Honor for having viewed the mushroom cloud over Japan. He was awarded the Distinguished Flying Cross and Air Medal for his combat flying in the Pacific.

On his way home, Beha became ill at Pearl Harbor and was admitted into the Navy hospital for about two weeks with pneumonia. When he reached San Francisco, he was admitted to a Navy hospital again for acute appendicitis for another two weeks.

Donald Beha received orders to inactive duty in late fall of 1945, and returned home. Beha joined the Marine Corps Reserves, and was recalled during the Korean War. Major Donald Beha was finally discharged in 1954 and worked for Sears Roebucks Co. until he retired.

His daughter said that her father's concept of being a good Marine (and about life) was that you do - "Whatever it takes to get the job done."

---

* Colonel Jeffrey DeBlanc (Retired), in a letter to the author granting permission to use excerpts of letter to Donald Beha, enclosed a copy of his Medal of Honor citation signed by President Truman.

70

Stuart Bogan

BATTLE OF IWO JIMA

The island of Iwo Jima, located about 600 miles South of Tokyo, was the next to the last major battle of the Pacific campaign and of World War II. The U.S. military leaders believed that it was necessary to invade and capture this volcanic island so that our fighter planes would have a base to protect our B-29 bombers and also provide a place for emergency landings as they carried out bombing missions to Japan from the islands of Tinian and Saipan (Pictorial 293).

On February 19, 1945, a sunny morning in the Pacific, 500 American ships under the Commander-in-Chief of the Pacific Fleet, Admiral Chester Nimitz, approached Iwo Jima and went ashore at 0900. At first the Japanese did not resist the American forces at the beachhead. Once established on the beach, the troops were met by deadly enemy mortar and artillery fire as they attempted to advance. Not a single Japanese was in sight. (Marling and Wetenhall 33).

On the fifth day of battle, the 28th Division placed the American flag on Mt. Suribachi. The first flag to be raised was small and a <u>Leatherneck </u>(Marine magazine) photographer Lou Lowery took the first photograph. This flag was considered too small so a second raising was needed so that everyone could see it. A larger flag was obtained from an LST and Joe Rosenthal of the Associated Press photographed the second raising. This became perhaps the most famous photograph of World War II. For this photograph Rosenthal won the Pulitzer Prize (Marling and Wetenhall 64-67).

On March 14, Admiral Nimitz declared that Iwo Jima had been conquered and there was a flag raising ceremony to raise the island flag. (Nimitz was criticized for this since the battle would go on for several more days.) Twenty-four men, eight from each division, made up the Honor Guard for the ceremony. [*]

Twenty-seven marines and navy men earned the Medal of Honor at Iwo Jima. Admiral Chester Nimitz issued a press release on March 16, 1945. "Among the Americans who served on Iwo Island, uncommon valor was a common

---

[*]   During the flag raising ceremony, "Private First Class Thomas Casale, 20, of Herkimer, NY, went to an 80 foot staff raised on top of a Japanese bunker. Two others from the Honor Guard accompanied him. Casale raised the flag and as the flag went up – the one on Suribachi came down. Iwo was now U.S. territory (Ross 322).

virtue (QTD. in Ross 322). About 6,000 Americans died at Iwo Jima and over 5,000 of the dead were from the 3ʳᵈ, 4ᵗʰ, and 5ᵗʰ Marine Divisions, which were commanded by General Howland Smith. (The Japanese fought bravely and would not surrender.). Of the 23,000 Japanese troops, only 216 were taken prisoners – many were non-combatant Korean laborers (Ross 336).

Stuart Bogan of Waterville was a veteran of Iwo Jima who landed on the first day of the battle as a member of a reconnaissance company attached to Battalion Headquarters of the 5ᵗʰ Marine Division.

* * * *

Bogan was drafted into the Marine Corps on February 12, 1943 and went to Paris Island, South Carolina for boot camp. There was no physical or brutal punishment while he was in "boot camp", but to say that Marine Corps boot camp was tough is an understatement, Bogan explained.

> *...One time when the company was being punished, they sent all these sergeants to train us and we didn't know nothing. The punishment consisted of eating hot dogs three meals a day for three days. The hot dogs were about 2 1/2 inches around. We went on strike. When the captain heard about this he checked it out and we were then transferred to another mess hall and the food improved. We were bothered by a lot of sand fleas. In boot camp there was no slapping at sand fleas or chewing gum while in ranks. We had to make sure we held our rifle up. There was this guy from Ohio who liked to chew tobacco until the drill instructor caught him. The DI made him swallow it. It didn't bother the guy who was caught chewing but six other guys threw up. There was no physical or brutal punishment while I was in boot camp.*

Following "boot camp", Bogan was transferred to the Philadelphia Naval Base while waiting for clerical school to begin. He was temporarily assigned as a guard at the naval prison located on the naval base. After completion of clerical school, he was then assigned as a drill instructor as part of the V-6 officer-training program located at Yale University. After six months as a DI, he was transferred to Quantico, Virginia for assignment to the fleet marine force. From Quantico, Bogan traveled to Camp Pendleton, California where he was assigned to the 5ᵗʰ Marine Division, Headquarters Battalion, Reconnaissance Company. The unit officers had not yet arrived at Pendleton. Consequently, no leave was granted since there were no officers present to sign leave papers.

While waiting for officers to arrive, he attended demolition school for two weeks. Bogan said that his funniest story occurred at demolition school. In demolition school everyone was required to take a stick of dynamite, prime it, light it, and set it in a shallow pit.

> *...After we had done it, the instructor asked if everyone had done it. We all agreed that one fellow hadn't. (He really had done it.) We convinced the instructor that he hadn't done it so the guy had to do it again. He said he didn't have a match so another guy gave him a matchbook. However, before passing the matchbook, the man who was handing it over had wet the striking part of the matchbook. Well, the guy who had to set this dynamite again started scratching the matches and he couldn't light them. Six other men were lighting theirs and they were going off, causing the man with the wet matchbook to jump and we were laughing our heads off since we knew there was no danger because the dynamite was laid in the pit and not covered. It would just go off like a firecracker. If it had been covered, it would have blown dirt to the sides.*

Following demolition school, Bogan boarded a ship that was bound for the island of Hawaii in the Hawaiian Islands. Arriving in Hawaii several days later, he was assigned to Camp Tarawa. On the island, as corporal of the guard, he had to travel across a volcanic mountain back and forth on a one-way road to Hilo. There was a guard posted on both ends of the one-way road to direct traffic.

On the island he had additional training in the Reconnaissance Company and boarded another ship in Hawaii traveling west across the Pacific. The destination was Iwo Jima.

It was February 19, 1945 and Bogan was on board an LST off Iwo Jima. No white man had been on Iwo Jima in 84 years. Between the first and second wave, he got aboard a small landing craft with the Assistant Division Commander, General Hermle, and a former headquarters battalion commander, a major. Bogan said he acted as a bodyguard for the major and they each had two canteens of water. The major, a big man, had gone through one canteen while on the boat and after landing a bullet had gone through the other and the water had dripped out of it. In giving one of his canteens to the major, Bogan said that he happened to look back. As he did, he saw a mortar hit in the middle of a boat that sent bodies flying in the air out of the boat. "I could really dig a hole deeper than anybody then. It was a whole different ballgame," Bogan remarked with a laugh.

"My shelter was a half-tent and while visiting a friend from Utica that I had met aboard ship, my poncho and half-tent that I used for shelter had disappeared. I noticed that it was being used to shelter a latrine for the General's privacy. It was mine so I took it off the line and put it back where it belonged." Bogan said that next morning after he awoke, he noticed that a shell had landed during the night and shrapnel had struck his rolled up pack hanging on the line. When he unrolled his poncho he saw that it was full of holes. "That was the closest anything came to me and I walked back and forth to headquarters every day," he added.

As a member of the Reconnaissance Company, one of the duties was to spot the location of Japanese snipers hidden in the numerous caves on the island. After locating the caves, bulldozers would be called in and the cave openings would be covered or marines carrying flamethrowers were called. Bogan recalled the use of flamethrowers by marines to flush out Japanese from the underground caves. The flamethrowers were directed at, and into the caves occupied by the enemy. The Japanese would come out screaming and he remembers seeing Japanese being shot by marines until they were ordered by the officers not to shoot them. The marines didn't want to take prisoners so they were placed in open areas and guards would shoot them. Intelligence personnel didn't want them shot so the shooting of prisoners was stopped.

One of Bogan's most memorable experiences was seeing the raising of the American flag on Mt. Suribachi by the 28th Marine Division. The author asked Bogan if he had seen the raising of the flag on Suribachi. "I sure did, he exclaimed. I saw both raisings of the flag."

At the conclusion of the battle of Iwo Jima, "The Navy picked us up and we ate Spam all the way back to Hawaii. I haven't eaten Spam since. In Hawaii we were making preparations for the invasion of Japan which was scheduled for November 1945," Bogan explained.

"When the war ended we went to Kyushu (one of the main islands of Japan). This was at Sasebo Harbor. We docked at a naval base for three days... Our job was to find the location of guns and then blow them up on the next day. It was there that I had my first taste of sake— rice wine — not bad."

Corporal Bogan said that a marine was arrested for engaging in the black market. "An investigation was conducted and the prisoner identified others in the black market ring. As the investigation was being conducted, one of the investigators was looking directly at me and I said, 'Keep moving! I'm not one of them.' " For several months after V-J Day, Bogan did guard duty and jeep patrol in Japan.

He was discharged on March 1946. He went to work for the New York Central Railroad and was also a village policeman in Waterville. He later went to work for Chicago Pneumatic (formerly of Utica) for 36 years before retiring.

Stuart Bogan passed away April 13, 2005

71

Stuart Cowen

BATTLE OF TARAWA

WRECKAGE OF JAPANESE PLANE AT BATTLE OF TARAWA-1943
(US. Marine Corps)

The Battle of Tarawa began on November 20, 1943. It lasted for three days and it has been remembered as one of the bloodiest battles in Marine Corps history. Located in the Central Pacific, Tarawa is an atoll but the battle was actually fought at Betio – a portion of the atoll. The late Stuart Cowen of Stockwell (a hamlet located between North Brookfield and Waterville, New York) participated in this battle and was severely wounded by Japanese snipers as he waded to the seawall or pier on the beach at Betio. Cowen said that he had received seven bullet wounds on the first day of the battle. Cowen's parents received the following telegram from the Commandant of the Marine Corps in 1943:

**I deeply regret to inform you that your son, Private Stuart L. Cowen, U. S. Marine Corps Reserve, has been wounded in action in the performance of duty and service of his country.........
Commandant U.S. Marine Corps.**

Hundreds of thousands of these Western Union telegrams were sent by the War Department (now the Defense Department) to fathers and mothers who had a son wounded, killed, or missing in action or held as a prisoner of war. Each day throughout the war mothers and fathers prayed that they would be spared this dreadful news.

****

During his school years, Cowen helped his father on the family dairy farm in Stockwell before he left home to enlist into the Marines in 1942 at the age of 18. Following a few weeks of rough and "old-fashioned" boot camp training at Paris Island, South Carolina, Cowen spent a few days at Camp LeJeune, North Carolina and then traveled to San Diego where he boarded a troop transport – bound for the South Pacific.

Thousands of miles from home in Stockwell, the slow moving transport crossed the equator in its lengthy voyage across the Pacific. Making stops in the British and Samoan Islands, the ship then crossed the International Date Line to Australia and New Zealand where the troops engaged in more combat training. More training followed in the South Pacific at New Caledonia and the Hebrides Islands.

With battle plans and training complete, the troops, tanks, weapons, fuel, and other equipment were loaded aboard the attack transports, LST's, and other amphibious warfare vessels. The amphibious vessels and warships entered into convoy formation and headed for the Tarawa atoll in the central pacific.

This was the beginning of the American offensive in the central Pacific. Because of the widely scattered islands, strong naval forces were needed to support the ground troops. For the first time in amphibious warfare history, the initial waves of the assault would go ashore in amphibious tractors launched from LST's. Tarawa (actually the island Betio of the Tarawa atoll) is located in the Gilbert Islands and Betio was the location of the airfield. The Second Marine Division was selected to begin the Central Pacific offensive. The battle plan established three beachheads – Red 1, Red 2, and Red 3 (Johnston 102).

It was predicted that the landing would be tough and it was not known how many Japanese inhabited Betio Island. It was estimated to be about 4,500 fighting troops (Vander Vat 299).

The enemy had constructed many fortifications on this island that was only two miles long and 600 yards wide. It was heavily fortified with many machine guns, automatic guns and artillery. This was to be the first time a landing would be made by American troops against a well-defended beach. (Vander Vat 299-300).

As the sun rose over the Central Pacific, preparations were underway for the landing. Boats were being loaded with troops as early as 0300 and the land battle began at 0910 on November 20, 1943 (Johnston 111-112).

Forty-two Amphibtracs (amphibious tractors) made up the first wave and were halted a few hundred yards from shore by a reef. As the marines left the Amtrak's, some died in the water before making the beach, sinking quickly under the weight of their equipment. The eighteen-year-old Cowen, a member of the mortar team carrying sights for mortars and with his M1 in hand, stepped off the Amtrak and headed for the beach and reached the pier at Betio. He was behind his sergeant and in a matter of moments was hit by sniper bullets in the leg, arm and buttocks. The author asked him, "How did you get hit by a sniper if the sergeant was just ahead of you? His answer: "One bullet went through the sergeant's head and hit me in the arm." Cowen was also hit in the leg and buttocks. The snipers, out to get the mortar men, were firing from more than one angle. "A corpsman was supposed to work on my wounds, but he got bumped off." Though wounded, Cowen was not immediately sent back to a transport ship, and said that he had to continue on duty that night —even standing guard duty.

The Marines sought protection at the crowded pier as the Japanese decided not to fight inland but on the beaches. Snipers were also firing from a damaged small Japanese vessel off the right flank. There was growing doubt that the battle would be won.

At the end of the first day, the marines had won one-tenth of a mile. Much blood had been lost and the smell of death permeated the tropical air. The Tarawa atoll is located on the equator and "the temperature never fell below 100 and there were dead bodies everywhere," he remarked. Amidst this intense equatorial heat, the deadly combat continued into the second day.

Cowen said the Navy had difficulty getting the troops ashore because of the reef and the small landing boats met heavy resistance. The Japanese defenses were tenacious and the Americans were engaged in a tough and bloody fight. Cowen commented that there wasn't "much ducking. Hell! You might duck and another bullet would come by." Snipers were everywhere. By the third day, the American forces were victorious. The battle lasted 76 hours until 24 November and during that time, according to official records; "the bitterest fighting in the history of the Marine Corps" had been encountered (Costello 438.) The ferocious resistance and strong defenses by the Japanese led to the deaths of over a thousand Marines.

Commanded by Rear Admiral Shibasaki Keyi, the Japanese troops were ordered to fight to the last man. The Japanese were to lose 4, 690 men and the Admiral himself was killed on the second day of the battle. Only 17 Japanese and 149 Korean laborers survived (Costello 438).

Much was to be learned from this first amphibious battle in the Central Pacific. Cowen points out how the Navy "screwed up." After the landing, Admiral Nimitz, Commander-in-Chief of the Pacific Fleet, had sent orders not to land since the Japanese were supposed to be in the Marshall Islands (according to the British) and not in the Gilbert Islands. One account of the battle indicates that there had been insufficient naval bombardment prior to the landings and too little air bombardment during the battle. This contributed significantly to the fierce Japanese resistance. Americans did not know the area and landing at low tide caused marines to wade across reefs to get ashore, which exposed them too long to the intense firing from the enemy (Johnston 114-115).

A valuable lesson from Tarawa would be learned and Admiral Nimitz would spend considerable time studying this invasion in an effort to avoid similar errors in the forthcoming battles in the Pacific.

Cowen said that the movie star Eddie Albert was a naval officer at the battle of Tarawa but was not one of those actually involved in the land battle. Percentage-wise, Cowen related, the officers took a heavy loss. "Snipers aimed at anyone using binoculars." (Used mainly by the officers). Cowen also said that a Cassville, New York marine was killed at Tarawa. It happened that the father of this boy came to Tarawa after the battle as a Navy Seabee (CB-Construction Battalion) to help construct a runway for airplanes. He later asked Cowen how he was ever able to get off that island alive.

Cowen was evacuated and returned to a transport ship that took him to a naval hospital at Pearl Harbor. He had been shot several times by snipers and he was to spend the remainder of the war in Hawaii recuperating from his wounds. Declared physically unfit, his leg continued to bother him for a long time. "I never had a day of furlough and I worked at an ammunition depot and did jeep patrol. Cowen said that while he was in the hospital, Eleanor Roosevelt visited. She shook my hand and the hands of all 2,000 in the hospital." He was in the hospital until January 1944 and while there, two brothers, Bill (a marine and Guadalcanal veteran, and Norm (a sailor), visited him. Two hometown friends, Bob Pierson who was on a ship and Bill Northrop, stationed aboard an aircraft carrier, also paid Stuart a visit.

Private Cowen was awarded the Purple Heart medal for his wounds. A veteran of one of the most controversial and memorable battles in world history, he was discharged on November 10, 1945 and returned to Stockwell and to farming, - -just a short distance down the road from the old homestead farm.

Stuart Cowen passed away May 21, 1999.

72

William Cowen

THE SOLOMON ISLANDS

Located below the equator in the Southwestern Pacific Ocean, the Solomon Islands are made up of the islands of Bougainville, Guadalcanal, and many smaller islands. They encompass almost 16,000 square miles and the people are mainly Melanesians. Prior to World War II, the Solomons were a British protectorate. The Japanese conquered the islands in 1942 and after the war; the northern part was made a United Nations trust territory governed by Australia. The southern part, which includes Guadalcanal, is presently a British protectorate. The climate is hot and damp and the islands are volcanic, mountainous and heavily wooded. Bitter fighting occurred in the Solomon Islands during World War II (Easy 476).

William Cowen of Stockwell and Clarence Raffauf of North Brookfield were two marines of the Waterville area that saw combat in the Solomons. William Cowen was trained to be a paramarine, but the island geography and lack of large open fields resulted in limited paratrooper operations. However, Pictorial History of World War II, Vol. 2, indicated that on October 27, 1943, a Marine parachute battalion staged a diversionary raid on Choiseul Island (35).

****

In September of 1941, when he was 20 years old, William "Bill" Cowen of Stockwell, enlisted in September of 1941 into the Marine Corps. After "boot camp" at Paris Island, South Carolina, he traveled to Camp Pendleton, California for paratrooper training. Cowen said that three battalions were formed and these were to be used on suicidal type missions, but he said that he never did jump into combat.

From Camp Pendleton, Cowen traveled across the Pacific to Hawaii where he had additional paratrooper training. Continuing on across the Pacific he arrived in Wellington, New Zealand where he had more infantry training.

From October 10 to October 27, 1943, he participated in the occupation of Vella Lavella, which is located in the Solomons near the Bismarck Archipelago. Cowen was also at Guadalcanal and Bougainvile where he served in a raider battalion. "At night the Japanese would crawl through the line and we used grenades but we couldn't find them," he recalled.

Cowen said that the hot and damp equatorial climate caused many of the troops to have jungle rot. He described the jungle living conditions where they had to live in jungle hammocks, and that he had acquired a fungus on both feet and hands at "the Canal" and at the other islands. He had to spend some time on a hospital ship and he still suffers from the fungus to this day.

Cowen discussed his sewing skills and how he obtained a sewing machine at Guadalcanal. The Japanese had a Singer sewing machine and he got it from the missionaries. He said that he packed it and carried it from place to place. While recuperating from jungle rot, he made curtains for the sick bay and also made nineteen baseball type hats. Making hats was his specialty and he made them out of old clothes and camouflage material. A native of Guadalcanal offered him $200 for the sewing machine.

One of his memorable experiences was seeing a Major Walsh jump from his burning airplane at Guadalcanal. He said that he had sent home two parachute panels cut from Walsh's parachute.

Another memorable experience, Cowen explained, was that he knew the Congressional Medal of Honor winner, Sgt. John Basilone. He had met him at Camp Pendleton and had attended his wedding in New Jersey. Basilone had won the medal for his bravery at Guadalcanal when Cowen was in New Zealand. "When the troops on a hill in Guadalcanal were out of ammunition after the landing, Basilone ran back alone to the beach and came back with a heavy case of the ammo, enough to stop the Japanese charge, Cowen explained. Basilone was later killed at Iwo Jima.

Cowen mentioned how difficult it was for him, after all of these years, to remember many of the details of his military experience. He did recall another interesting incident when one time, while on maneuvers, his commanding officer was injured. Cowen was on one end of the stretcher helping to carry his commanding officer that was the father of a recent Marine Corps Commandant, General Krulac.

He also remembered that on his way home on a cross-country medical troop train, he met the late Bill Veeck, former owner of the Chicago Cubs baseball team. Veeck had lost his leg while serving with the Marines and was on this medical troop train, which was letting off men in its journey across the country.

Corporal Cowen was discharged in December of 1945 and returned to live in Waterville where he became a self-employed house painter.

He passed away January 5, 2005.

73

Harold "Red" Maine

BATTLE OF OKINAWA

It was Easter Sunday, the first of April 1945. The hour was 0830. The last and largest amphibious battle of World War II was about to take place. Over 1200 ships carrying over 450,000 troops were ready to assault the island located about 500 miles south of Kyushu, the southernmost island of Japan. The 10th U.S. Army, 3rd Marine Amphibious Corps, the XXIII Corps, Tactical Air Force, and other units went ashore on the western beach. During the battle, four Army and four Marine divisions would participate in the battle. Marine General Simon Buckner was the commander in charge (Sheperd 315).

Okinawa is an island of the Ryukyu Islands located in what was considered a strategic area near Kyushu and Honshu, two main islands of the Japanese homeland. U.S. forces felt it needed Okinawa for anchorages and airfield sites.

The landing on that Easter morning was uneventful since the Japanese were located away from the beach. Nevertheless, events followed which would make Okinawa one of the bloodiest battles of World War II.

The 82-day battle finally ended June 21, 1945 after the Japanese had fought desperately to protect their homeland. Kamikaze planes sank 36 vessels and damaged 322. In their desperation, the Japanese were looking for another "divine wind"* to save their homeland (Sheperd 316).

A Japanese machine gun sniper on the island of Ie Shima off the coast of Okinawa killed Ernie Pyle, a famous war correspondent, columnist, and author. He had been at many of the great battles of World War II in Africa, Sicily, and the Pacific.

There were 49,000 American casualties at Okinawa and seven thousand soldiers and Marines died. One hundred and nine thousand Japanese lost their lives (Ropp 407).

Harold "Red" Maine of Brookfield, New York was assigned to the Sixth Division, 29th Infantry Regiment in the summer of 1944. As a sergeant he was in charge of a machine gun squad and participated in the Battle of Okinawa and later assigned to duty in China.

---

*   In the late 13th century as the Mongols were invading Japan, a typhoon destroyed the Mongol fleet. The Japanese called this a divine wind. (kami=divine – kaze=wind).

* * * *

Maine was born in Brookfield and attended school at Leonardsville, New York and before the war was employed as a carpenter. At age 17 on March 18, 1943 he joined the Marines and went through "boot camp" at Paris Island, South Carolina.

> *..Training was pretty rough. I had five carbuncles taken off my neck and the collars aggravated them. Since I had to spend two weeks in the hospital my boot camp had to start over. I was at Paris Island a total of thirteen weeks and I was then transferred to the Naval Air Station at Floyd Bennett Field in Brooklyn. I met my wife there. I did guard duty at Floyd Bennett Field for nine months.*

Following his duty at Floyd Bennett, he was transferred to Camp LeJeune, North Carolina and following that duty, he traveled to Camp Linda Vista, California. This base was located on a high mountain and he stayed in a bivouac area for about ten days. While there, it was necessary to repeat seven or eight inoculations, since records of these shots had been lost enroute to California.

In late July or early August of 1944, Maine boarded the USS MORTON, a troop transport bound for Guadalcanal in the Solomon Islands. There were no stops along the way but there was plenty of excitement and aches and pains when the equator was crossed. An initiation was the order of the day. "That was an awful initiation," Maine exclaimed. "They beat the devil out of us, knocked us down, used electric swords, rapped us with brooms and beat us all around the ship running on wet decks without shoes. We had wet socks. The sailors, all shellbacks, were in charge and they put several guys in sickbay. They were really rough on us but worse on the officers," Maine recalled with a dry laugh. He proudly showed the author his shellback certificate that bears a portrait of Neptune, the mythological Roman god of the sea.

The USS MORTON arrived at Guadalcanal shortly after his birthday, which is August 10 and with the exception of a few Japanese hiding out in the jungle, the fighting on Guadalcanal had ended by August of 1944.

The troops engaged in real hard training at Guadalcanal for six months. "At that time we thought we were invincible and we were waiting for the invasion of Okinawa. We were over-trained since we had reached our peak but the training continued," Maine recalled.

Maine said the division was established at Guadalcanal in September and he was assigned to the 29th Infantry Regiment -the last of the three-infantry regiments in the Sixth Division to be formed. He was assigned to the 2nd Battalion, E Company and was a machine gunner and later advanced to squad leader in a machine gun squad.

In March of 1945, as the time of departure for Okinawa arrived, the division boarded their ships, which then rendezvoused at various locations to form the invasion convoy. "The ocean was full of ships," Maine remarked. (1,200 ships participated in the battle of Okinawa.) "On board the ships there were false alarms, air raid and submarine drills — one or two a day."

On April 1, 1945, Easter Sunday, the ships arrived off Okinawa and Maine climbed down the net, which draped the side of the ship, and he stepped on board the Higgins boat, which would take him ashore on the second wave.

> *…Everybody was apprehensive and pretty scared. My big thought was to get my feet on dry land out of the water. I never was a good swimmer. I wanted to get on dry land so I could take care of myself. The landing itself was unopposed. Naval ships and airplanes had bombarded the shoreline very much.*

Maine said that they had to get up one side of the island and they progressed about 125 miles in the first five days with very little resistance.

> *…I actually wore out a new pair of shoes in five days carrying that equipment and guns as we moved up one side of the island and than started down the other side before we ran into the Japanese. There were snipers along the way but no serious fighting for five days. Then all hell broke loose – we found the Japs. The Japanese were concealed in caves and the Navy shelled us. The Navy didn't have enough elevation set on their guns and they directed shells right in on you. "Friendly fire" they called it. It killed a few of our men. The Navy had sent in white phosphorus shells and they burned personnel. They would light up and you could tell where they hit and it also sent up a lot of smoke. From there on it was rough going. Phosphorus shells were sent in so ships could see where they fell. It took time to get messages back to them to let them know our location. It was pretty rough the rest of the time and there was constant fighting with very little rest in between. The troops ate C-rations and K-rations and stayed in foxholes at times. Machine gun positions were set up and every night the guns would be set up on the perimeter of the platoon. Each rifle platoon had a machine gun squad assigned to it. So wherever*

that rifle platoon was located the machine guns would be set up in the wings. There were 48 riflemen in a rifle platoon and 52 men in a machine gun platoon. The squad was made up of a gunner, assistant gunner, and nine ammunition carriers. There was a squad leader, two men to carry the gun and nine carrying ammunition. I was the squad leader directing the one gun. One carried the tripod. It took two men to carry the gun and each carrier carried 500 rounds of ammunition – two belts of 250 shells each. It weighed forty pounds – two boxes of twenty pounds. Each marine also carried a pack and a .30-caliber carbine. (Small carbine and not considered very accurate). Rifle platoon members carried M-1's.

Maine further explained that there was also one or two BAR (Browning Automatic Riflemen) in a rifle platoon. He said that there were about 250 men in a Marine company and that he was squad leader all the while on Okinawa. As a squad leader, he had to fire the machine gun at times. "I was promoted to 'buck' sergeant because all of the other non-commissioned officers had been killed or wounded, he added. As a general rule a machine gunner's longevity was not long, since one of the goals was to knock out the machine guns fast. "We had to be very careful where the guns would be set up and sometimes we had no choice," he said.

Many accounts say the Battle of Okinawa lasted eighty-two days. Maine explained that it actually lasted about ninety-three days before the island was finally secured. "On the ninety-first day of the battle, I could see the beach where I set up the gun and I could see a lot of Japanese between us and the beach. I was lucky that day."

The next day, Maine turned himself into the hospital. He wasn't wounded but he had a temperature of 104°.

…I just couldn't go any further. I rested for three days in sickbay and then went back to my outfit. I was talking to my Corporal as we were setting up the two guns and talking to the Lieutenant as to where to place the two guns and a sniper picked off the corporal. While we were setting up the gun for the night we were both standing up and talking to the Lieutenant. It was then that the corporal was killed.

One of the bloodiest battles of World War II was over. Maine displayed a copy of a Sixth Marine Division newsletter pointing out that his 29th Regiment, which was given credit for capturing Sugar Loaf Hill, suffered the highest rate of casualties ever sustained by a U.S. Marine Corps Regiment in one battle. In the eighty-two days of the Okinawa campaign, there were 2,821 casualties out of 3,512 in the regiment (Sixth 22).

Maine returned to Guam for rehabilitation and he was there on V-J Day when the war with Japan ended. Everyone thought they were finally going home. However, the division got news that they had to go to China to accept the surrender of China from the Japanese and that duty would last six months. "When we got news that we were going to China, my buddy and I spent $40 for a quart of whisky, sat down on a cocoanut log and drank it," he said laughing.

The division went to Tsingtao, and there was a big Japanese garrison there, which had been in China for four years. The Japanese stacked up their arms and surrendered to us. Maine showed the author a pamphlet entitled "North China" which included pictures of his duty in China. One picture was of the formal surrender, and the other was a picture of the Commanding General, Lemuel Shepherd.

While in China, Maine and four Marines escorted Japanese prisoners to Japan by way of a cargo ship but they did not go ashore. They returned to China but the ship was diverted leaving them at Shanghai and they had to hitchhike to Tsingtao.

After six months in China, Maine was given orders to go home. Once again, fate would cause another delay. When the ship came into Tsingtao, it was quarantined for thirty days because of a chicken pox outbreak, so Maine had to wait another thirty days. He had written to his wife that he was leaving tomorrow but the ship didn't leave for a month. When the ship did leave it took twenty-seven days to get to California and another five days on board a troop train to return to the east coast.

Maine displayed some service medals he received in Brookfield in 1999 when a Cancer Run was held to honor his late wife. His son had made arrangements with the Marine Recruiting Detachment in Albany and they sent two marines for the presentation of the medals. "That was really impressive," he said.

Sergeant Harold "Red" Maine was discharged on April 6, 1946 at the Naval Training Center in Bainbridge, Maryland. His days as a marine and machine gunner were over. Returning home to Brookfield, he became a self-employed contractor.

He passed away January 29, 2010

74

Charles Rigaud

GUADALCANAL "INTO THE VALLEY"

The well-known writer, John Hersey, author of <u>Hiroshima</u> and <u>Bell For Adano</u>
also wrote <u>Into the Valley</u>, an account of a skirmish at Guadalcanal in the Solomon
Islands in the South Pacific. Employed by "Time-Life Magazines" in October of
1942, he accompanied Company H, a Marine Corps unit as it advanced toward
the Japanese in the vicinity of the Matanikau River close to what is now Henderson
Field. Captain Charles Rigaud, who was born and raised in Oriskany Falls, NY,
commanded company H.

* * * *

Prior to the Battle of Guadalcanal, Rigaud had participated in the Battle
of Tulagi, and for both of these battles he was cited for bravery and fine
leadership while under fire everyday for five months.

Retired Colonel Charles A. Rigaud died on December 2, 2000 and much
of the following account is the result of an interview with his sister, Phyllis
Rigaud McNamara, and passages from the book, <u>Into the Valley.</u>

After graduation as valedictorian from high school, Rigaud wanted to
attend West Point. Unsuccessful in obtaining a congressional appointment
he attended college and graduated from the College of Forestry at Syracuse
University in 1939. While in college, he was a member of ROTC. After
graduation, the Colonel could appoint two-second lieutenants to the Army,
but Rigaud opted for the Marine Corps.

The newly commissioned second lieutenant traveled to Camp LeJeune,
North Carolina and Quantico, Virginia for marine training. He was stationed
at Quantico for a long time and was promoted to captain. Following his
promotion, he was married. His sister, Phyllis mentioned that Charles always
said that he would not marry until he was promoted to captain.

Following his training at Quantico, Rigaud then shipped out to the
Solomon Islands in the South Pacific, and participated in the battle of Tulagi
on August 7, 1942. While on Tulagi, he said that his biggest thrill was
watching some Navy warships shoot down 24 of 25 Japanese airplanes. That
Japanese attack had occurred on the second day that the American forces

had occupied the islands. After engaging in combat at Tulagi, where he was cited for bravery and fine leadership, he landed at Guadalcanal. Commanding Company H on Guadalcanal, he carried a BAR (Browning Automatic Rifle) into combat with the enemy.

His sister, Phyllis, said that when she was in Rochester during the War, she had gone into a drug store for a cup of coffee. She picked up a "Life" magazine and saw a picture of Captain Charles Rigaud. "I almost fell out of my seat," she exclaimed. That was when we first found out where he was. All that time he was in Guadalcanal we had not heard from him so I called home. The "Life" magazine article dealt with John Hersey's book, Into the Valley. Hersey came to Oriskany Falls and visited his mother and told her that Charles was okay," Phyllis added.

Into the Valley is an account of Hersey accompanying Captain Rigaud for two weeks as Rigaud's company faced the enemy in combat October 8, 1942 – the early days of World War II. Hersey called the skirmish part of an insignificant battle but "it showed how the war feels to men everywhere"(QTD. in Hersey 4). The object of the battle at the Matanikau River was to drive the enemy back, but the Japanese snipers created a major problem. Rigaud's mission was to rid the valley of snipers, get to the Matanikau River, and force a crossing (25).

Rigaud ordered the men to proceed in single file fashion into the valley. The Japanese lurked in the valley waiting to ambush the Marines. Rigaud gave the order. "Keep five paces." Bunching up would make them too large a target for the Japanese.

Advancing into the valley they were met by sniper fire, and deadly machine gun and mortar fire. To their disappointment, Company H was only able to set up two machine guns. The Marines were trapped and someone shouted, "Withdraw!" Rigaud yelled, "Who in Christ's name gave that order?" Rigaud succeeded in stopping his men from retreating and they then regrouped and held their position. Greatly impressed with Rigaud's leadership, Hersey wrote, "As cool a performance as you can imagine"(QTD. in Hersey 90).

Observing that it would be senseless to remain trapped, Rigaud dispatched a runner to request permission from his superior to withdraw. However, not receiving an answer, he made the decision himself to withdraw. (Rigaud did not know at the time that his superior had been wounded). An orderly withdrawal then took place.

When Rigaud learned that Hersey would be returning to the States, and feeling somewhat homesick, he said to the correspondent, "What I'd give to be you." Hersey's admiration for the Oriskany Falls marine is illustrated in the following words: "After what I had seen him do in the valley that afternoon, in the face of fear in his ranks and in his own heart, I would have given something to be Captain Rigaud, homesickness and all"(QTD. in Hersey 117).

Despite the failure of the skirmish in the valley, the Marines did succeed in winning the three-day battle against the Japanese. Phyllis McNamara recalled that from Guadalcanal Rigaud was transported by submarine to New Zealand or Australia.

After the war, Rigaud remained in the military and one of his major assignments was, Chief of the Naval Prison at Portsmouth, New Hampshire. From Portsmouth he was transferred to Okinawa and it was on Okinawa where he was advanced to the rank of colonel.

Phyllis McNamara proudly displayed an American history textbook that is used by the Waterville Central School. The author turned to a page in the text and read several facts similar to her own recollections and passages from the Hersey book.

Okinawa was his last duty station and he decided to retire in 1966 at the age of 48. He had spent 27 dedicated and glorious years of service in the Marine Corps that included the Korean War and part of the Viet Nam War.

He returned to Oriskany Falls and later moved with his second wife to North Carolina. Colonel Charles A. Rigaud died on December 2, 2000 and is buried at Hillside Cemetery in Oriskany Falls.

75

Clarence Raffauf

SIXTH MARINE DIVISION

During World War II four Marine divisions were formed. The Sixth Marine Division, the last to be formed, was established at Guadalcanal in September of 1944. It was the only Marine division that was made up of battle- seasoned veterans. The division consisted of three infantry regiments that were organized in the summer of 1944. The Sixth Division participated in only one battle, Okinawa. In existence for 19 months, it was deactivated at Tsingtao, China. The division never had duty in the United States (Cass 1 and 221).

Clarence Raffauf, a Marine from North Brookfield, served in the Pacific Theater of Operations and was assigned to the Sixth Marine Division when it was formed on Guadalcanal. (In addition to interviewing Raffauf, excerpts from his personal notes recorded October 26, 1943 to December 4 are quoted in the account).

* * * *

Before enlisting into the Marines, Clarence Raffauf of North Brookfield worked in New Berlin, New York where they made powdered eggs and put them into 55-gallon drums. The powdered eggs were then sent to England as part of the Lend-Lease Program before World War II. "Of course, we ate a lot of powdered eggs in the service," he laughed. He said that he, Stuart Cowen, Rodney Pierson and one of Pierson's sisters, used to ride together to New Berlin. Raffauf also worked on the old Delaware Lackawanna & Western Railroad and for Savage Arms before enlisting at age 19 in 1942.

After one month of "boot camp" aorth Carolina for three weeks on the rifle range. "All they had there was a rifle range and 'tent city.'" He said that this place was later called Camp LeJeune, a well-known Marine training facility.

Raffauf remembered how the recruits were scared most of the time of the drill instructors. After basic training, he boarded a troop train bound for San Diego, California. It took five days to go across the country.

At San Diego, he boarded a merchant vessel, a converted luxury liner of the Matsonia Line. Its destination was Pago Pago, in the British Samoan

Islands in the South Pacific. He went over as part of a regiment replacement battalion. After arriving in January of 1943, the group was split up and assigned to various units. A great tourist place today, "it was a great tourist place even before the war - the Dorothy Lamour islands," he said with a grin.

This was a defense battalion, which engaged in anti-aircraft and shore artillery. All of the islands including Guam and Wake Island had defense battalions and the 3rd Defense Battalion had put up quite a defense at Guam.

He was assigned to the 7th Defense Battalion and was there for about eight weeks of advanced training. There were about 80 of us in this small battalion.

Traveling aboard a Liberty ship, Raffauf's next duty station was in New Zealand. He was to be one of the replacements for troops in New Zealand, which had just left Henderson Field at Guadalcanal. Those troops had also done base defense duty at Midway Island. As a member of the 3rd Defense Battalion, he went back to Guadalcanal and was there for five to six months to replace some troops who were going home on leave. At Guadalcanal, the troops were getting ready to make a landing at another island in the Solomons - Bougainville. This was the last of the Solomon Island invasions and was called the "Consolidation of the Solomons." "At that time the Americans had not done much offensively against the Japanese. This was the beginning of the offensive to drive the Japanese back," Raffauf explained.

On October 26, Raffauf left Guadalcanal aboard the USS LIHA bound for Bougainville. There was a dummy run made at the "Canal" and they left on October 30 for the invasion. All leave was cancelled and he was working in the mess hall aboard ship.

It was November 1, 1943 and Vice Admiral William "Bull" Halsey was the over-all commander of the invasion. "Bougainville was my first landing and from the transports we climbed down the nets and into the Higgins boats, (LCVP's) and then we hit the beach on D-Day," he recalled. On that day he was working on a loading barge, which sank because of the bad seas. "The waves were terrific that day and it made the landing more difficult," he emphasized. After landing, he hunted up the rest of his outfit. Each outfit had landed according to specific colors on the beach and there were snipers shooting all around.

On the next day, Raffauf noted that they moved forward with the front lines until they got to their position was obtained and then had to protect the beach from bombs and landings. Raffauf indicated in his notes that a Japanese task force was moving up but "thanks to the Navy they didn't reach us." On November 4, he noted that they found a chicken the Japanese had so they enjoyed a chicken dinner, and on November 6 the LST's were bringing in CB's and "they stole plenty of chow." "On Bougainville we manned the 90mm anti-aircraft guns. It took about an 18-20-man crew to man the guns and handle the ammunition," Raffauf added.

Raffauf's notes also indicated that:

...On November 7 there were heavy air raids. Two P-40's were knocked out. There were a lot of enemy aircraft there - about 50 Japanese planes in the raid. The Japs really had the power then and they bombed us every night. On November 10 one of our planes was shot down by mistake by D or F Battery. We got one Jap plane but it was credited to another battery. Some of Admiral Halsey's staff came ashore November 12 and looked over the beachhead. I think one of the great sea battles was going on at the time and the ships' guns were knocking planes out of the sky. Both sides lost a lot of ships. The Japanese were trying to drive us back with their airplanes and Navy. The Merchant Marines rolled barrels of oil and gasoline ashore. Things were kind of crude regarding the storage of fuel. In those days there was lots of oil and gasoline at the gasoline dumps and it was very hazardous to be in the area...

On November 14, he worked all day cutting out the jungle for new gun positions. One observation plane sneaked over the island took pictures and got away. "We can standby for one hell of a bombing now. "Up every damned night on alerts," Raffauf had recorded in his notes.

On November 17, reinforcements came in and there was a big air raid and there was a direct hit on a 155 director and all were killed in the pit. There was heavy bombing between the 19th and 23rd of November. Why, oh why, did we let that Jap observation plane sneak in? On the 23rd we got credit for knocking down one and one-third planes..

Raffauf's notes illustrated another example of cruelty by the enemy during World War II. There were stories of Marine raiders being tortured by the Japanese. "That was a long time ago. We can leave out the details," he directed.

On November 24 according to Raffauf's personal notes, "a Jap task force is headed our way. We have lugged all sorts of ammo into our pit and ready to fight them. It is going to cost them if they do come. Every man is prepared to stay in the pit and fight to the last man." His notes state that, "on the next day the Jap task force hadn't come yet but field pieces from the hills shelled the shit out of the fighter strip last night. This morning they shelled the shit out of us, coming as close as 15 feet."

He noted that on November 26 only five prisoners had been taken on the island and none of them would talk.

There was more shelling on the 29ᵗʰ. "At the airport, at the gas dump, there were awful flames all morning. On November 30, "the infantry is making a great push." Raffauf"'s last entry in his notes is dated December 4. "Up all night. On Condition Red. Big convoy was headed in and Jap bombers were after it."

Raffauf said that the Marines took only seven to eight square miles of Bougainville. The U.S. wanted only enough to build an airstrip. The 77ᵗʰ CB's (Construction Battalions) built an airstrip in the jungle using sheet metal. The airstrip would be built primarily for damaged carrier fighters to land because attempting to land back on their carriers could endanger the ship. The CB's also dug all of the gun emplacements. Raffauf praised the CB's. "They were a great outfit," he commented..

"We were at Bougainville for about 2-3 months and then we went back to Guadalcanal," he said. At Guadalcanal they did away with the defense battalions and anti-aircraft units. In the summer of 1944, the 6ᵗʰ Marine Division was formed and was undergoing training for Okinawa. Raffauf was assigned to the 15th Marine Regiment - a field artillery unit made up of 105-mm howitzers transported by trucks. There was a howitzer for each truck and the division had four battalions. Each battalion was in support of one infantry regiment. Men transported the 105mm guns. "My outfit supported the 27ᵗʰ Infantry Regiment. At Bougainville, we had placed spotters at the front lines. The spotters would try to fix positions or directions for us by firing a shot. We would then send a shot back (at a safe distance from our troops). After three or four shots from us, a position could be established and then we would fire several to hit the enemy. The infantry would use us at times to stop the Japanese Banzai attacks," he explained.

At Guadalcanal the troops trained and worked together for Okinawa. During that time, the Tarawa and Marianas campaigns occurred. Raffauf said that he spent all of 1944 and part of 1945 training for Okinawa.

As the date for the invasion of Okinawa approached, Raffauf boarded a liberty ship bound for Ulithi, a small island about 1,200 miles from Okinawa. At Ulithi ammunition and guns were loaded on to LST's (Landing Ship Tank) before leaving for Okinawa on March 27. The 105's and ammunition were loaded in the bottom of the LSD's on top of Army Ducks. Raffauf said that Ducks were different from AMTRACS, which had caterpillar treads. The amphibious Duck was like a truck.

On April 1, 1945 the battle of Okinawa began. Raffauf explained that about twelve hundred ships were ready for battle.

Raffauf described how he went ashore on a DUKWS, (a Duck), and he said it was his first experience on a "Duck" stating that it was a very simple landing. "Very simple. We went ashore easily", he exclaimed. "The worst fighting came later."

Raffauf said that there were many Army men also fighting on Okinawa. A month after the landing, the island was cut in two by the 10th Army Division that was led by Gen. Buckner, who was killed by a sniper during the battle. A sniper on an island off Okinawa also killed Ernie Pyle.

Okinawa was a dirty battle, Raffauf recalled, as he described the Japanese use of suicide planes.

They didn't miss. The Japanese knew it was their last attempt to stop us. We were lucky to get ashore but we had heavy support from the Navy. The Japanese were in caves and flame-thrower tanks had to be used. This sealed a lot of them in their caves and then the caves would be blown up. The Navy was protecting us but they dumped us ashore as fast as they could in order to get back away from the beach.

Raffauf was asked whether there were many in the division who died during the battle. Opening a book entitled History of the Sixth Marine Division, he indicated that 1,697 members of the division were buried in a cemetery on Okinawa (Cass 182). A total of 8,227 members of the division had been killed and wounded (177).

Raffauf went back to Guam in July of 1945 where the troops were being trained for the invasion of Japan, which was scheduled for November 1, 1945. "That was to be the next jump. The plan was to land at two different places with three divisions for each landing and the predictions were 80% casualties. We were at Guam when the Truman bomb was dropped in two different places," he said.

Private First Class Raffauf left Guam on November 1945 on a transport and the destination was San Pedro, California. He was discharged at San Diego on November 4, 1945.

The author asked Raffauf what it was like to be in combat. "It was scary but it climatizes you and they brainwash you. I was there for almost three years. I went along with the tide and you begin to harden into it," he replied.

Returning to North Brookfield, he joined his father's business in the grocery store and after the store was sold in 1976, he went to work for the American Management Association for about seven years before he retired.

He passed away June 9, 2007.

Epilogue

Now we are old, but if the word were passed,
We'd go again, knowing the die was cast,
And ride machines all bareback in the sun,
Repel invaders, put them on the run.

(Commander George King qtd. in Prados 8)

Appendix
Lists of World War II Veterans

Waterville Area

Name	Branch	Rank	Dates of Service	Significant Facts
Acker, Walter	Navy	Seaman 2/C	05-05-45- 46	Enlisted at age 16. CB's, Acorn 54. Asiatic-Pacific Theater. Saipan, Guam
Allen, Stuart	Army	2nd Lt.		
Alsheimer, Carlton	Army	Corporal	1941 to 10-18-45	#ETO – Army Musician
Angier, Charles	AAF	Sgt.		
Angier, Robert	Army	Corporal		
Avery, Elizabeth	Army	Corporal		Womens Army Corps
Avery, John R.	AAF	Private		
Bancroft, Edwin S.	Army	Staff Sgt.		ETO –Silver Star
Baron, Edmund	AAF	Sgt.		
Bates, Glenn	Army	Private		
Bett, Amos	Marines	Private		
Beck, Gilbert	Army	Private First Class		
Beha, Donald A.	Marines	Second Lt.	10-40-1945	Asiatic-Pacific Theater – Corsair Pilot
Beha, Joseph	AAF	Staff Sgt.	01-43 to 01-29-46	Airways Communications – Brazil

Name	Branch	Rank	Dates of Service	Significant Facts
Belfield, Ebenezer	AAF	Private.		ETO. 3881ˢᵗ Quartermaster Co. Three Battle Stars. Normandy,N. France, Battle of Bulge.
Belfield, Ora H.	Army	Corporal		
Bellamy, Elwyn	Army	Corporal		
Bellamy, Robert	Army	Private.		
Bellingham, Esther				
Benjamin, B. Wesley	Navy	Seaman 1/C		
Berry, Charlon	Navy	SK 3/C		
Birmingham, Francis	Army	Corporal		
Bissell, Joseph	Army	Corporal		
Blair, Henry	Army	Sgt.		
*Blair, Robert	Army	Private		
Boff, Gordon F.	Army	Captain		
Boff, Richard R.	Army	Staff Sgt.		
Bourke, Norman F.	AAF	Staff Sgt.		

Name	Branch	Rank	Dates of Service	Significant Facts
Brady, Charles J.	Army	Captain		
Brady, Robert T.	AAF	Staff Sgt.		
Brewer, Melvin	AAF	Tech Sgt.	8-30-42 to 10-27-45	ETO 375th fighter squadron. .Radio repair. .Four battle stars
Brocker, Paul Jr.	Army	Corporal		
Browne, Charles D.	Navy	Chief Yeoman	1939 to -09-21-47	Asiatic-Pacific – USS JACK –Submarine
Brownell, Charles E.	Army	Corporal		
Budlong, Robert	Marines	Private		
Burdick, Elmer	Navy	Seaman 2/C		
Burdick, Jack	Army	Private		
Burgess, Arthur H.	Army	Private		
Burkert, Frank D.	Army	Private First Class		22nd Infantry Regiment
Burlingame, Eldon W.	Army	Private		
Burlingame, Elmo	Army	First Lieut.		

Name	Branch	Rank	Dates of Service	Significant Facts
Byrnes, Frederick J.	Coast Guard	Lieut. (j.g.)		
Byrnes, Lawrence	Army	Sgt.		
Byrnes, Norman	Army	Second Lieut..	03-07-43 to 1945	ETO. 44th Infantry Division 324th Infantry. Regiment, France, Germany, Austria, Combat Infantry Badge. Battle Stars, Bronze Star, and Purple Heart.
Byrnes, William	Navy	Seaman 2/C		
Carey, John	Army	Corporal		
Carney, Tobias Glenn	Army	Corporal		
Carr, Ralph	Navy	AS		
Cash, Roger	AAF	Lieut.		
Cebrat, Ernest J.	Army	Sgt.		
Cebrat, Rosemary	WAVE	Seaman 1/C		
Chamberlain, George	Army	Private First Class		
Chamberlain, Lester	Navy	C.S.F		
Chamberlain, Roland	Army	Staff Sgt.		

Name	Branch	Rank	Dates of Service	Significant Facts
Chamberlain, Stanley	Army	Private. First Class		
*Chrzanowski, Stanley	Army	Private. First. Class	01-26-41	ETO. KIA in North Africa (Tunisia).
Ciocca, Rocco	Army	Private.FirstClass		
Clark, Roy O.	Army	Corporal		
Cleary, Margaret	Army	First Lt.	1942-1945	ETO/ Africa. Nurse Corps.
Clemens, Ralph L.	Army	Tech Corporal		
Coggeshall, Peter	Army	Private		
Cole, Glenn	Army	Lieut.. Colonel		
Cole, H. Bradford	Army	Private First Class		
Cole, Otis R.	Army	Colonel		
Cole, Otis R. Jr.	Navy	Commander.		
Condon, Daniel	Navy	Seaman 1/C	06- 44 to 07-46	USS ANDOMEDA. AKA-15 (Attack Cargo Amphibious Forces.) Asiatic- Pacific. Philippines- Iwo Jima- Okinawa- Nagasaki- USS DEVICE. AMS 220. (Minesweeper.)
Cook, Clesson L.	Army	Corporal		

Name	Branch	Rank	Dates of Service	Significant Facts
*Cook, Royce G.	Army	Private		
Coon, Robert E.	Army	First Lt.		
Corbin, Robert	Navy	Fireman 2/C		
Cowen, Charles	Army	Staff Sgt.	1944- 1946	Paratrooper. 503rd Airborne Reg. Asiatic Pacific. Philippine Islands. Combat Infantry Badge. Battle Stars.
Cowen, Clement	Army	First Sgt.	12-39-1945	Paratrooper. 11th Airborne. Sicily and Philippines.
Cowen, Norman, Jr.	Navy	AMM 1/C	12-40 to '61 .	Asiatic- Pacific. Retired from Navy as MMC. In1961
**Cowen, Richard J.	AAF	Master Sgt..	1-20-40 to '68	Asiatic-Pacific P.O.W. -Bataan Death March Retired from Air Force in 1968.
Cowen, Stuart	Marines	Private First Class		Asiatic-Pacific. Battle ofTarawa. Purple Heart.
Cowen, William	Marines l	Corporal	9-41 to 12-45	Asiatic-Pacific. Para marine Infantry. Solomon Islands (Guadalcanal, Vella Lavella, Bougainville)
Creedon, Edward F.	Navy	Seaman 1/C		
Creedon, John	Army	Corporal		

Name	Branch	Rank	Dates of Service	Significant Facts
Davidson, Charles	Army	Private		
Davis, Jay L.	Army	Private.		
Dempsey, Harold	Army	Corporal		
Doyle, Edward	Navy	AMM 2/C		
Draheim, Dorman	Navy	Seaman 1/C		
Dann, Earl W.	Army	Corporal		
Dunn, George	Army	Private First Class	06-28-43 to 11-03-45	Asiatic- Pacific.27th Infantry .. Tank Bn.. Tank Bow Gunner/ Driver.Okinawa American Defense.
Dunn, Raymond	Army	Corporal	01-18-42 to 03-46	
Dunster, Donald	Navy	QM 3/C		
Dunster, Richard	AAF	Tech Sgt.		
Duvelow, William	Marines	Private First Class		First Marine Division. Guadalcanal.
*Dyman, Benjamin	Army	Tech. Sgt.		
Dyman, Peter	Marines	Sgt.		
Dyman, Walter	Army	Tech Sgt.		
Eastman, Beverly	Navy	Seaman 1/C	11-02-44 to 01-03-46	WAVES.U.S.Naval Barracks, Wash,D.C.

Name	Branch	Rank	Dates of Service	Significant Facts
Edwards, Albert C. Jr.	Marines	Sgt		
*Ekstrand, Louis	Army	Private.		
Ekstrand, Oscar	Army	Private		
*Ekstrand, Robert E.	Army	Private		
Ernst, Theodore	Army	Private		
Ferrucci, Anthony	Marines	Private		
Ferrucci, Michael	AAF	Staff Sgt		
Foppes, Luke	Navy	EN1		Asiatic-Pacific Theater – Amphibious Navy. LSD-vessel.
Ford, Robert	AAF	Corporal	09-07-42 to 11-45	American Theater. A/C Mechanic. P38, P-47, P-51,
Ford, Vincent	AAF	Sgt	10-06-42- 04-1-46.	ETO. Mechanic P40 Aircraft. 9th AF C47 Crew. Flt Troop carrier.
Franko, Michael	Army	Private		
Frederick, Edward	Army	Private		
Friedman, Gabriel	Army	Private`		
Fuess, John L.	Army	Captain		

Name	Branch	Rank	Dates of Service	Significant Facts
Fuess, Frederick	AAF	AC		
Fuess, Kenneth	Army	Staff Sgt.		
Fuess, Stuart	Navy	RT 3rd Class		
Fusek, Daniel	Army	Private		
Fulmer, J. Willard	Navy	Seaman 1/C		
Furner, Gerald	Navy	Seaman 1/C	11-42- to 3-46	Minesweeper. Asiatic- Guam Pacific, Okinawa, and East China Sea. Japan. Two Battle Stars.
Gallagher, John	AAF	First Lieut.	7-04-45 to 04-04-45	ETO. 15th Air Force. 20th Bomber Squadron.B-17 Pilot. 35 missions- Central Europe. Distinguished Flying Cross and Air Medals
Gallup, Gerald	Coast Guard	AS		
Gardner, Henry	Navy	Seaman 2/C	04-43 to 19-46	Asiatic- Pacific Theater. USS MERRICK AKA (Attack Cargo) Amphibious Forces
Gates, Edmund	AAF	Private		
Gates, Gilman M.	AAF	Sgt.		
Gates, Stephan	Navy	Ensign		
Gibbons, Frank R.	Army	Sgt.		

Name	Branch	Rank	Dates of Service	Significant Facts
**Gibbons, John	Army	Corporal	04-06-43 to 11-17-45	ETO. 5th Army. North Africa, Italy. German Prisoner of War. Stalag II
Gibbons, Leo .	Army	2nd Lt		
Gilliland, Elizabeth	Army	Tech. Sgt.		WAC
Gilliland, John T.	Army	Corporal		
Gorton, Jack	Army	Private.		
Gorton, Milton C.	Army	Corporal		
Gorton, Robert	Army	Private		
Goulette, Louis K.	Army	Private First Class		
Green, Richard	Army	Private		
Hahle, Roger	Navy	SK 3/C		
Harris, Edward J.	Navy	GM 3/C		
Head, John	Army	Sgt.		
Heidel, Edward M.	Army	Private		ETO. North Africa.
Helmes, Frank O.	Army	Corporal		
Helmes, Fred	Army	Private		

Name	Branch	Rank	Dates of Service	Significant Facts
Helmes, William	Army	Private		
Helterline, Frederick	AAF	Lieut.		
Hilsinger, Frederick	AAF	Tech. 3	02-02-42- 10-02-45	ETO. EBS-Sos HDQTRS 28th Infantry division. Two battle stars.
Hilsinger, Harry	AAF	Corporal		
Hilsinger, Paul	Army	Private.		
Hilsinger, Richard	AAF	Tech. Sgt	06-30- 42- 09-20-45	ETO. 8th Air Force FLT Engineer and Top Turret on B-17. 33 Combat Missions. Medals: DFC and four Air medals.
Hoffman, Elmer	Navy	MM 2/C		
Holmes, Tilford R.	Navy	YN 2/C		
Howe, William J.	Army	Corporal		ETO-748th Tank Battalion. Four battle stars N. France, Ardennes, Rhineland, central Europe
Huff, Leeman C.	Army	Sgt	08-42 to 11-09-45	ETO. 26th Infantry division. Battle of Bulge, Rhineland Bronze Star. Purple Hear. Two battle stars
Hughes, Richard	Army	First Sgt	11-11-43 to 01-02-46	ETO. 276th Combat Eng.Combat BN. Central Europe Rhineland. Two battle stars

Name	Branch	Rank	Dates of Service	Significant Facts
Hughes, Robert	Navy	Seaman 1/C	02-05-43 to 01-17-46	Asiatic-Pacific. USS Canberra. Eniwetok, Philippine Sea
Hunter, Lawrence	Marines	Private First Class		
Huntington, Collis V.	Army	2nd. Lt.		
Ingalls, George L.	Army	Private		
Ingalls, William	Army	Private		
Ireland, Milton L.	Navy			
Jackson, Albert C. Jr.	Army	Private		
Jackson, Charles	Navy	A.S.		
Jackson, Francis	Navy	Seaman 2/C		
Jannone, Milton	Navy	Lieut (j.g.)	07-43 to 03-05-46	ETO. Officer Candidate School. Destroyer escort North Africa. Presidential Unit Citation. Battle Star.
Jannone, William	Army	Private First Class	06- 28-43-46	Pacific Theater of Operations. 170th Engineer Combat Battalion. Truck Driver.
Jenkins, Milton	Army	2nd.Lieut.		
Johnstone, Alastair	Navy	A.S.		

Name	Branch	Rank	Dates of Service	Significant Facts
Jones, Almon	Army	Private		
Jones, Roger	Army	Corporal		
Jones, Thomas	Army	Private First Class		
Joy, James	Army	Private		
Karram, Fred J.	Navy	Seaman 2/C		
Kehoe, Robert T.	AAF	S/Sgt.		
Kelley, Francis	Navy	SM3	1943 to 12-30-45	ETO. USS Howard F. Clark DE-533, USS Hanover
Kelmurray, James M.	Army	5th. Tech.		
King, Harold C.	Army	Captain		
King, Laurence T.	Army	Major		
King, Norman	Navy	Fireman 3/C		
Lally, Howard H.	Army	Sgt.		
Lally, John	Navy	Ensign		
Lally, Robert	Army	Private		
Langone, Anthony D.	Navy	SF 3/C	05-18-44- 6-15-46	ETO. Asiatic- Pacific Theater. LST 988

Name	Branch	Rank	Dates of Service	Significant Facts
Langone, John W.	Army	5th Tech	03-03-43- 12-45	China- Burma India Theater. Truck Driver. 1st Convoy over Ledo Road to Kunming, China. Two Battle Stars
Langone, Rocco	Army	Private First Class	12-01-42 to-12-04-45	ETO. 748th Tank Battalion. Truck driver. Four battle stars. Northern France- Ardennes (Battle of Bulge) Rhineland- Central Europe
Lapham, Granville L.	Army	Tech. Sgt	03-03-43 - 03-02-46	American Defense. 46th Coast Artillery BN. Supervised location of Gun positions in U.S. (Coastal Guns.)
Lapham, Walter	Army	Private		
La Vallee, Richard	Army	Private		
La Vallee, Theodore	Army	Private First Class		
Lawrence, James	Navy	Ensign		
Letson, Frederick	AAF	Corporal		
Lewis, Edward	Army	Private		
Lewis, Hubert	Army			
Lewis, Raymond	AAF	Staff Sgt.		
Lewis, Robert	Army	Private.		

Name	Branch	Rank	Dates of Service	Significant Facts
Lewis, Stuart V.	Army	PrivateFirst Class		
Lindsay, Benjamin F.	Army	Sgt.		
Loftus, Fred J.	Army	Staff Sgt.		
Lynch, Robert	Navy	AS		
+Madsen, Harry E.	Army	Corporal		
Mango, John	Army	Private First Class		
Manion, John Edward	AAF	Staff Sgt	0 8-44 - 8-27-46	Pacific Theater of Operations. Philippines Islands. Transferred to Army Air Force. 20th Air Force
Manion, Joseph	Army	Private First Class		
Manion, Robert	AAF	Staff Sgt.		
Manion, Royce	Navy	AS		
Marscher, William	Navy	Seaman 2/C		
Martin, Stuart	Army	Private		
Martin, Victor	Army	Private		
Mayne, Hubert	Army	T-5	12-4-42- 12-9-45	ETO/Africa.Rifleman/Auto.Mech. Normandy,Ardennes, Rhineland.Three battle stars

Name	Branch	Rank	Dates of Service	Significant Facts
McCabe, Kenneth B.	Navy	SK 3/C		
McCartney, David S.	Marines	Private		
McCartney, Stephan	Army	Private First Class		
McLean, Bruce	AAF	Sgt	11-08-42 to 02-46	Sixth Air Force. Howard AFB, Panama. Meteorology
McLean, Roderick	Navy	Lieut. (j.g.)	05-42 to 1944.	V-125 Program. Medical Corps. . St. Albans& Veterans Hospital in TN.
McTigue, James	Army			
Miller, George N.	Army	Private		
Morgan, Harold T.	Army	5th. Tech.		
Nichols, Peter	AAF	Corporal		
Nieters, John M.	AAF	Corporal		
Nolan, Charles	Army	Private First Class		
Nolan, Charlotte	Navy	Ensign		
Nolan, George	Army	Private		
Nolan, Peter	AAF	Sgt.		

Name	Branch	Rank	Dates of Service	Significant Facts
*Noon, Elizabeth	Navy	Lieutenant		
Noon, Thomas	AAF	Lt. Col.		
Northrop, Harry	Army	Private		
Northrop, J. Howard	Navy	Lieut. (j.g.)		
Northrop, William	Navy	Yeoman 1/C	06-23-43 to 1969	Asiatic-Pacific. USS WASP(CV-18). Eight battle stars. Retired as CWO3.
O'Connor, Dr. Harold	Navy	Lieut (j.g.)		
O'Dowd, William	Army	Private First Class	0 6-18-45 to10-46	ETO Infantry Replacement. Occupation Duty. 379th Railway Security Group. Visited Nuremberg Trial Proceedings.
Owens, Joseph	Army	Corporal		
Penree, William A.	Army	AC		
Pesto, Kenneth D.	Army	Corporal		
Pesto, Lawrence F.	Army	Private		
Pierson, Robert	Navy	Seaman 1/C	06-24-43 to 9-43	Armed Guard on merchant vessels and USS BEN FRANKLIN
Plante, J. Royal	AAF	Sgt.		ETO 303rd Bomb Group, Eighth Air Force.B-17 Ball Turret Gunner. 27 missions. DFC. Four Air Medal

Name	Branch	Rank	Dates of Service	Significant Facts
Potter, Gordon Jr.	Army	Corporal		
Pughe, Kenneth F.	Army	Lt. Col.		
Quillman, John	Army	Private	1943-1945	ETO. Infantry. Battle of the Bulge. . Purple Heart.
Reagan, Edward	Army	Corporal		
Reagan, Thomas	Army	Corporal		
+Redmond, J. Lincoln	Navy	Seaman 1/C		Asiatic-Pacific USS TICONDEROGA. Missing in action. South Pacific
Redmond, Rodney	Navy	AS		
Redmond, Wendell J.	Navy	A.S.		
Reynolds, George Jr.	AAF	Sgt.		
Rider, John W.	Army	Corporal		
Ridings, Lawrence	Army	Private		
Rienzo, Alphonso	Army	Sgt.		
Riesterer, Francis	Army	Private First class		
Riesterer, Harold	AAF	F. O.		
*Roche, James L.	Army	Private first Class		

Name	Branch	Rank	Dates of Service	Significant Facts
Roberts, Arthur J.	AAF	Staff Sgt.	04-42 to 09-45	ETO. Radioman on C-47.
Roberts, Aubrey	Navy	Mo. Mach. 2/C		
Roberts, Charles	Army	Private		
Roberts, Ralph M.	AAF	Captain		Physical Training Officer. Griffis AFB.
Roberts, Thomas	Army			
Roberts, William	Army	Private First Class		
Rollband, Hyman	Navy	Seaman 1/C		
Rooks, Ralph	Army	Private		
Roskam, George	AAF	Corporal		
Ruane, Edward	Navy	Seaman 1/C	09-21-42 to 01-46	Submarine Base . Coco Solo, Canal Zone. Electrician's Mate– Charged submarine batteries
Ruane, Leo C.	Army	Private first Class	12-01-42 to 12-04-45	ETO. 748th Tank Battalion. 2-½ Ton Truck driver. Four battle stars. Northern France, Ardennes, Rhineland, C. Europe.
Ruane, Robert I.	Army	Private First Class	12-01-42 to 12-04-45	ETO. 748th Tank Battalion. 2 ½ Ton Truck Driver. Four battle stars. Northern France, Ardennes, Rhineland, C. Europe
Rubel, Philip	Army	2nd Lieut.		

Name	Branch	Rank	Dates of Service	Significant Facts
Ryder, John	AAF	Staff Sgt.	10-0642 to 08-31-45	Asiatic-Pacific Theater. Tail Gunner on B-24. 35 missions.
Salm, Earl	Navy	Seaman 1/C		Asiatic-Pacific Theater. USS CANBERRA (CL-13)
Schroeder, Paul	Army	Private First Class		
Scott, Russell	Army	Corporal		
Shoemaker, Neil C.	Army	Corporal		
Sinclair, Harry	Army	Private		
Smith, Bentley F.	Army	Tech. Sgt.		
Snow, Daniel	Army	Sgt.		
Snyder, Harry	Army	Private First Class		
Snyder, Lester	Navy	AOM 3		
Snyder, Roy	Army	Private First Class		American Defense. Aleutian Islands
Stafford, Lincoln	Army	Private	02-06-42 to 09-22-45	ETO. 8th Infantry Division.Field Artillery
Stafford, William	Army	Private		
Stephenson, Roberta G	Marines	Sgt		Women Marines

Name	Branch	Rank	Dates of Service	Significant Facts
Sterling, Elwyn	Army	Tech. Sgt.	09-43 to 01-46	ETO. Infantry. 302nd Infantry,94th Infantry Division. Four Battle Stars. Northern France,Ardennes(Bulge), Rhineland, Central Europe.Combat Infantry Badge.
Stricker, Ernest W.	Army	Tech. Sgt.		
Strong, Charles	Marines	Staff Sgt		
Stukey, Albert	Army	Corporal		
Stukey, Edwin	AAF	Corporal		
Stukey, Fred W.	Navy	Seaman 2/C		
Stukey, Raymond	Army	1st. Lieut.		
Sullivan, Ruth G.	Army		10-22-43 to 12-15-45	Womens Army Corps. Clerk - Tilton General Hospital
Suters, Philip	AAF	Private		
Tarbox, Albert Jr.	AAF	Master Sgt		
Tarbox, Leroy	Navy			
Tarbox, Reginald	Army	Private First Class.		
Teefey, John	Army	Private First Class.		
Terry, Donald	AAF	Private		

Name	Branch	Rank	Dates of Service	Significant Facts
Terry, Horace	Army	Captain		
Tepolt, Florian E.	AAF	Tech. Sgt.		
Townsend, Ted H.	Navy	Seaman 2/C		
Treen, Robert	Army	Corporal		
*Tuffey, Delos J.	AAF	Sgt.		Killed in action in Solomon Islands. 1943
**Tuffey, Francis	AAF	Private		Asiatic-Pacific Theater. Bataan Death March. Died in Prisoner of War camp at Davao, Mindanao, Philippines.
Tuffey, Verne	Marines	Sgt.		
Tyler, Harold R Jr.	Army	Captain	1940(Reserves) to 3-46	ETO –Third Army- Artillery, HQ Co., 76th Division, Battle of Falaise Gap, Ardennes (Battle of the Bulge)- Bronze Star with Cluster.
Vining, Guy Jr.	AAF-	Corporal		North Africa.
Vining, Leland	AAF	Captain		Asiatic-Pacific Theater. P-47 Pilot. 100 combat missions. DFC.
Volkman, Floyd	Army	Corporal		
Volkman, Francis A.	Army	Corporal		
Waterman, Richard	Army	Tech.Sgt.		

Name	Branch	Rank	Dates of Service	Significant Facts
Wedgren, Herman	Army	Sgt.		
Wedgren, William	Army	Private		Retired. Thirty years service.
Welch, Harold	Navy	Chief Warrant Officer		
Weissmuller, John	Army	Private		
Westcott, Horace T.	Army	Sgt.		
Wilbur, Clarence	Navy	AS		Const. Battalion. (Seabees).
+Wilbur, Max E.	AAF	F. O.		China-Burma-India Theater.C-46 Pilot. Flew "Hump." Missing in Action
Wilkinson, Glenn	Navy	MM 3rd Class		
Williams, Donald E.	AAF	1st Lieut.	02-42 to 08-45	ETO. P-51 Pilot. Several battle stars including Battle of Bulge.
Williams, Glenn	Army	Private.		
Williams, John F.	Army	1st. Lieut.	06-42 to 01-46	ETO. Anti-Aircraft Unit. Invasion of Normandy - First Army, Northern France, Ardennes (Battle of Bulge) Rhineland, Central Europe. Four battle stars.
*Williams, John H.	AAF	Corporal		
Williams, John R.				
Williams, Norman Jr.	AAF	Lieut.		

Name	Branch	Rank	Dates of Service	Significant Facts
Williams, William H.	AAF	Sgt.		
Woodhouse, George	Army	Private		
Woodman, Richard	Army	1st. Lieut.	08-23-43 to 04-46	Asiatic-Pacific Theater. Invasion of Lingayan Gulf. Judge Advocate
York, Murray B.	Army	Captain		
Youngs, Harold	Army	Corporal	12-01-42 to 1945	ETO. 748TH tank Battalion. Tank Driver. Purple Heart-Northern France, Ardennes (Battle of Bulge), Rhineland, and Central Europe Four battle stars.
Youngs, John R.	Army	Private	06-44 to 04-46	ETO. 84th Infantry Division. 638th Tank Destroyer Battalion
Zinkevitch, Michael	Navy			
Zweifel, John	Army	Private		
Zweifel, Leo	Army	Private First Class	11-06-42 to 09-22-45	ETO. 82nd Airborne. Dist. Service Medal
Zweifel, William	Army	Private		

FOOTNOTES REFERRING TO ABOVE LIST OF VETERANS.

\# ETO = European Theater of Operations. European-Africa-Middle East Campaign Ribbon.

* Deceased.

** Prisoner of War

+ Missing In Action

Source: <u>Waterville Times</u>, August 23, 1945. (Some modifications and additions were made by author.. Dates of service and significant fact were added to list by author).

ADDENDUM TO WATERVILLE LIST OF WW II VETERANS.

The following were not on the Waterville Honor Roll but questionnaires were completed and/or were interviewed.

Name	Branch	Rank	Dates of Service	Significant Facts
Barnes, Willis G	Navy	Ensign (during World War II)	06-41 to 1977	Attended U. S. Naval Academy ETO. USS WOOLSEY (DD) Retired as Rear Admiral in 1977
Battaglia, Salvatore Sr.	Army	Private First Class	1941 to 11-45	Asiatic-Pacific. Hawaiian Islands.
Brennan, Francis	Navy	Seaman 1/C	04-27-44 to 06-46	American Defense. NROTC AT Yale U. Submarine School.
Garrett, Robert	Army	Private First Class	11-44 to 1946	ETO.103rd and 42nd Infantry. Prisoner of War Guard and Mail Guard
Cooper, Forrest	Navy	Lieut. (j.g.)	09-21-44 to1946	Asiatic-Pacific. DD(692). Electronics Maintenance Officer
Ford, Elmer	Army	Corporal	02-24-43- 12-04-45	ETO. 3806th Quartermaster Truck Regiment. Northern France- Ardennes- Rhineland- Central Europe. Four Battle stars
Lundt, Robert	Navy	EMP 2	01-26-43 to 03-02-46	ETO – Asiatic-Pacific. Three battle stars-Philippine Liberation
McNamara, Thomas	Army	Tech. 4	01-13-42 - 10-03-45	Battle Stars- Bronze Star and Purple Heart. Combat Infantry Badge."

Name	Branch	Rank	Dates of Service	Significant Facts
Paulson, Arthur T.	Army	Private First Class	07-7-43 to 12-10-45	ETO. 440th Anti-Aircraft and Artillery BN. Utah beach 6-9-44. Normandy – Aachen Hurtgen Forest. Unit shot down 21 planes including 1st German jet. Five battle stars.
Spearing, Arthur E.	Army	T-5	10-05-43 to 04-05-46	ETO-Central Europe Campaign. 86th ("Black Hawk") Division..Asiatic-Pacific
Upcraft, John	AAF	Corporal	04-01-42 to 11-11-45	American Theater. Celestial Navigation Trainer Department
Voll, Helen	AAF	Tech. Sgt.	10-42 to 11-45	Women's Army Corps. American Defense. WAC Supervisor.

DEANSBORO AREA

Name	Branch	Rank	Dates of Service	Significant Facts
Adams, John S.	Army			Signal Corps - Intelligence
Bellamy, Elwyn S.	Army			
Birdsall, Wilmer	Army			
Blunt, Robert H.	Navy	Machinist Mate 1/C	Inducted 10-39	
Catlin, Robert H.	Army	Sgt	05-19-43 to 04-24-46	Asiatic Pacific Theater
Christeler, Armin	Army	Tech Sgt.	Inducted 1943	Medical Corps
Christeler, Hans	AAF	Staff Sgt.	04-42 to 11-14-45	Weather Observer Two Battle Stars

Name	Branch	Rank	Dates of Service	Significant Facts
Cichon, Isabelle	Navy			WAVES
Clifford, Levis E.	Navy			
Cloute, George	Army	T/4	Inducted 2-05-43	
Clute, Howard				
Conklin, John H.	Army	Corporal	Inducted 10-11-39	
Conklin, George E.	Army	Corporal	Inducted 08-04-42	
Converse, Frederick L.	AAF	Second Lieut..	Inducted 10-14-43	Instructor
#Cornett, Winslow	Army	Colonel		Asiatic-Pacific.26th Infantry. Marshall Islands.
Dawes, Robert				
Diehl, William C.	Navy	Seaman 1/C	Inducted –5-20-44	
Eisele, Alfred A.	Army		02-24-43 to 12-08-44	
Finch, George C.	AAF	Sgt.	08-21-41	
Finch, Leo W.	Navy	Seaman	Inducted 12-22-43	Construction Battalion (Seabees)
Finch, Myrtle	Navy			WAVES
Fuess, Kenneth P.	Army	Staff Sgt.	Inducted 01-20-40	
Girius, Roland	Army	Private	Inducted 06-01-43	

Name	Branch	Rank	Dates of Service	Significant Facts
Givens, Rolland	Army			
Goodson, Harry	Army			
Greene, Robert	Army			
Hinman, Alton F.	Navy			
Hitchcock, Harold L.	Army	Staff Sgt.	01-13-44	
Hitchcock, Howard R.	Army	Private First Class	01-29-43 to 12-45	Medical Corps
Hitchcock, Robert W.	Army	Staff Sgt.	10-13-41 to 10-29-45	China- Burma- India Theater overseas 33 Months- Three Battle Stars- Presidential Unit Citation
Hughes, David	AAF	First Lieut.	Inducted 06-42	
*Huther, William	Army			
Ingersoll, R.obert	Army			
Jones, William T	AAF	First Lieut.	Enlisted 02-42	
Keller, Clarence	Army			
Kelsey, Francis Norman,	Navy	Carpenters Mate 1/C	Inducted 11-18-40	
Kelsey, Robert			Inducted 06-20-45	
Kelsey, Willard W.	Army	Corporal	Inducted 12-01-42	

Name	Branch	Rank	Dates of Service	Significant Facts
Kennard, George W.	Army	Sgt.	01-13-41 to 03-02-44	European-African-Middle East Campaign- Purple Heart. Kasserine Pass. Squad Leader. 9th Division.
Kennard, Raymond F.	Army	Staff Sgt.	12-05-40 to 06-17-45	European-African-Middle East Campaign- 1st Infantry Div - Purple Heart -Combat Infantry Badge
Kimball Alton	AAF	Staff Sgt.	09-11-42 to 10-18-45	European-African-Middle East Campaign- B-24/B-26 Flight Engineer and Turret Gunner – 28 Missions over Germany- Air Medal with three Oak Leaf Clusters
Kimball, James G.	Army	Private	Inducted March 1943	
Lloyd, Robert	Army	Private First Class		
Luenberger, Otto	Army			
Lyszczarz, Frank				
Lyszczarz, Stanley				
Mace, Clifford E.	Army	Private	11-24-42 to 10-4-45	Two Battle Stars
*Madden, Mae	Army			Womens Army Corps
Mara, Thomas J.	Navy	Musician 1/C		Drummer

Name	Branch	Rank	Dates of Service	Significant Facts
Mara, Jack L.	AAF	Corporal	Inducted 10-23-43	ETO.B-24 Turret Gunner-Air Medal
#McConnell, George	Army	T/5	12-42 to 11-45	European Theater – Motor Vehicle Co.
Mc Mullen, Gerald G.	Navy	Machinist Mate 3/C	01-02-45 to 07-22-46	Asiatic Pacific Theater
Miller, Mary L.	Army			Womens Army Corps
Montigny, Edward	Navy			
Montigny, William	Navy			
Palmer, Spencer	Army			
Pasiak, Anthony	Army	T/5	06-24-42 to 08-15-45	ETO.Truck Driver. Combat Infantry Badge. Tunisia. Italy. Four battle stars.
Risley, Howard Stuart	Army	Sgt.	02-24-4305-14-46	Asiatic Pacific Theater-Engineer- Two Battle Stars- Philippine Liberation-
Roberts, E	Army			
Seelow, William F.	Army	Sgt.	10-12-43 to 05-03-46	ETO. ArmyEngineers/Transportation Corps- Three Battle Stars
Spencer, Harold	Navy			
Steinman, Gilbert	Navy			
Steinman, Howard	Army			

Name	Branch	Rank	Dates of Service	Significant Facts
Stricker, Ernest	Army			
Sweet, George	Army			
Sweet, Paul	Army			
Taylor, Stuart	Army			
Thompson, Charles S.	AAF	Staff Sgt.	10 -09-43 to 03-24-46	China Burma India Theater- Engineer Aviation Battalion HQ and Service Company- Ledo-Burma Road- Two Battle Stars
*Tritton, Herman	Army	Private First Class	Enlisted 11-24-42	European Theater. Killed in Action in France -08-20-43
Tritton, Walter	Army	Private First Class	Enlisted 04- 25-42	Three Battle Stars
Tritton, Werner	Army3	Private First Class	Enlisted 04-25-42	Artillery Three Battle Stars
Uhlig, Clyde L.	AAF	Corporal	02-08-43 to 01-08-46	Engineer- 2 ½ years overseas
Uhlig, Paul R. Jr.	Navy	Seaman 1/C	11-08-43 to 04-27-46	Asiatic Pacific Theater- Three Battle Stars 18 Months overseas
Uhlig, Robert	Army			
Warriner, Victor B.	AAF	Major	Inducted 08-42	European Africa-Middle East Theater Combat Glider Pilot. –Troop Carrier Force Distinguished Flying Cross

Name	Branch	Rank	Dates of Service	Significant Facts
Waterman, Harold	Army			
Waterman, Myrtle	Army			WACS
Welch, Jack D.	Marines	Private First Class	Inducted10-25-43	
White, John	Army			
Williams, Donald C.	Navy	Machinist Mate 1/C	12-22-42 to 04-04-46	American Theater -Naval Aviation. Plane
Wilmot, Byron E.	Navy		Enlisted 2-12-40	Captain(Crew Chief) on Navy Patrol Bombers.
Winfield, Theron	AAF	Tech Sgt.	06-28-43 to 09-16-45	European Theater of Operations
Zeires, Harold E.	Army	Corporal	11-10-42 to 11-28-45	Aviation Engineer- Signal Corps

*Killed in Action

Data compiled from Honor Roll list of September 1946 and from booklet, "World War II Veterans" by Dorothy McConnell Town Clerk Marshall. The author has included some information compiled from veterans or families.

#Not listed on Deansboro Honor Roll. Submitted by family.

TOWN OF AUGUSTA AND ORISKANY FALLS

Name	Branch	Rank	Dates of Service	Significant Facts
Alberding, Glen A.	Navy	Lieut. (Junior Grade)	05-05-43	Asiatic-Pacific Theater. Seabees
Anderson, John	AAF+	T/Sgt.	07-05-42	
Anderson, Sidney W.	Army	Private First Class.	02-05-43	
Babcock, Henry J.	Army	Private First class	04-26-43	
Babcock, James J.	Army	T/5 Cpl.	12-26-42	
Bachelder, Leo	Army	Private First Class		
Bardrof, Frank Jr.	Army	Corporal	10-01-42	
Barrows, Donald E.	Army		08-21-39 to 12-18-43	
Bean, Donald	Army	Private First Class	03-03-42	
Bean, William	Army	Private First Class	09-20-44 to 07-46	
Bellinger, Raymond Ed.	Army	Sgt.	03-26-43-to 01-19-46	Asiatic-Pacific. Co.A, 264th Medical Battalion, 4th Engineer Special Brigade (the "Army's Navy"). Evacuated wounded from beachhead. Northern Solomon's, New Guinea, Luzon, Lingayen Gulf, Philippine Liberation Ribbon, Meritorious Service Unit Award.

Name	Branch	Rank	Dates of Service	Significant Facts
Belois, Francis W.	Army		09-01-40 to 04-07-46	
Beiderman, Albert	Navy	Seaman 2/c.	01-03-44	Asiatic-Pacific. LST 661 & 588. Okinawa-Iwo Jima. Lingayen Gulf and Leyte. Beach Party.
Beiderman, Harold	Navy	Seaman 2/c.	12-03-43	
Billings, Joseph	Army	Staff Sgt.	10-10-39	ETO++. North Africa. Purple Heart with Oak Leaf Cluster.
Buckoski, William F. Jr.	Army		12-20-44 to 12-06-46	Aleutian Islands
Carney, Donald				ETO
Carney, Herbert	Army			ETO
Carney, Lee				
Carney, Raymond F.				
Carney, Walter				
Castellucci, Matthew	AAF		02-16-43 to 02-17-46	
Charboneau, John	Army	Private First Class	06-12-42	ETO
Cieslak, Leo J.	Navy	Seaman First Class	12-27-43 to12-22-46	American Defense.Aviation Machinist Mate Aerial Gunner.Fleet Air Wing Six. Serviced fighter Planes and PBY's

Name	Branch	Rank	Dates of Service	Significant Facts
Clair, John	Army	Private First Class	04-05-43	
Clair, Henry (Toots)				
Clark, Oliver	Army	Corporal	10-27-42 to 10-26-45	ETO
Connors, Daniel R.	AAF	Private First Class	08-08-42	
Cook, Warren	AAF	First Lieut.	01-05-43	
Cowles, Francis L.	Navy`	Seaman 2/C	04-05-43	
Cowles, Robert Jr.	Army	Private First Class	12-04-42	
Cox, Joseph James, Jr.	Army	Staff Sgt.	02——43to 01-09-46	ETO. Infantry
Dapson, Melvin	Navy	FC 3/C	12-07-43	
Davies, Archibald	Army	Private First Class	05-29-43	
Denauro, Anthony	Army	Corporal		Asiatic-Pacific Theater. Philippines
Denny, Douglas	Army	Private		Infantry
Dolan, Edward	Army	Corporal	04-27-43	
Dolan, John A.	Army	Sgt.	06-16-44	ETO. Armored Division
Dovi, John	Army	Private	01-02-42	
Dovi, Sebastian (Buster)	AAF	First Lieut.	01-42	

Name	Branch	Rank	Dates of Service	Significant Facts
Duell, Charles		Lieut.		
Duell Frederick		Lieut.		
#Dziekan, Mathew	Army	Sgt.		ETO. 7th Armored Division. Ardennes (Battle Of Bulge). Bronze Star.
Eddy, Evelyn				
Eddy, Richard	AAF	Staff Sgt.	02-02-43	
Elliot, Roderick	Marines	Private First Class	12-19-44to 07-04-45	
Elmer, Bernard	Army	Private	03-06-45	
Engle, James	Navy	Seaman 2/C	10-06-44	
Eychner, Ellsworth	Navy	Seaman 1/C	01-45	
Fairbrother, Walter	Navy	Apprentice Seaman	03-12-45	
Findlay, Lawrence	Army	Tech. Sgt.	03-28-41	Infantry
Findley, James	Army	Tech. Sgt.		Infantry
Folts, Gordon	AAF	Staff Sgt		ETO.
Folts, LeRoy	Army	Private		ETO. Infantry
Fredericks, Edward	Army	Corporal		ETO

Name	Branch	Rank	Dates of Service	Significant Facts
Fuller, Ronald	Navy	EM3	06-09-44	
Furness, Charles	Army	Private	01-04-43	
Furness, Raymond J.	Navy	Apprentice seaman		
Genske, Ted				
Godfrey, Melville C.	Army		06-16-44	
Godfrey, Raymond	AAF	Flight. Officer	02-18-43	
Godfrey, Reginald	Army	Private	12-02-44	
Grossman, Alfred DDS	Army	Major	09-01-42-to 07-06-46	Dentist.
Grossman, Dorothy	Army Nurse	Lieut.	07-02-45 to 06-26-46	
Harney, Halsey	Army	Private First Class	11-17-44	
Harney, James H.	Army		09 -43	
Hayward, Robert W.	Army	Private	06-12-43 to 04-03-46	
Hennessy, John A.	AAF		08-14-43 to 11-10-45	ETO. –B-24 Radio Operator. Prisoner of War. Bronze Star with Oak Leaf Cluster.
Hoch, Armand				
Hoch, Kurt				

Name	Branch	Rank	Dates of Service	Significant Facts
Howe, William C.	Navy	Motor Machinist 2C	03-30-43	
Huntley, Lyle	Army	Private	06-28-44	
Hynes, Francis	Army	Staff Sgt.	01-02-43	
Ingalls, Newell	Army	Private	05-21-45 to 01-02-47	
Ingalls, Newton	Navy	Seaman 2/C	02-20-45	
Isley, Edward	Navy	Motor Machinist Mate 2/C	43-46	Asiatic-Pacific. Amphinious – LCT.
Jeffers, Gordon	Navy	Seaman 2/C	06-22-44	Asiatic- Pacific Theater
**Jeffers, Kenneth A.	AAF	Tech. Sgt	09-18-41 to	ETO. 8th Air Force. Radio technician and Gunner. Died in plane crash in Iceland May 1943. Air Medal with Oak Leaf Cluster.
Jipson, Dan L.	Army	Tech. Sgt.	11-11-43	
Kennett, Donald	Navy	Seaman 1/C	10-28-43	
Keyser, Walter	Army	Corporal	01-08-43 to 12-08-43	
Kilts, William	Army	Staff Sgt.	10-28-38	
Kimball, T. Alton	AAF	Staff Sgt.	09-10-42	
King, Charles	AAF	Tech. Sgt.	12-11-41	
King, Harold	Army	Corporal	10-26-38	Infantry

Name	Branch	Rank	Dates of Service	Significant Facts
Kirley, Bernard	Army	Private First Class	12-01-42	
Kirley, Donald	Army		03-22-45	
Koenig, Stanley	Army	Corporal	01-01-42	
Krohn, Lionel Everett	Navy	Apprentice Seaman	03-22-45	
LaPree, William	Navy	Seaman 2/C	12-23-43	
Legacy, Harold	Army	Tech Sgt.	01-20-42	
Legacy, Lloyd	Army	Private First Class	12-07-40 to 06-17-45	ETO. Invasions of Africa, Sicily, and Normandy. Bronze Star and Purple Heart.
Legacy, Wilfred	Army	Private First class	08-15-42	
Litz, John	Navy	Coxswain		Asiatic-Pacific Theater.
Litz, Richard	Navy	Apprentice Seaman		
Luenberger, Otto E.	Army	Tech. Sgt.	03-03-43	
Martel, Robert	Navy	L. Seaman	06-02-41	Canadian Navy
McNamara, James	Army	Corporal		
Miller, George N.			10-28-38	
Miner, Charles B.	Army	Second Lieut..	05-22-04 to 02-02-46	

Name	Branch	Rank	Dates of Service	Significant Facts
Moon, Fred, Jr.	Navy	Hospitalman 1/C	09-05-43	
Moon, George	Army	Sgt.	04-26-39	
Moon, Theodore			03-22-45	
McLaughlin, Richard	Army	Private First Class	02-12-44	ETO
Nodecker, Deforest	Army	T/5	02-10-41	ETO. Armored Division
Nodecker, Leo	AAF	Sgt.	10-01-42	ETO
Norton, Paul	Army	Private First Class.	12-09-42	
O' Day, Edward S.	Army		05-29-42	
Oliver, Cloyce	AAF	Private First Class	09-07-42	
Onyan, Blaine	Army			Asiatic-Pacific Theater.
**Owen, David C.	Army	Private First class	06-02-44	ETO. Killed in Action
Owen, Gilbert	Army	Private	03-23-45	Infantry
Parker, John W.	Mer. Marine		42	
Pasiak, Anthony	Army		06-42 to 08-15-45	
Pexton, Robert B.			10-27-42	

- 426 -

Name	Branch	Rank	Dates of Service	Significant Facts
**Phillips, Frances E.			10-28-38	Africa. Killed in Action.
Plumley, Gordon	AAF	Corporal	08-42	
Plumley, Howard J.	AAF	Sgt.	04-42	
Plumley, Lawrence	Navy	Seaman 2/c	01-24-45	
Plumley, Orville	AAF	Sgt.	05-42	
Quackenbush, Byron	Marines	Captain	11-20-40	Asiatic-Pacific Theater. Retired Major - 1959
Quackenbush, Glenn	AAF	Private.	06-02-45	
Reihl, Carl			08-23-38	
Reihl, Charles W.			10-28-38	
Reynolds, Earl	Army	Private First Class	03-01-43	
Reilly, Raymond	Army	Private.	09-20-42	ETO
Rhiel, Leonard	Marines	Private		
Rice, Stanley	Army	Private	12-23-43	ETO. Infantry
Rigaud, Charles Alfred	Marines	Captain	07-01-39 to 06-65	Asiatic-Pacific Theater. Guadalcanal. Retired
Rigaud, Ralph E.	AAF	Staff Sgt	09-24-41 to 3-45	ETO
Rigaud, Sidney	Mer. Marines		1-3-45	

Name	Branch	Rank	Dates of Service	Significant Facts
Riordan, Francis	AAF	Private First Class	12-11-41	
Roberts, Donald	Army	Corporal - T/5	8-23-42	ETO. Engineering Division
Rockwell, Burton L., Jr.	Army	Captain.	1-1-42	American Theater. Military Police.
Scerbo, Guy	Army	Corporal	08-21-44-to 0 6-27-46	
Schindler, Kenneth	Marines	Corporal	10-8-42	
Sefcheck, Joseph	Navy		06-01-43-to 03-01-46	
Sherman, Clifford Clark	Navy	Seaman 1C	03-23-43	Asiatic-Pacific Theater
Sherman, Harold Phillip	Navy	ARM 1/C	01-07-41	
Silver, Clarence Burr	Marines	Sgt.	05-11-43 to 1946	Asiatic-Pacific Theater
Silver, Raymond L., Jr.	AAF		7-12-46 to 0 7-10-49	
Sitts, Irving	Army	Sgt.		ETO. Infantry
Sitts, Kenneth	Navy	Seaman 2/C	04-27-44	
Sitts, William	Army	Private First Class		ETO. Armored Division.
Slocum, Charles R.	Army	Sgt.	03-22-45	Asiatic-Pacific Theater
Slocum, Robert W.	Army	Private.		

Name	Branch	Rank	Dates of Service	Significant Facts
Smith, Bernard C.	Army	Private First Class	05-27-42 to 06-12-46	Panama. Infantry.
Socha, Walter	AAF	Staff Sgt.	04-27-42	
Squires, David	Army	Tech. Sgt.		Engineers.
Stabb, Henry	Army	First Lieut.		ETO. North Africa
Stebb, Camillus	Marines		10-28-38	
Strong, Charles	Marines	Sgt.	10-07-42	
Strong, Keith	Navy	Seaman 2/C	01-24-45	Seabees
Swift, Howard	Army	Staff Sgt.	12-01-42	ETO. North Africa. Died 1945.
Sykes, Donald	AAF	Corporal	05-12-42	
Sykes, Max	AAF	First Lieut..	12-07-42 to 05-18-45	ETO
Tallman, Frank	Army	Corporal		
Tallman, James Leland	Navy	Seaman 1/C	09-17 to 1943	
Tallman, Robert W.				
Tanner, Almon	AAF	Sgt.	02-43	
Tanner, William	Marines	Private	01-24 to 1944	
Tastor, Robert				

Name	Branch	Rank	Dates of Service	Significant Facts
Thomas, Richard	Marines	Sgt..	10-07 to 1942	
Titsworth, Martin E.	Navy		07-2-47 to4-10-50	
Todd, Alfred James	AAF	Tech. Sgt.	09-27 to 1940	ETO
Towns, Roy Arthur	Navy	Seaman 2C	11-20 to 1944	
Towns, William Oliver	Army	Staff Sgt.	4-2-43	ETO. Chemical Warfare.
#Tucker, George	AAF	Sgt.	09-42 to 01-06-46	China-Burma-India. Radio Operator on C-47. Several missions over "the Hump." Rode on Ledo Road from India to China.
Vair, Thomas	Coast Guard		2-24 to 1943	
Van Hooten, Earl R.	Army		5-6-4 to 2-2-46	
VanHyning, Raymond	Navy	Coxswain		
Vaughn, Franklin	Army	First Lieut.	5-20 to 1941	
Waterman, Richard	Army	Tech. Sgt.	3-22-45	
Williams, Darwin W.	Army	Private	12-2-42-KIA 11-13	ETO.
Williams, Erwin B.	Army	Tech. Sgt.	10-28-42	Panama
Williams, John				
Williams, Lee P.	Army	Corporal		

Name	Branch	Rank	Dates of Service	Significant Facts
Williams, Millard R.	AAF	Staff Sgt.	1-41	Asiatic-Pacific Theater
Wilmot, Byron E.	Navy	Chief Radioman	2-12-40	
Wilson, Thomas Edward	Navy	Seaman 2/C	3-20-45- 7-19-50	
Zarod, Felix	Army	Staff Sgt.		

*Missing in Action.
**Killed in plane crash in Iceland.
Not on original honor roll list. Information provided by personal interview, or family member.
Sources: "A Listing of World War II Service People from the Town of Augusta." Data collected from individuals or their families and compiled by the Limestone Ridge Historical Society. 1992. Some modifications and additions made by author and by the historical society including the Armed Forces page of the 1944-45 Oriskany Falls school yearbook compiled by Elsie Ames
+ AAF – Army Air Forces. (Prior to 1942 – Army Air Corps).
++ ETO – (European Theater of Operations). Europe- Middle East-Africa Campaign Ribbon.

NORTH BROOKFIELD

Name	Rank	Name	Rank
Barnes,R.Lester	Sergeant	Pierson, Robert	Seaman 1/C
Birmingham, Francis	Corporal	Raffauf, Clarence	Private First Class
Boutwell, Oscar	Private	Smith, Harmon E.	Staff Sergeant
Chesebro, Orthello	Private First Class.	Smith, Howard P.	Corporal
Clark, Elmer	Private First Class	Swider, Joseph	Corporal
Clemens, Calvin	Private First Class	Tyzick, Clifford	Yeoman 3/C
Clemens, Ralph	Staff Sergeant	Wages, John	
Cook, Ola	Lieutenant	Warner, Worth F.	T/4
Cook, Olive	Lieutenant	Wilcox, Howard	Sergeant
Cowen, Charles	Staff Sergeant		
Cowen, Clement	First Sergeant		
Cowen, Norman	Aviation MMC.		
Cowen, Richard	Sergeant		
Cowen, Stuart	Private First class		
Cowen, William	Corporal		
Furner, Fred	Private		
Furner, Gerald	Coxswain		
Furner, Walter	Coxswain		
*Hawkridge, Earl			
Helmes, Frank	Corporal		
Hutchins, Guy	Private First Class		
Hutchins, Nelson	Private		
Jory, Arthur	T/4		
Jory, Donald	Aviation Ordnance 2		
Jory, Francis	Lieutenant		
Lamaitis, Ralph	Technical Sergeant		
Larkin, Edwin	Corporal		

Name	Rank	Name	Rank
Livermore, Elroy	Corporal		
Main, Lyle H.	Master Sergeant		
Mason, Herbert	Private		
Palmiter, James	Sergeant		

Names taken from Roll of Honor in <u>A Book of Remembrance</u> –p.19 In Loving Memory

BROOKFIELD

Name	Rank	Name	Rank
Alderman, Clair	T/5	Merrill, Edgar	Sergeant
Baldwin, Edwin L.	Sergeant	Millard, Lester	First Lieutenant
Baldwin, Laurence	T/Corporal	Morse, Gerald E.	Private First Class
Beach, Raymond	Corporal	Morse, Harold	Seaman First Class
Becraft, Alvin	Technical Sergeant	Morse, Kenneth	Private First Class
Bellamy, Elwyn	Private First Class	McClintock,Bernard	Private
Booth Joseph A.	T/5	McIntyre, Francis	AviationOrdnance3
Brinkerhoff, Eri	Corporal	McIntyre, Lewis	Private
Brinkerhoff, Forest	Private first Class	McIntyre, Norman	Seaman First Class
Brinkerhoff, Leonard	Corporal	Nickerson, Curtis	First Lieutenant
Bryant, Charles Jr.	Lieutenant	Osborne, Gerald	T/5
Carey, Kay F.	Seaman First Class	Owens, Gordon	Private
Carey, Walter L.	Sergeant	Page, George T.	Technical Sergeant
Case, Kenneth	GM3	Palmiter,Russell B.	Captain
Chesebro, Paul	Private	Pederson, Evelyn M.	Aviation MM1
Corbin, Ellison	Staff Sergeant	Pederson, Floyd	Private First Class
Corbin, Victor	T/Corporal	*Polan, Dighton	Lieutenant Jr. Grade
Craine, Harold w.	Private First Class	Reid, Clifford	Private
Crandall, George*	Staff Sergeant	Rice, Douglas I.	Motor Mach.1
Crandall, C.I.	Staff Sergeant	*Rice, Victor Lee	Motor Mach.1
Crandall, Wheeler	Private	Rogers, Douglas C.	Corporal
Cross, Clair	Sergeant	*Rogers, Royce H.	Private First Class
Curtis, Clifton, R.	Sergeant	Rollins, Harold	Private
Davis, Joseph F.	T/4	Saulis, Edward	Pharmacist Mate 2
Dougherty. Kenneth J.	Seaman First Class	Silknetter, George	Second Lieutenant
Dougherty, J. Russell	Seaman First Class	Snow, Jason S.	Private
Dye, Merton	Sergeant	Spooner, Dick L.	Private

Edick, Arthur	Private First class	Spooner, Malcolm	Lieut. Colonel
Edick, Floyd	Private First Class	Spooner, Robert B.	Seaman Second Class
Elliott.Edward	Private	Stanbro, H. J.	Sp. (A) Second Class.
Gerhardt, Carl F.	Sergeant	Stillman, John K.	Private First Class
Hall, Clifton	Private First Class	*Stone, Hugh Jr.	Private
Hodge, Alton	PTR Third Class	Whitford, C.Calvin	Private
Hoover, Frank	Private First Class	Wilkinson, Irwin	
Hunter, Lawrence	Private First Class	Wilkinson, Walter	
Ingalls, George	Private	Witter, Willis	Captain
Ingalls, William	Private		
Jaquay, Alfred	Private First Class		
Johnson, Edward	Sergeant		
Johnson, Elmer F.	Private First Class		
Johnson, William	Private		
Jones, Francis C.	Private First Class		
Kenyon, Kenneth	Sergeant		
Knefley, Paul	Staff Sergeant		
Maxwell, Dean I.	Corporal		
Maxwell,Raymond	Private		
Maxwell, Stanley	Private		

*In Loving Memory
Names taken from Brookfield Honor Roll in A Book of Remembrance. P.11

BRIDGEWATER

Albin, Joseph

Albin, William

Belfield, Ebenezer

Belfield, Harold

Belfield, Ora

Bell, Ward

Bishop, Donald

Blaettler, Walter

Brown, Elizabeth

Buckley, Augustine

Carey, Kay

Carey, Roy

Carr, Ralph

Chapin, Frederick Jr.

Clark, Bernard

Clark, Harold

Clark, Raymond

Clark, Roy

Clarke, Elmer

Colling, Wesley

Dwyer, Edward

Dwyer, John

Dye, Harland

Edick, Arthur

Edick, Floyd

*Edick, Robert

Edwards, Irving

Evans, Arthur

Inman, Charles

Janicki, John

Janicki, Stephen

Kantor, Mathew

Kehoe, Andrew

Kehoe, Vincent

Keiser, Hubert

Kennedy, William

Key, Edwin

Kilbourne, Judson Sr.

King, Harold

Kran, Henry

Kran, John

LaQuay, Lauren

Larsen, Bert

Lenard, Charles

Lenard, Francis

Lenard, John

Letson, Frederic Jr.

Livermore, Alfred

Loomis, Frederick

Loomis, Gordon

Lowell, Kenneth

Lowell, Lawrence

MacLeod, Ian

Macner, Henry

Macner, John

Meck, Mark

Parkinson, William

Perlman, Nathan

Pickering, Clarence

Pierce, Ruth E.

*Purpura, Charles

Roberts, Glenn

Roberts, Leon

Rowlands, Warren

Saxton, Wilbur

Schermmerhorn, Carl

Scott, Hosner

Sheridan, Charles

Snow, Daniel

Snow, Eugene

Southworth, John M.

Spooner, Andrew

Spooner, Joseph

Spooner, Stephen

Stephenson, Roberta

Stephenson, Roland

Stevens, Robert

Stickles, Lester

Stickles, Lynn

Tilbe, Carlton

Trippe, Gordon M.

Tuckerman, George Jr.

Tuttle, Casper

Uccen, Chester

Evans, Charles

Evans, Everett

Hansen, Robert

Harvey, James Sr.

Harvey, Robert

Harvey, William

Hastings, Charles

Hazard, George

Hazard, Raymond

Herboldt, August

Holmes, Carrol

Horrigan, Henry

Howard, Douglas

Hungerford, Gilbert

Hungerford, Harold

Hungerford, Marion

Melvin, Jay

Mollaly, Thomas

Moran, Donald

Morgan, Charles

Morgan, Forest

Morgan, Sewell

Morse, Charles

Myers, Harry

Nolan, John

North, Stanley

North, Theodore

North, Walter

Orcutt, Raymond

Owens, Donald

Palmer, Frederick Jr.

Parkinson, Willard

Walker, Jamon

Wheeldon, Wallace

**Wheeler, Elmer

Wiencek, Vincent

Wilkinson, Bliss

Wilkinson, Eleanor

Wilkinson, Glenn

Williams, John

Williams, Robert

Wright, Howard

Wrobel, Frank

Wrobel, Joseph

Yettru, Carl Robert

Zweifel, Harry Robert

Zweifel, Leo

*Missing in Action
List compiled by past historian of the Town of Bridgewater, Stanley Owen.

**Killed in Action

LEONARDSVILLE

Name	Rank	Name	Rank
Allen, Richard	Corporal	LaShure, Donald	Private First Class
Allen, William E.	T/3	Lee, Walter W.	S.C. (B)Second Class
Baldwin, Dean	Private	Maine, Floyd	Private First Class
Ballard, Norman*	Sergeant	Maine, H.G.	Sergeant
Ballard, Theodore	Private First Class	Manchester, Robert E.	Sergeant
Barrell, Claire	Yeoman 2/C Class	Matteson, Eldon F.	Lieutenant Jr. Grade
Barrell, Claude	Corporal	Matteson, Lyle	Technical Sergeant
Blaettler, Walter	Corporal	McCarthy, Keith	
Brand, Fred E.	T/5	McNamara, Edward	Private First Class
Brown, Ina Allen	Lieutenant	Owens, Frank A. Jr.	C.M.M.
Brown, Kent H.	Sergeant	Owens, Fred	Private
Brown, Paul A.	Technical Sergeant	Palmer, Fred	Staff Sergeant
Bundy, Sheldon	Private	Price, Rowland	Corporal
Burch, Beulah	Private First Class	Pritchard, David	Seaman First Class
Burch, David Lynn	Private	Ray, Albert Kenneth	B Second Class
Burch, Francis H.	Seaman First Class	Ray, Elmer	Private First Class
Carr, Harry F.	Private First Class	Ray, John D.	T/5
Chambers, Robert	"	Ray, Linden	Private First Class
Chase, Roger	Staff Sergeant	Ray, Winfield Jr.	Private First Class
Clark, Harold	T/5	Ritchey, Bernard W.	Sergeant
Clarke, Dana		Roberts, Clyde	Corporal
Clarke, W. Russell	Staff Sergeant	Roberts, Leon	Corporal
Colgrove, George	Corporal	Rogers, Jason D.	T/5
Crumb, Lloyd P.	Lieutenant	Rogers, Larry	Seaman Second Class
Cursh, Alexander		Rogers, N.B.	Corporal
Degan, Daniel J.	Seaman First Class	Salamacha, Joseph	Private First Class
Dutcher, Stewart	T/4	Schumaker, George,	N.C.B.

Name	Rank	Name	Rank
Ellsworth, Carl L.	Captain, MC	Scott, Glenn H.	Private
Ellsworth, Donald	Private	Smith, Perriam	Seaman First Class
Ellsworth, John	Corporal	Smith, Richard	Aviation MM1
Fleming, Jacob C.		Stillman, Fremont	Lieutenant
Frost, Stephen	Corporal	Sweet, Legrand	Captain
Gaynor, Edward M. Jr.	QMC	Walker, Florence E.	Sergeant
Gaynor, Eleanor M.	HA First Class	Walker, John D.	
Gould, Kendrick M.	Staff sergeant	Weaver, Quentin	
Gustin, Raymond E.	Corporal	Weaver, Walter	Sergeant
Hawver, Wilbert L.	Sergeant	Welch, Lynn R.	Private First Class
Holk, Aage	Private First Class	Whaley, John H.	Private
Howard, Douglas J.	Lieutenant	Wheeldon, Clifford	Private First Class
Howard, Robert	Corporal	Wheeler, Elmer*	Corporal
Hughes, John B.	Master Sergeant	White, Paul E	Staff Sergeant
Hughes, Roland		Williams, Al	Corporal
Johnson, Devillo	Corporal	Williams, John D.	Seaman Second Class
Johnson, Earl C.	Corporal	Williams, Lloyd G.	Corporal
Johnson, Erford M. *.		Williams, Robert	Aviation Radioman 2
Johnson, Leo Leslie Jr.	Technical Sergeant	Wilson, Carey M.	Lieutenant
Jones, Gordon D.	Sergeant	Wilson, John H.	A/S
Jones, F.O. Keith	G.P.	Wright, Alton	
Langworthy, Robert S.	Corporal	York, Marion	Corporal

TOWN OF WINFIELD

Albin, William J.
Armstrong, Clyde R.
Armstrong, Floyd D.
Austin, Harry E.
Austin, Robert D.
Barnes, Ernest A.
Barnes, James
Beal, Charles S.
Bell, Franklin W.
Benedict, Paul
Bennett, Floyd
Berberick, William D.
Berrie, Donald W.
Blowers, Lucian
Blowers, Paul
Blowers, Shirley C.
Blowers, Wayne W.
Bonsteel, Stanley
Boorn, Clifford W.
Brown, Vernal C.
Burke, Gerald L.
Burke, Walter E.
Burnett, Willis E.
Burns, James
Carson, Andrew J.
Castronover, Dominic
Castronover, James L.
Cembrinski, Mary
Cembrinski, Stephen
Chase, John K.
Christian, Lester
Clark, Francis T.
Clark, John B.
Clayton, Richard
Crandall, Otis D.
Davis, Harold F.
Davis, John
Derosia, Melvin C.
Doran, James E.
Dutton, Fred J.
Dye, Homer W.
Dye, Raymond
Dye, Richard I.

Evans, Earle C.
Evans, Robert M.
Folds, David P. Jr.
Folds, John A.
Ford, Archie R.
Goodheart, Bruce
Green, George M.
Griffiths, Owen W.
Harvey, Edward E.
Holmes, Jerry G.
Hunter, Robert C.
Hyde, Robert
  Hyde, Thomas J.
Johnson, Henry
Jones, Harold T.
Kelderhouse, Harold
Kelly, Francis K.
Knowles, H Henry
Koenig, John H.
Koenig, Josephine
Krause, Marshall
Landphere, Ernest
Landphere, Royce
Leogrande, Anthony
Leogrande, John J.
Leogrande, Joseph F.
Leogrande, Nicholas
Leonard, Charles E.
Lohnas, Leslie
MacDaughton, James F.
Mahon, Thomas
Matteson, Raymond K.
Matthews, Edward
McCoy, Clyde Jr.
McCoy, William
McCredy, David
McCredy, George
McCredy, Robert
McCredy, Warren
Midzinski, Joseph
Miller, Arthur F.
Moran, Albert
Moran, Arthur

Murphy Edward J.
Owens, Earl B.
Palmer, Charles
Palmer, Fred
Palmer, John
Palmer, Stanley
Pelky, Bernard J.
Perkins, Herman
Pollard, Curtis B.
Pollard, Harry W.
Pollard, Henry G.
Radley, William F.
Reader, Robert A.
Rhoda, Kenneth
Salisbury, Roland W.
Santo, George
Santo, Nicholas A.
Saunders, Morris.
Schmid, James
Selch, Rev. Grant M.
Senif, Howard C.
Senif, Thomas
Sheridan, Charles
Sherwood, Arthur
Sherwood, Raymond
Shirley, Addie
Slade, Lynn R.
Smith, Alfred J.
Smith, Fred N.
Smith, James A.
*Smith, John W.
Smith, Walter A.
Sullivan, Lawrence F.
Sullivan, Louis J..
Sullivan, Michael.
Swanson, Frederick J.
Tarcza, Frank J.
Tarcza, Fred
Tarcza, Henry A.
Tofalo, Dominick A.
Tofalo, Francis
Truex, Will C.
Van Atta, Lawrence B.

Vermilya, Leroy
Waldruff, Ernest
Waldruff, Frederick
Welch, Leonard A.
Wheeler, Charles K.
Wheeler, Lynn D.
Wheeler, Russell
Wickwire, Raymond
Will, Albert K.
**Will, Walter J.
Willems, Henry
Willems, Matthew

*Willems, William J.
Williams, Charles R.
Wilson, Carey M.
Wright, John
Wright, Parke G.

*Died while in service **Killed in Action

Source: 1944 photograph (Courtesy of Florence Senif and Stephen Evans) of Winfield Honor Roll . (List modified by author and Stephen Evans)

Books

Ambrose, Stephen E. D-Day– June 6, 1944, The Climactic Battle of World War II. NY:Simon and Schuster. 1994

Anders, Leslie. The Ledo Road. Norman, OK.University of Oklahoma Press. 1965.

Bowman, Martin. B-24 Liberator, 1939-45.

Burger, Melvin D. Large Slow Target, A History of the LST. Toledo, Ohio. U.S. LST Association. 1986.

Butler, John A. Sailing On Friday. Washington, DC. Brassey's. 1997.

Cass, Bevan (Ed.). History of the Sixth Marine Division. Washington, DC. Infantry Journal Press. 1948.

Chang, Iris. The Chinese in America. The Viking Press, The Penquin Group,NY:2003

Costello, John. The Pacific War: 1941-1945. NewYork: Wm. Morrow & Co., 1981.

DeMond, J. What the Hell! Baton Rouge, LA.(Self-Published).

Eisenhower, Dwight D. Crusade in Europe. New York. Doubleday &Co., Inc.1948.

Falk, Stanley L. Bataan: The March of Death. New York: W.W. Norton Co., Inc. 1962.

Ferris, J.S. and W. Wheeler. The Wasp. Boston: George E. Crosby Co.1945-6.

Fischer, Edward. The Chancy War. New York: Orion Books.1991.

Garrec, Rene. I Remember Normandy, The Regional Council of Normandy, June 1944.

Gotts, Steve. Little Friends, 361st Fighter Group. Dallas Taylor Publishing Co. 1993

Hersey, John. Into the Valley. New York: Alfred Knopf Publishing Co. 1943.

Houston, Robert. D-Day to Bastogne. Smithtown, NY: Exposition Press. 1980.

Huff, Richard A. (ed.). The Fighting 36th. Austin,Tx: 36th Division Association.1945.

Jones, David E. Women Warriors. London: Brassey's. 1997.

Johnson, Clayton, F. and John Roberts. Dictionary of American Naval Fighting Ships.Vol.3.Washington: Navy Department. Office of CNO, Naval History Division. 1968.

Johnston, Richard W. Follow Me! The Story of the Second Marine Division in World War II. NY:Random House. 1948

Knickerbocker, H. R., Introduction by Hanson Baldwin, and Jack Belden, R.E. Depuy, Iris Carpenter, Drew Middleton, A.J. Liebling, Cy Peterman, Jack Thompson, Mark Watson, Don Whitehead, and formerofficers of the Division.. Danger Forward, The Story of the First Division In World War II. Washington: Society of the First Division. 1947. Reprinted by the Battery Press, Inc. Nashville: 1980.

Leckie, Robert. Delivered From Evil. The Saga of World War II. NY:Harper & Row. 1987.

Lowder, Hughston. The Silent Service. U.S. Submarines in World War II. Baltimore: Silent Service Books. 1987.

Marling, K. A. and Wetenhall, J. Iwo Jima. Cambridge: Harvard University Press.1991.

McGuire, Melvin. Bloody Skies. Las Cruces, NM: Yucca Tree Press. 1991.

Miller, Francis T. The Complete History of World War II. Chicago: Armed Service Memorial Edition. Readers service Bureau.1948.

Mooney, James,(Ed.). Dictionary of American Naval fighting Ships. Vol. 1,2,3,5,6 and8.Washington: Navy Department, Office of CNO, Naval History Division. 1959-1981.

Newcombe, Richard F. Battle of Iwo Jima. New York, Holt Rhinehart & Winston. 1965.

O'Neill, Brian D. Half A Wing, Three Engines and A Prayer. B-17's Over Germany. Summit, PA: TAB Aero Books, McGraw Hill, and Inc. 1980.

Pictorial History of World War II - The War in Europe and The War in the Pacific, Volumes 1 and 2. (Anonymous) Veterans Historical Book Services. Memorial Edition. VFW.1951.

Pyle, Ernie. Here Is Your War. Chicago: Henry Holt Co. 1943.

Quick, John. Dictionary of Weapons and Military Terms. NY:McGraw-HillBookCo.1973

Richardson, Robert C. "The War in the Central Pacific." Pictorial History of World War II. The War in the Pacific. Vol.2. Veterans Historical Book Service, Inc.. Memorial Edition. VFW. 1951.

'Roscoe, Theodore, et al. The U. S. Submarine Operation in World War II. Washington: U.S. Naval Institute.

Ross, Bill D. Iwo Jima New York. First Vintage Books. 1986.

Sharpe, Richard. Jane's Fighting Ships. Coulldon, Surrey, UK. Jane's Information Group LTD.98th Edition. 1955-6.

Taylor, Michael J.H. Jane's Encyclopedia of Aviation. New York: Portland House (divisionOf Lithium Press) Random House Company. 1980.

Trevelyan, R. Rome '44, The Battle for the Eternal City. New York: Viking Press. 1981.

---

* The U.S. Submarine Operations in World War II. RADM R.G. Voge,USN, CAPT W.J. Homes, USN, CDR W.H. Hazzard, USN, LCDR D.S. Graham, USN and LT H.J. Kuehn, USNR contributed to the Foreward and page 7.

Vander Vat, Dan. The Pacific Campaign -World War II. New York: Simon and Schuster. 1991.

Vey, W.D. and O.J.Elliott. The Beach Boys. A Narrative of the First Beach Battalion (Self-Published). 1996.

Wheal, Elizabeth A. and Stephen Pope and James Taylor. Encyclopedia of the Second World War. Secaucus, NJ:Castle Books. 1989.

Wong, K. Scott. First Chinese-Americans and the Second World War. Asian American History and Culture. Cambridge, MA: Harvard University Press. 2005

Pamphlets

Buchanan, C.M. and John R. McDowell and Sidney Kotler. "The Stilwell Road." Office of Public."Relations, USF in IBT with the information and Education Division. 1945.

, Live, a Publication of Project Liberty Ship, Baltimore, MD.

, "Saga of the Rhinos. A Short History of the 748th Tank Battalion."

Encyclopedias

Cass, Edward C."Artillery." Encarta 2001. CD-Rom.Redmond WA. Microsoft Corporation (2001 Ed).

"Cavalry." Encarta 2001.CD-Rom. Redmond, WA. Microsoft Corporation 2001.

Cole, Hugh M. "Tank Destroyers." World Book, Vol. 19. 1973 ed.

Deasy, George F."Solomon Islands." World Book, Vol. 18. 1973 ed.

Lough, Frederick C. "Judge Advocate." World Book, Vol. 11, 1973 ed.

Newsletter

Prados, Edward. "Facts and Memories of the War Years." The Lone Sailor. Washington: U.S.Navy Memorial Foundation. Summer 1999

Sixth Newsletter. 1st Provisional Marine Brigade, Vol.18, Number 1. March 1992.- Quotation from the "World War II Quiz and Fact Book". Vol.2, by Timothy B. Benford.

Periodicals

"Chief Yeoman Charles Browne Receives Citation From Navy." Waterville Times 4 April 1946, 1.

Cook, Jud. "Ledo Road – The Background." Yank, The Army Weekly. 10 Mar., 1945.

Doyle, Robert. "Forgotten Warriors. Voices From Captivity." American Legion." Sept.2001

MacDonald, Charles B. "Slapton Sands: The Cover Up That Never Was." Army. June 1988.

"Military Honors at Funeral of Charles D. Browne Monday." Waterville Times 2 Oct 1947, 1.

"On the Fifth Army's Beachhead North of Rome." Utica Daily Press. January 1944. Utica, New York.

Parshall, Gerald. "Special Report." U.S. News & World Report. 31 July 1995.

Stars and Stripes. (European Ed.) 4,, no. 237, August 7, 1944.

"T-5 John Langone in First Convoy on Stilwell Road." Waterville Times, Apr 5, 1945.

Turbak, Gary. "Death March." Veterans of Foreign Wars. April. 1999.

"Utica WAC Will Perform in Waco, Texas." Utica Daily Press. August 1943.

Vey, W.D. "Operation Beachhead." Veterans of Foreign Wars. Mar. 1981.

"WAC Corporal Learns Her Riding Tricks From Father and Trooper.Waco Star,Aug.43

Walker, Howell. "The Making of a West Pointer." National Geographic. May 1951.

"Waterville Man Serves On the JACK." Waterville Times. 28 Feb 1946, 1.

"Waterville's Honor Roll." Waterville Times. August 23, 1945.

World Wide Web

Anderson, Richard "The United States Army in World War. Military History. [Online]. http://www.military history online.comwwii/usarmy/ logistics.htm.

"Army Bands in World War II." [Online] Available http://bands.army.mil/ history/21.asp, 06/21/001.

B-17 Flying Fortress." [Online]. http:// www.B-17.org/flying_fortress.html. 01/08/02.

"B-24D Liberator Specifications." [Online].Available http://www.planestuff. com/b2libspec.html.

Bellafaire, Judith A. "The Women's Army Corps." CMH Publication72-15, [Online]   http://www.army.mil/cmh/pg/brochures/wac/wac-htm.7/19/02.

"BlueStarServiceBannersFactSheet."[Online].Available
http://www.legion.org/downloads/bluebannerfact.htm
http://www.chemical warfare
http://www.citizendium.org/wik://ammunition ship

"ConvoyPQ-17,June–July1942."Online] Available.http://www.history.navy. mil/faqs/faq104-2.htm. 2/23/2002.

Crosby, H. (Ed.) "Splasher Six of the 100th Bomb Group." [Online] Available http://www.webbirds.com/8th/100/100.html

"Destroyers Online – Destroyer Escort." [Online].http://www.plateau.net/ usndd//detyes.htm.

Eckstam, Eugene Dr. "Recollections by LT Eugene Eckstam", MC, USNR (Ret.)[Online]. http://www.history.navy.mil/faqs/faq87.3g.htm. 02/20/02.

"Enterprise - specifications." [Online]Available.http://home.att.net/~enterprise/1701/Cvn-65/tech.html.

Gasque, Steve. "In Memory of the 9th Armored Division." The Bridge. Printed in Germany.CarlGiessel. [Online]http://www.mindspring.com/~sgasque/army/army.htm.

"German Prisoners of War." [Online].Available http://www.rootsweb.com/~txgray/german.html. 12/07/0

Greisbach, Marc Lt(ed.) "Combat History of the Eighth Infantry Division in World "War II. Rob Oliver-Transcriber.[Online]. Available:http:// www.militaria.com/8th/8thid.html.

http://www.history.navy/mil.)

Holbert, Linda F. and La Juan R. Watson, "U. S. Army Center of Military History." [Online]. http://www.army.mil/cmh-pg/brochures/ indiaburma/indiaburma.htm.

Merchant Marine. "American Merchant Marine Men & Ships in World War II. "Liberty Ships." Online]. Available.http://www.USMM.org/ men_ships.html. 1999. 05/08/02.

MerchantMarine."ShipsSunk.."[Online].Available. http://www.USMM.org/ shipssunkdamagedf.html..02/15/01.

Merchant Marine. "Mine warfare."[Online].Available. http://www.USMM. org.

Naval Academy Admissions" [Online] http://www.nadn.navy.mil/admissions/ faq.htm.
[Online]. http://dir.yahoo.com/government/us.

"Old Hickory." [Online]. Available http://home.nc.rr.com/oldhickory/index. shtml.

Pixler,DennisDidYouKnow?"[Online]. http://www.personal.trxinc.com/ dpixler/December 28, 2001

Rainbow. [Online] Available. http://www.rainbowvets.org/Default.htm.

"Records of the U.S. Army Forces in the China-Burma-India Theater of Operations (Record Group 493)." National Archives and records Administration. [Online] http://www.nara.gov/iwg/declass/rg 493. html.

Reis, Guy, "History of the 104th Infantry Regiment of the 26th Infantry Division. [Online] Available http:// go.to/26YD (Excerpts from Grapevine, 26th Infantry division Newsletter, Vol II/ No.35, October 21, 1945. Courtesy of George C. Lithicum).

http://sampa.org/show__article.php?display

"Tiger – The E-Boat Attack." [Online]. http://www.qmmuseum.lee.army. mil/d/tiger.htm

"Twenty-Eighth Infantry Division." [Online] Available http://sites.pa.us/PA-Exec/military-Affairs/discl.htm. December 17,2001.

"Twenty-Sixth Infantry Division History - WW II." (Compiled and edited by G-3 – Section 26th Infantry, Druck:Bch-undKundstdruckerei, Weisermahl, Wels Klishee-Krammer Linz-(Courtesy of David J. Clymer, 101st Infantry Regiment veteran).[Online].Availablehttp:// geocities.com/pentagonbarracks/2422/104th.ireg.html. April 4 2001.

"U.S.HorseCavalry,1941."[Online]Available   http://www.geocities.com/
Pentagon/Barracks/2189/2001. 6/11/2001.

http://www.usmilitary/about.com/library/milinfo/navyfacts/blammoships.
htm http://wikepedia.anti-aircraft

"WorldWarIIAviation."SmithonianInstitution.   [Online}.Available.http://
www.si.edu/Harcourt/nasm/gal205/gal205.html.

Miscellaneous

Armstrong, R. G. Mrs.. and Mrs. Charles E. Foster. A Book of Remembrance,
Wives and Members Service Club.

Arn, Edward Col.. Letter to editor of Waterville Times regarding Charles
Miner.

Cowen, Richard. Letters to Mr. and Mrs. Norman Cowen, Sr. April 1941
and September 2, 1945.

Cowen, Richard. Hand-Written Narrative including the Bataan Death March.
Post-1945(no date).

DeBlanc, Jeffrey Col. Copy of his Medal of Honor citation and excerpt from
letter to Donald Beha

Dictionary of American Naval Fighting Ships, Vol. 8,

Ships, Vol.1 and V.3.Navy Department.

"Five Hundred Ninth Composite Pictorial Album" The 509th Composite
Group, Tinian: 1945.

Glass, Robert R. Col. "So Long Tankers." (A Farewell to the 748th Tank
Battalion). June 22, 1945.

Hapsworth, Kenneth Col. "472nd Q.M. Regiment." (Mimeographed
History).

Langone, Anthony, Letter to Gerald Furner, May 4, 1945.

Moyer, Francis. Diary notes recorded aboard the USS ASTORIA (CL-90) between May 1944 to 23 July 1945.

Nelson, James. <u>Memoirs.</u> March 1979.

Palmer, Marjorie. Letter with information regarding Walter J. Will. December 19, 2001.

Santo, Judy. Summary of family information regarding military experience of Donald Beha. March 19, 2000.

Letter with additional information on military experience of Donald Beha. August 24, 2001.

Vitucci, Raymond. War Memoirs.

Williamson, John Lt. Col.. Letter to Mrs. Theresa Will dated 8 April 1945

Yearbooks

1944-45 Oriskany Falls Central School Yearbook. Page entitled "Armed Forces" by Elsie Ames.

Pictorial Album

509TH Composite Group Pictorial Album., The 509th Composite Group. Tinian 1945.

Electronic Mail – E-Mail

Hilsinger, Richard. World War II Experiences (Questionnaire Answers) E-Mail to Louis C. Langone, January 21, 2001, July 9, 2001, and January 2002.

Personal and Telephone Interviews

Alsheimer, C.	Personal Interview	July 23-1999
Barnes, Frederick	"	January 6, 2005
Barnes, Iris	"	January 6-2005
Barnes, Lester	"	March10, 2000
Barnes, W.	"	August 2, 2000
Belfield, Ebenezer	"	May 27, 2002
	"	March 21, 2009
Beha, J.	. "	February 11-2000.
Bellinger,Raymond E.	Phone Interview	May 2, 2002
Benjamin, F.	Personal Interview	January 19, 2001
Billings, J.	"	January 5, 2001
Bogan, S.	"	January 15, 1999
Brewer, M.	"	April 10, 2001
Butrym, R	"	February 22, 2000
Campese, L..	"	June13,,2001
Cieslak, Leo	Personal Interview	January 19, 2001
Cooper, F.	"	July 20, 2000
Cowen, C.	"	July 21998
Cowen, S.	"	June 28, 1998
Cowen, W.	"	August 14,1998
Cucci, A.	"	January 15, 2001
Excell, E.	"	April 9 2001
Farrall, Clarence	"	April 24, 2009
Ford, E	"	April 2, 2000
Ford, R.	"	May 10, 2002
Gallagher, J..	Personal interviews	May 12, 1998
Garrett, R.	"	May 6, 2002
Guidera, T.	"	January 29, 2001
Hilsinger, F.	"	October 13, 2001
Howe, Donald	"	September -2010
Huff, L..	"	May 31, 2000
Hughes,R.	"	May 29, 2001
Isley, E.	"	January 4, 2001
Jamieson, A.	"	May 30, 2001
Jannone, M.	"	July 18, 2001

Kane, E./Cowen, F. "   Oct9,2001, Jan.30,2002

Kelley, F. " October 17, 2000

Kennard, R.. " October18, 1998

Koenig, J. " May 19, 2001

Kucirka, M. " April 4, 2001

Lim, G. " March 24.2009

Mahoney, D. " December 1, 2001

Maine, H. ". January 20, 2001

McNamara, P. " February 24,2001

Michel, W " July 25, 1999

Miner, C. " October 3, 2001

Mondo, A.. " February 23, 2001

Morgan, Sewall " October 17, 2009

Moon, F. " May 10, 2000

Moyer, B. " January 16, 2002

Nelsom, James Personal interview January.2001

Northrop, W. " February 13, 2001

O'Dowd, W. Personal interview August 21999

Pardee, N. " Jan.23,2001 –

Pierson, R. " Feb.27,2002

Puccio, Sylvester " December-11-2009

Raffauf, C " April19, 2001

Randazzo, L. " January 13, 2001

Roberts, A. " August 16, 2001

Roberts, K.. " November 26, 2001

Rogers, Royce " July 20, 2009

Ryder, J. " June 1999

Sadlon, S. " January 23, 2001

Sango, N. Phone Interview October 10, 2001

Sinnot, M: PhoneInterview/Questionnaire November 3 2001

Sliter, Ken Personal Interview. November 28, 2001.

Smith, L. " August 2, 2001

Southwick, Calvin " May 11, 2006

Stafford, W " January 17, 2001

Taibi, John Jr. " May 2010

Thompson, C. Personal interview July 23, 1998

Tonetti, O	"	November 3, 1999
Treen, R Jr.	"	April 30, 2008
Tucker, G.	"	January 25, 2001
Vitucci, R.	Phone Interview	May20, 2002
Voll, H.	Personal Interiew	October 19, 2001
Wazenkewitz, E	"	February 7, 2001
Williams, D.C	Interview/Questionnaire	April 10, 2000
Williams, J.	Personal Interview	April 20, 2000
Woodman, R.	"	March 29, 1999
Youngs, J.	"	May 18, 2002
Zito,, R.	"	January 29, 2001

RETURNED QUESTIONNAIRES BY VETERANS (OR BY FAMILY MEMBERS - BUT NOT LISTED IN ABOVE LIST OF INTERVIEWS.

Acker, W
Battaglia, S
Beha, D.
Cleary, M
Condon, D.
Cowen, C..
Cowen, N.
Dolan, J.
Dunn, G..
Dunn, R.
Dziekan, M
Ford,V.
Gardner, H
Gibbons, J.
Hughes, Richard.
Huntley, R.
Jannone, W.
Kennard, G.
Lapham G.
Lundt, R.
Manfredo, Ruth (Sullivan)
Manion, J. Edward
Mayne, H.
McConnell, G.
McLean, B.
McLean,R.
McNamara, F.
Pasiak, A.
Paulson, A.
Quillman, J.
Scerbo, G.
Spearing, A.
Sterling, E.
Tyler, H.
Upcraft, J.

Index

W

Wainwright, General Jonathan 279
Wendover Field 149, 150, 151

BOOK REVIEW
First Printing.2002
Second Printing-2003
Revised Edition 2011

"Lou's meticulous research offers a much-needed collection of stories about how Central New Yorkers served their country during World War II.

Jack Behrens, Readers' Digest Professor of Magazine author of America's Music Makers: Big Bands and Ballrooms 1912-2011

The Star in the Window is a powerful, compelling, and by turns, bittersweet (even, on occasion, amusing) account of the real world of WWII, in the words, and through the eyes, of dozens of Central New York veterans. The difficulties in producing this collection of interviews, and background checking and Honor Rolls, were sometimes daunting, but not nearly so much as the actual individual experiences recounted from fighter and bomber pilots to infantrymen, prisoners of war, submariners, and living Pearl Harbor survivors, to name a few. Without this record, by author, teacher, and Navy veteran, Louis Langone, their stories might have become lost to future generations. But time cannot diminish their sacrifice."

—Richard Searles, Retired English Teacher, Mount Markham Central School, West Winfield, NY.

"The Star in the Window offers a unique view into life during World War II. I especially enjoyed reading the unusual stories from around the world, i.e., building the Ledo Road in the China-Burma-India Theater of Operations in fighting on the beaches of a Pacific island or manning a gun from a plane over Europe or the Pacific Ocean. While reading a chapter you feel connected to the veteran and are able to relate to their feelings and experiences. The book offers an interesting way to learn more about this very complex war through the eyes of actual veterans."
—Kim Todd, Annapolis, MD